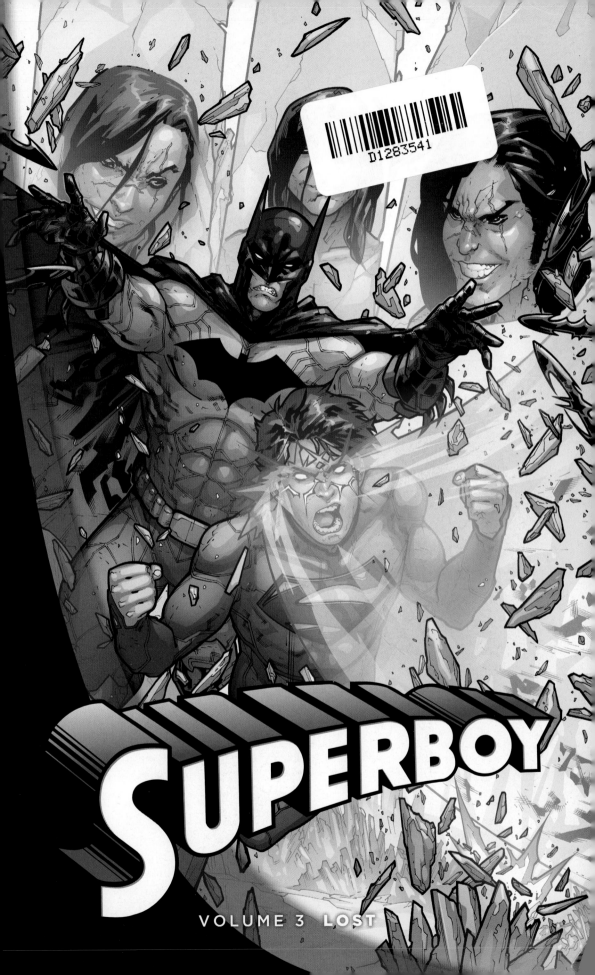

SUPERBOY

VOLUME 3   LOST

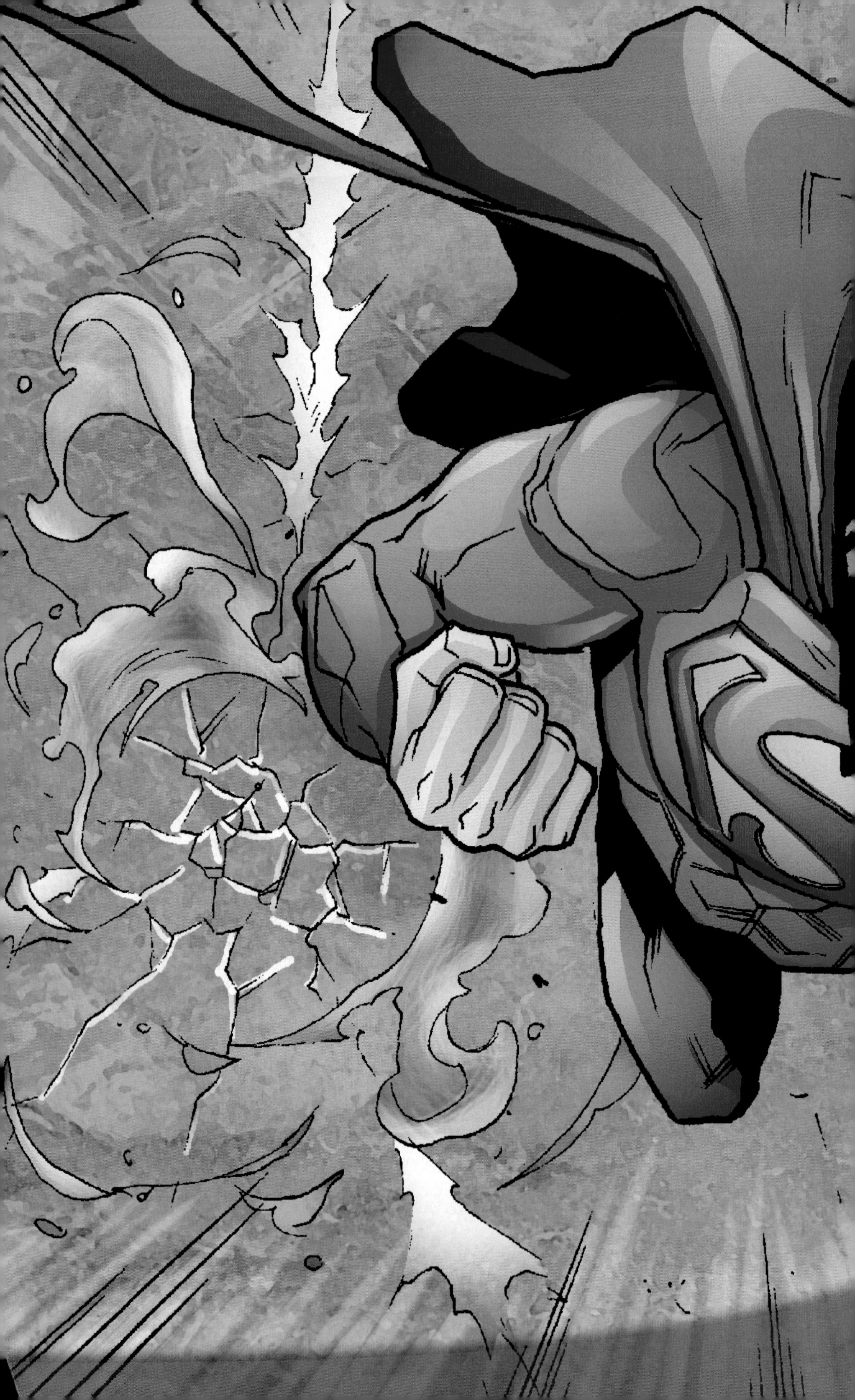

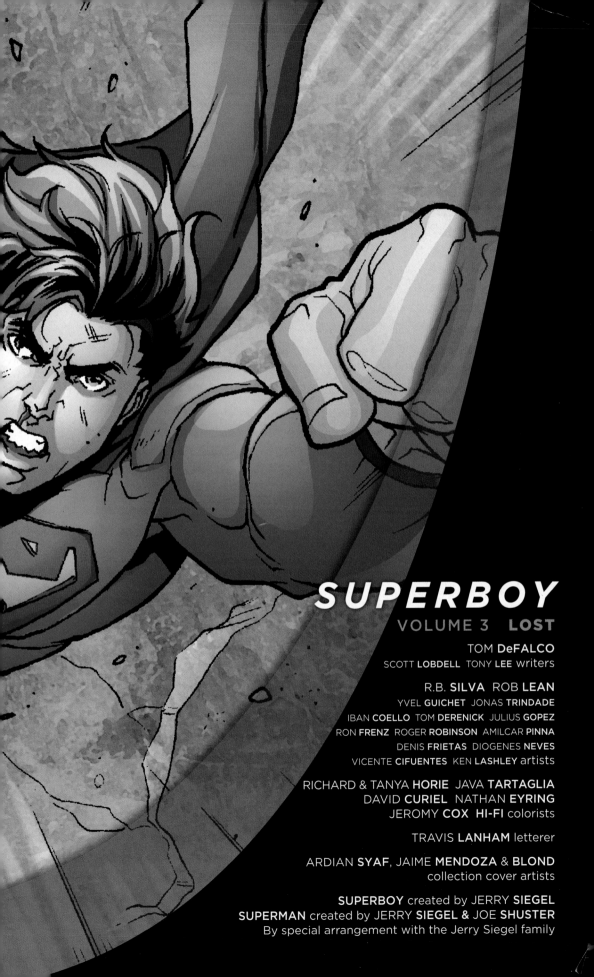

SUPERBOY

VOLUME 3   LOST

TOM DeFALCO
SCOTT LOBDELL TONY LEE writers

R.B. SILVA ROB LEAN
YVEL GUICHET JONAS TRINDADE
IBAN COELLO TOM DERENICK JULIUS GOPEZ
RON FRENZ ROGER ROBINSON AMILCAR PINNA
DENIS FRIETAS DIOGENES NEVES
VICENTE CIFUENTES KEN LASHLEY artists

RICHARD & TANYA HORIE JAVA TARTAGLIA
DAVID CURIEL NATHAN EYRING
JEROMY COX HI-FI colorists

TRAVIS LANHAM letterer

ARDIAN SYAF, JAIME MENDOZA & BLOND
collection cover artists

SUPERBOY created by JERRY SIEGEL
SUPERMAN created by JERRY SIEGEL & JOE SHUSTER
By special arrangement with the Jerry Siegel family

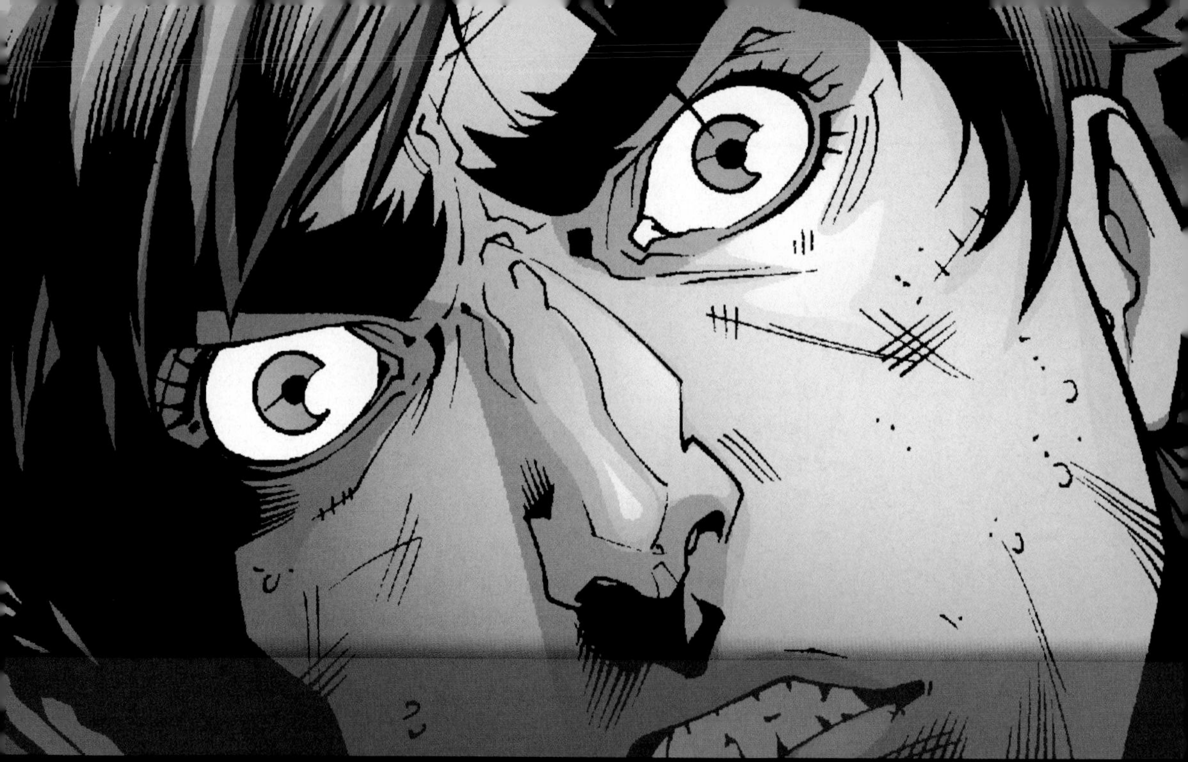

CHRIS CONROY EDDIE BERGANZA Editors - Original Series RICKEY PURDIN Associate Editor - Original Series ROWENA YOW Editor
ROBBIN BROSTERMAN Design Director - Books ROBBIE BIEDERMAN Publication Design

BOB HARRAS Senior VP - Editor-in-Chief, DC Comics

DIANE NELSON President DAN DIDIO and JIM LEE Co-Publishers GEOFF JOHNS Chief Creative Officer
JOHN ROOD Executive VP - Sales, Marketing and Business Development AMY GENKINS Senior VP - Business and Legal Affairs
NAIRI GARDINER Senior VP - Finance JEFF BOISON VP - Publishing Planning
MARK CHIARELLO VP - Art Direction and Design JOHN CUNNINGHAM VP - Marketing
TERRI CUNNINGHAM VP - Editorial Administration ALISON GILL Senior VP - Manufacturing and Operations
HANK KANALZ Senior VP - Vertigo and Integrated Publishing JAY KOGAN VP - Business and Legal Affairs, Publishing
JACK MAHAN VP - Business Affairs, Talent NICK NAPOLITANO VP - Manufacturing Administration
SUE POHJA VP - Book Sales COURTNEY SIMMONS Senior VP - Publicity BOB WAYNE Senior VP - Sales

SUPERBOY VOLUME 3: LOST

DC Comics, 1700 Broadway, New York, NY 10019
A Warner Bros. Entertainment Company.
Printed by RR Donnelley, Salem, VA, USA. 11/29/13. First Printing

ISBN: 978-1-4012-4317-3

Library of Congress Cataloging-in-Publication Data

DeFalco, Tom, author.
Superboy. Volume 3, Lost / Tom DeFalco, R.B. Silva, Rob Lean.
pages cm. — (The New 52!)
ISBN 978-1-4012-4317-3 (pbk.)
1. Graphic novels. I. Silva, R. B., 1985- illustrator. II. Lean, Rob, illustrator. III. Title. IV. Title: Lost.
PN6728.S87D44 2014
741.5'973—dc23
2013035929

SUSTAINABLE FORESTRY INITIATIVE
Certified Chain of Custody
At Least 20% Certified Forest Content
www.sfiprogram.org
SFI-01042
APPLIES TO TEXT STOCK ONLY

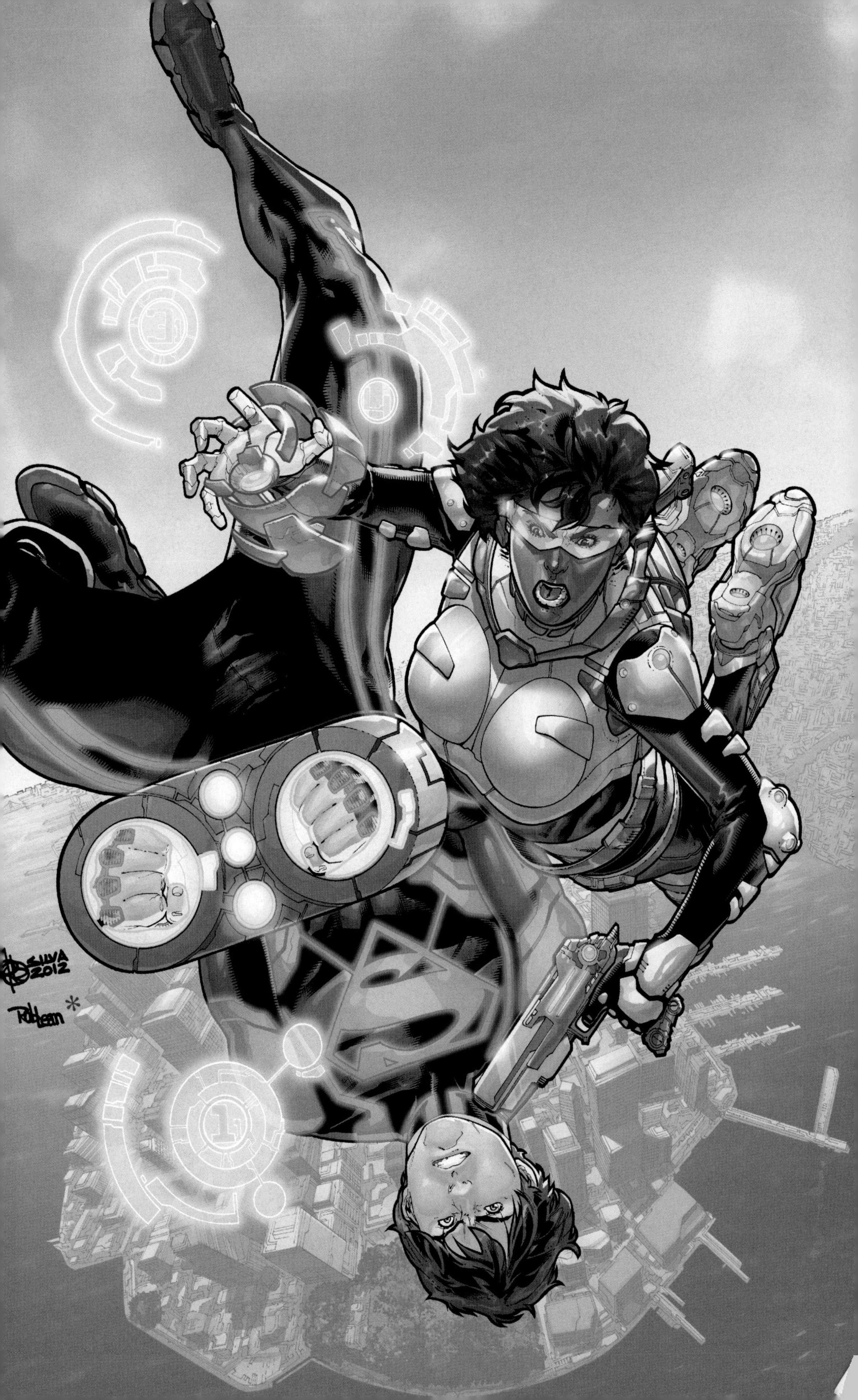

LAW AND DISORDER!

TOM DeFALCO writer **R.B. SILVA** penciller **ROB LEAN** inker cover art by **R. B. SILVA, ROB LEAN & HI-FI**

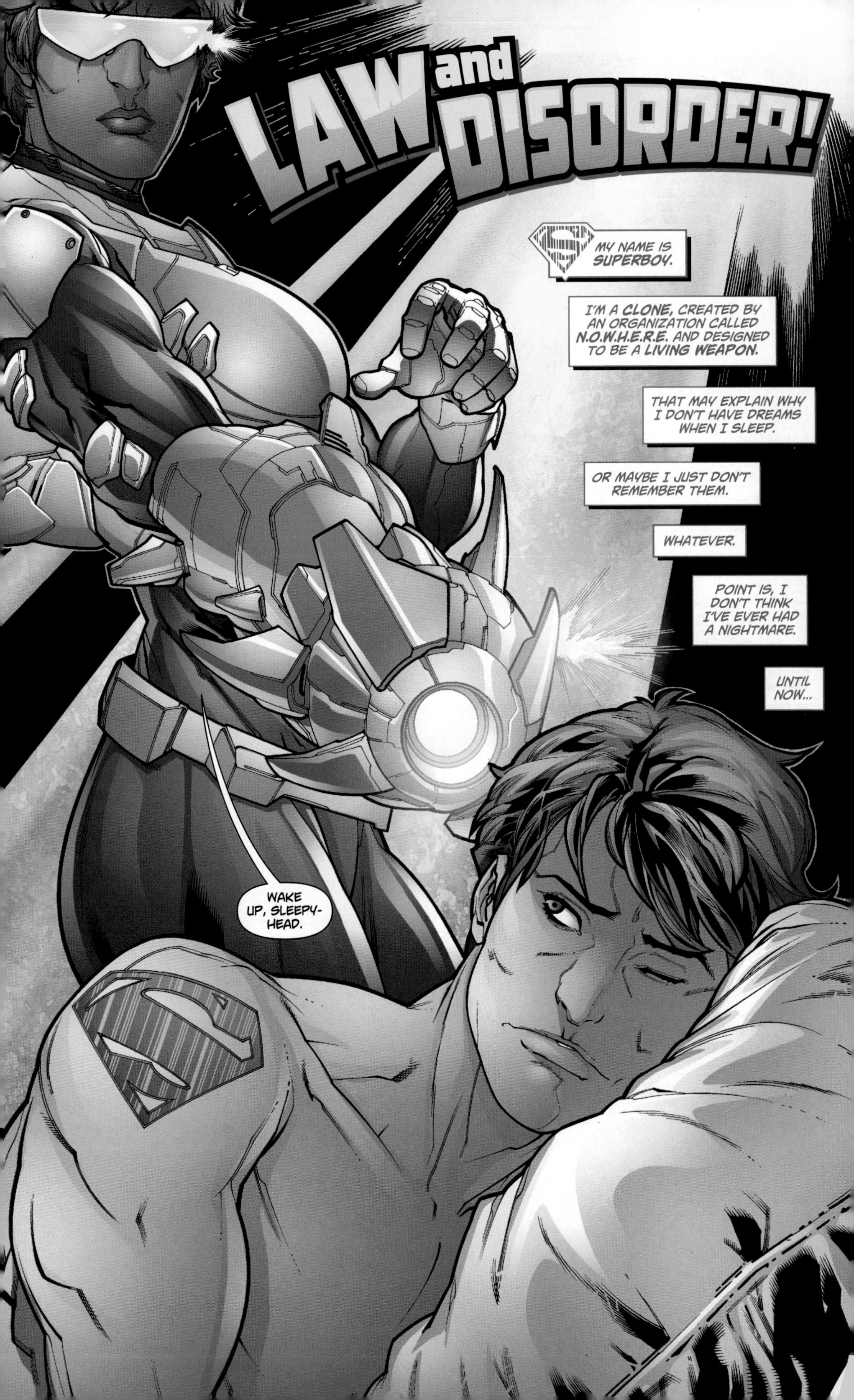
LAW and DISORDER!
MY NAME IS SUPERBOY.
I'M A CLONE, CREATED BY AN ORGANIZATION CALLED N.O.W.H.E.R.E. AND DESIGNED TO BE A LIVING WEAPON.
THAT MAY EXPLAIN WHY I DON'T HAVE DREAMS WHEN I SLEEP.
OR MAYBE I JUST DON'T REMEMBER THEM.
WHATEVER.
POINT IS, I DON'T THINK I'VE EVER HAD A NIGHTMARE.
UNTIL NOW...
WAKE UP, SLEEPY-HEAD.

RUDE! COMMON COURTESY DEMANDS YOU WAKE ME UP *BEFORE* SCREWING A GUN INTO MY HEAD.

I'VE ACTUALLY READ ALL THE CURRENT BOOKS ON ETIQUETTE, BUT NONE OF THEM COVER--

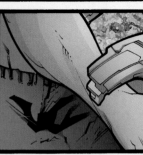

?!?

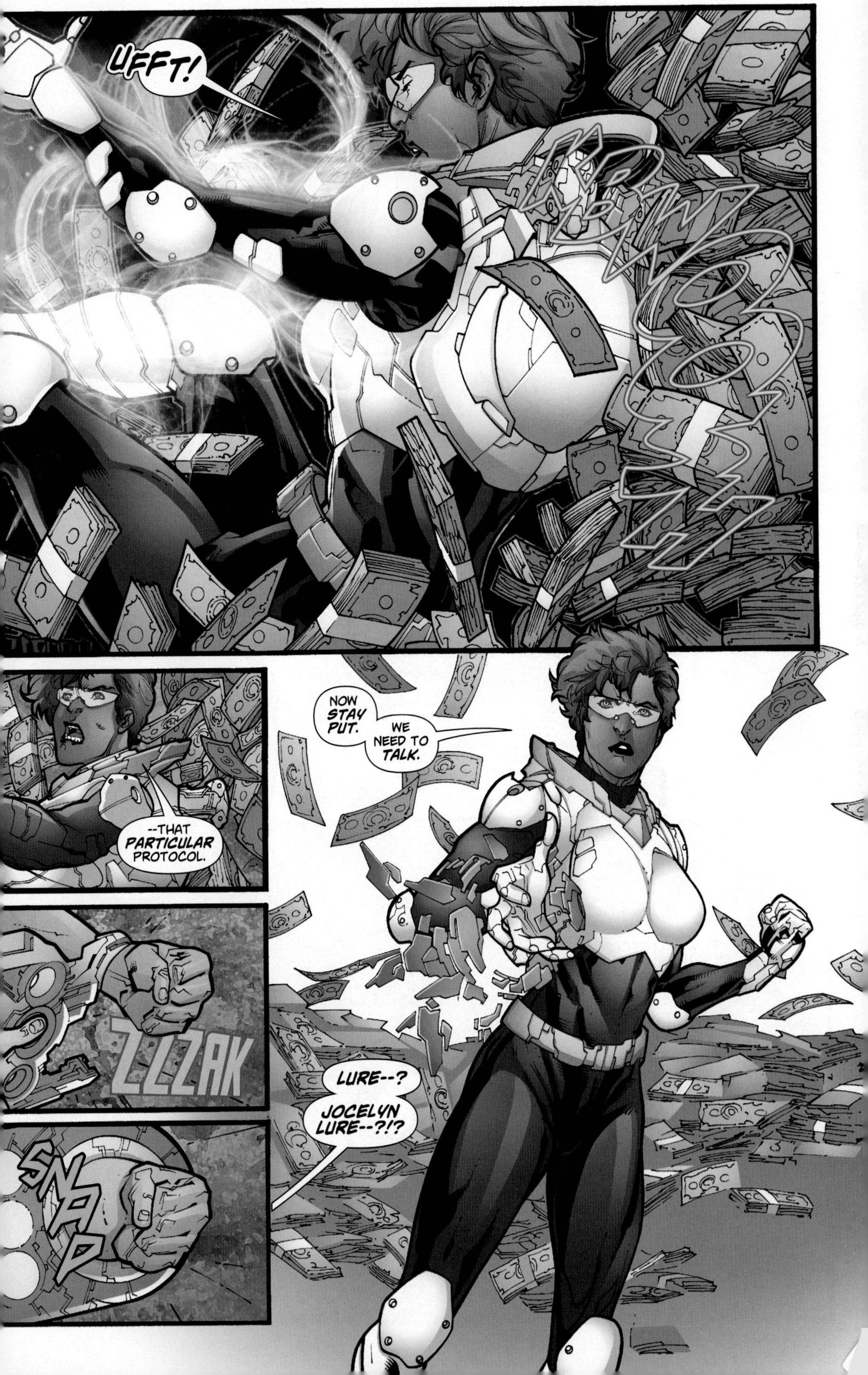
UFFT!
--THAT PARTICULAR PROTOCOL.
NOW STAY PUT.
WE NEED TO TALK.
ZZZAK
SNAP
LURE--?
JOCELYN LURE--?!?

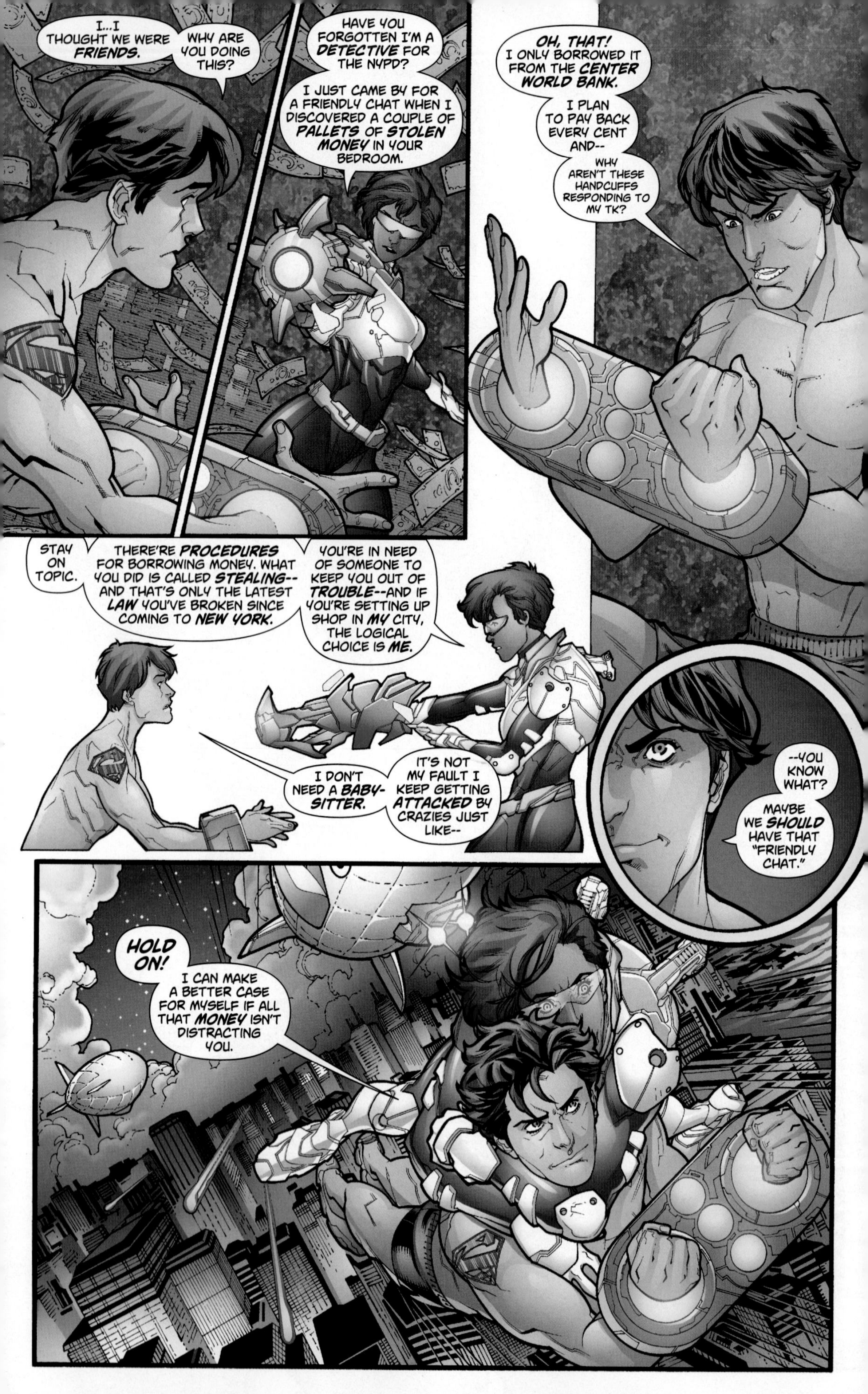
I...I THOUGHT WE WERE FRIENDS.
WHY ARE YOU DOING THIS?
HAVE YOU FORGOTTEN I'M A DETECTIVE FOR THE NYPD?
I JUST CAME BY FOR A FRIENDLY CHAT WHEN I DISCOVERED A COUPLE OF PALLETS OF STOLEN MONEY IN YOUR BEDROOM.
OH, THAT! I ONLY BORROWED IT FROM THE CENTER WORLD BANK.
I PLAN TO PAY BACK EVERY CENT AND--
WHY AREN'T THESE HANDCUFFS RESPONDING TO MY TK?
STAY ON TOPIC.
THERE'RE PROCEDURES FOR BORROWING MONEY. WHAT YOU DID IS CALLED STEALING-- AND THAT'S ONLY THE LATEST LAW YOU'VE BROKEN SINCE COMING TO NEW YORK.
YOU'RE IN NEED OF SOMEONE TO KEEP YOU OUT OF TROUBLE--AND IF YOU'RE SETTING UP SHOP IN MY CITY, THE LOGICAL CHOICE IS ME.
I DON'T NEED A BABY-SITTER.
IT'S NOT MY FAULT I KEEP GETTING ATTACKED BY CRAZIES JUST LIKE--
--YOU KNOW WHAT?
MAYBE WE SHOULD HAVE THAT "FRIENDLY CHAT."
HOLD ON!
I CAN MAKE A BETTER CASE FOR MYSELF IF ALL THAT MONEY ISN'T DISTRACTING YOU.

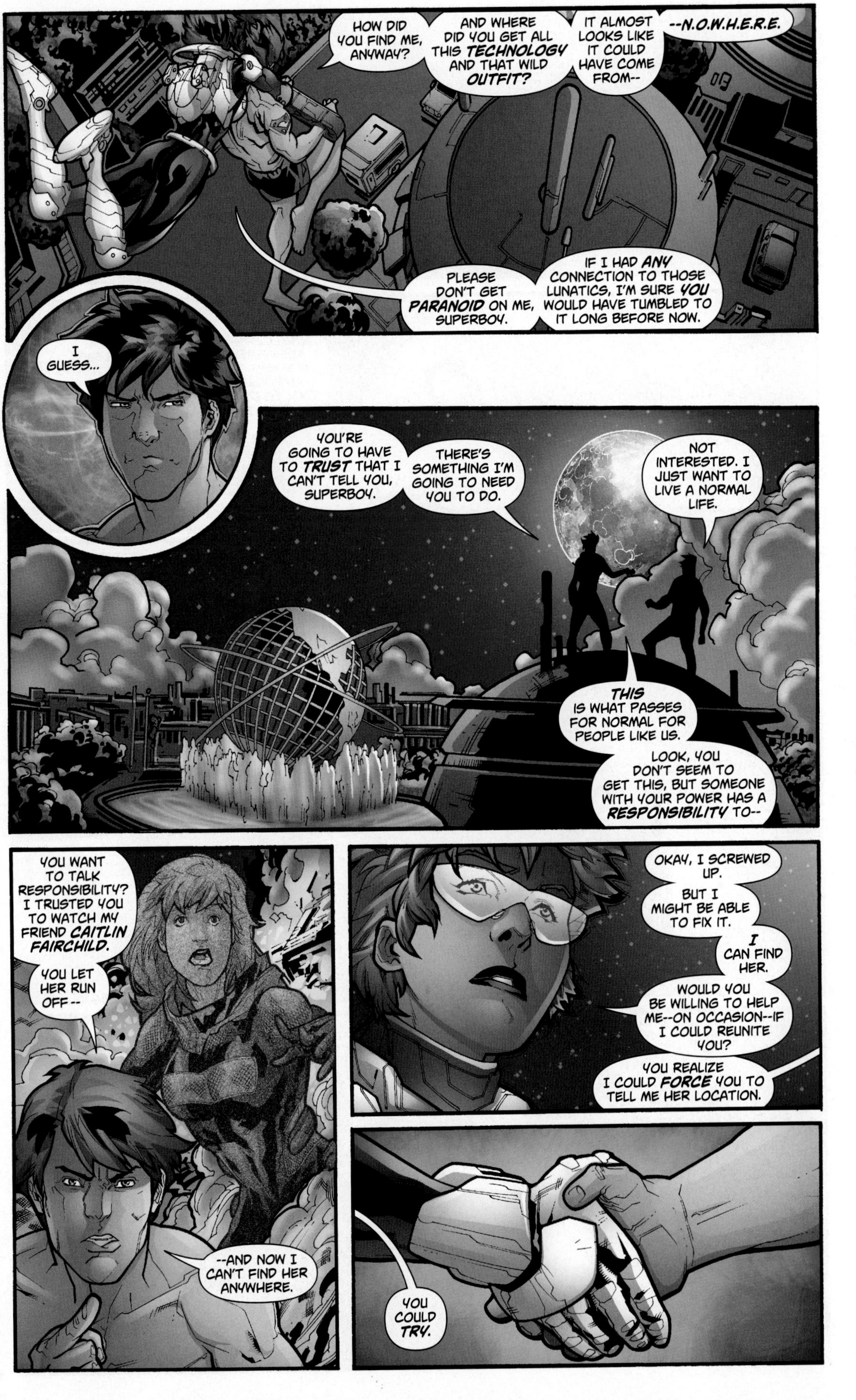
HOW DID YOU FIND ME, ANYWAY?
AND WHERE DID YOU GET ALL THIS TECHNOLOGY AND THAT WILD OUTFIT?
IT ALMOST LOOKS LIKE IT COULD HAVE COME FROM--
--N.O.W.H.E.R.E.
PLEASE DON'T GET PARANOID ON ME, SUPERBOY.
IF I HAD ANY CONNECTION TO THOSE LUNATICS, I'M SURE YOU WOULD HAVE TUMBLED TO IT LONG BEFORE NOW.
I GUESS...
YOU'RE GOING TO HAVE TO TRUST THAT I CAN'T TELL YOU, SUPERBOY.
THERE'S SOMETHING I'M GOING TO NEED YOU TO DO.
NOT INTERESTED. I JUST WANT TO LIVE A NORMAL LIFE.
THIS IS WHAT PASSES FOR NORMAL FOR PEOPLE LIKE US.
LOOK, YOU DON'T SEEM TO GET THIS, BUT SOMEONE WITH YOUR POWER HAS A RESPONSIBILITY TO--
YOU WANT TO TALK RESPONSIBILITY? I TRUSTED YOU TO WATCH MY FRIEND CAITLIN FAIRCHILD.
YOU LET HER RUN OFF--
--AND NOW I CAN'T FIND HER ANYWHERE.
OKAY, I SCREWED UP.
BUT I MIGHT BE ABLE TO FIX IT.
I CAN FIND HER.
WOULD YOU BE WILLING TO HELP ME--ON OCCASION--IF I COULD REUNITE YOU?
YOU REALIZE I COULD FORCE YOU TO TELL ME HER LOCATION.
YOU COULD TRY.

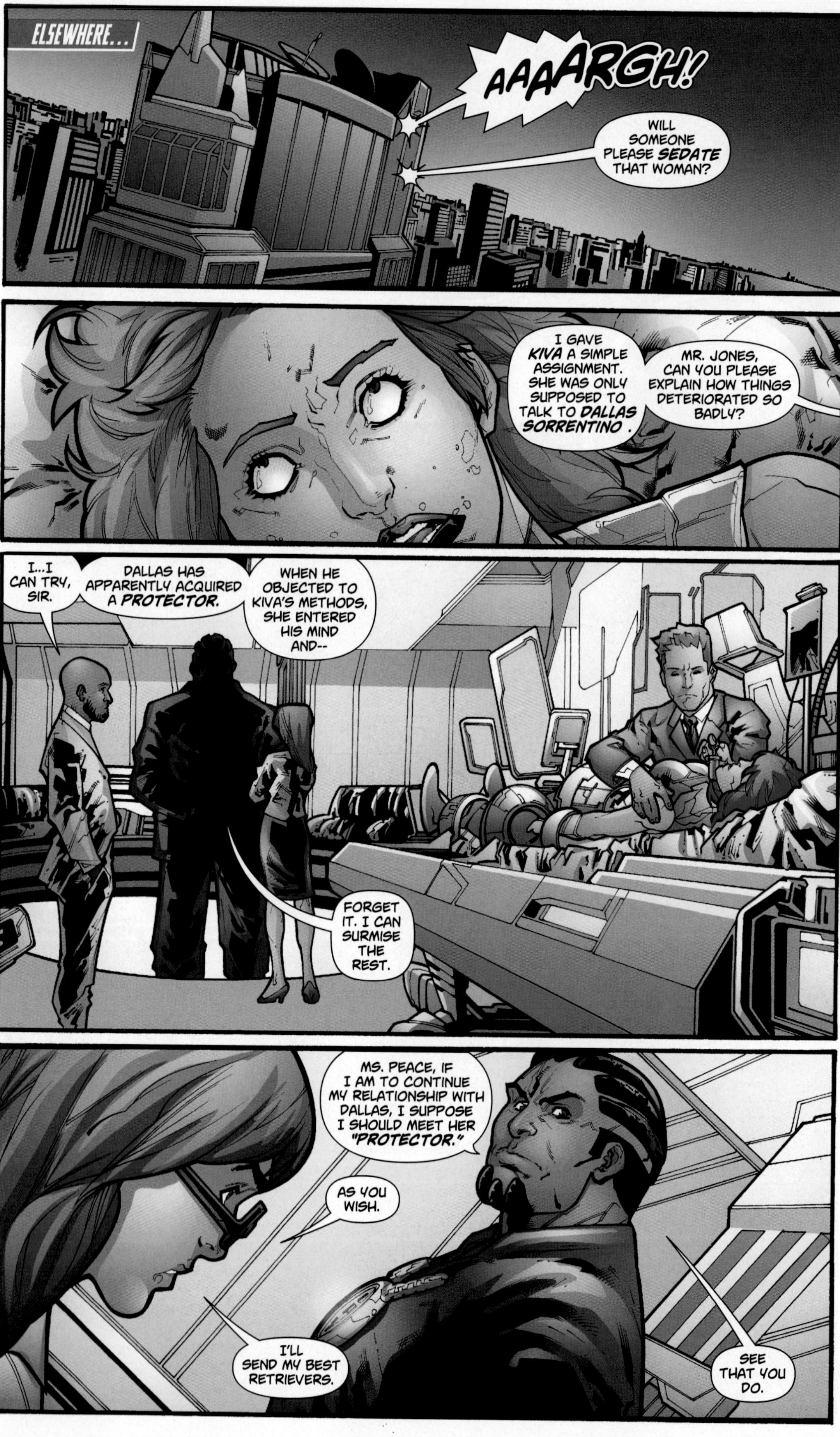
ELSEWHERE...
AAAARGH!
WILL SOMEONE PLEASE SEDATE THAT WOMAN?
I GAVE KIVA A SIMPLE ASSIGNMENT. SHE WAS ONLY SUPPOSED TO TALK TO DALLAS SORRENTINO.
MR. JONES, CAN YOU PLEASE EXPLAIN HOW THINGS DETERIORATED SO BADLY?
I...I CAN TRY, SIR.
DALLAS HAS APPARENTLY ACQUIRED A PROTECTOR.
WHEN HE OBJECTED TO KIVA'S METHODS, SHE ENTERED HIS MIND AND--
FORGET IT. I CAN SURMISE THE REST.
MS. PEACE, IF I AM TO CONTINUE MY RELATIONSHIP WITH DALLAS, I SUPPOSE I SHOULD MEET HER "PROTECTOR."
AS YOU WISH.
I'LL SEND MY BEST RETRIEVERS.
SEE THAT YOU DO.

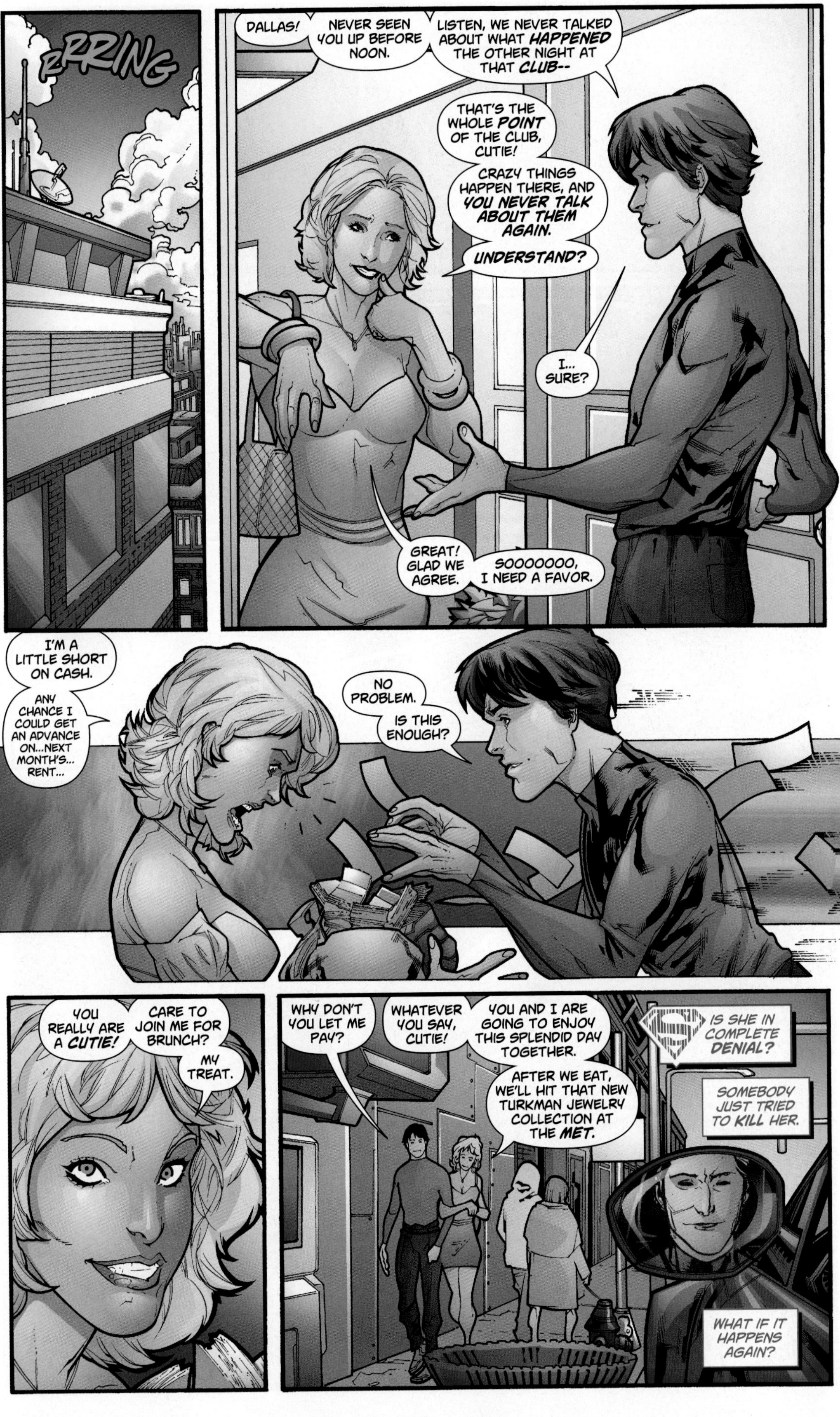
rRRING
DALLAS!
NEVER SEEN YOU UP BEFORE NOON.
LISTEN, WE NEVER TALKED ABOUT WHAT HAPPENED THE OTHER NIGHT AT THAT CLUB--
THAT'S THE WHOLE POINT OF THE CLUB, CUTIE!
CRAZY THINGS HAPPEN THERE, AND YOU NEVER TALK ABOUT THEM AGAIN.
UNDERSTAND?
I... SURE?
GREAT! GLAD WE AGREE.
SOOOOOOO, I NEED A FAVOR.
I'M A LITTLE SHORT ON CASH.
ANY CHANCE I COULD GET AN ADVANCE ON...NEXT MONTH'S... RENT...
NO PROBLEM.
IS THIS ENOUGH?
YOU REALLY ARE A CUTIE!
CARE TO JOIN ME FOR BRUNCH?
MY TREAT.
WHY DON'T YOU LET ME PAY?
WHATEVER YOU SAY, CUTIE!
YOU AND I ARE GOING TO ENJOY THIS SPLENDID DAY TOGETHER.
AFTER WE EAT, WE'LL HIT THAT NEW TURKMAN JEWELRY COLLECTION AT THE MET.
IS SHE IN COMPLETE DENIAL?
SOMEBODY JUST TRIED TO KILL HER.
WHAT IF IT HAPPENS AGAIN?

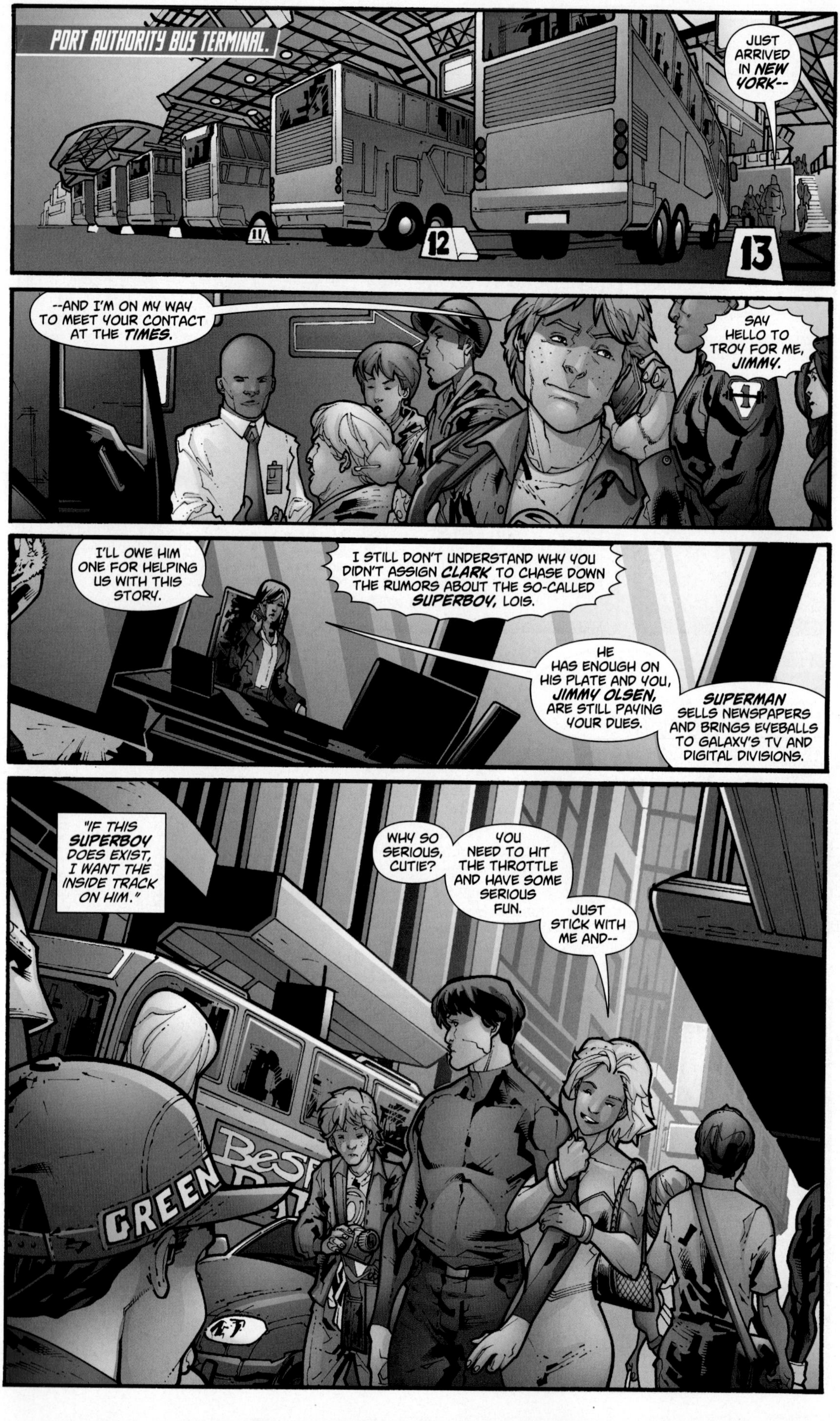
PORT AUTHORITY BUS TERMINAL.
JUST ARRIVED IN NEW YORK--
12
13
--AND I'M ON MY WAY TO MEET YOUR CONTACT AT THE TIMES.
SAY HELLO TO TROY FOR ME, JIMMY.
I'LL OWE HIM ONE FOR HELPING US WITH THIS STORY.
I STILL DON'T UNDERSTAND WHY YOU DIDN'T ASSIGN CLARK TO CHASE DOWN THE RUMORS ABOUT THE SO-CALLED SUPERBOY, LOIS.
HE HAS ENOUGH ON HIS PLATE AND YOU, JIMMY OLSEN, ARE STILL PAYING YOUR DUES.
SUPERMAN SELLS NEWSPAPERS AND BRINGS EYEBALLS TO GALAXY'S TV AND DIGITAL DIVISIONS.
"IF THIS SUPERBOY DOES EXIST, I WANT THE INSIDE TRACK ON HIM."
WHY SO SERIOUS, CUTIE?
YOU NEED TO HIT THE THROTTLE AND HAVE SOME SERIOUS FUN.
JUST STICK WITH ME AND--
GREEN

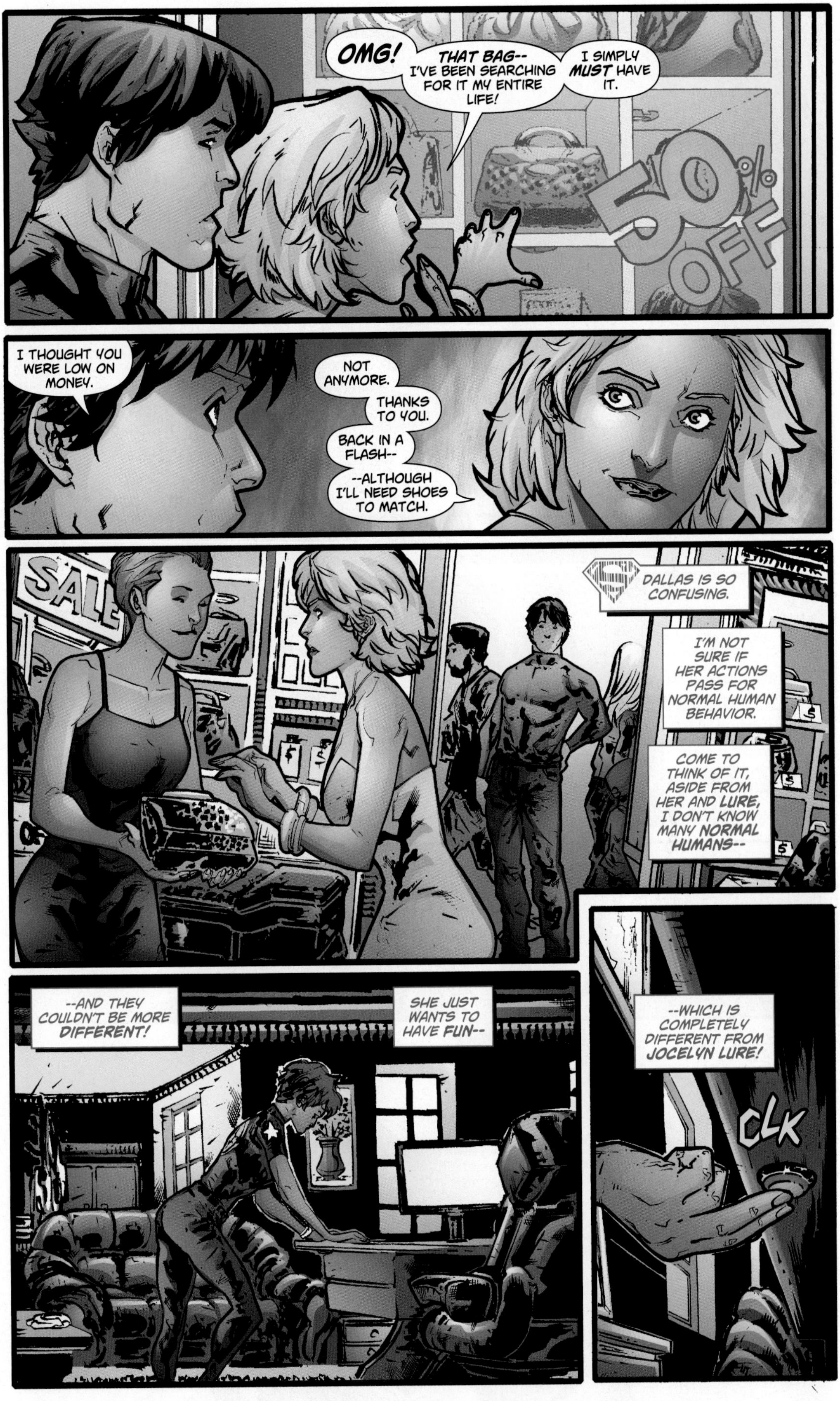
OMG!
THAT BAG-- I'VE BEEN SEARCHING FOR IT MY ENTIRE LIFE!
I SIMPLY MUST HAVE IT.
50% OFF
I THOUGHT YOU WERE LOW ON MONEY.
NOT ANYMORE.
THANKS TO YOU.
BACK IN A FLASH--
--ALTHOUGH I'LL NEED SHOES TO MATCH.
SALE
DALLAS IS SO CONFUSING.
I'M NOT SURE IF HER ACTIONS PASS FOR NORMAL HUMAN BEHAVIOR.
COME TO THINK OF IT, ASIDE FROM HER AND LURE, I DON'T KNOW MANY NORMAL HUMANS--
--AND THEY COULDN'T BE MORE DIFFERENT!
SHE JUST WANTS TO HAVE FUN--
--WHICH IS COMPLETELY DIFFERENT FROM JOCELYN LURE!
CLK

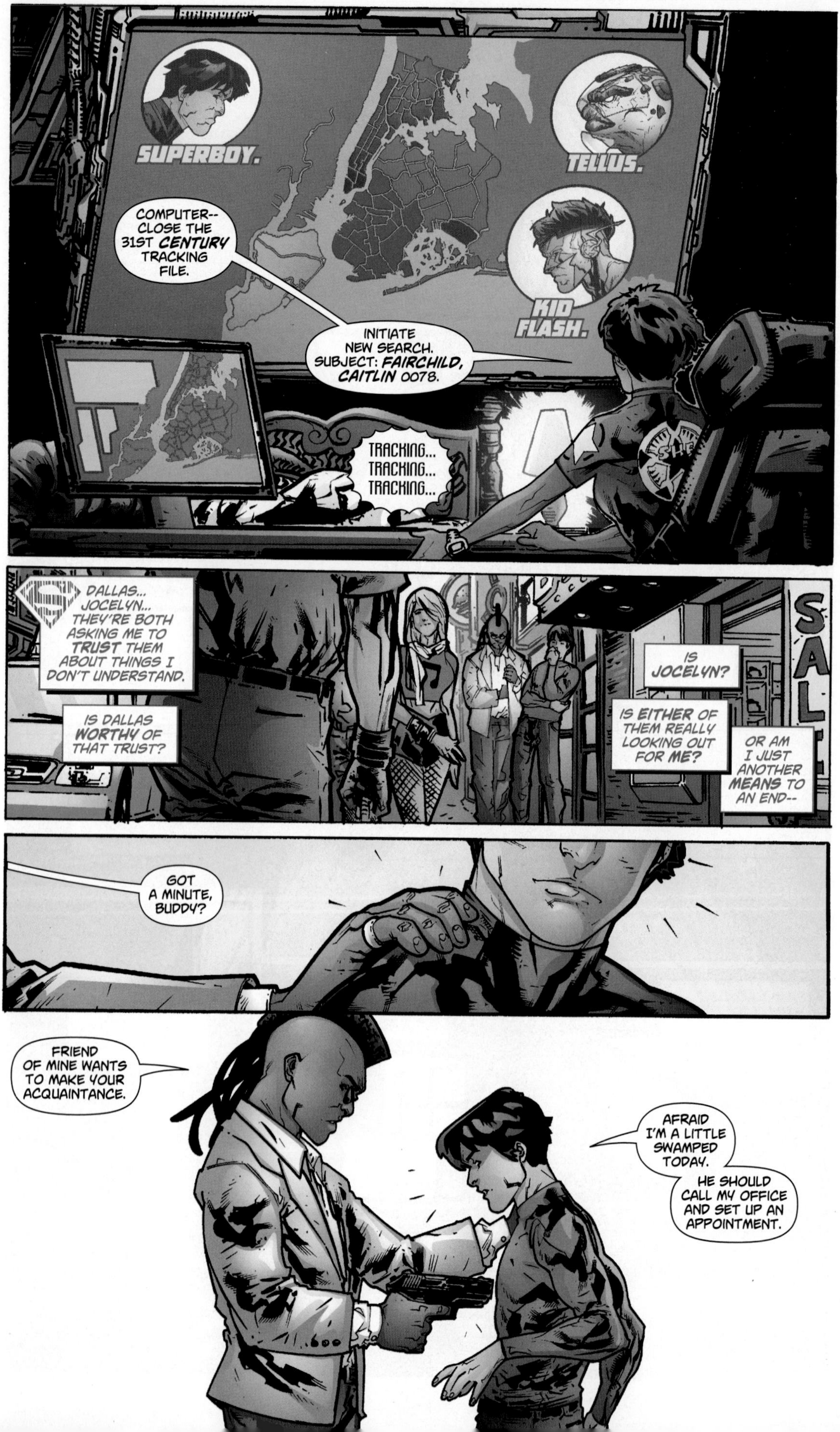
SUPERBOY.
TELLUS.
KID FLASH.
COMPUTER--CLOSE THE 31ST CENTURY TRACKING FILE.
INITIATE NEW SEARCH. SUBJECT: FAIRCHILD, CAITLIN 0078.
TRACKING... TRACKING... TRACKING...
DALLAS... JOCELYN... THEY'RE BOTH ASKING ME TO TRUST THEM ABOUT THINGS I DON'T UNDERSTAND.
IS DALLAS WORTHY OF THAT TRUST?
IS JOCELYN?
IS EITHER OF THEM REALLY LOOKING OUT FOR ME?
OR AM I JUST ANOTHER MEANS TO AN END--
GOT A MINUTE, BUDDY?
FRIEND OF MINE WANTS TO MAKE YOUR ACQUAINTANCE.
AFRAID I'M A LITTLE SWAMPED TODAY.
HE SHOULD CALL MY OFFICE AND SET UP AN APPOINTMENT.

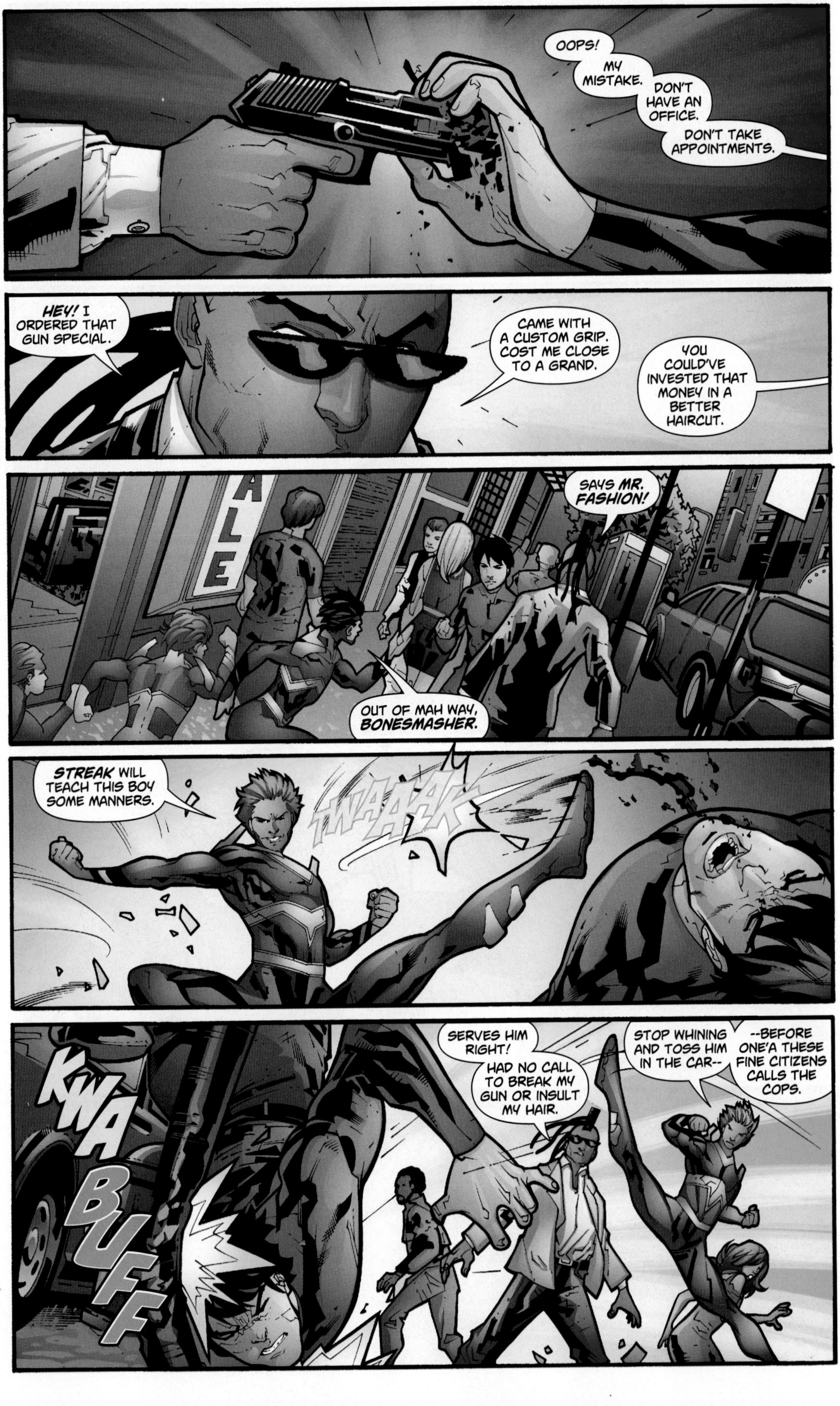

OOPS!
MY MISTAKE.
DON'T HAVE AN OFFICE.
DON'T TAKE APPOINTMENTS.
HEY! I ORDERED THAT GUN SPECIAL.
CAME WITH A CUSTOM GRIP. COST ME CLOSE TO A GRAND.
YOU COULD'VE INVESTED THAT MONEY IN A BETTER HAIRCUT.
SAYS MR. FASHION!
OUT OF MAH WAY, BONESMASHER.
STREAK WILL TEACH THIS BOY SOME MANNERS.
TWAAAK
KWABUFF
SERVES HIM RIGHT!
HAD NO CALL TO BREAK MY GUN OR INSULT MY HAIR.
STOP WHINING AND TOSS HIM IN THE CAR--
--BEFORE ONE'A THESE FINE CITIZENS CALLS THE COPS.

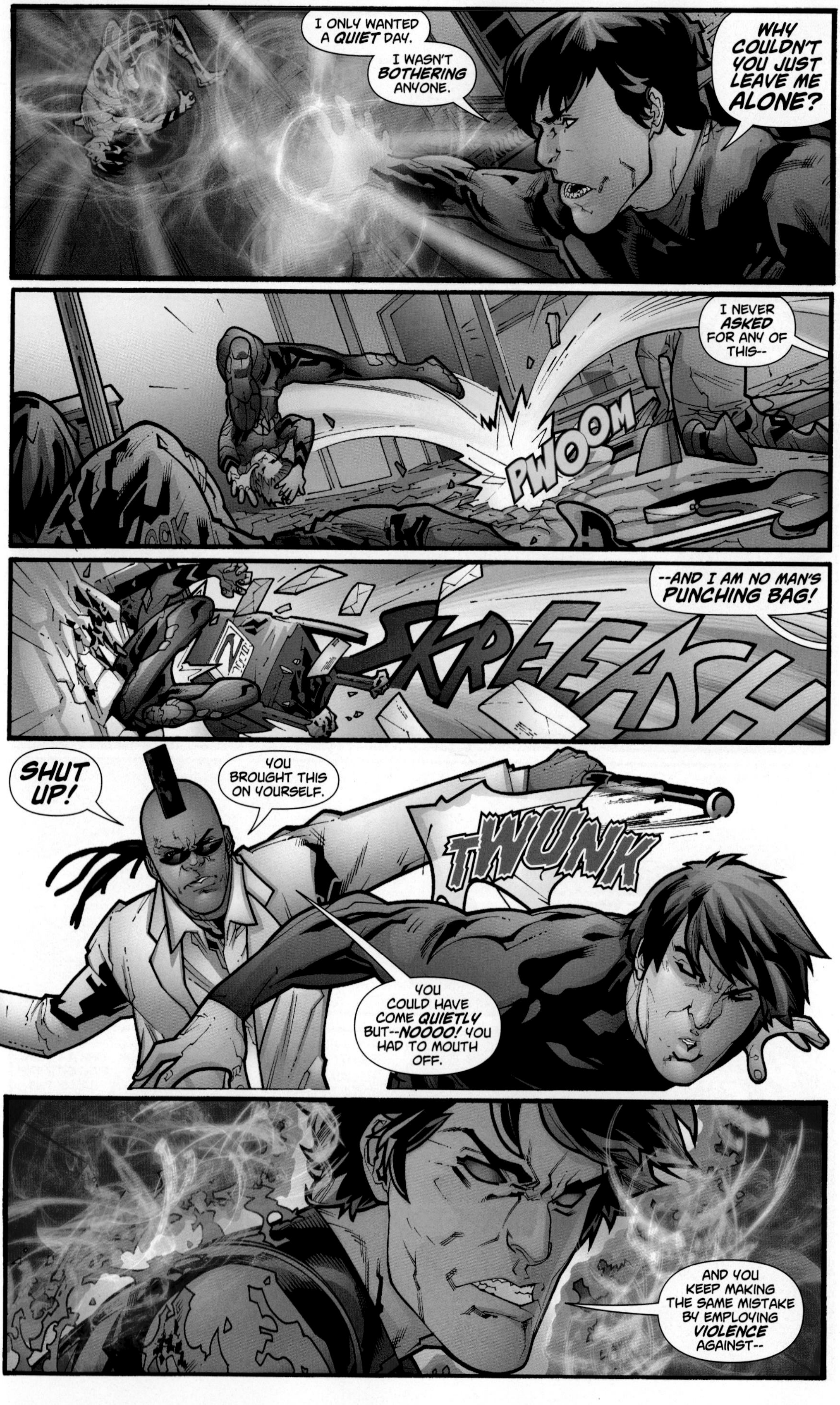
I ONLY WANTED A QUIET DAY.
I WASN'T BOTHERING ANYONE.
WHY COULDN'T YOU JUST LEAVE ME ALONE?
I NEVER ASKED FOR ANY OF THIS--
PWOOM
--AND I AM NO MAN'S PUNCHING BAG!
SKREEEASH
SHUT UP!
YOU BROUGHT THIS ON YOURSELF.
TWUNK
YOU COULD HAVE COME QUIETLY BUT--NOOOO! YOU HAD TO MOUTH OFF.
AND YOU KEEP MAKING THE SAME MISTAKE BY EMPLOYING VIOLENCE AGAINST--

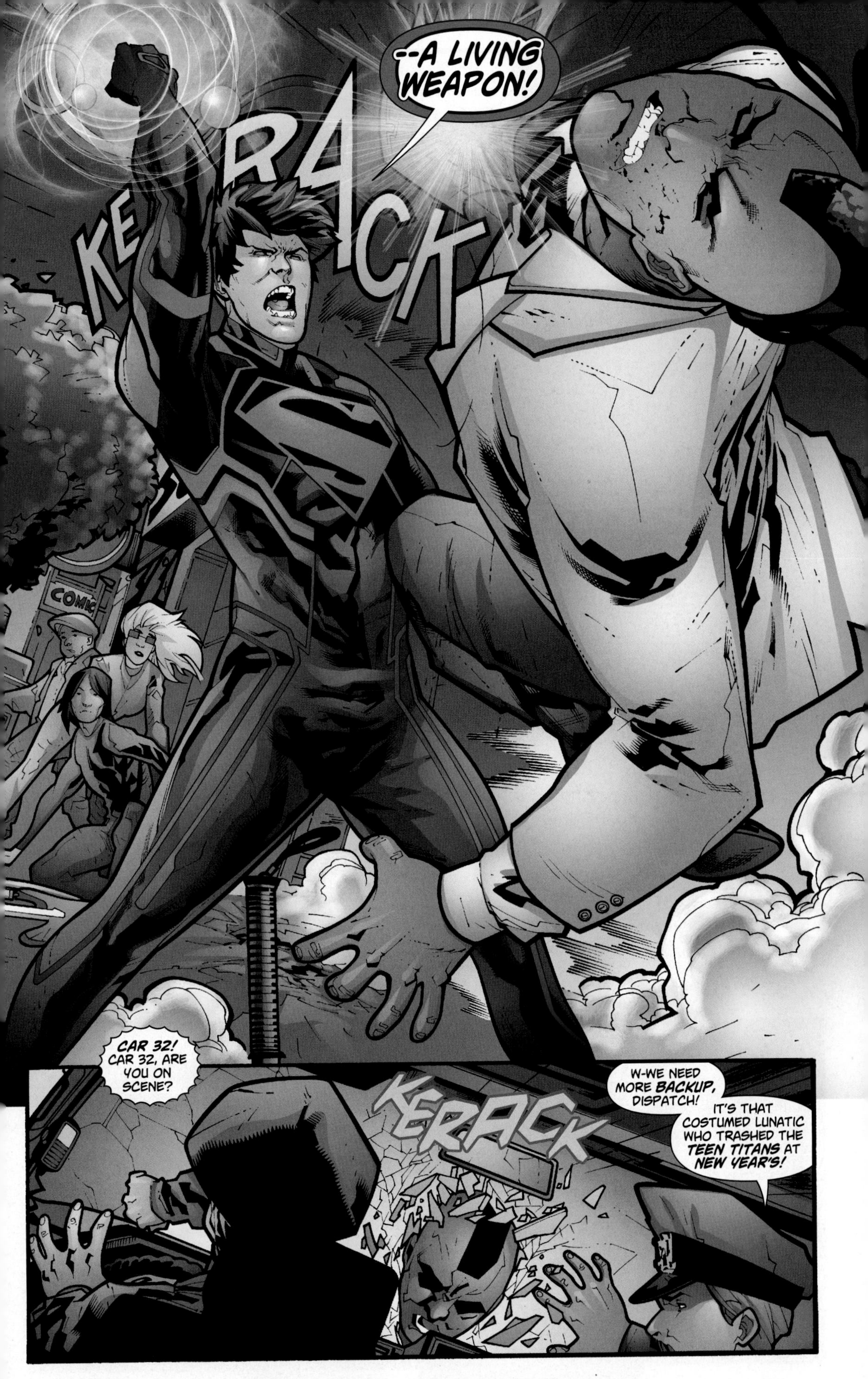
--A LIVING WEAPON!
KERACK
COMIC
CAR 32! CAR 32, ARE YOU ON SCENE?
KERACK
W-WE NEED MORE BACKUP, DISPATCH!
IT'S THAT COSTUMED LUNATIC WHO TRASHED THE TEEN TITANS AT NEW YEAR'S!

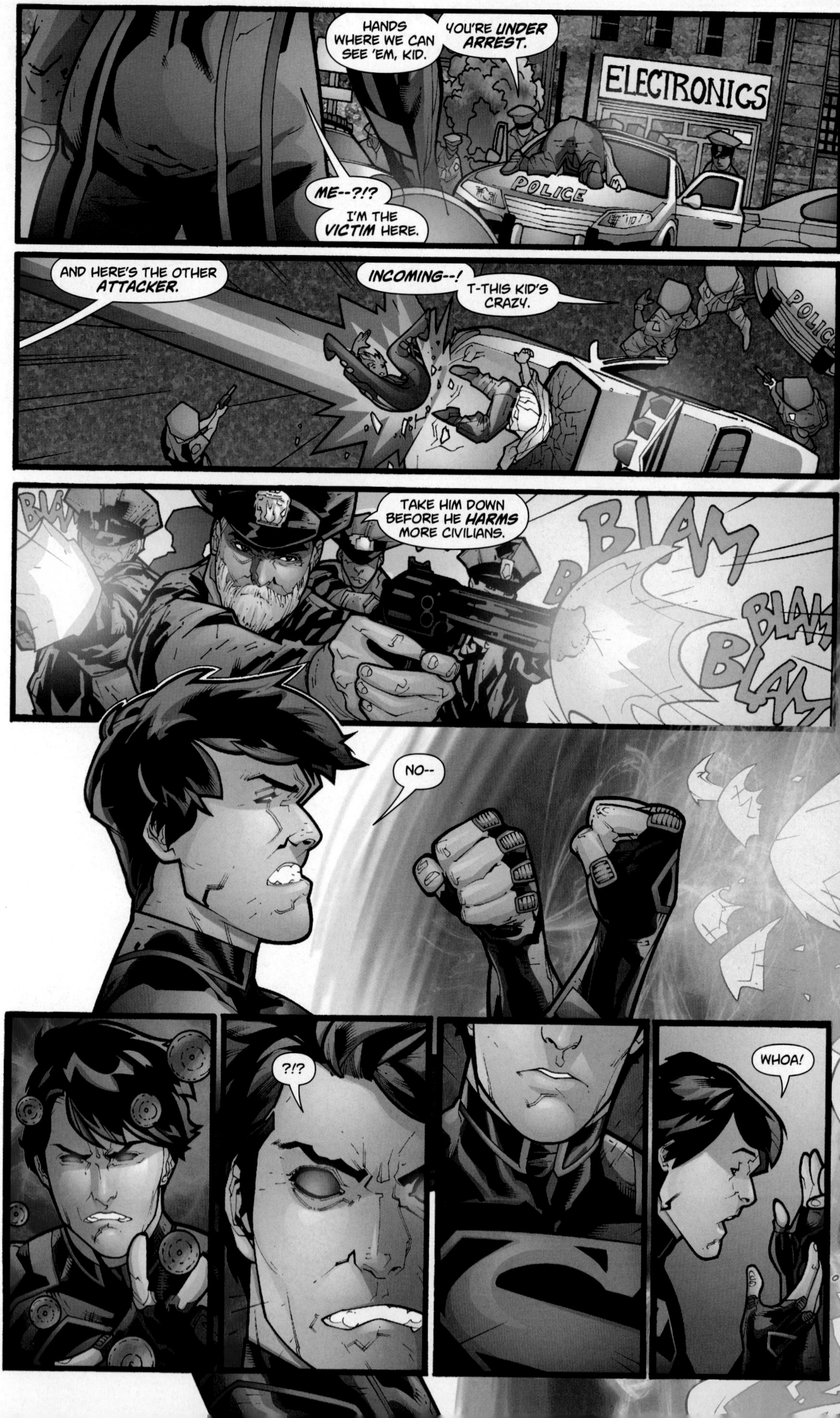
HANDS WHERE WE CAN SEE 'EM, KID.
YOU'RE UNDER ARREST.
ELECTRONICS
POLICE
ME--?!? I'M THE VICTIM HERE.
AND HERE'S THE OTHER ATTACKER.
INCOMING--!
T-THIS KID'S CRAZY.
POLICE
TAKE HIM DOWN BEFORE HE HARMS MORE CIVILIANS.
BLAM
BLAM
BLAM
NO--
?!?
WHOA!

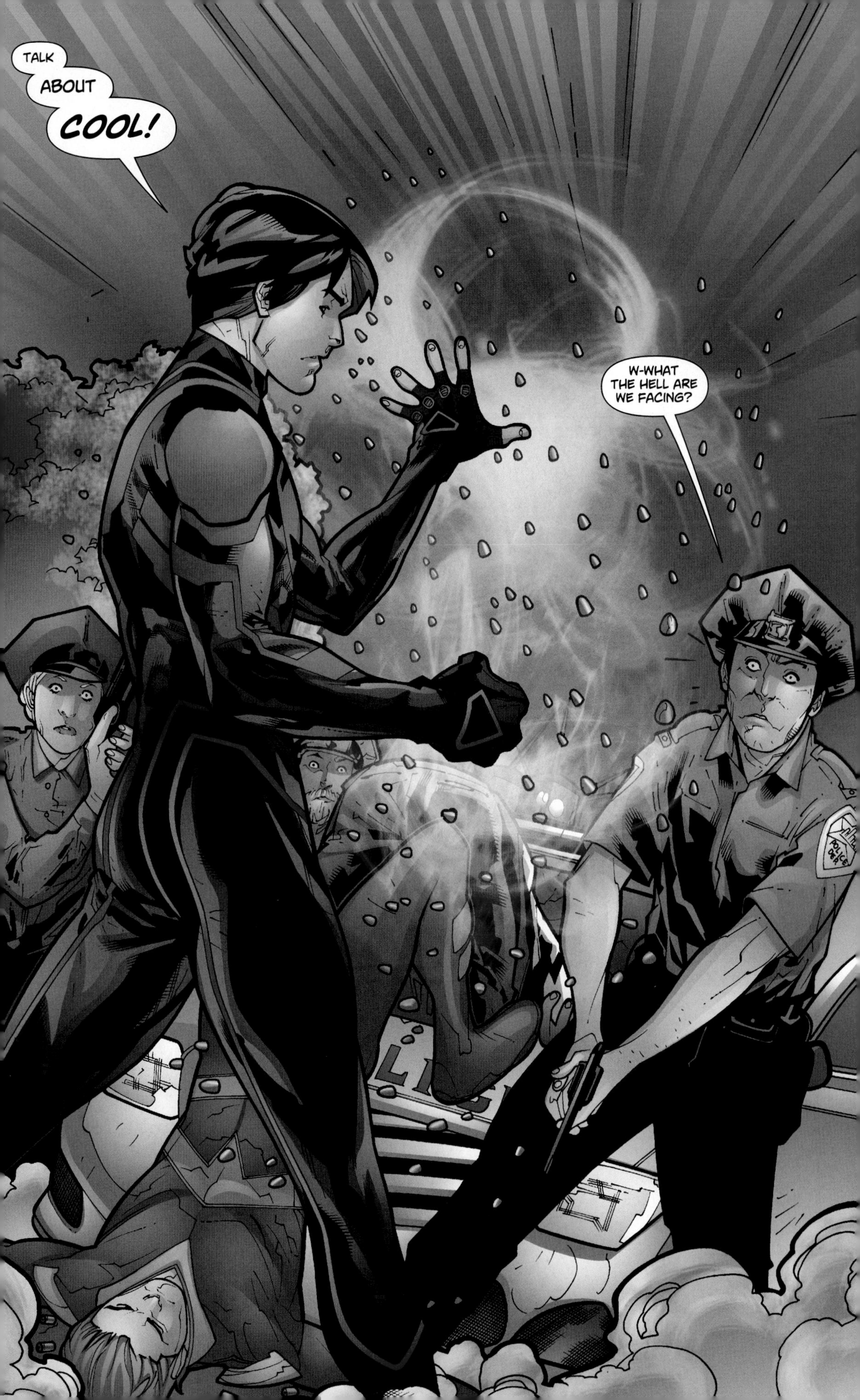
TALK ABOUT COOL!
W-WHAT THE HELL ARE WE FACING?

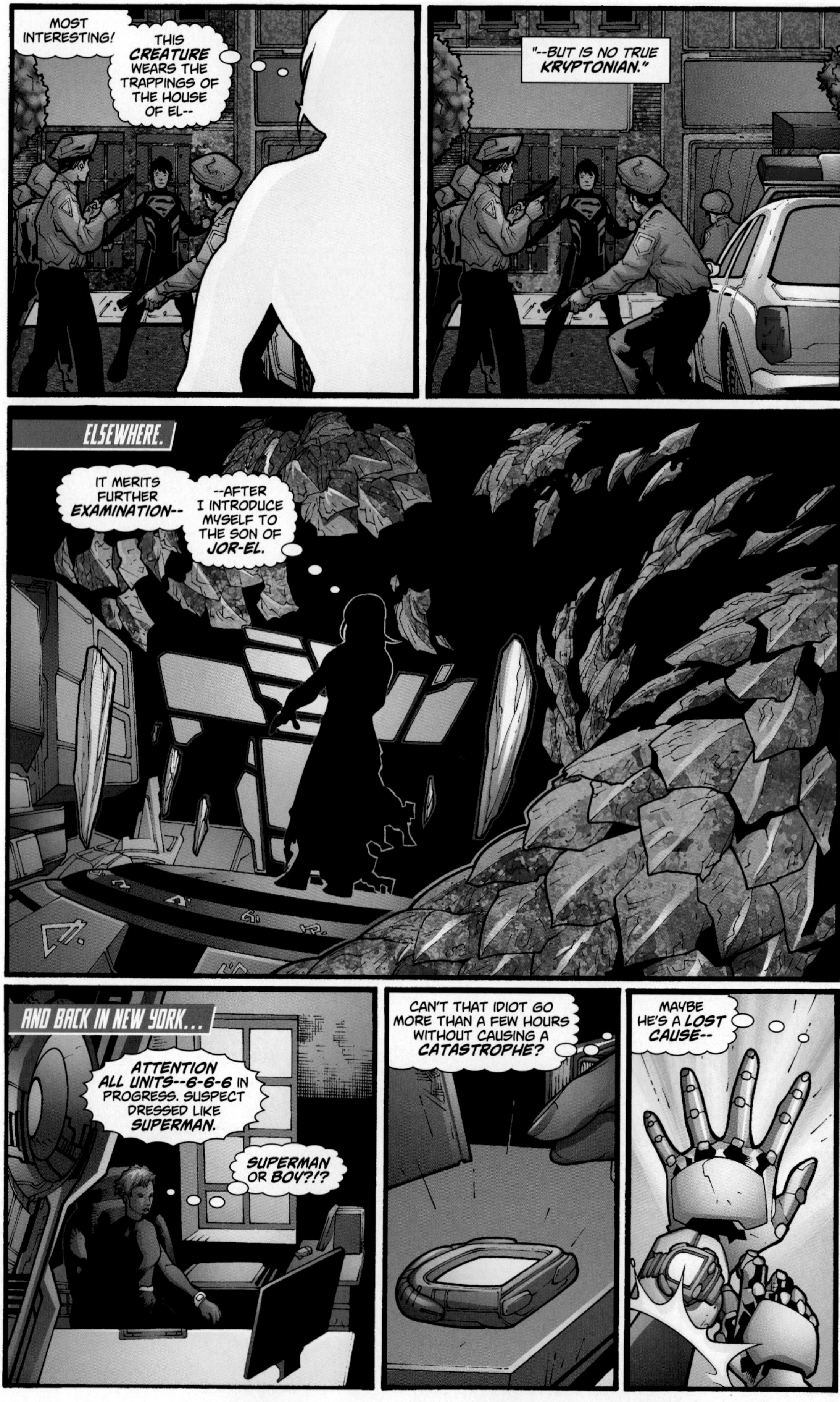
MOST INTERESTING!
THIS CREATURE WEARS THE TRAPPINGS OF THE HOUSE OF EL--
"--BUT IS NO TRUE KRYPTONIAN."
ELSEWHERE.
IT MERITS FURTHER EXAMINATION--
--AFTER I INTRODUCE MYSELF TO THE SON OF JOR-EL.
AND BACK IN NEW YORK...
ATTENTION ALL UNITS--6-6-6 IN PROGRESS. SUSPECT DRESSED LIKE SUPERMAN.
SUPERMAN OR BOY?!?
CAN'T THAT IDIOT GO MORE THAN A FEW HOURS WITHOUT CAUSING A CATASTROPHE?
MAYBE HE'S A LOST CAUSE--

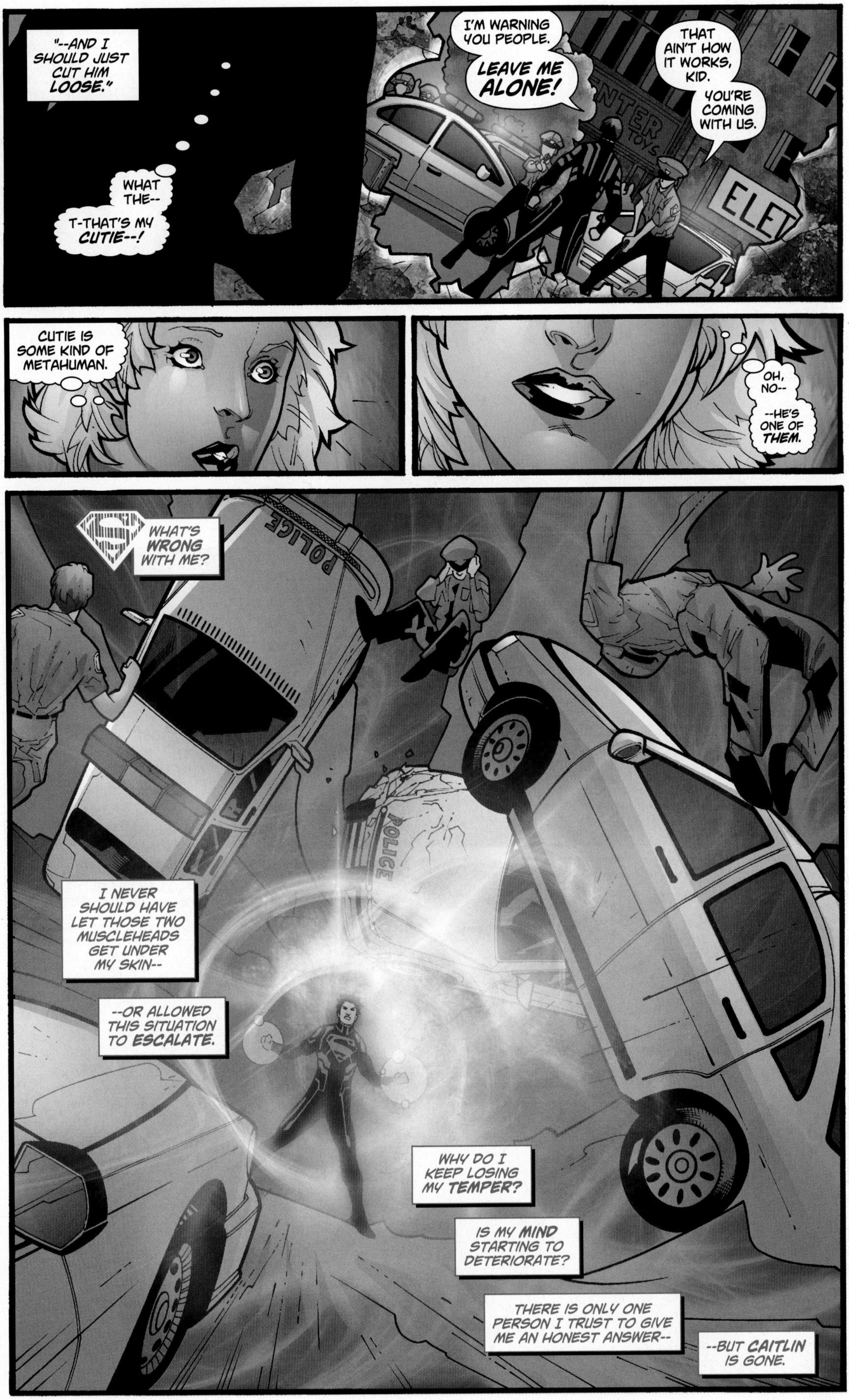

"--AND I SHOULD JUST CUT HIM LOOSE."
WHAT THE--
T-THAT'S MY CUTIE--!
I'M WARNING YOU PEOPLE.
LEAVE ME ALONE!
THAT AIN'T HOW IT WORKS, KID.
YOU'RE COMING WITH US.
CUTIE IS SOME KIND OF METAHUMAN.
OH, NO--
--HE'S ONE OF THEM.
WHAT'S WRONG WITH ME?
POLICE
I NEVER SHOULD HAVE LET THOSE TWO MUSCLEHEADS GET UNDER MY SKIN--
--OR ALLOWED THIS SITUATION TO ESCALATE.
WHY DO I KEEP LOSING MY TEMPER?
IS MY MIND STARTING TO DETERIORATE?
THERE IS ONLY ONE PERSON I TRUST TO GIVE ME AN HONEST ANSWER--
--BUT CAITLIN IS GONE.

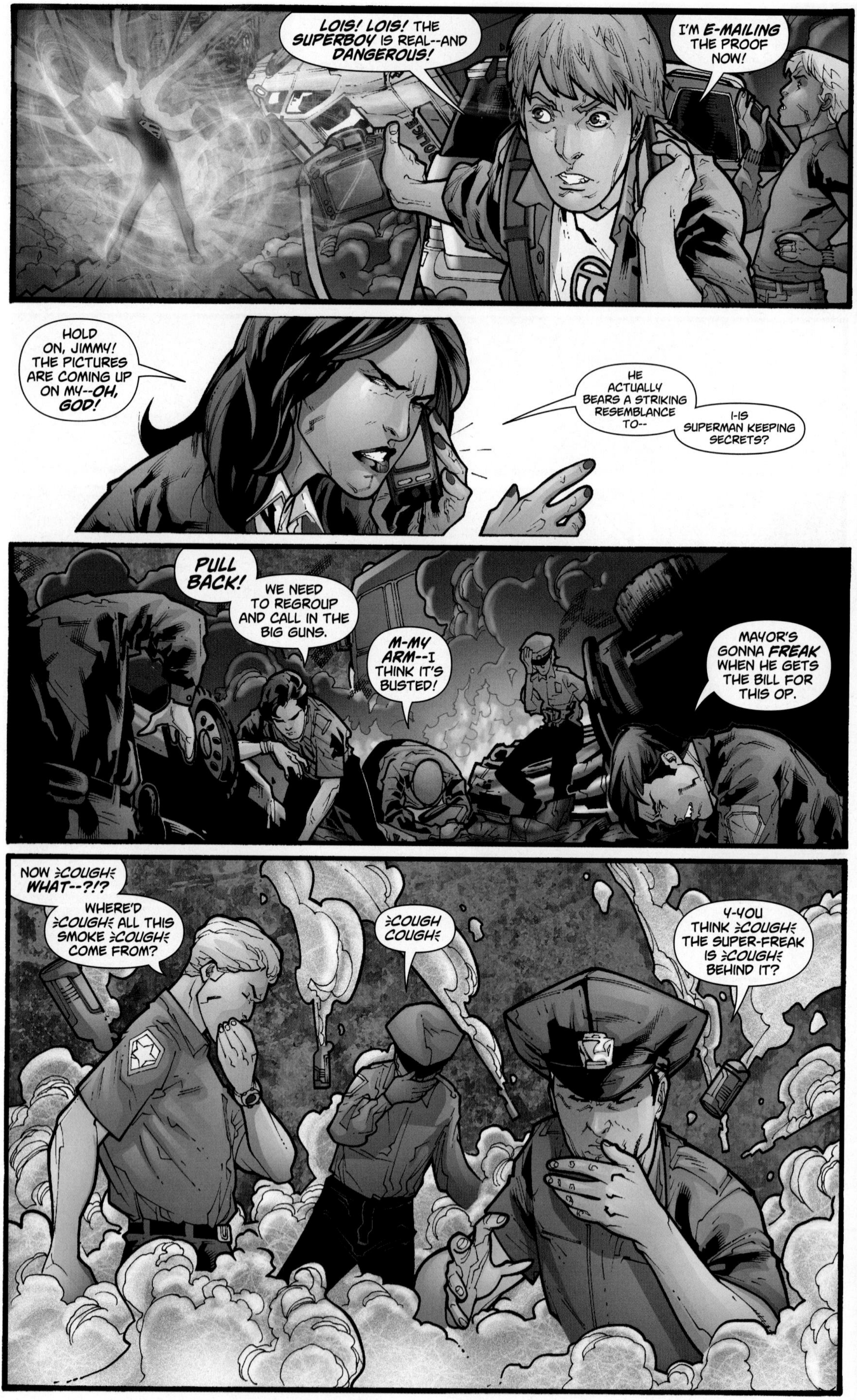
LOIS! LOIS! THE SUPERBOY IS REAL--AND DANGEROUS!
I'M E-MAILING THE PROOF NOW!
HOLD ON, JIMMY! THE PICTURES ARE COMING UP ON MY--OH, GOD!
HE ACTUALLY BEARS A STRIKING RESEMBLANCE TO--
I-IS SUPERMAN KEEPING SECRETS?
PULL BACK!
WE NEED TO REGROUP AND CALL IN THE BIG GUNS.
M-MY ARM--I THINK IT'S BUSTED!
MAYOR'S GONNA FREAK WHEN HE GETS THE BILL FOR THIS OP.
NOW ≻COUGH≺ WHAT--?!?
WHERE'D ≻COUGH≺ ALL THIS SMOKE ≻COUGH≺ COME FROM?
≻COUGH COUGH≺
Y-YOU THINK ≻COUGH≺ THE SUPER-FREAK IS ≻COUGH≺ BEHIND IT?

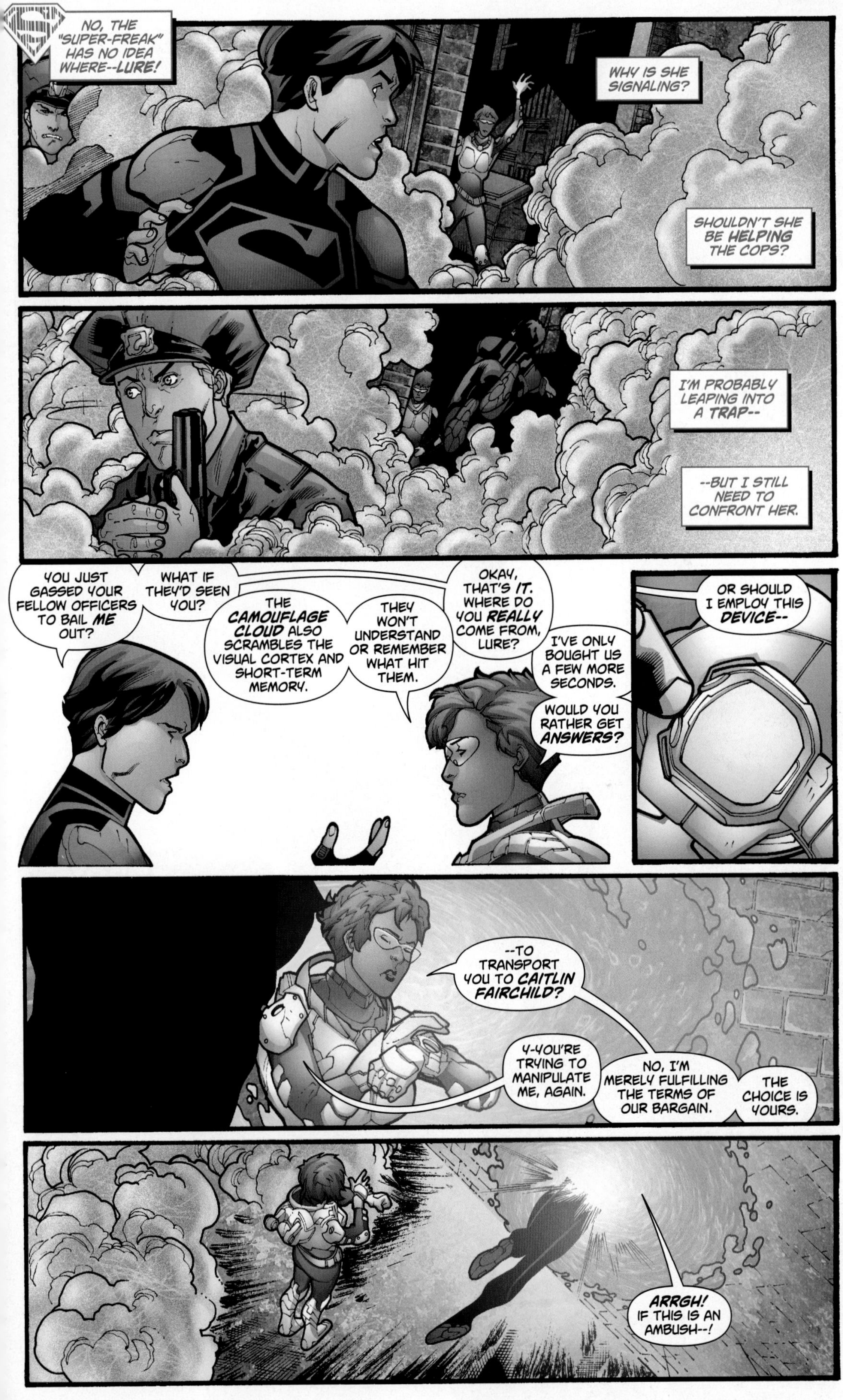
NO, THE "SUPER-FREAK" HAS NO IDEA WHERE--LURE!
WHY IS SHE SIGNALING?
SHOULDN'T SHE BE HELPING THE COPS?
I'M PROBABLY LEAPING INTO A TRAP--
--BUT I STILL NEED TO CONFRONT HER.
YOU JUST GASSED YOUR FELLOW OFFICERS TO BAIL ME OUT?
WHAT IF THEY'D SEEN YOU?
THE CAMOUFLAGE CLOUD ALSO SCRAMBLES THE VISUAL CORTEX AND SHORT-TERM MEMORY.
THEY WON'T UNDERSTAND OR REMEMBER WHAT HIT THEM.
OKAY, THAT'S IT. WHERE DO YOU REALLY COME FROM, LURE?
I'VE ONLY BOUGHT US A FEW MORE SECONDS.
WOULD YOU RATHER GET ANSWERS?
OR SHOULD I EMPLOY THIS DEVICE--
--TO TRANSPORT YOU TO CAITLIN FAIRCHILD?
Y-YOU'RE TRYING TO MANIPULATE ME, AGAIN.
NO, I'M MERELY FULFILLING THE TERMS OF OUR BARGAIN.
THE CHOICE IS YOURS.
ARRGH! IF THIS IS AN AMBUSH--!

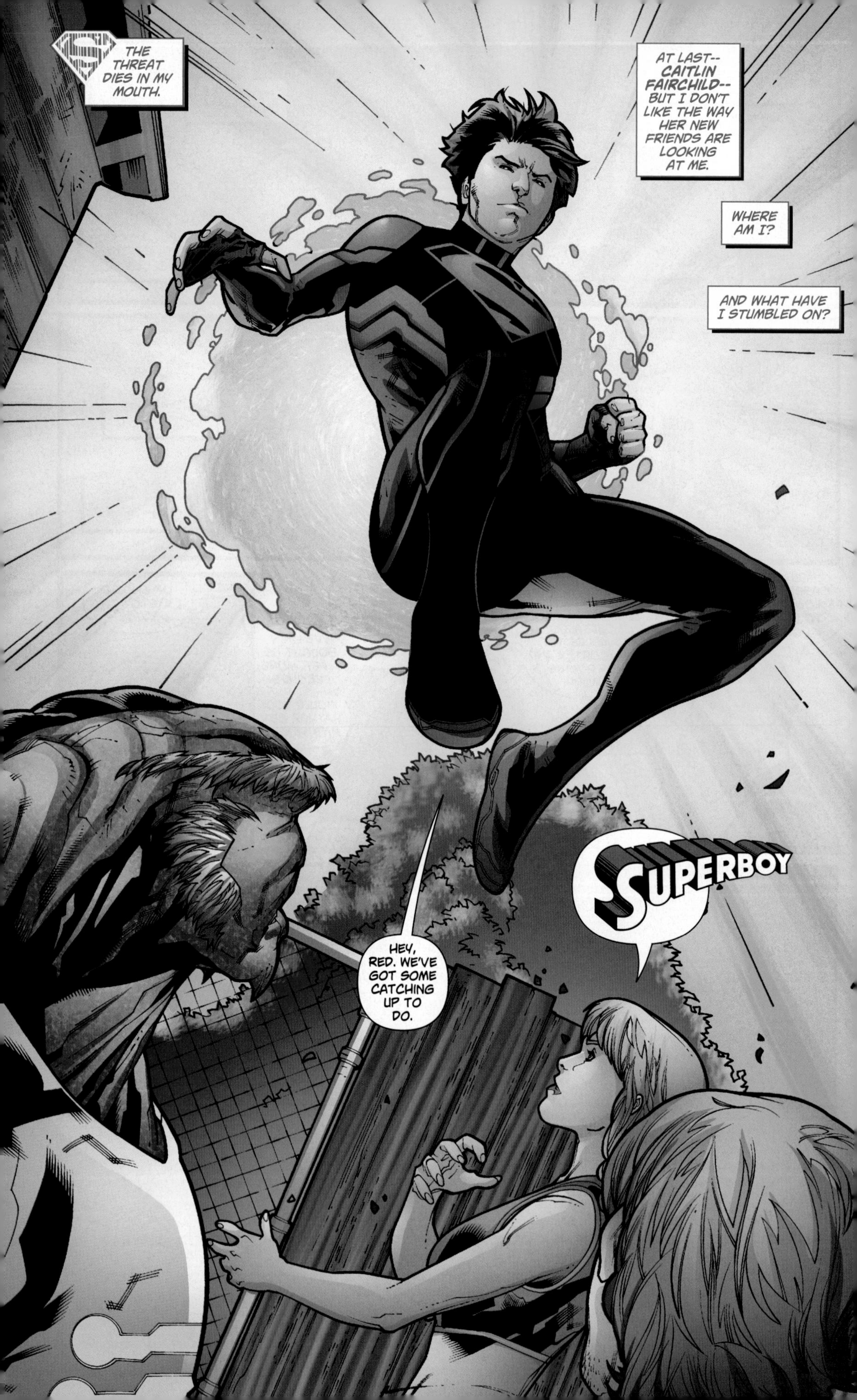
THE THREAT DIES IN MY MOUTH.
AT LAST-- CAITLIN FAIRCHILD-- BUT I DON'T LIKE THE WAY HER NEW FRIENDS ARE LOOKING AT ME.
WHERE AM I?
AND WHAT HAVE I STUMBLED ON?
HEY, RED. WE'VE GOT SOME CATCHING UP TO DO.
SUPERBOY

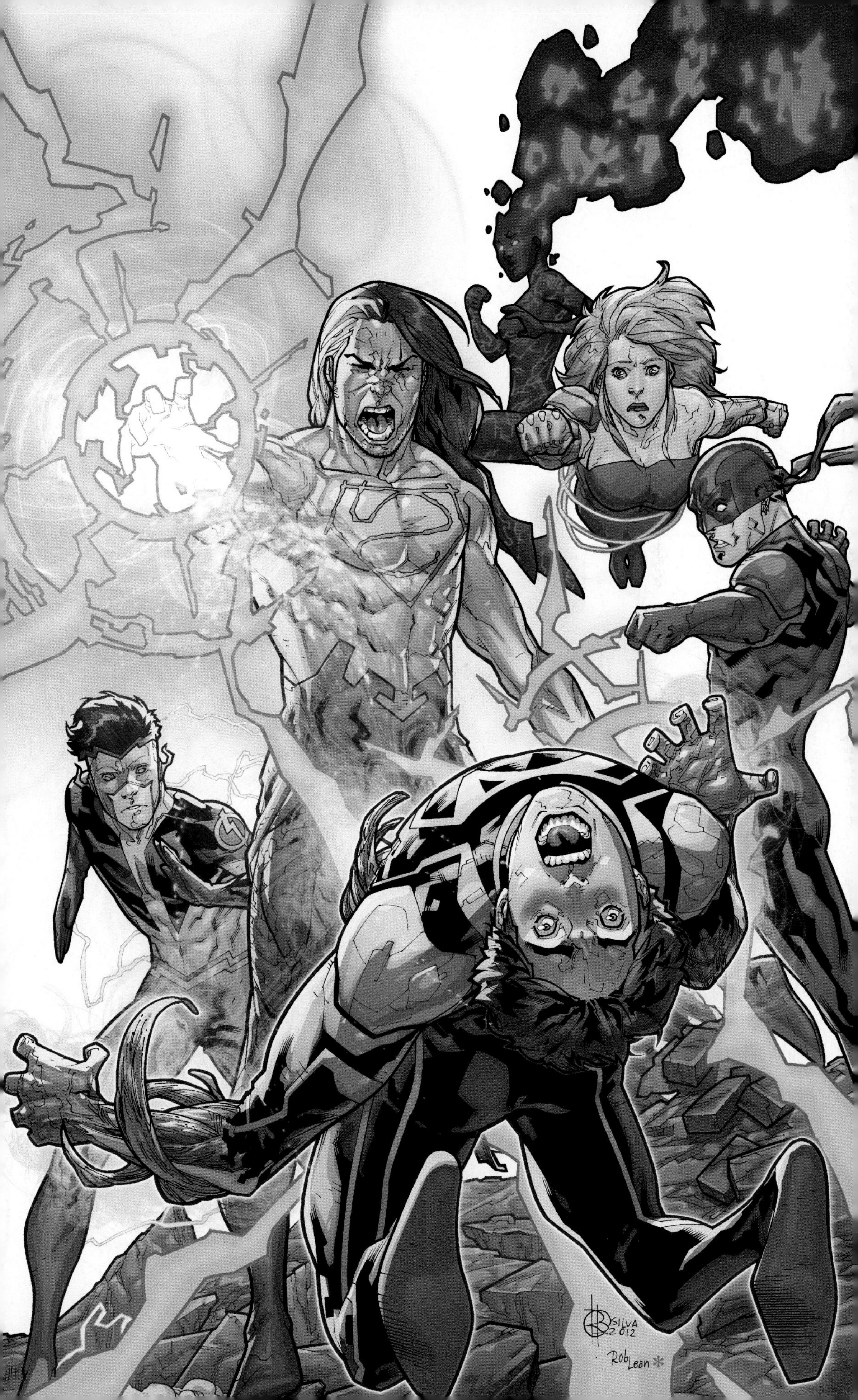
SILVA 2012
Rob Lean

THE FACE OF H'EL!

TOM DeFALCO writer **R.B. SILVA** penciller **ROB LEAN** inker cover art by **R. B. SILVA, ROB LEAN & HI-FI**

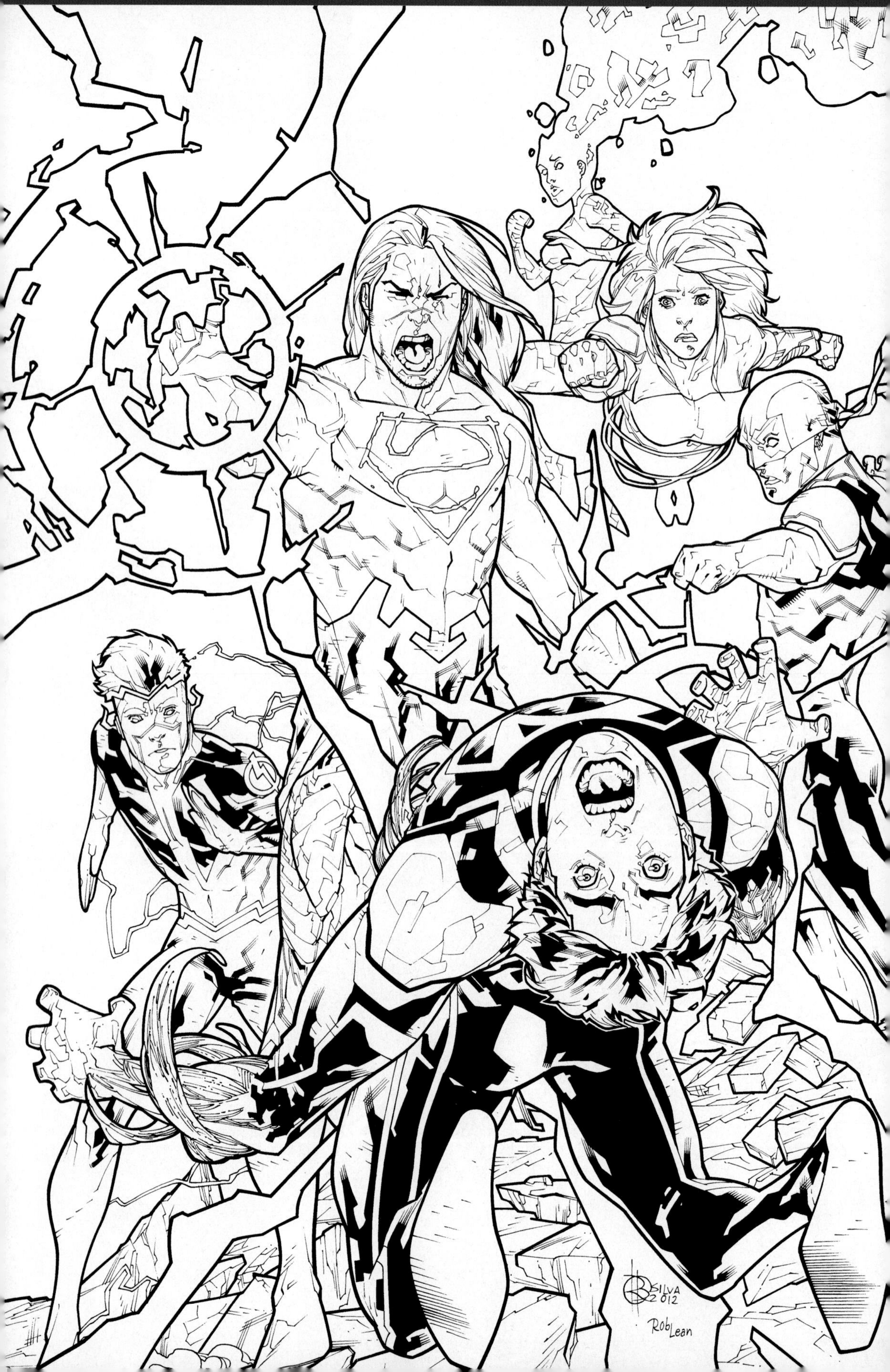

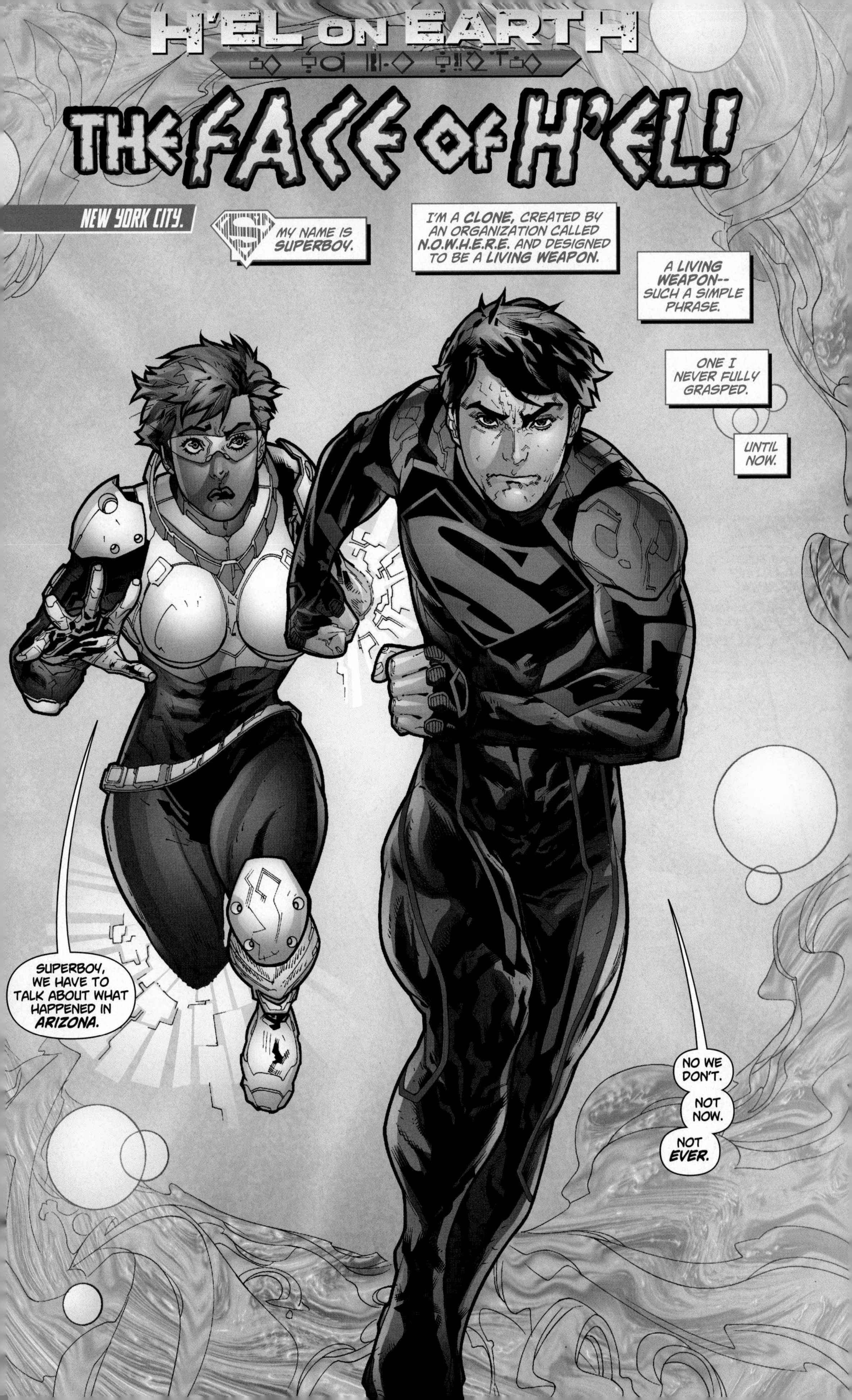
H'EL ON EARTH
THE FACE OF H'EL!
NEW YORK CITY.
MY NAME IS SUPERBOY.
I'M A CLONE, CREATED BY AN ORGANIZATION CALLED N.O.W.H.E.R.E. AND DESIGNED TO BE A LIVING WEAPON.
A LIVING WEAPON-- SUCH A SIMPLE PHRASE.
ONE I NEVER FULLY GRASPED.
UNTIL NOW.
SUPERBOY, WE HAVE TO TALK ABOUT WHAT HAPPENED IN ARIZONA.
NO WE DON'T.
NOT NOW.
NOT EVER.

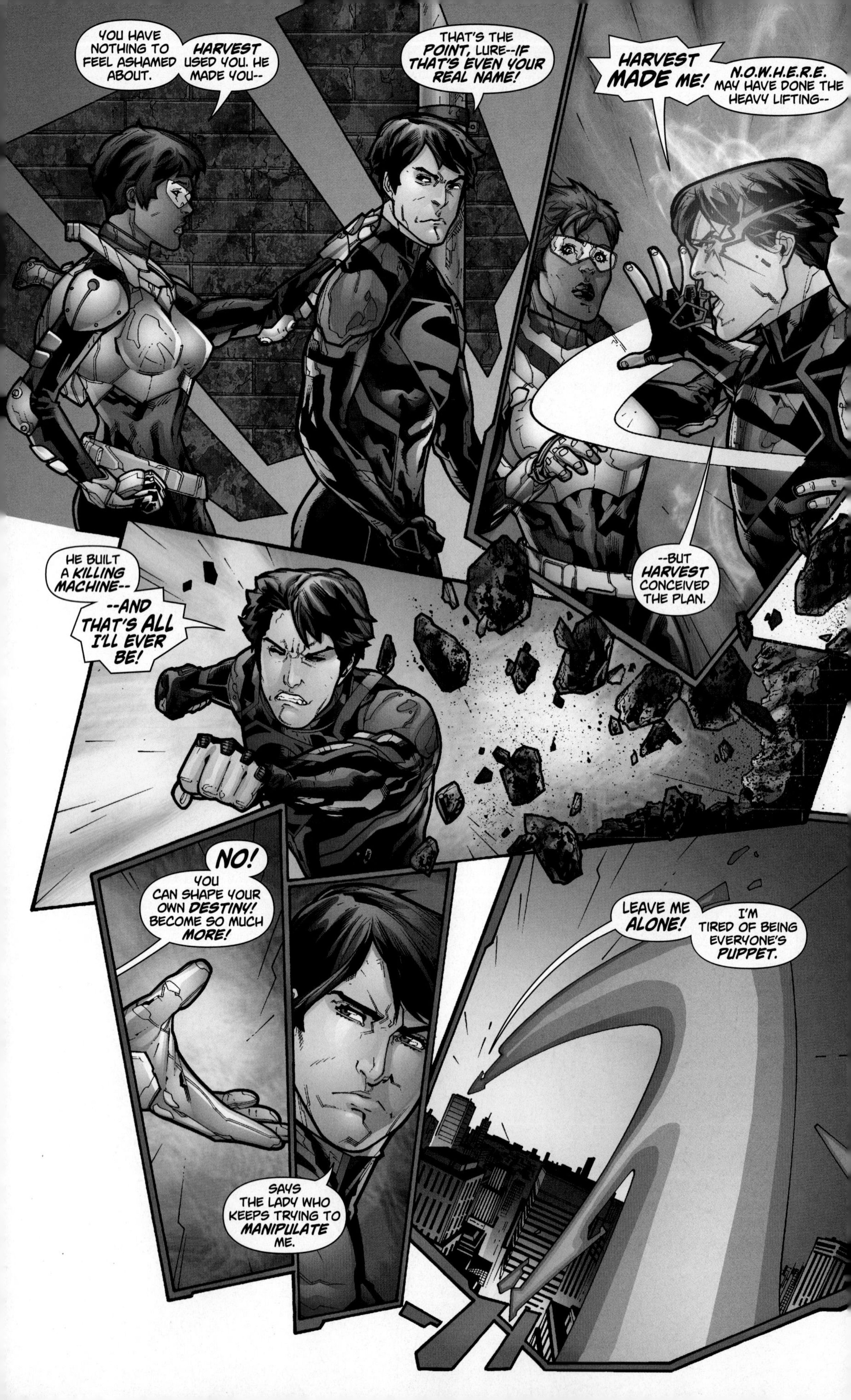

YOU HAVE NOTHING TO FEEL ASHAMED ABOUT.
HARVEST USED YOU. HE MADE YOU--
THAT'S THE POINT, LURE--IF THAT'S EVEN YOUR REAL NAME!
HARVEST MADE ME!
N.O.W.H.E.R.E. MAY HAVE DONE THE HEAVY LIFTING--
--BUT HARVEST CONCEIVED THE PLAN.
HE BUILT A KILLING MACHINE--
--AND THAT'S ALL I'LL EVER BE!
NO!
YOU CAN SHAPE YOUR OWN DESTINY! BECOME SO MUCH MORE!
SAYS THE LADY WHO KEEPS TRYING TO MANIPULATE ME.
LEAVE ME ALONE!
I'M TIRED OF BEING EVERYONE'S PUPPET.

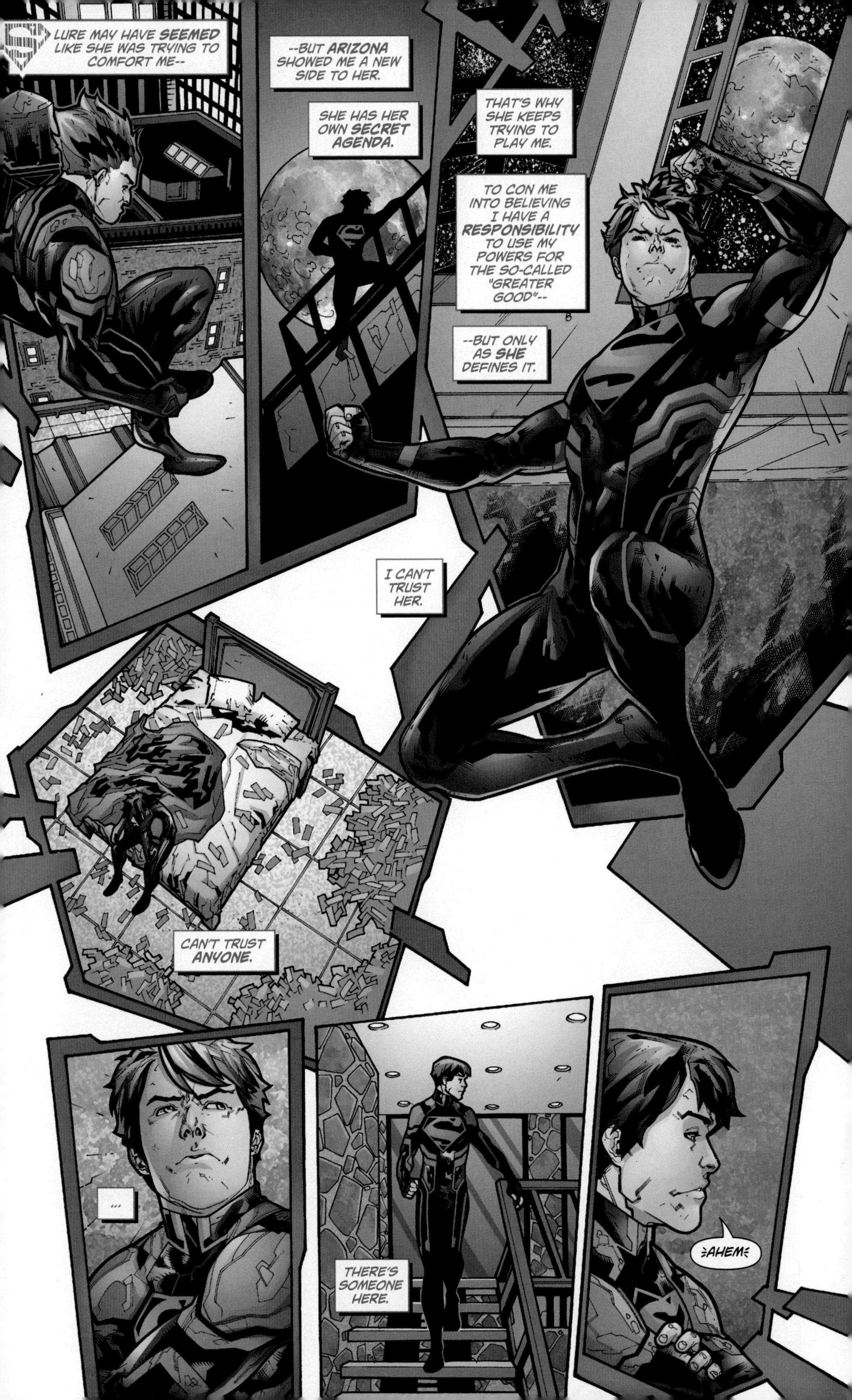

LURE MAY HAVE SEEMED LIKE SHE WAS TRYING TO COMFORT ME--
--BUT ARIZONA SHOWED ME A NEW SIDE TO HER.
SHE HAS HER OWN SECRET AGENDA.
THAT'S WHY SHE KEEPS TRYING TO PLAY ME.
TO CON ME INTO BELIEVING I HAVE A RESPONSIBILITY TO USE MY POWERS FOR THE SO-CALLED "GREATER GOOD"--
--BUT ONLY AS SHE DEFINES IT.
I CAN'T TRUST HER.
CAN'T TRUST ANYONE.
...
THERE'S SOMEONE HERE.
AHEM

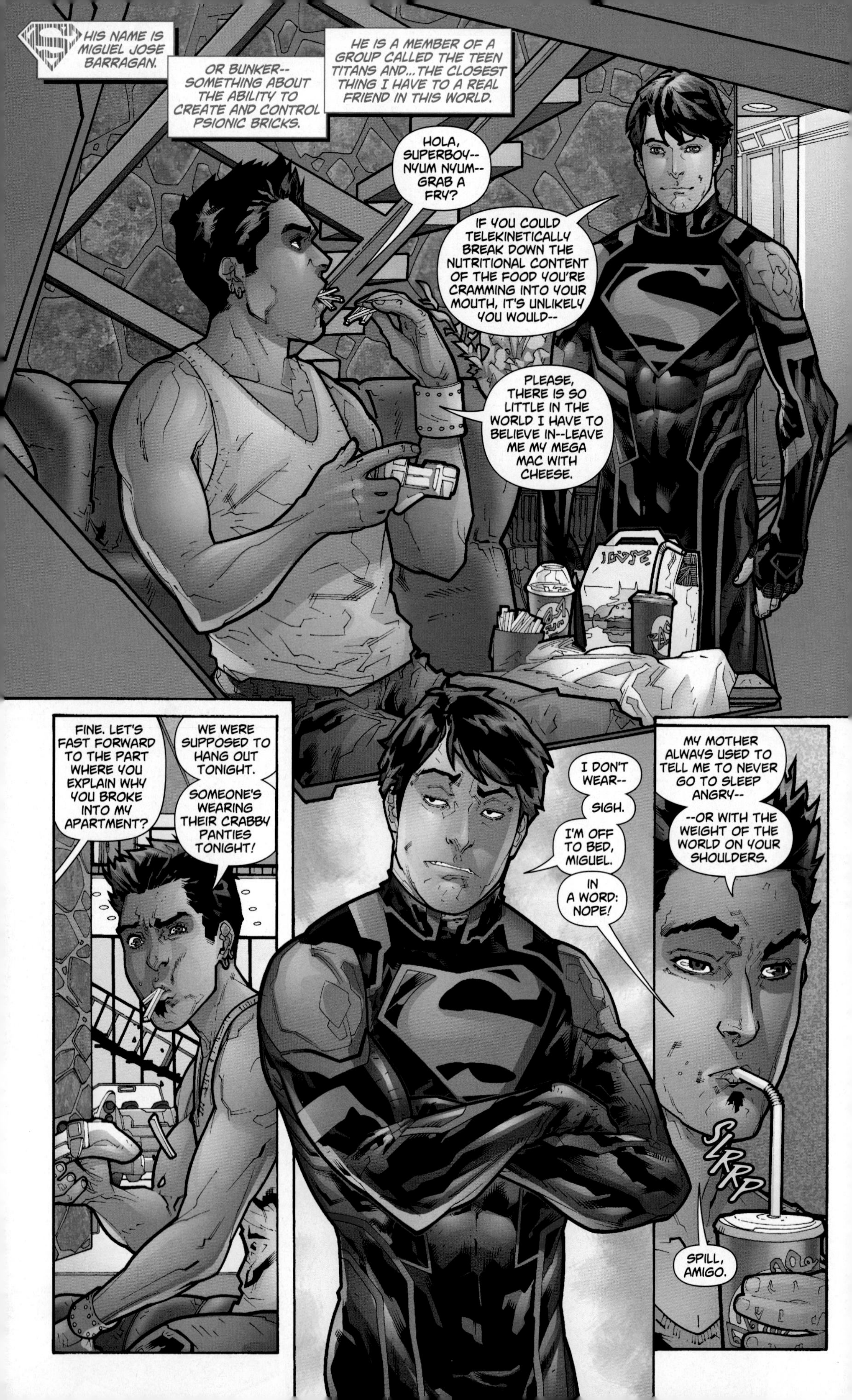
HIS NAME IS MIGUEL JOSE BARRAGAN.
OR BUNKER--SOMETHING ABOUT THE ABILITY TO CREATE AND CONTROL PSIONIC BRICKS.
HE IS A MEMBER OF A GROUP CALLED THE TEEN TITANS AND...THE CLOSEST THING I HAVE TO A REAL FRIEND IN THIS WORLD.
HOLA, SUPERBOY--NYUM NYUM--GRAB A FRY?
IF YOU COULD TELEKINETICALLY BREAK DOWN THE NUTRITIONAL CONTENT OF THE FOOD YOU'RE CRAMMING INTO YOUR MOUTH, IT'S UNLIKELY YOU WOULD--
PLEASE, THERE IS SO LITTLE IN THE WORLD I HAVE TO BELIEVE IN--LEAVE ME MY MEGA MAC WITH CHEESE.
FINE. LET'S FAST FORWARD TO THE PART WHERE YOU EXPLAIN WHY YOU BROKE INTO MY APARTMENT?
WE WERE SUPPOSED TO HANG OUT TONIGHT.
SOMEONE'S WEARING THEIR CRABBY PANTIES TONIGHT!
I DON'T WEAR--
SIGH.
I'M OFF TO BED, MIGUEL.
IN A WORD: NOPE!
MY MOTHER ALWAYS USED TO TELL ME TO NEVER GO TO SLEEP ANGRY--
--OR WITH THE WEIGHT OF THE WORLD ON YOUR SHOULDERS.
SLRRP
SPILL, AMIGO.

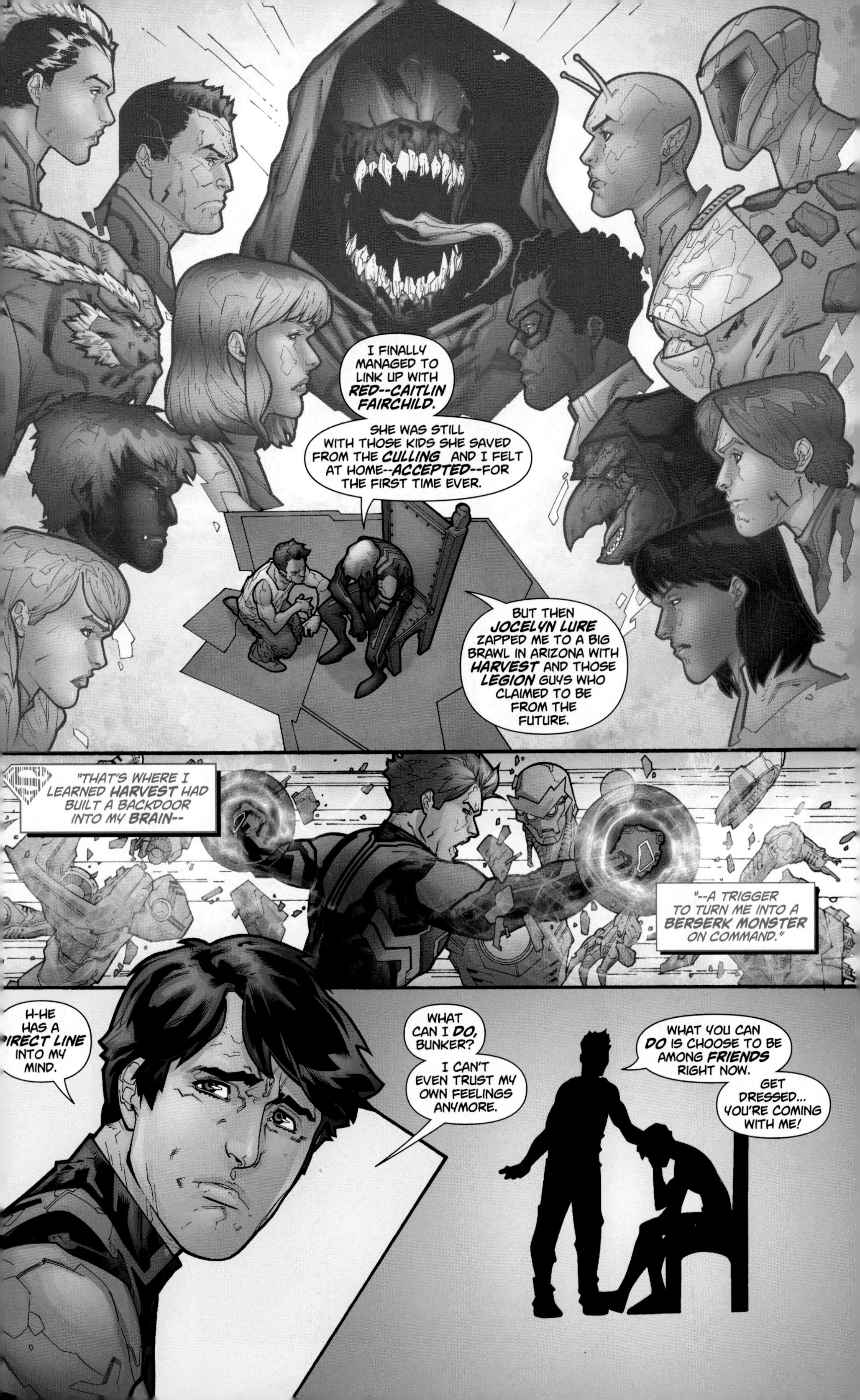
I FINALLY MANAGED TO LINK UP WITH RED--CAITLIN FAIRCHILD.
SHE WAS STILL WITH THOSE KIDS SHE SAVED FROM THE CULLING AND I FELT AT HOME--ACCEPTED--FOR THE FIRST TIME EVER.
BUT THEN JOCELYN LURE ZAPPED ME TO A BIG BRAWL IN ARIZONA WITH HARVEST AND THOSE LEGION GUYS WHO CLAIMED TO BE FROM THE FUTURE.
"THAT'S WHERE I LEARNED HARVEST HAD BUILT A BACKDOOR INTO MY BRAIN--
"--A TRIGGER TO TURN ME INTO A BERSERK MONSTER ON COMMAND."
H-HE HAS A DIRECT LINE INTO MY MIND.
WHAT CAN I DO, BUNKER?
I CAN'T EVEN TRUST MY OWN FEELINGS ANYMORE.
WHAT YOU CAN DO IS CHOOSE TO BE AMONG FRIENDS RIGHT NOW.
GET DRESSED... YOU'RE COMING WITH ME!

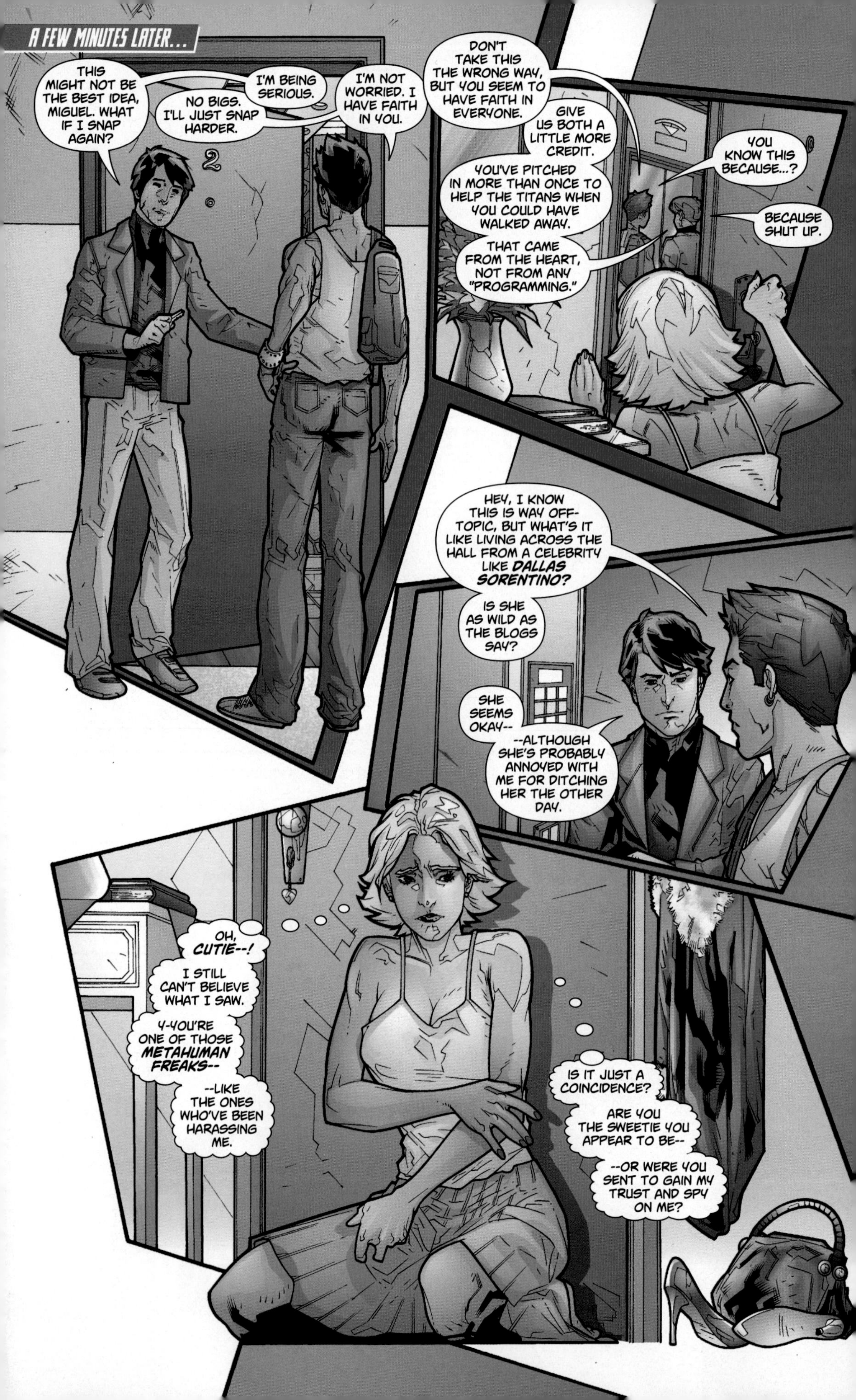
A FEW MINUTES LATER...
THIS MIGHT NOT BE THE BEST IDEA, MIGUEL. WHAT IF I SNAP AGAIN?
NO BIGS. I'LL JUST SNAP HARDER.
I'M BEING SERIOUS.
I'M NOT WORRIED. I HAVE FAITH IN YOU.
DON'T TAKE THIS THE WRONG WAY, BUT YOU SEEM TO HAVE FAITH IN EVERYONE.
GIVE US BOTH A LITTLE MORE CREDIT.
YOU'VE PITCHED IN MORE THAN ONCE TO HELP THE TITANS WHEN YOU COULD HAVE WALKED AWAY.
THAT CAME FROM THE HEART, NOT FROM ANY "PROGRAMMING."
YOU KNOW THIS BECAUSE...?
BECAUSE SHUT UP.
HEY, I KNOW THIS IS WAY OFF-TOPIC, BUT WHAT'S IT LIKE LIVING ACROSS THE HALL FROM A CELEBRITY LIKE DALLAS SORENTINO?
IS SHE AS WILD AS THE BLOGS SAY?
SHE SEEMS OKAY--
--ALTHOUGH SHE'S PROBABLY ANNOYED WITH ME FOR DITCHING HER THE OTHER DAY.
OH, CUTIE--!
I STILL CAN'T BELIEVE WHAT I SAW.
Y-YOU'RE ONE OF THOSE METAHUMAN FREAKS--
--LIKE THE ONES WHO'VE BEEN HARASSING ME.
IS IT JUST A COINCIDENCE?
ARE YOU THE SWEETIE YOU APPEAR TO BE--
--OR WERE YOU SENT TO GAIN MY TRUST AND SPY ON ME?

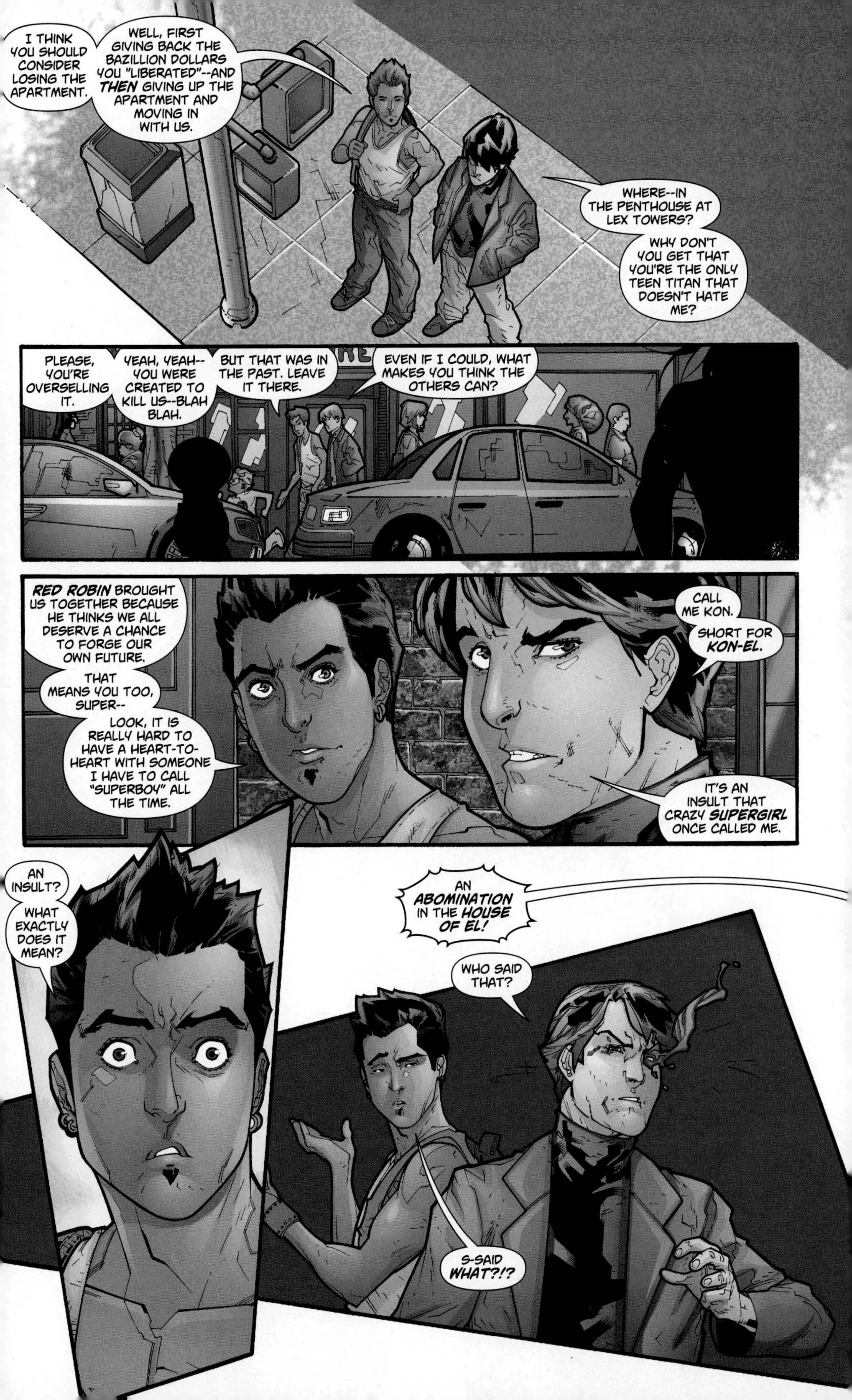
I THINK YOU SHOULD CONSIDER LOSING THE APARTMENT.
WELL, FIRST GIVING BACK THE BAZILLION DOLLARS YOU "LIBERATED"--AND THEN GIVING UP THE APARTMENT AND MOVING IN WITH US.
WHERE--IN THE PENTHOUSE AT LEX TOWERS?
WHY DON'T YOU GET THAT YOU'RE THE ONLY TEEN TITAN THAT DOESN'T HATE ME?
PLEASE, YOU'RE OVERSELLING IT.
YEAH, YEAH-- YOU WERE CREATED TO KILL US--BLAH BLAH.
BUT THAT WAS IN THE PAST. LEAVE IT THERE.
EVEN IF I COULD, WHAT MAKES YOU THINK THE OTHERS CAN?
RED ROBIN BROUGHT US TOGETHER BECAUSE HE THINKS WE ALL DESERVE A CHANCE TO FORGE OUR OWN FUTURE.
THAT MEANS YOU TOO, SUPER--
LOOK, IT IS REALLY HARD TO HAVE A HEART-TO-HEART WITH SOMEONE I HAVE TO CALL "SUPERBOY" ALL THE TIME.
CALL ME KON.
SHORT FOR KON-EL.
IT'S AN INSULT THAT CRAZY SUPERGIRL ONCE CALLED ME.
AN INSULT?
WHAT EXACTLY DOES IT MEAN?
AN ABOMINATION IN THE HOUSE OF EL!
WHO SAID THAT?
S-SAID WHAT?!?

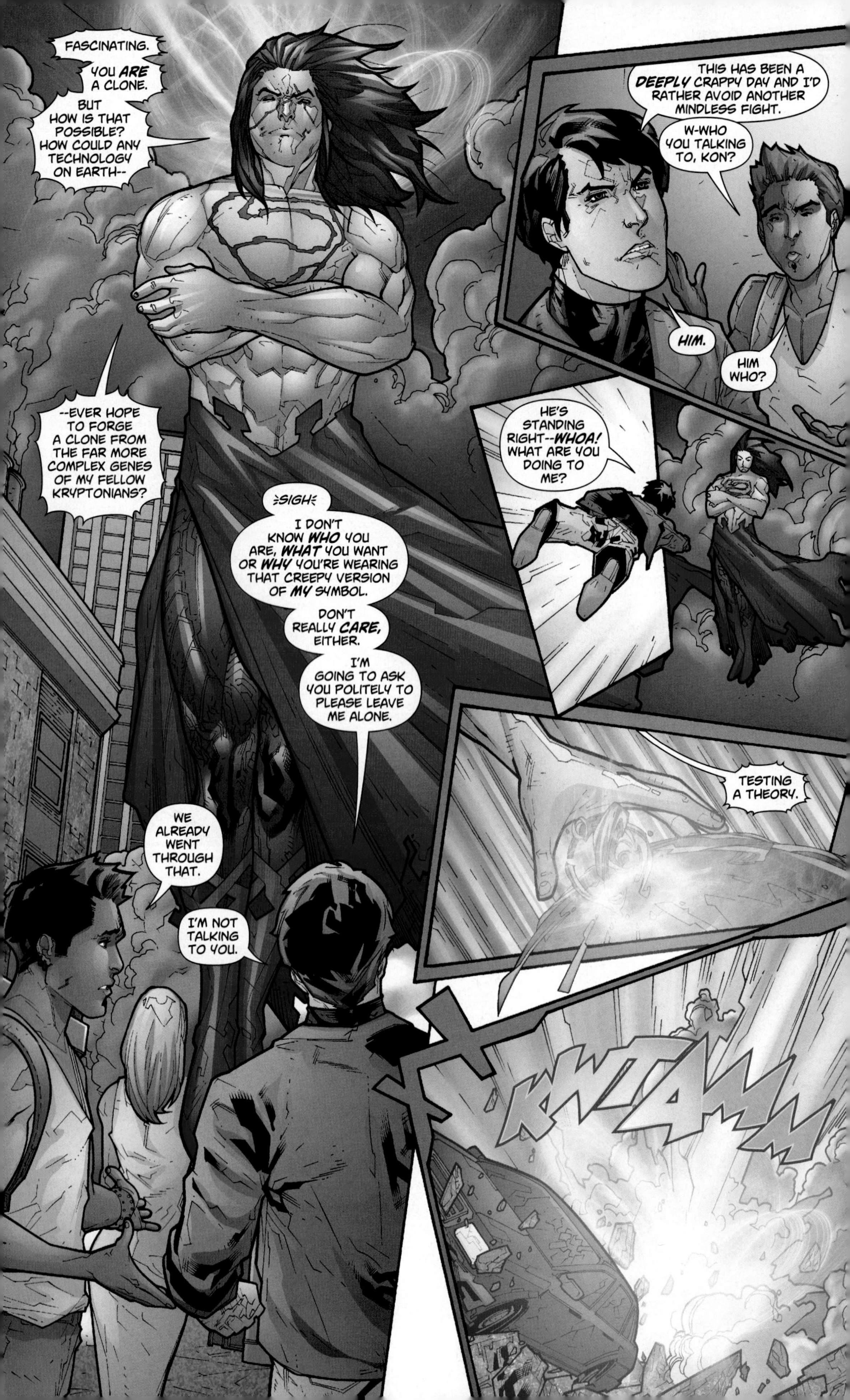
FASCINATING.
YOU ARE A CLONE.
BUT HOW IS THAT POSSIBLE? HOW COULD ANY TECHNOLOGY ON EARTH--
--EVER HOPE TO FORGE A CLONE FROM THE FAR MORE COMPLEX GENES OF MY FELLOW KRYPTONIANS?
SIGH
I DON'T KNOW WHO YOU ARE, WHAT YOU WANT OR WHY YOU'RE WEARING THAT CREEPY VERSION OF MY SYMBOL.
DON'T REALLY CARE, EITHER.
I'M GOING TO ASK YOU POLITELY TO PLEASE LEAVE ME ALONE.
WE ALREADY WENT THROUGH THAT.
I'M NOT TALKING TO YOU.
THIS HAS BEEN A DEEPLY CRAPPY DAY AND I'D RATHER AVOID ANOTHER MINDLESS FIGHT.
W-WHO YOU TALKING TO, KON?
HIM.
HIM WHO?
HE'S STANDING RIGHT--WHOA! WHAT ARE YOU DOING TO ME?
TESTING A THEORY.
KWTAMM

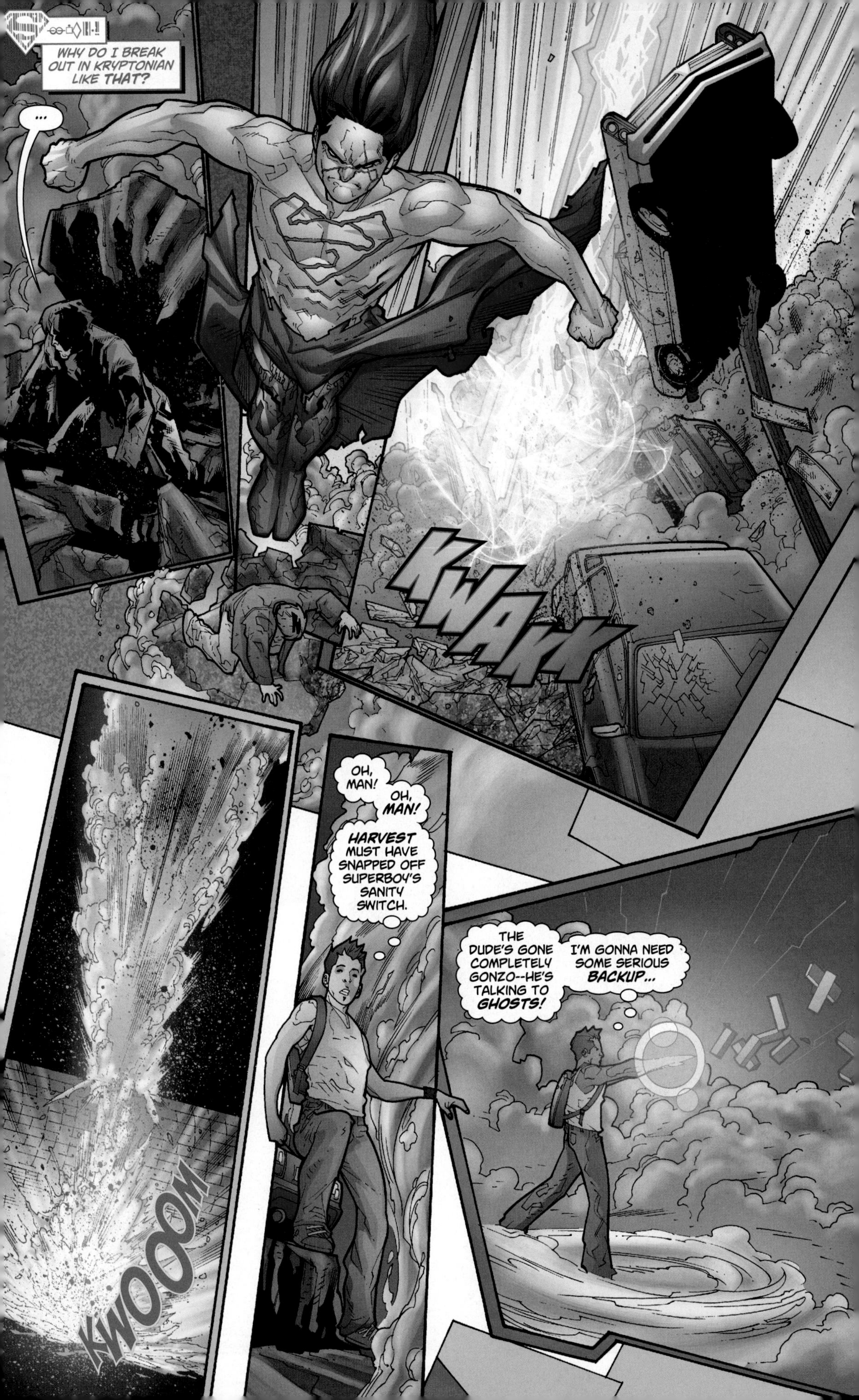
WHY DO I BREAK OUT IN KRYPTONIAN LIKE THAT?
...
KWAKK
KWOOOM
OH, MAN!
OH, MAN!
HARVEST MUST HAVE SNAPPED OFF SUPERBOY'S SANITY SWITCH.
THE DUDE'S GONE COMPLETELY GONZO--HE'S TALKING TO GHOSTS!
I'M GONNA NEED SOME SERIOUS BACKUP...

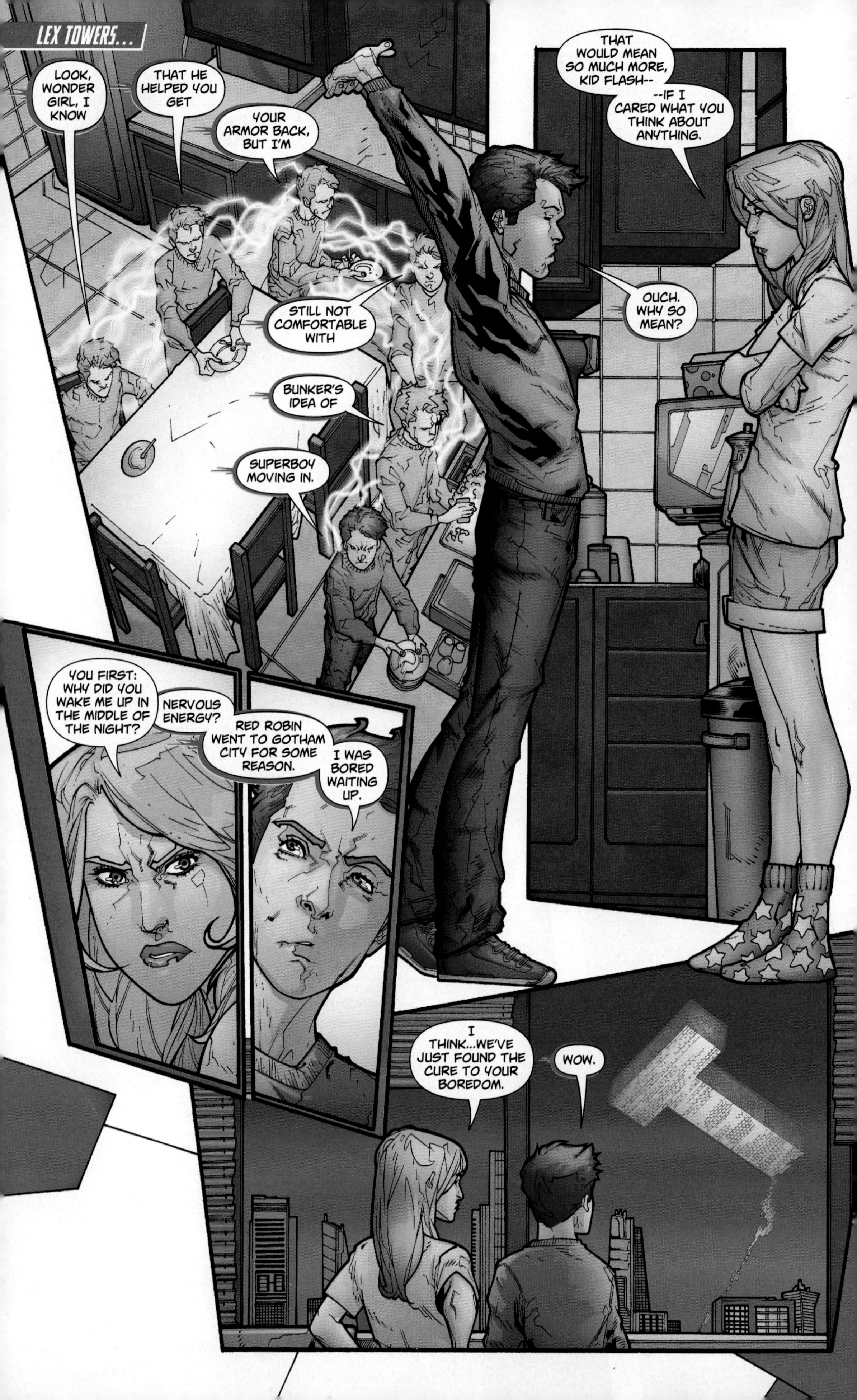
LEX TOWERS...
LOOK, WONDER GIRL, I KNOW
THAT HE HELPED YOU GET
YOUR ARMOR BACK, BUT I'M
STILL NOT COMFORTABLE WITH
BUNKER'S IDEA OF
SUPERBOY MOVING IN.
THAT WOULD MEAN SO MUCH MORE, KID FLASH--
--IF I CARED WHAT YOU THINK ABOUT ANYTHING.
OUCH. WHY SO MEAN?
YOU FIRST: WHY DID YOU WAKE ME UP IN THE MIDDLE OF THE NIGHT?
NERVOUS ENERGY?
RED ROBIN WENT TO GOTHAM CITY FOR SOME REASON.
I WAS BORED WAITING UP.
I THINK...WE'VE JUST FOUND THE CURE TO YOUR BOREDOM.
WOW.

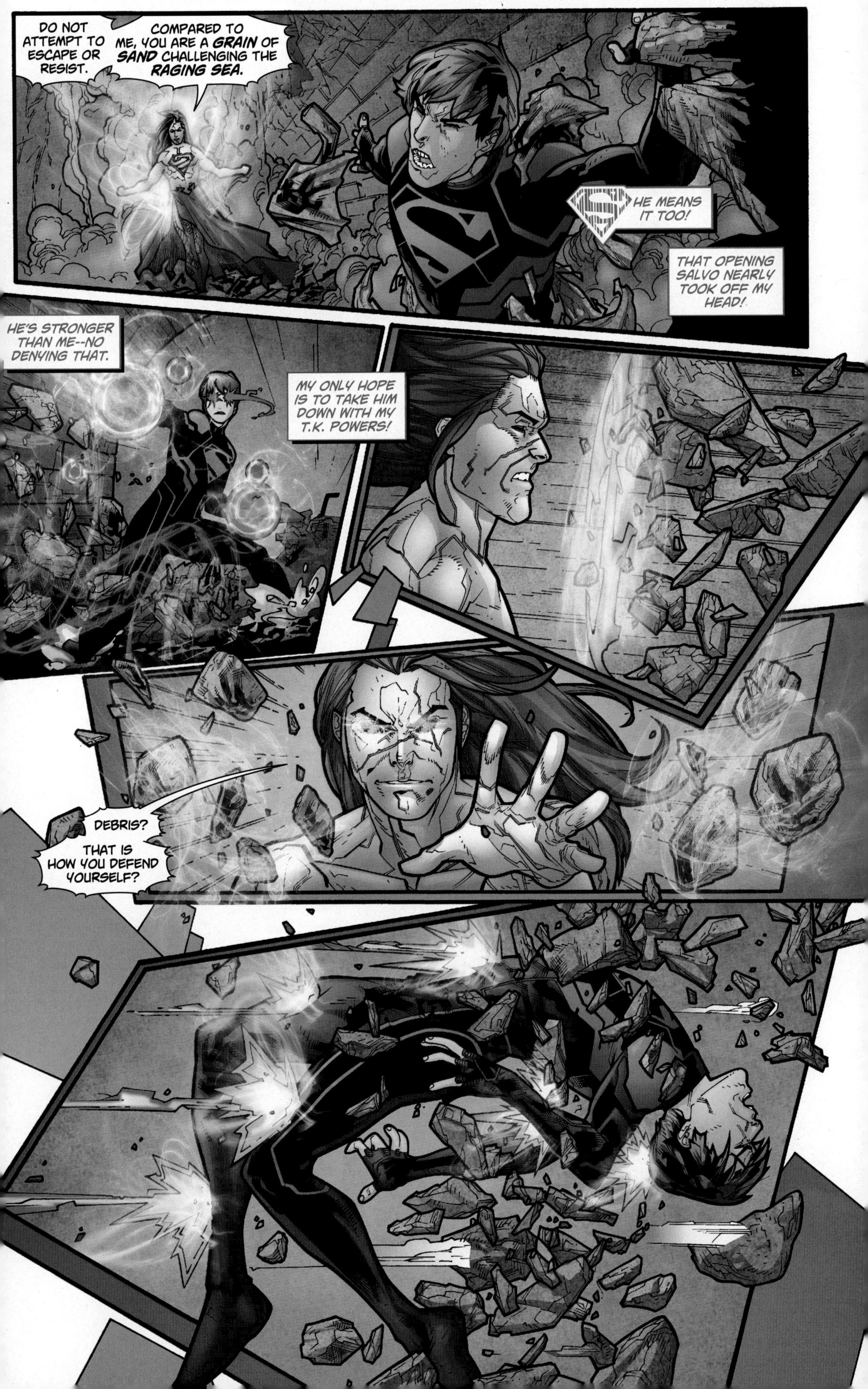
DO NOT ATTEMPT TO ESCAPE OR RESIST.
COMPARED TO ME, YOU ARE A GRAIN OF SAND CHALLENGING THE RAGING SEA.
HE MEANS IT TOO!
THAT OPENING SALVO NEARLY TOOK OFF MY HEAD!
HE'S STRONGER THAN ME--NO DENYING THAT.
MY ONLY HOPE IS TO TAKE HIM DOWN WITH MY T.K. POWERS!
DEBRIS?
THAT IS HOW YOU DEFEND YOURSELF?

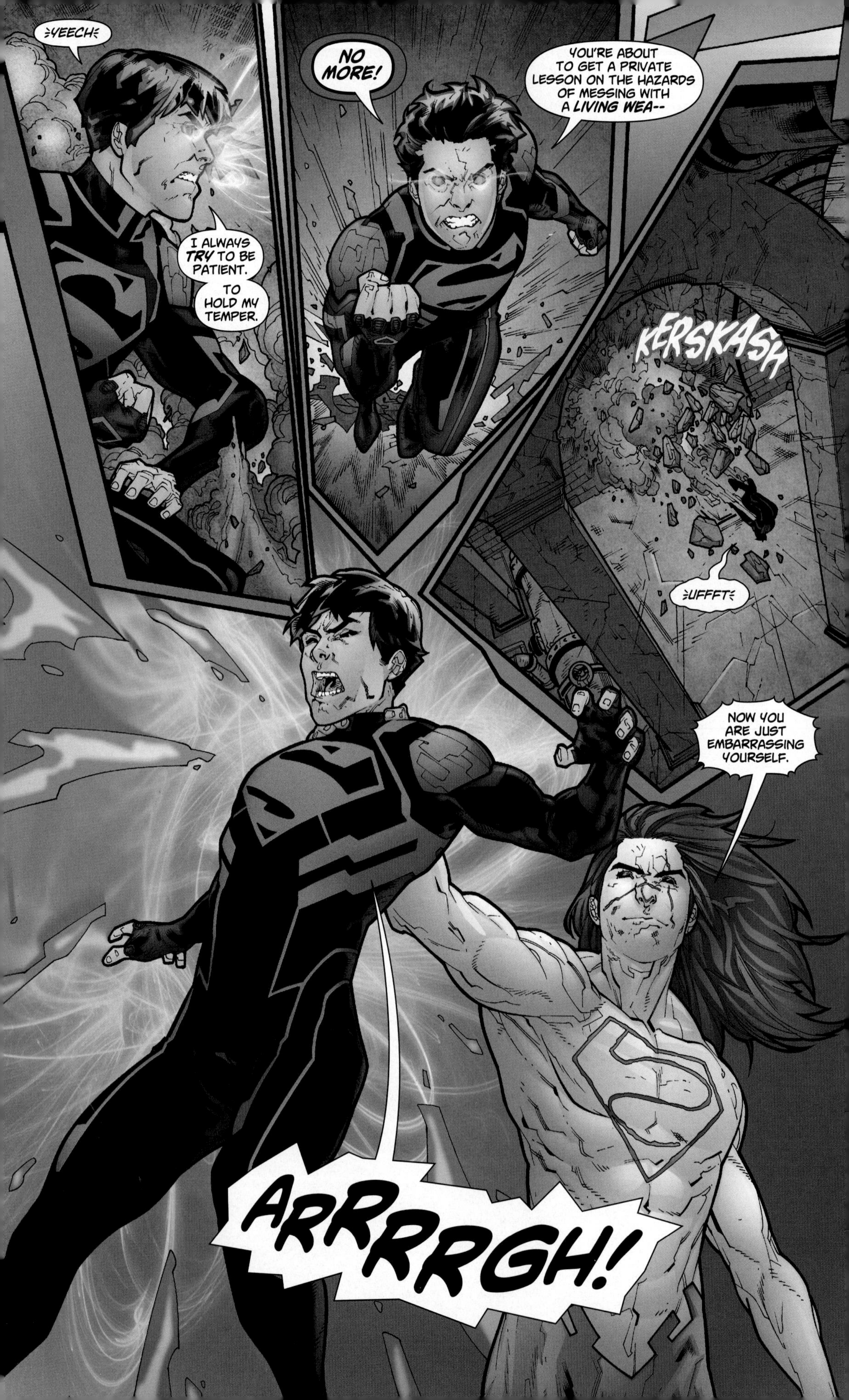
YEECH
I ALWAYS TRY TO BE PATIENT.
TO HOLD MY TEMPER.
NO MORE!
YOU'RE ABOUT TO GET A PRIVATE LESSON ON THE HAZARDS OF MESSING WITH A LIVING WEA--
KERSKASH
UFFFT
NOW YOU ARE JUST EMBARRASSING YOURSELF.
ARRRRGH!

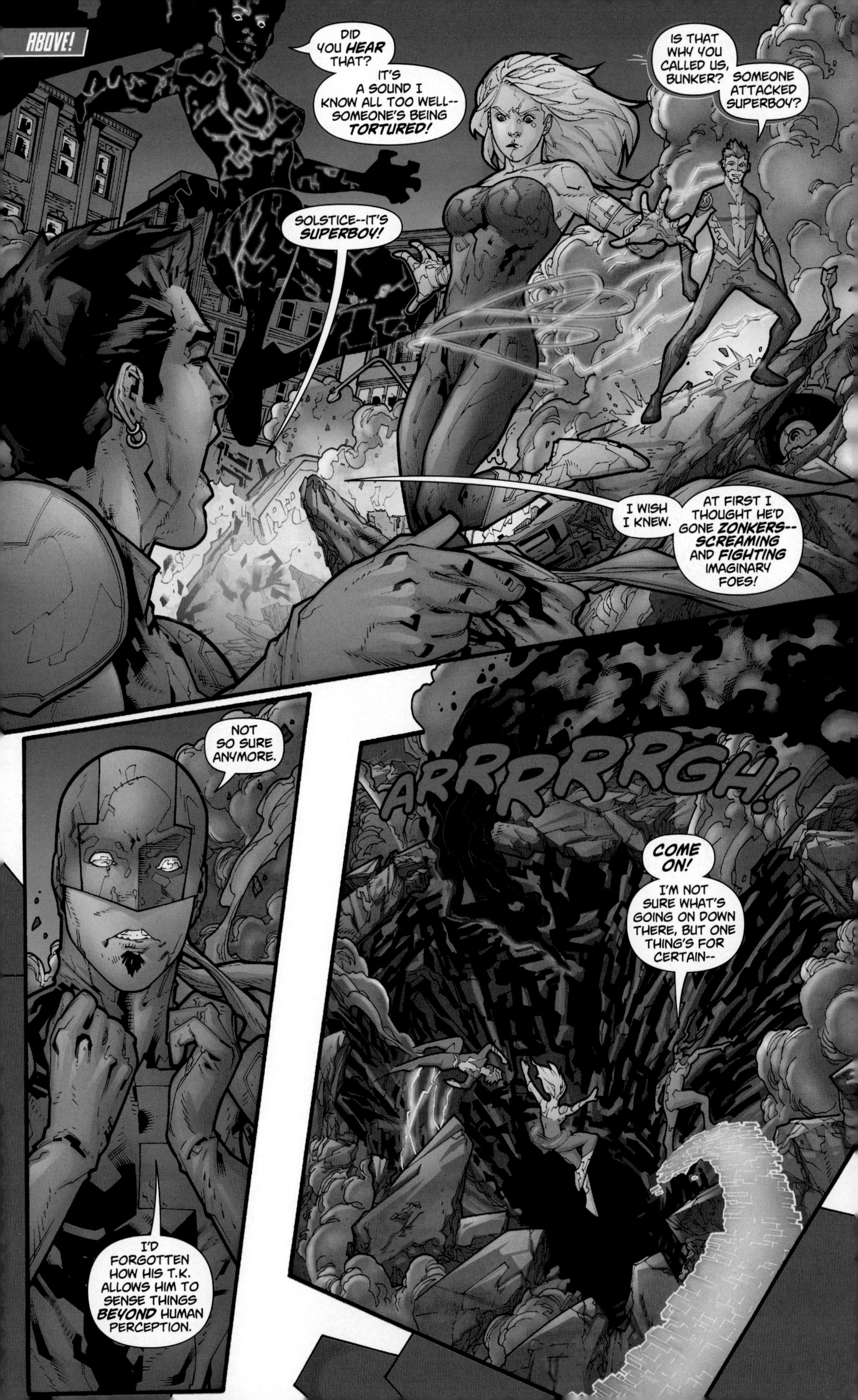
ABOVE!
DID YOU HEAR THAT?
IT'S A SOUND I KNOW ALL TOO WELL-- SOMEONE'S BEING TORTURED!
IS THAT WHY YOU CALLED US, BUNKER?
SOMEONE ATTACKED SUPERBOY?
SOLSTICE--IT'S SUPERBOY!
I WISH I KNEW.
AT FIRST I THOUGHT HE'D GONE ZONKERS-- SCREAMING AND FIGHTING IMAGINARY FOES!
NOT SO SURE ANYMORE.
I'D FORGOTTEN HOW HIS T.K. ALLOWS HIM TO SENSE THINGS BEYOND HUMAN PERCEPTION.
ARRRRRGH!
COME ON!
I'M NOT SURE WHAT'S GOING ON DOWN THERE, BUT ONE THING'S FOR CERTAIN--

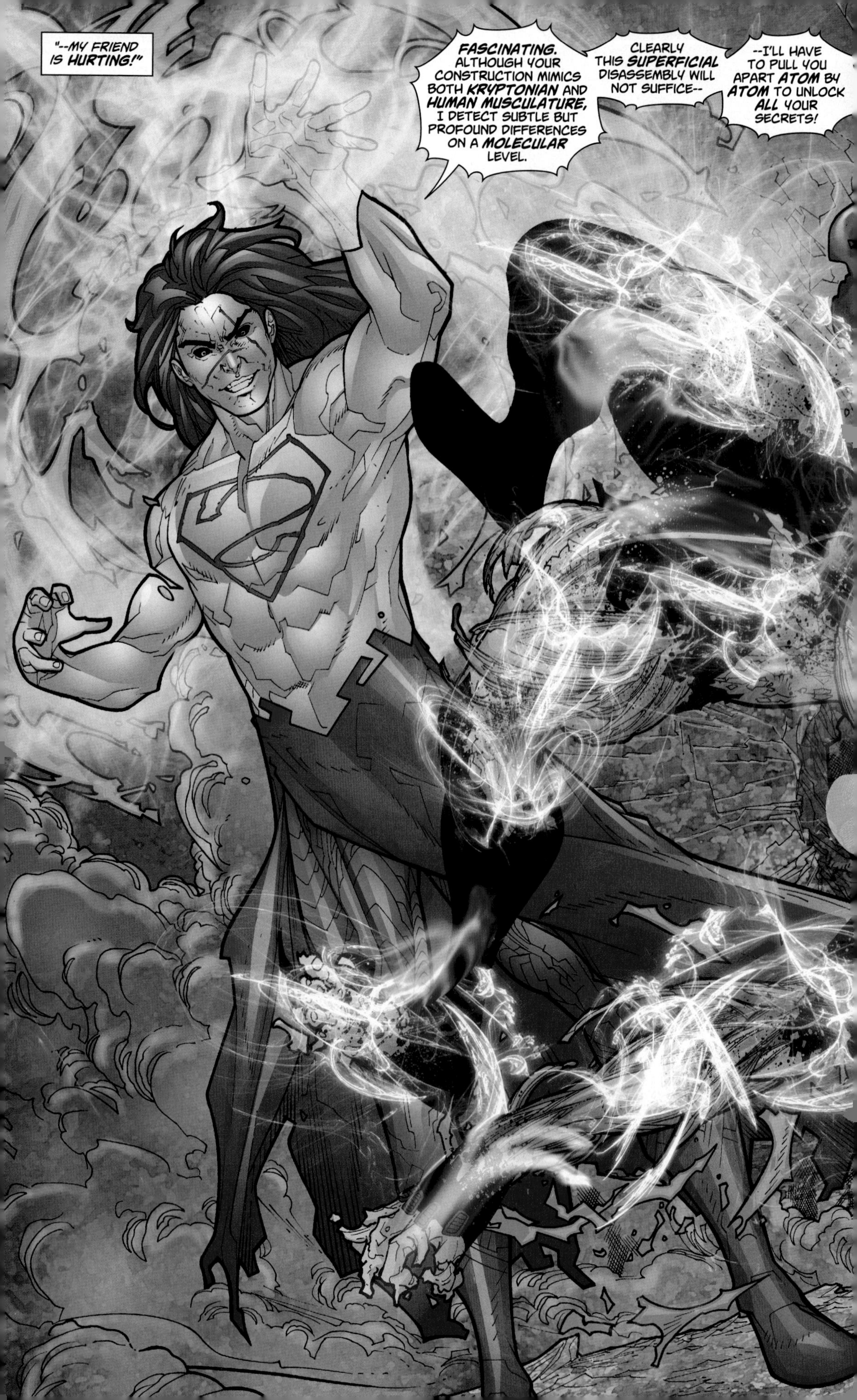
"--MY FRIEND IS HURTING!"
FASCINATING. ALTHOUGH YOUR CONSTRUCTION MIMICS BOTH KRYPTONIAN AND HUMAN MUSCULATURE, I DETECT SUBTLE BUT PROFOUND DIFFERENCES ON A MOLECULAR LEVEL.
CLEARLY THIS SUPERFICIAL DISASSEMBLY WILL NOT SUFFICE--
--I'LL HAVE TO PULL YOU APART ATOM BY ATOM TO UNLOCK ALL YOUR SECRETS!

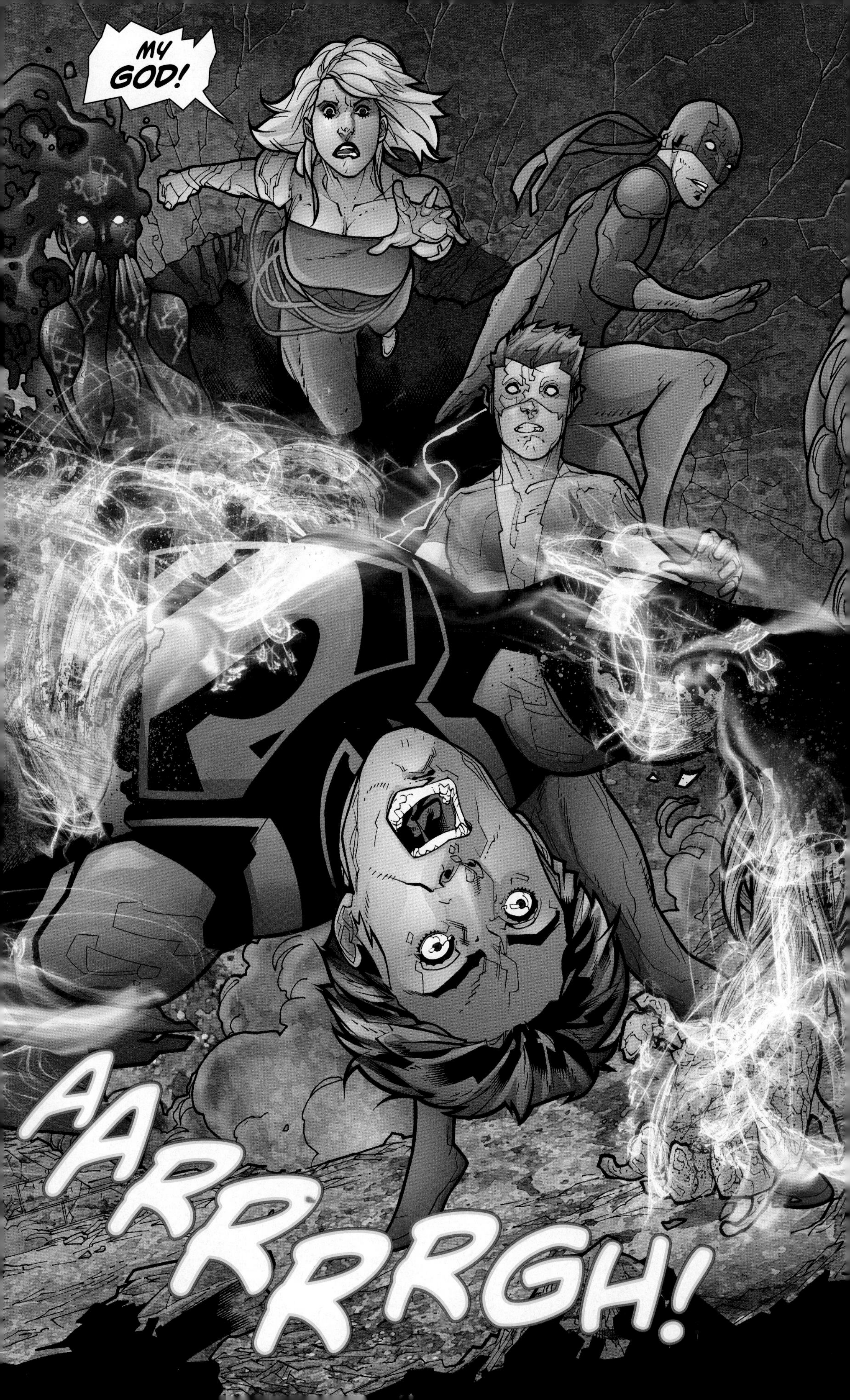
MY GOD!
AARRRRGH!

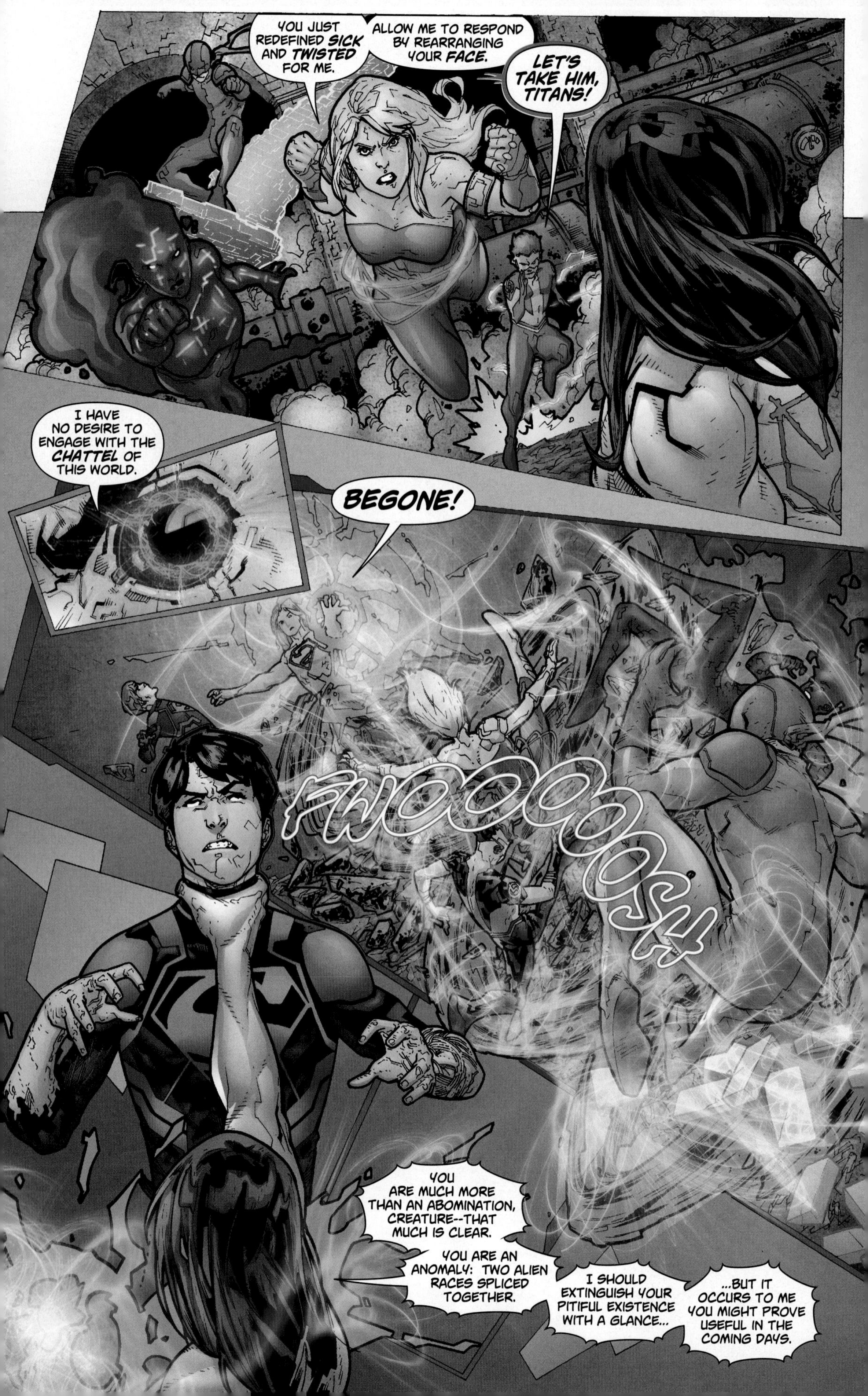

YOU JUST REDEFINED SICK AND TWISTED FOR ME.
ALLOW ME TO RESPOND BY REARRANGING YOUR FACE.
LET'S TAKE HIM, TITANS!
I HAVE NO DESIRE TO ENGAGE WITH THE CHATTEL OF THIS WORLD.
BEGONE!
FWOOOOOSH
YOU ARE MUCH MORE THAN AN ABOMINATION, CREATURE--THAT MUCH IS CLEAR.
YOU ARE AN ANOMALY: TWO ALIEN RACES SPLICED TOGETHER.
I SHOULD EXTINGUISH YOUR PITIFUL EXISTENCE WITH A GLANCE...
...BUT IT OCCURS TO ME YOU MIGHT PROVE USEFUL IN THE COMING DAYS.

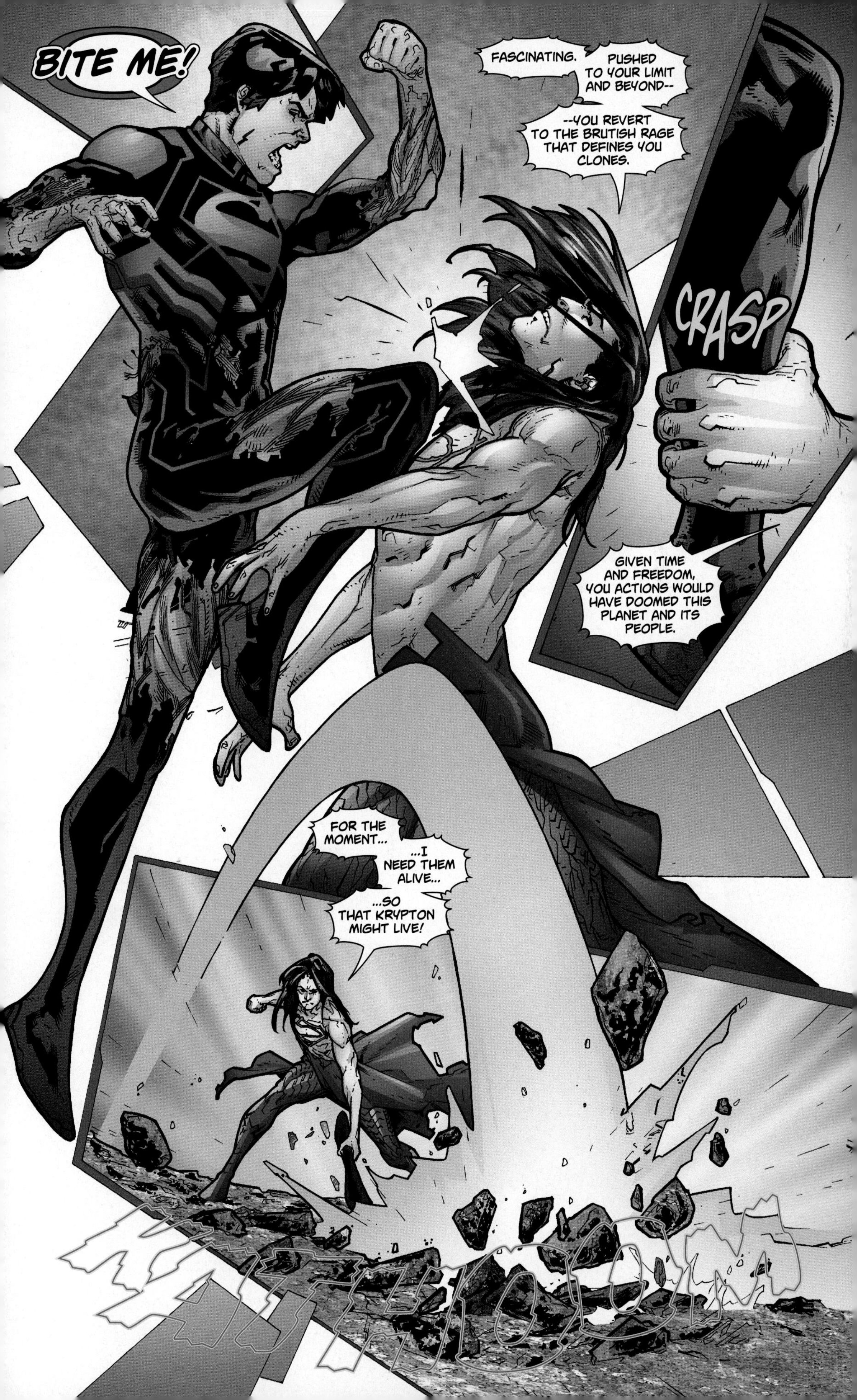
BITE ME!
FASCINATING.
PUSHED TO YOUR LIMIT AND BEYOND--
--YOU REVERT TO THE BRUTISH RAGE THAT DEFINES YOU CLONES.
CRASP
GIVEN TIME AND FREEDOM, YOU ACTIONS WOULD HAVE DOOMED THIS PLANET AND ITS PEOPLE.
FOR THE MOMENT...
...I NEED THEM ALIVE...
...SO THAT KRYPTON MIGHT LIVE!

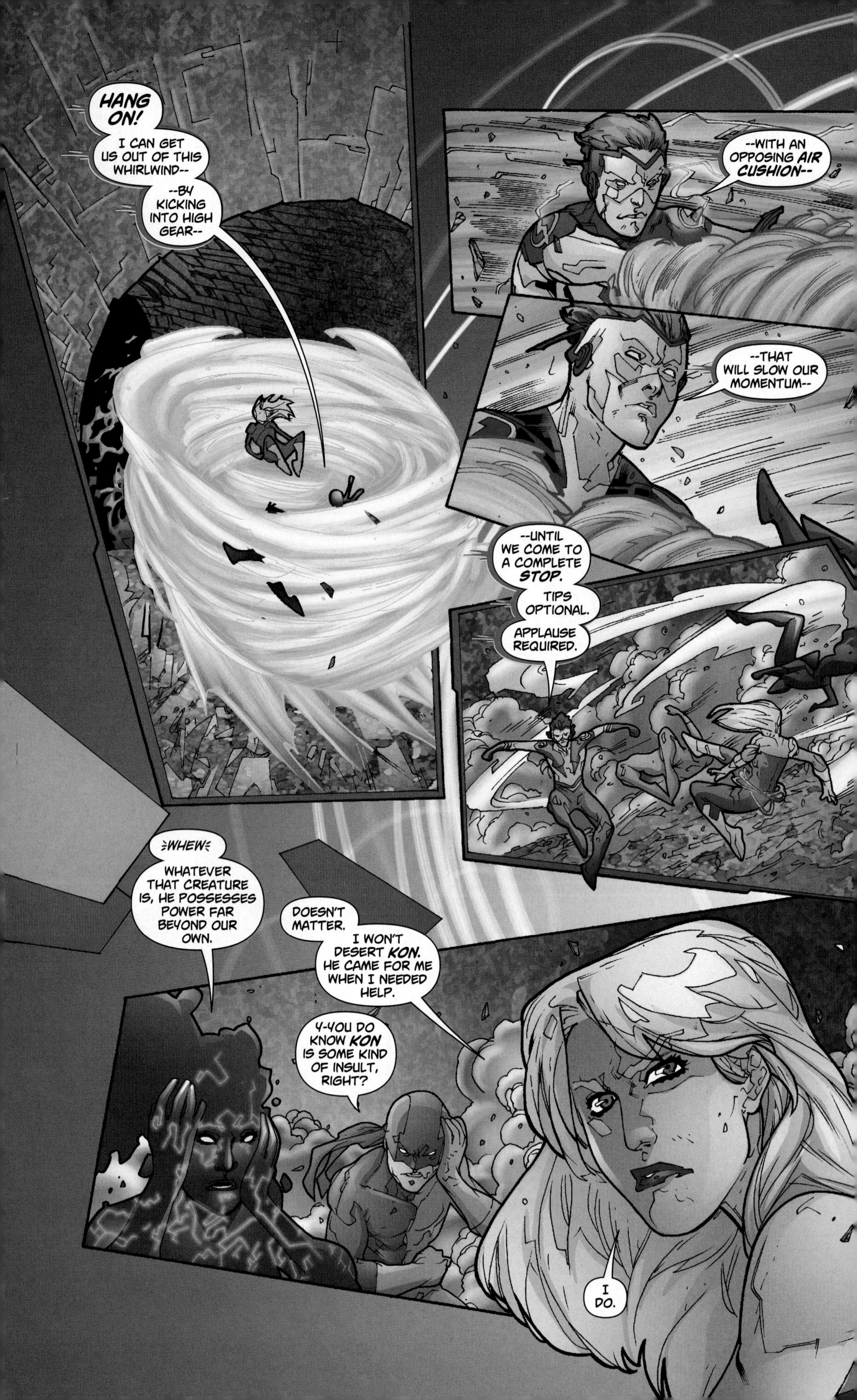
HANG ON!
I CAN GET US OUT OF THIS WHIRLWIND--
--BY KICKING INTO HIGH GEAR--
--WITH AN OPPOSING AIR CUSHION--
--THAT WILL SLOW OUR MOMENTUM--
--UNTIL WE COME TO A COMPLETE STOP.
TIPS OPTIONAL.
APPLAUSE REQUIRED.
WHEW
WHATEVER THAT CREATURE IS, HE POSSESSES POWER FAR BEYOND OUR OWN.
DOESN'T MATTER.
I WON'T DESERT KON. HE CAME FOR ME WHEN I NEEDED HELP.
Y-YOU DO KNOW KON IS SOME KIND OF INSULT, RIGHT?
I DO.

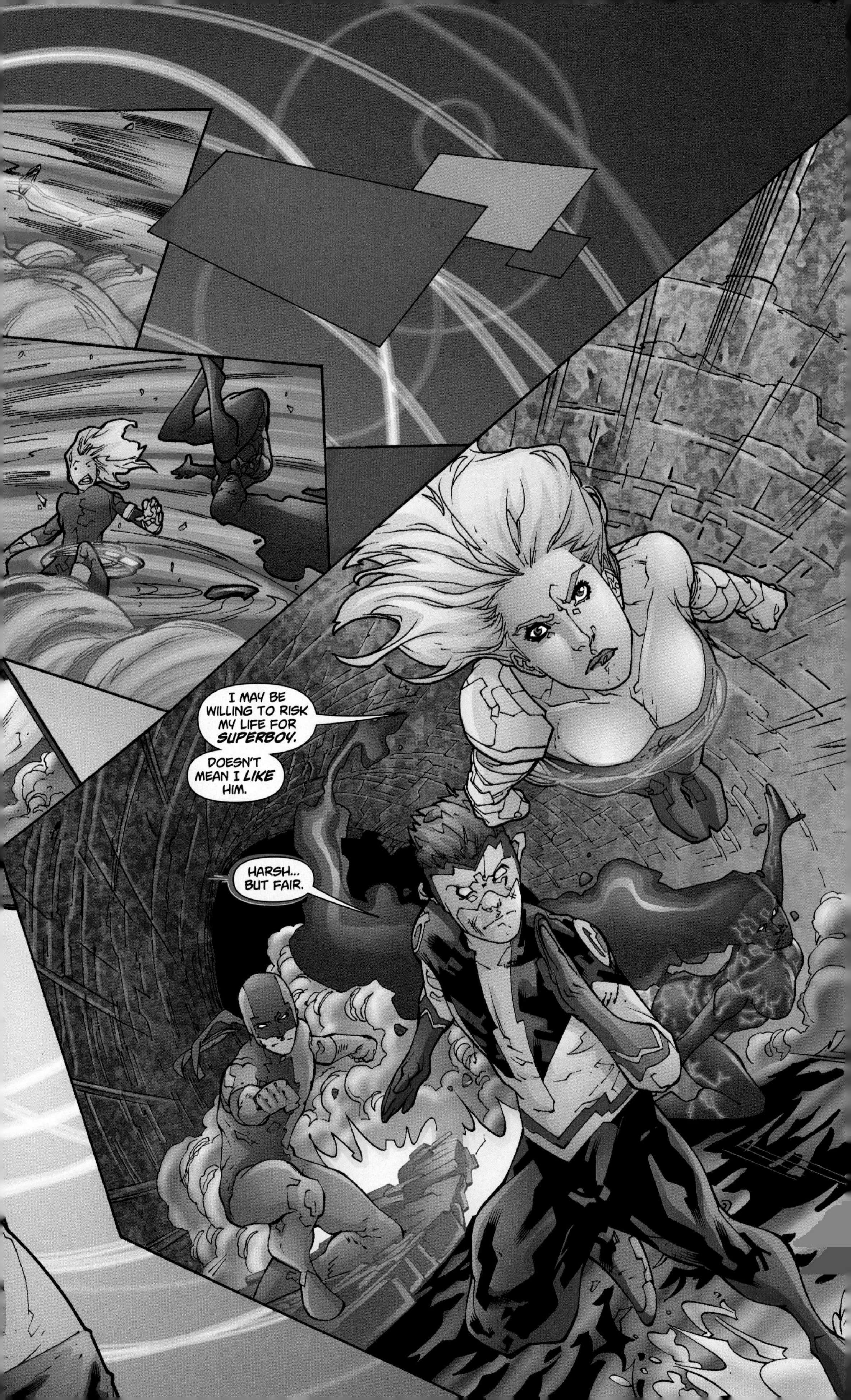
I MAY BE WILLING TO RISK MY LIFE FOR SUPERBOY.
DOESN'T MEAN I LIKE HIM.
HARSH... BUT FAIR.

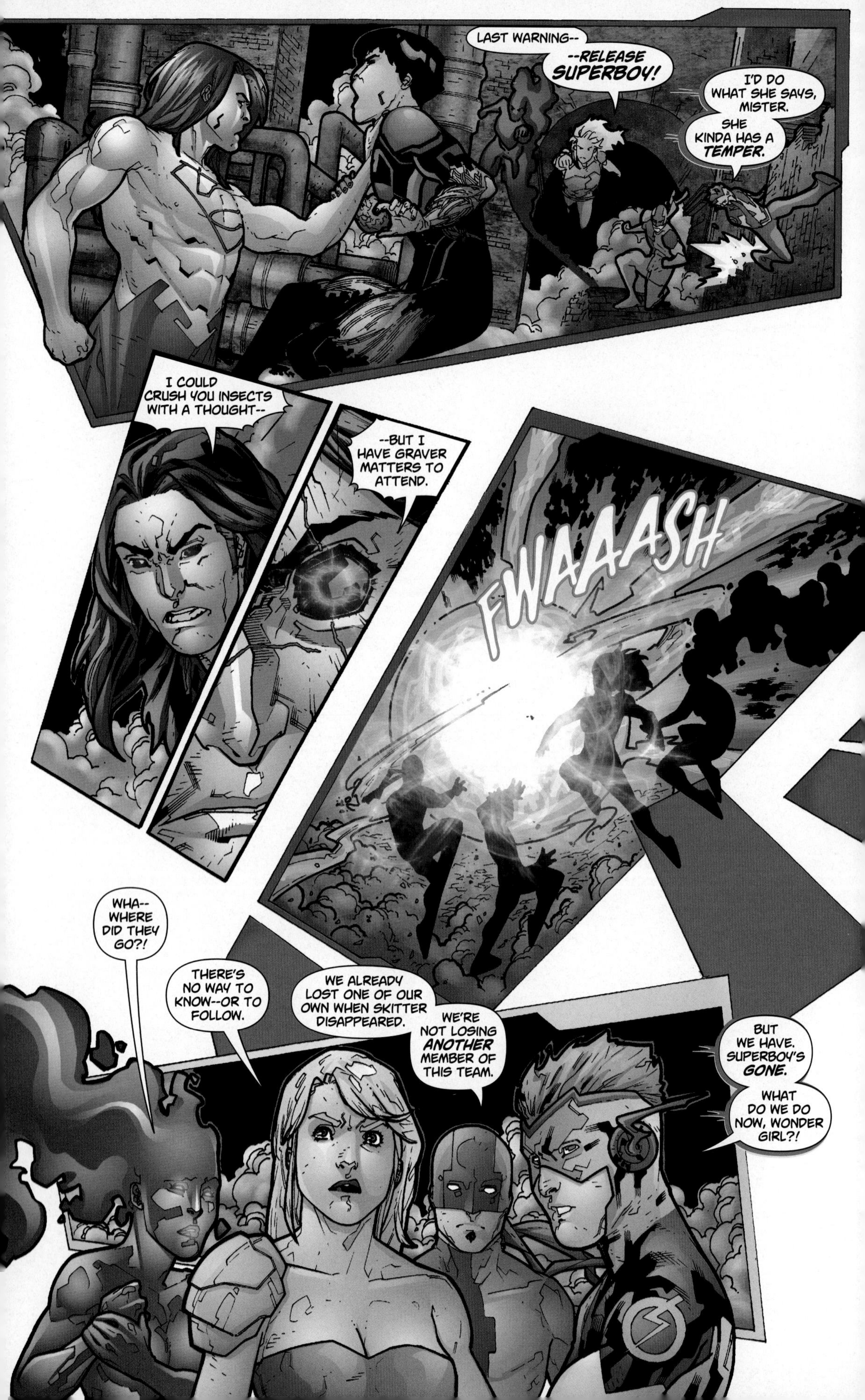
LAST WARNING--
--RELEASE SUPERBOY!
I'D DO WHAT SHE SAYS, MISTER.
SHE KINDA HAS A TEMPER.
I COULD CRUSH YOU INSECTS WITH A THOUGHT--
--BUT I HAVE GRAVER MATTERS TO ATTEND.
FWAAASH
WHA-- WHERE DID THEY GO?!
THERE'S NO WAY TO KNOW--OR TO FOLLOW.
WE ALREADY LOST ONE OF OUR OWN WHEN SKITTER DISAPPEARED.
WE'RE NOT LOSING ANOTHER MEMBER OF THIS TEAM.
BUT WE HAVE. SUPERBOY'S GONE.
WHAT DO WE DO NOW, WONDER GIRL?!

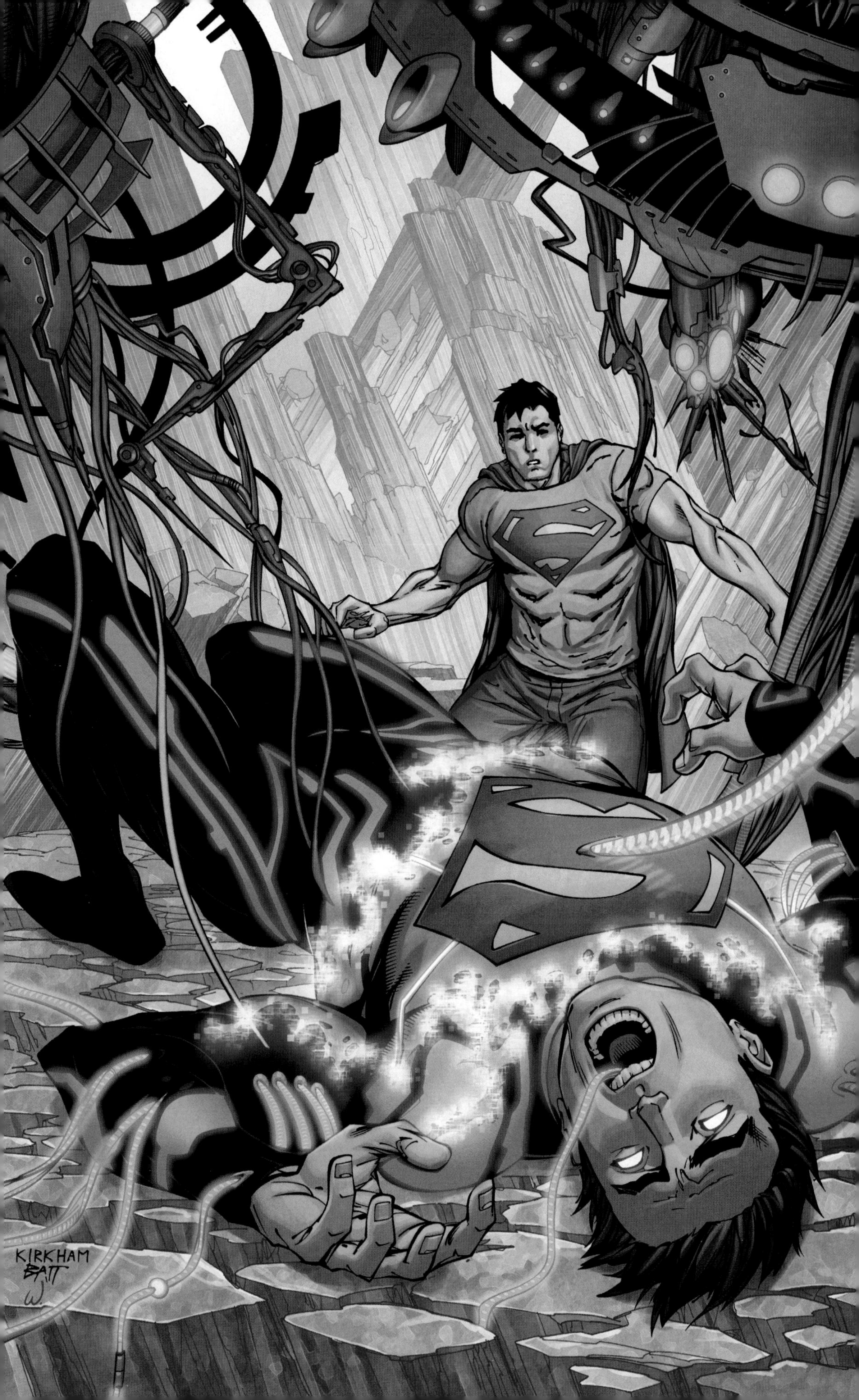
KIRKHAM
BATT
W.

SHATTERED STEEL!

TOM DeFALCO writer **RON FRENZ, ROGER ROBINSON, IBAN COELLO & AMILCAR PINNA** artists

cover art by **TYLER KIRKHAM, BATT & JASON WRIGHT**

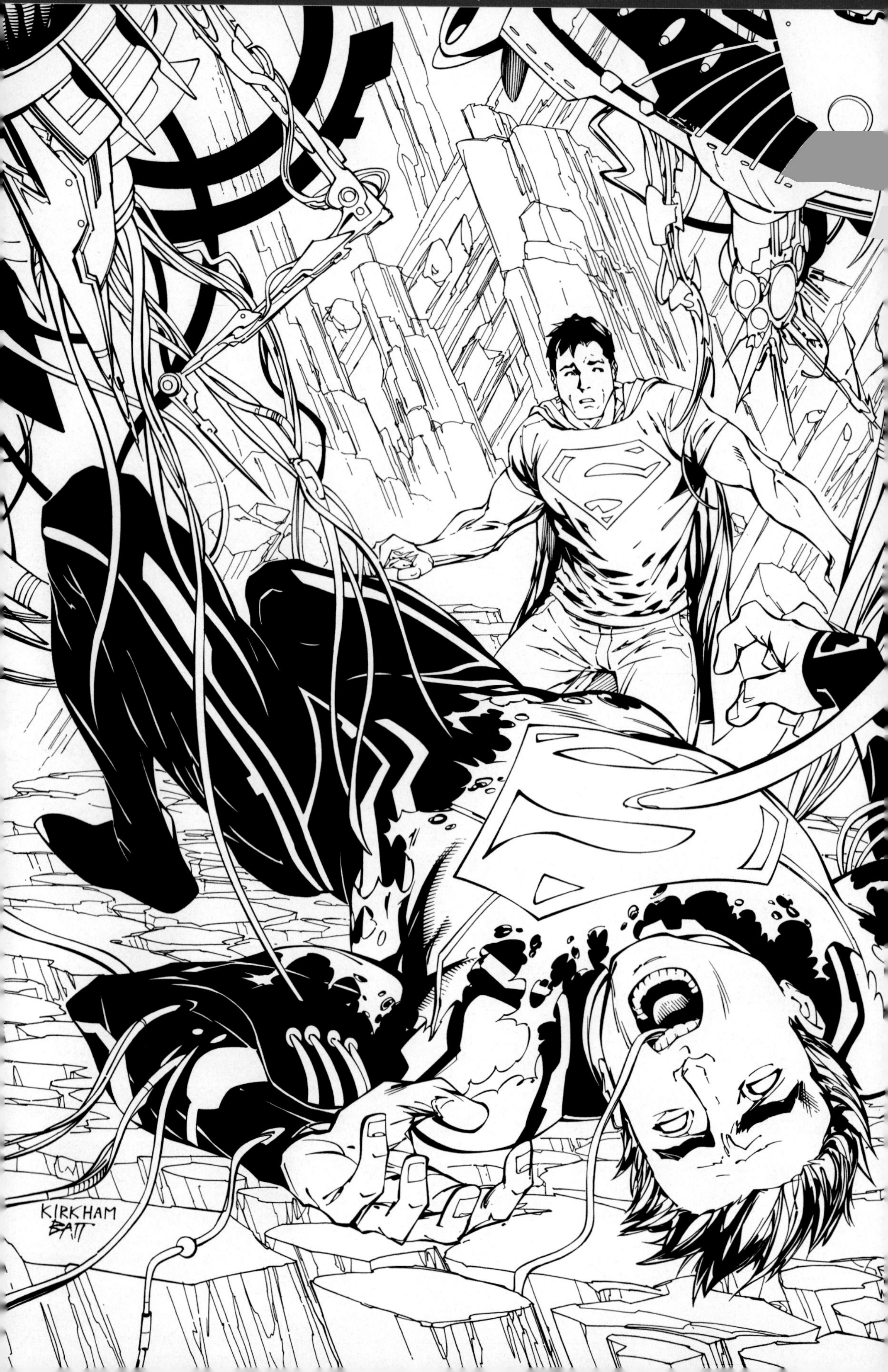
KIRKHAM
BATT

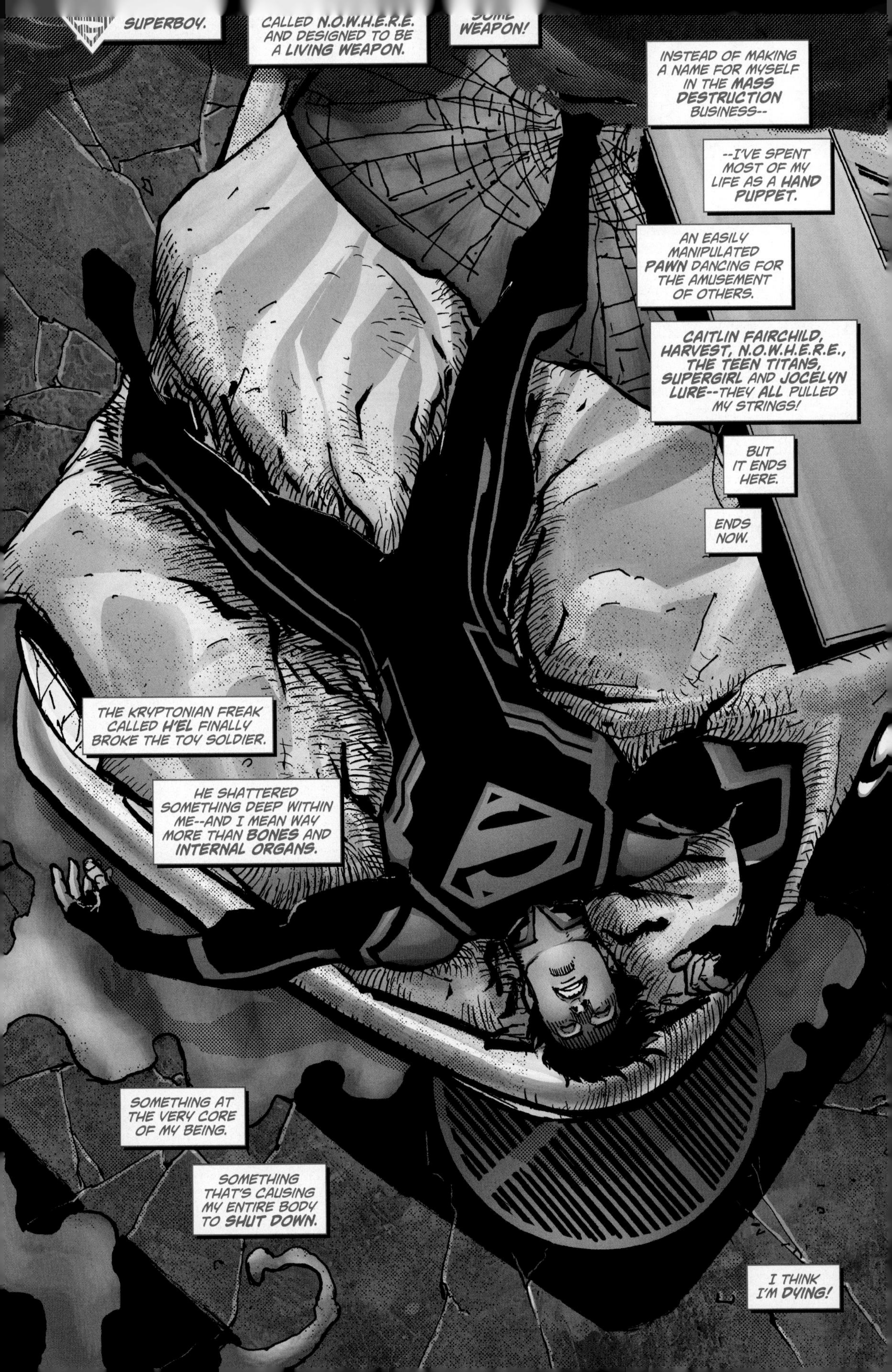
SUPERBOY.
CALLED N.O.W.H.E.R.E. AND DESIGNED TO BE A LIVING WEAPON.
WEAPON!
INSTEAD OF MAKING A NAME FOR MYSELF IN THE MASS DESTRUCTION BUSINESS--
--I'VE SPENT MOST OF MY LIFE AS A HAND PUPPET.
AN EASILY MANIPULATED PAWN DANCING FOR THE AMUSEMENT OF OTHERS.
CAITLIN FAIRCHILD, HARVEST, N.O.W.H.E.R.E., THE TEEN TITANS, SUPERGIRL AND JOCELYN LURE--THEY ALL PULLED MY STRINGS!
BUT IT ENDS HERE.
ENDS NOW.
THE KRYPTONIAN FREAK CALLED H'EL FINALLY BROKE THE TOY SOLDIER.
HE SHATTERED SOMETHING DEEP WITHIN ME--AND I MEAN WAY MORE THAN BONES AND INTERNAL ORGANS.
SOMETHING AT THE VERY CORE OF MY BEING.
SOMETHING THAT'S CAUSING MY ENTIRE BODY TO SHUT DOWN.
I THINK I'M DYING!

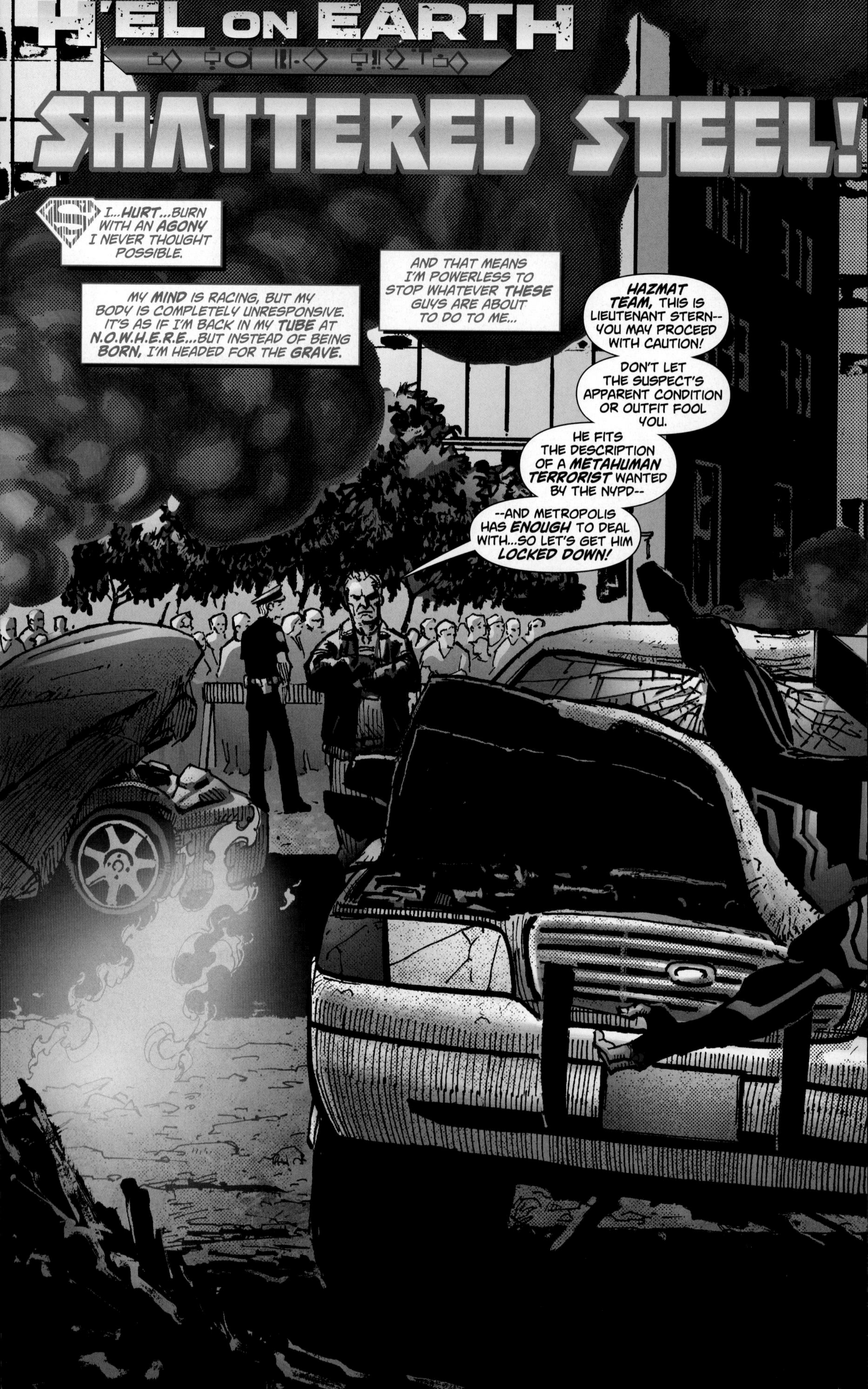
H'EL ON EARTH
SHATTERED STEEL!
I...HURT...BURN WITH AN AGONY I NEVER THOUGHT POSSIBLE.
MY MIND IS RACING, BUT MY BODY IS COMPLETELY UNRESPONSIVE. IT'S AS IF I'M BACK IN MY TUBE AT N.O.W.H.E.R.E...BUT INSTEAD OF BEING BORN, I'M HEADED FOR THE GRAVE.
AND THAT MEANS I'M POWERLESS TO STOP WHATEVER THESE GUYS ARE ABOUT TO DO TO ME...
HAZMAT TEAM, THIS IS LIEUTENANT STERN-- YOU MAY PROCEED WITH CAUTION!
DON'T LET THE SUSPECT'S APPARENT CONDITION OR OUTFIT FOOL YOU.
HE FITS THE DESCRIPTION OF A METAHUMAN TERRORIST WANTED BY THE NYPD--
--AND METROPOLIS HAS ENOUGH TO DEAL WITH...SO LET'S GET HIM LOCKED DOWN!

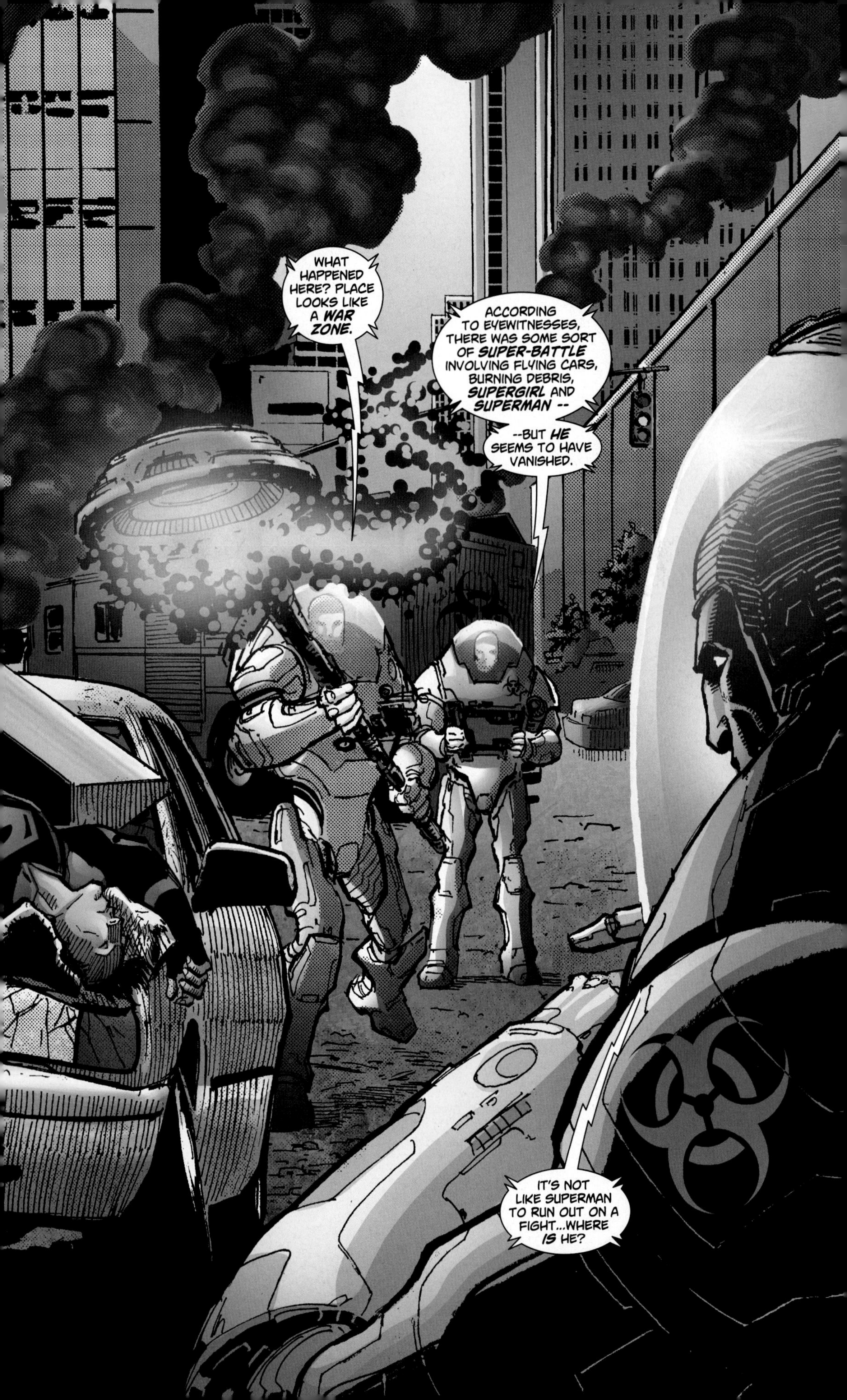
WHAT HAPPENED HERE? PLACE LOOKS LIKE A WAR ZONE.
ACCORDING TO EYEWITNESSES, THERE WAS SOME SORT OF SUPER-BATTLE INVOLVING FLYING CARS, BURNING DEBRIS, SUPERGIRL AND SUPERMAN --
--BUT HE SEEMS TO HAVE VANISHED.
IT'S NOT LIKE SUPERMAN TO RUN OUT ON A FIGHT...WHERE IS HE?

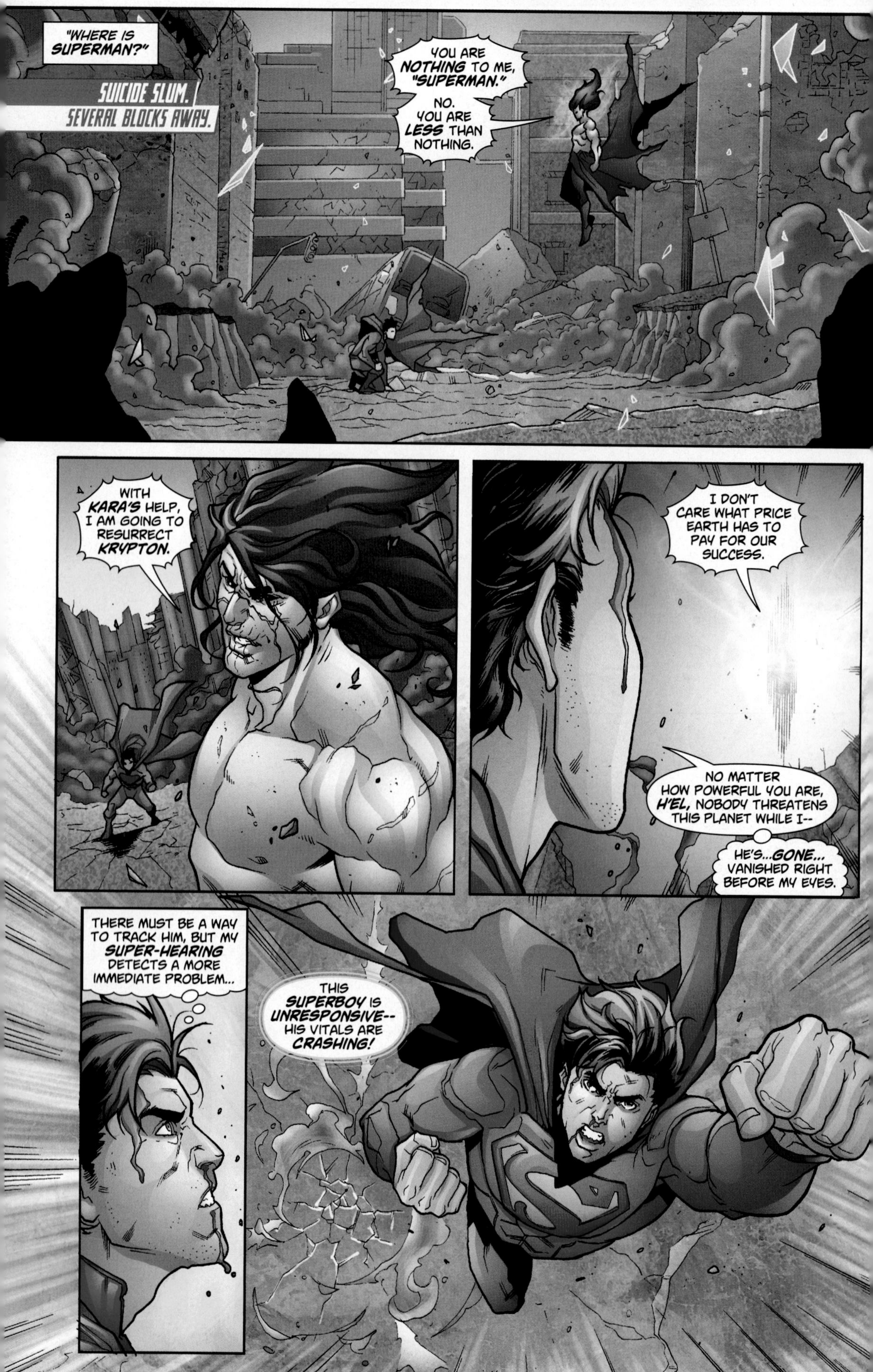
"WHERE IS SUPERMAN?"
SUICIDE SLUM. SEVERAL BLOCKS AWAY.
YOU ARE NOTHING TO ME, "SUPERMAN."
NO. YOU ARE LESS THAN NOTHING.
WITH KARA'S HELP, I AM GOING TO RESURRECT KRYPTON.
I DON'T CARE WHAT PRICE EARTH HAS TO PAY FOR OUR SUCCESS.
NO MATTER HOW POWERFUL YOU ARE, H'EL, NOBODY THREATENS THIS PLANET WHILE I--
HE'S...GONE... VANISHED RIGHT BEFORE MY EYES.
THERE MUST BE A WAY TO TRACK HIM, BUT MY SUPER-HEARING DETECTS A MORE IMMEDIATE PROBLEM...
THIS SUPERBOY IS UNRESPONSIVE-- HIS VITALS ARE CRASHING!

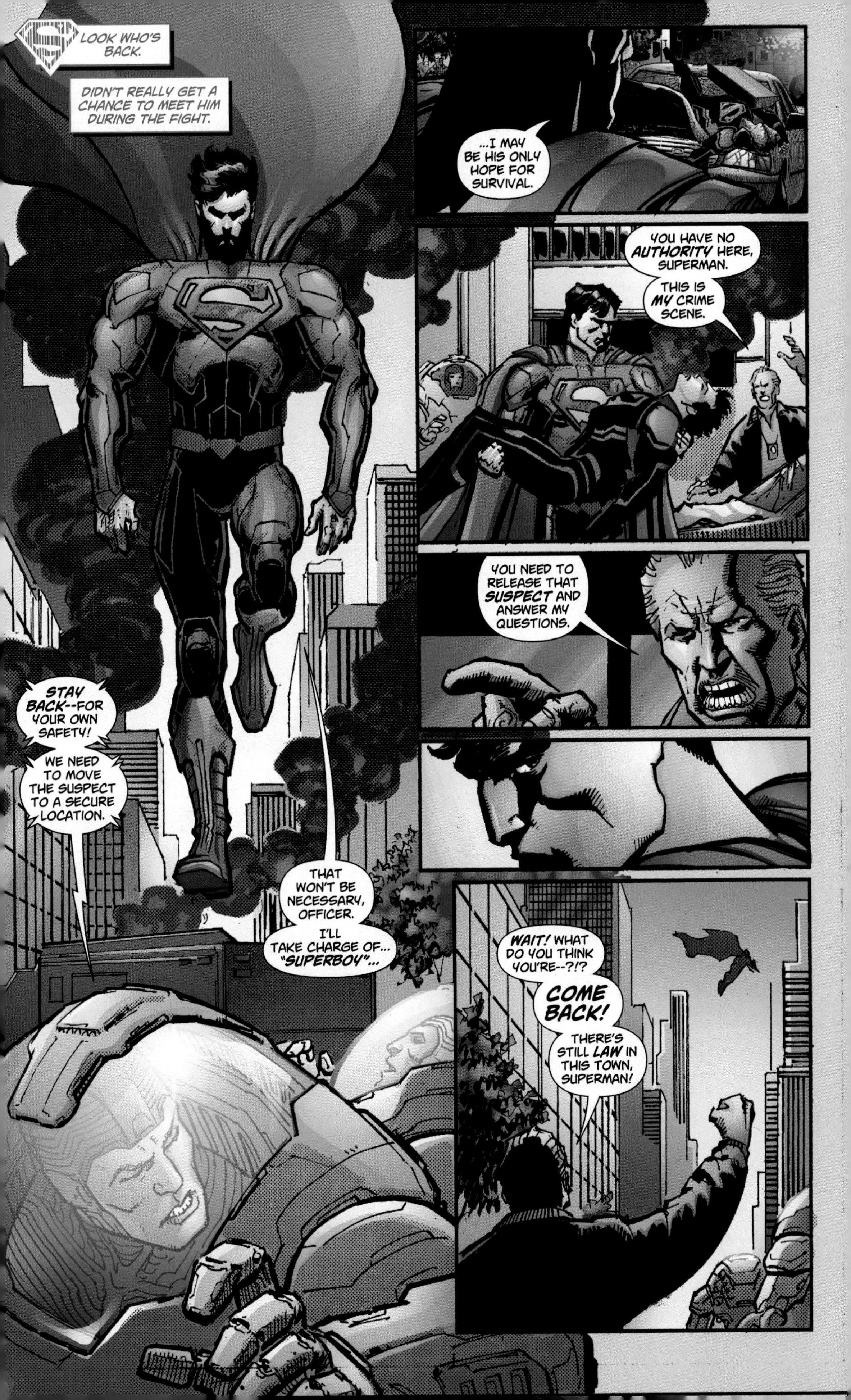
LOOK WHO'S BACK.
DIDN'T REALLY GET A CHANCE TO MEET HIM DURING THE FIGHT.
STAY BACK--FOR YOUR OWN SAFETY!
WE NEED TO MOVE THE SUSPECT TO A SECURE LOCATION.
THAT WON'T BE NECESSARY, OFFICER.
I'LL TAKE CHARGE OF... "SUPERBOY"...
...I MAY BE HIS ONLY HOPE FOR SURVIVAL.
YOU HAVE NO AUTHORITY HERE, SUPERMAN.
THIS IS MY CRIME SCENE.
YOU NEED TO RELEASE THAT SUSPECT AND ANSWER MY QUESTIONS.
WAIT! WHAT DO YOU THINK YOU'RE--?!?
COME BACK!
THERE'S STILL LAW IN THIS TOWN, SUPERMAN!

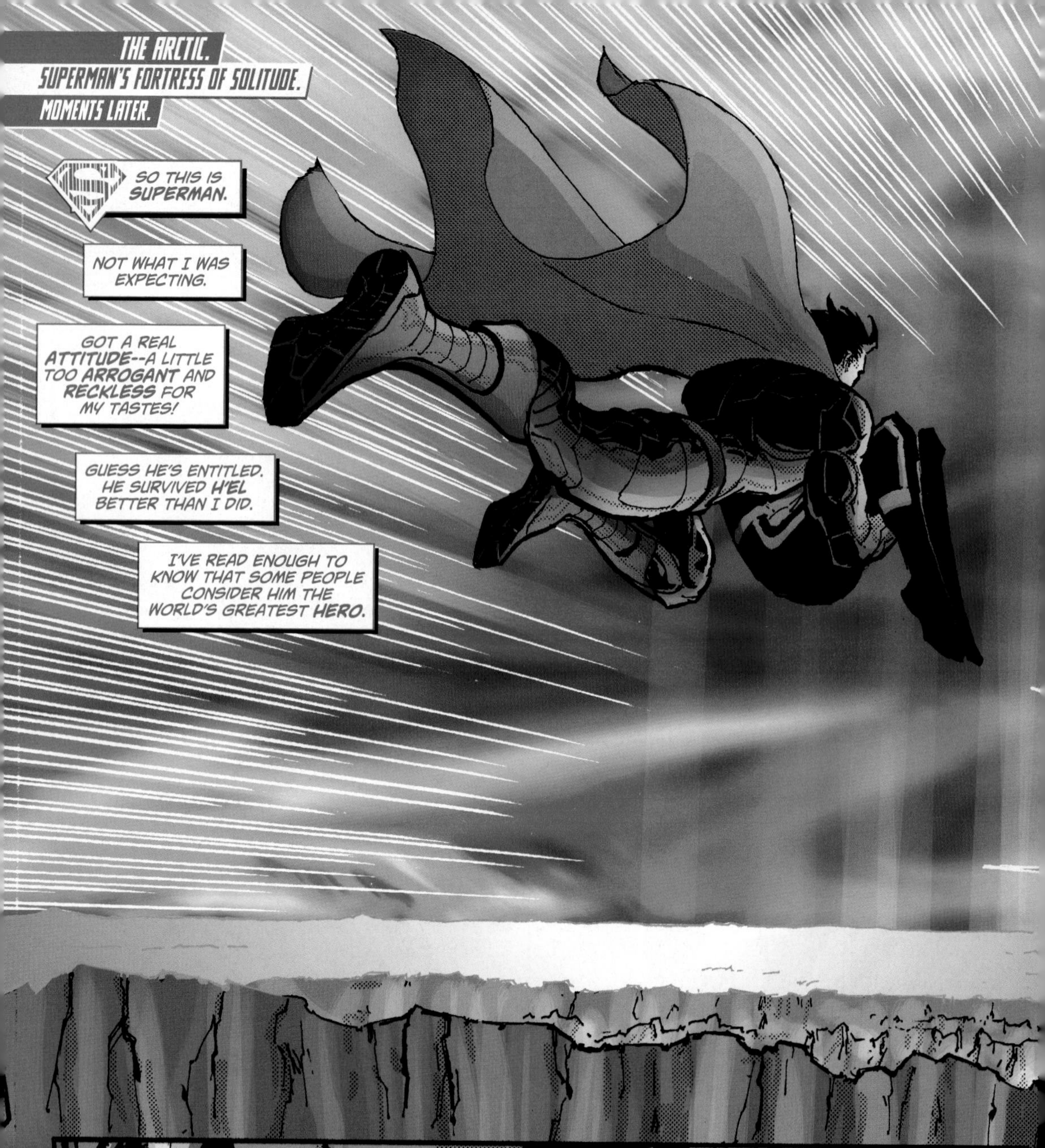
THE ARCTIC.
SUPERMAN'S FORTRESS OF SOLITUDE.
MOMENTS LATER.
SO THIS IS SUPERMAN.
NOT WHAT I WAS EXPECTING.
GOT A REAL ATTITUDE--A LITTLE TOO ARROGANT AND RECKLESS FOR MY TASTES!
GUESS HE'S ENTITLED. HE SURVIVED H'EL BETTER THAN I DID.
I'VE READ ENOUGH TO KNOW THAT SOME PEOPLE CONSIDER HIM THE WORLD'S GREATEST HERO.

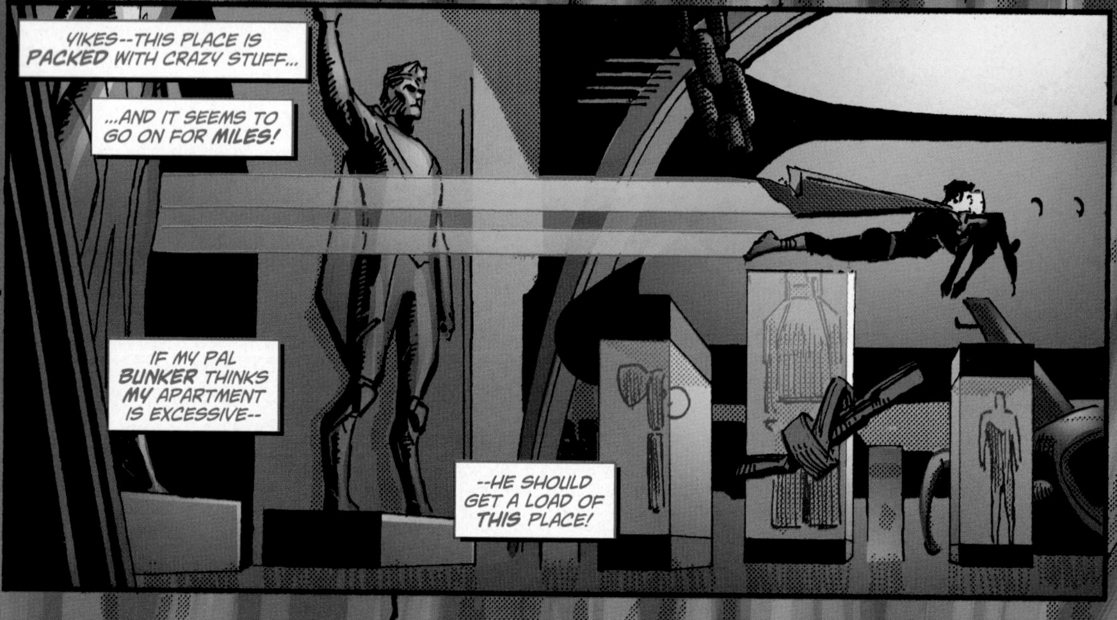
YIKES--THIS PLACE IS PACKED WITH CRAZY STUFF...
...AND IT SEEMS TO GO ON FOR MILES!
IF MY PAL BUNKER THINKS MY APARTMENT IS EXCESSIVE--
--HE SHOULD GET A LOAD OF THIS PLACE!

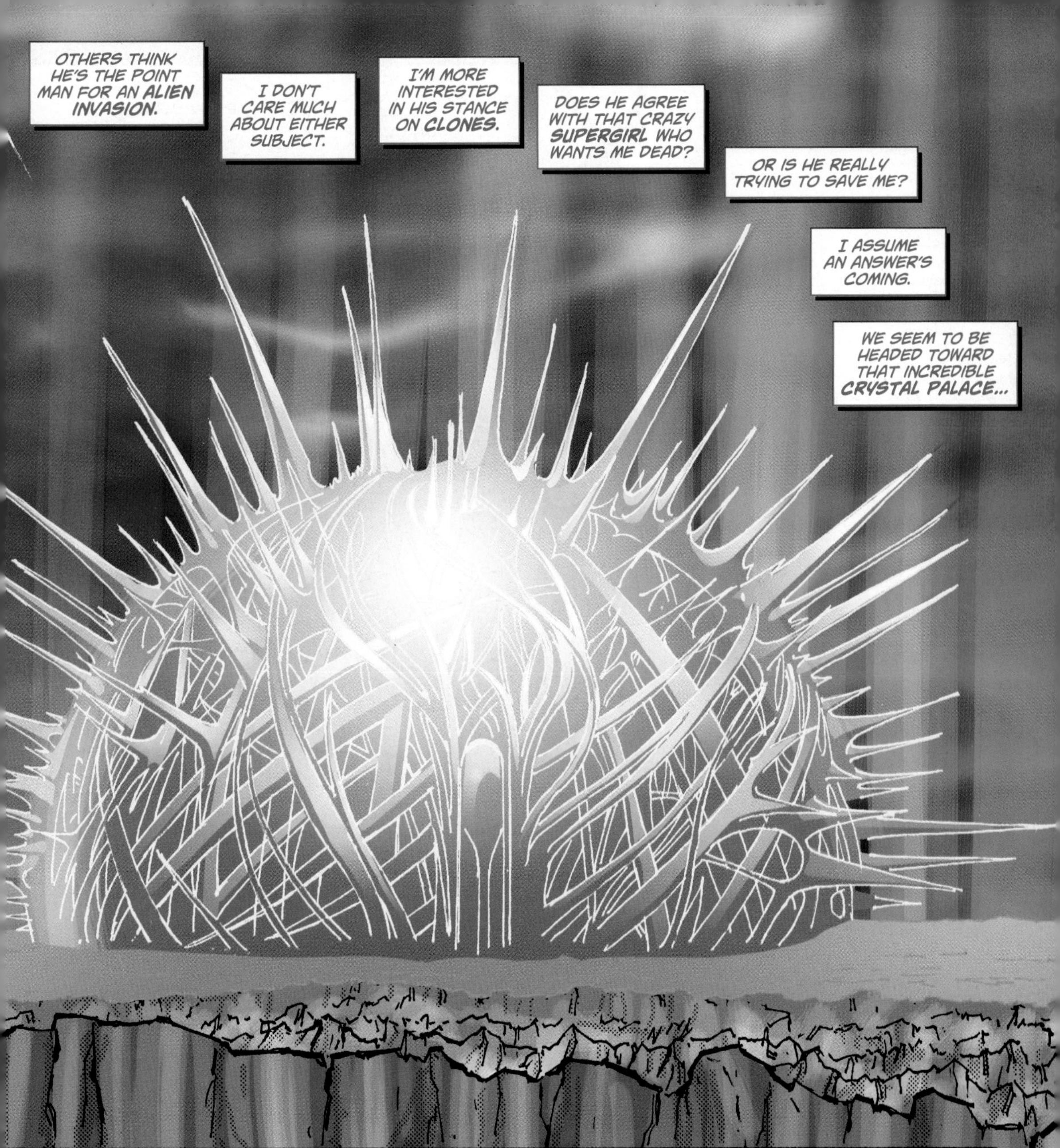
OTHERS THINK HE'S THE POINT MAN FOR AN ALIEN INVASION.
I DON'T CARE MUCH ABOUT EITHER SUBJECT.
I'M MORE INTERESTED IN HIS STANCE ON CLONES.
DOES HE AGREE WITH THAT CRAZY SUPERGIRL WHO WANTS ME DEAD?
OR IS HE REALLY TRYING TO SAVE ME?
I ASSUME AN ANSWER'S COMING.
WE SEEM TO BE HEADED TOWARD THAT INCREDIBLE CRYSTAL PALACE...
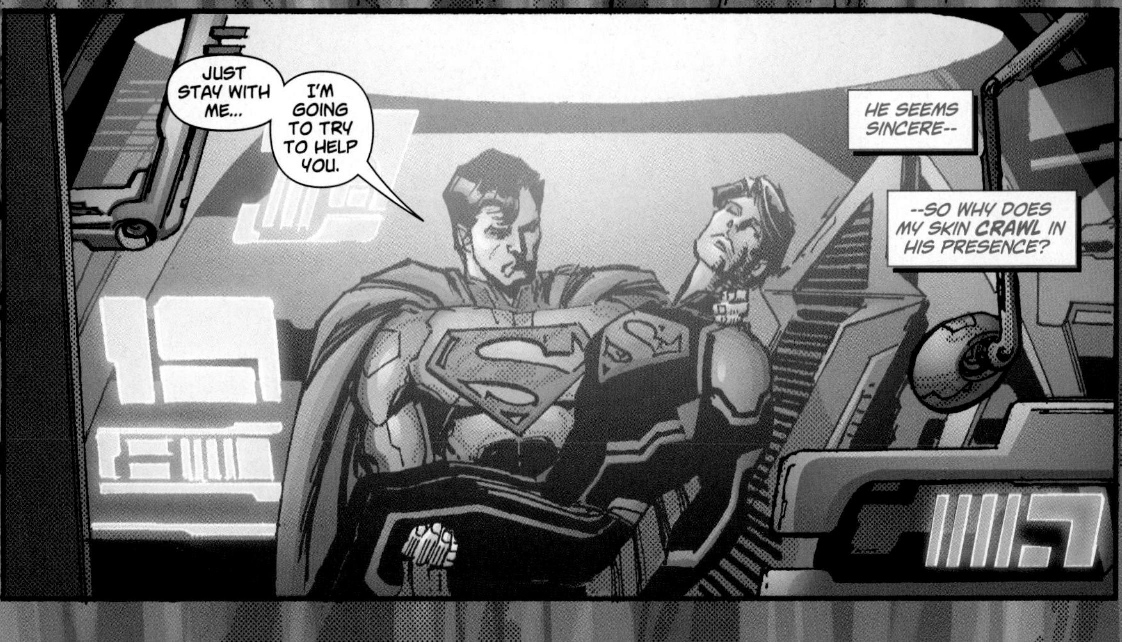
JUST STAY WITH ME...
I'M GOING TO TRY TO HELP YOU.
HE SEEMS SINCERE--
--SO WHY DOES MY SKIN CRAWL IN HIS PRESENCE?

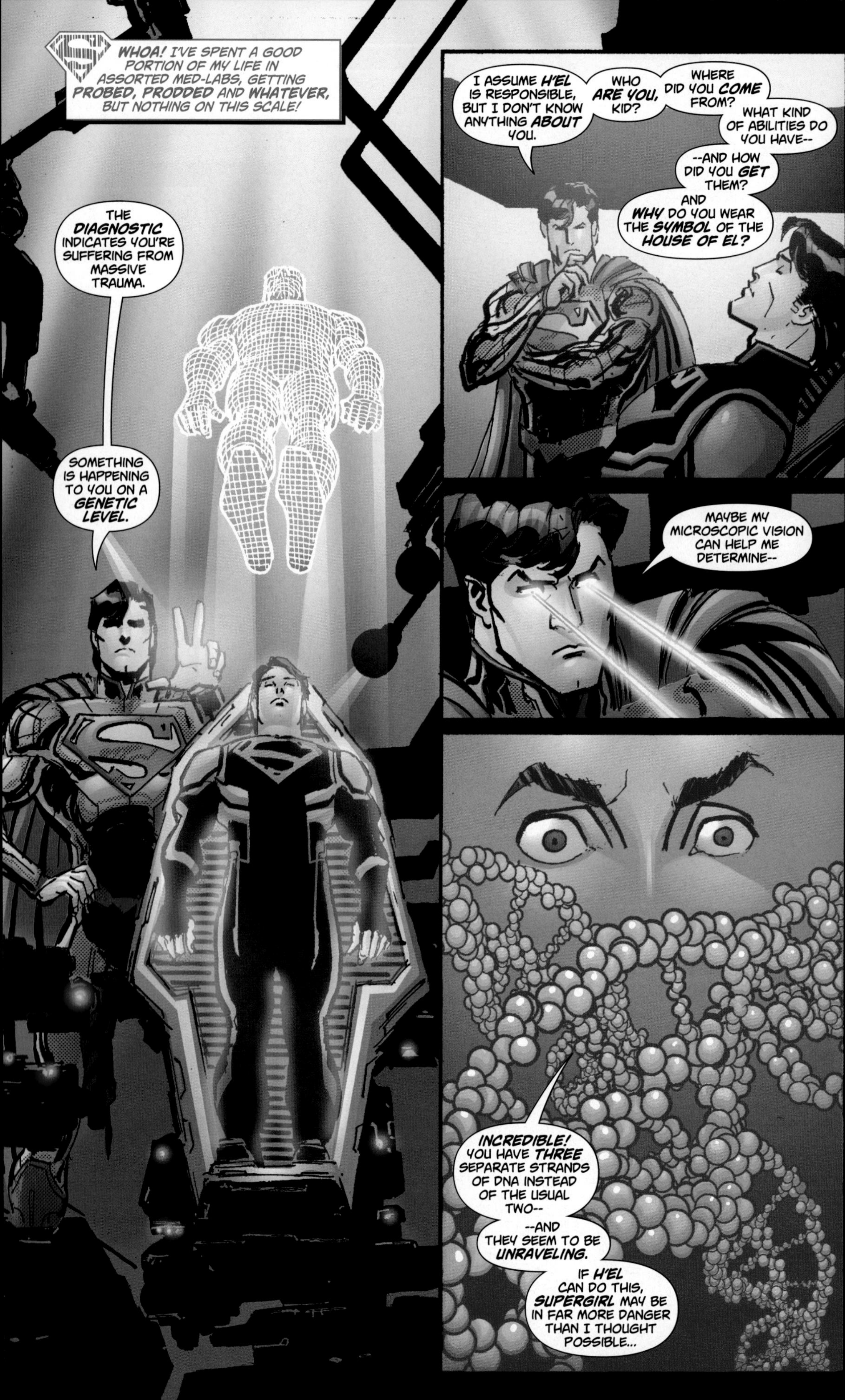
WHOA! I'VE SPENT A GOOD PORTION OF MY LIFE IN ASSORTED MED-LABS, GETTING PROBED, PRODDED AND WHATEVER, BUT NOTHING ON THIS SCALE!
THE DIAGNOSTIC INDICATES YOU'RE SUFFERING FROM MASSIVE TRAUMA.
SOMETHING IS HAPPENING TO YOU ON A GENETIC LEVEL.
I ASSUME H'EL IS RESPONSIBLE, BUT I DON'T KNOW ANYTHING ABOUT YOU.
WHO ARE YOU, KID?
WHERE DID YOU COME FROM?
WHAT KIND OF ABILITIES DO YOU HAVE--
--AND HOW DID YOU GET THEM?
AND WHY DO YOU WEAR THE SYMBOL OF THE HOUSE OF EL?
MAYBE MY MICROSCOPIC VISION CAN HELP ME DETERMINE--
INCREDIBLE! YOU HAVE THREE SEPARATE STRANDS OF DNA INSTEAD OF THE USUAL TWO--
--AND THEY SEEM TO BE UNRAVELING.
IF H'EL CAN DO THIS, SUPERGIRL MAY BE IN FAR MORE DANGER THAN I THOUGHT POSSIBLE...

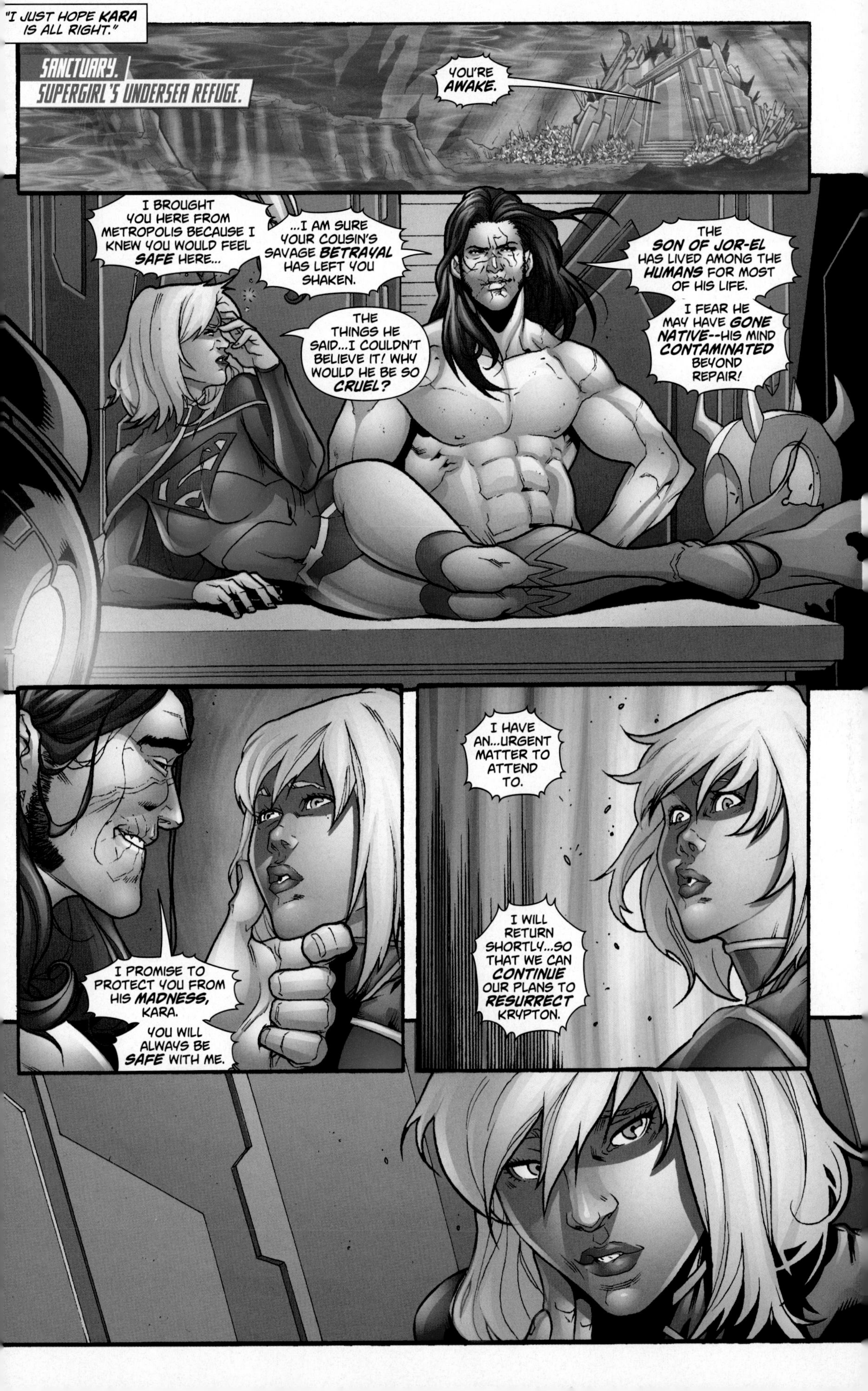

"I JUST HOPE KARA IS ALL RIGHT."
SANCTUARY. SUPERGIRL'S UNDERSEA REFUGE.
YOU'RE AWAKE.
I BROUGHT YOU HERE FROM METROPOLIS BECAUSE I KNEW YOU WOULD FEEL SAFE HERE...
...I AM SURE YOUR COUSIN'S SAVAGE BETRAYAL HAS LEFT YOU SHAKEN.
THE THINGS HE SAID...I COULDN'T BELIEVE IT! WHY WOULD HE BE SO CRUEL?
THE SON OF JOR-EL HAS LIVED AMONG THE HUMANS FOR MOST OF HIS LIFE.
I FEAR HE MAY HAVE GONE NATIVE--HIS MIND CONTAMINATED BEYOND REPAIR!
I PROMISE TO PROTECT YOU FROM HIS MADNESS, KARA.
YOU WILL ALWAYS BE SAFE WITH ME.
I HAVE AN...URGENT MATTER TO ATTEND TO.
I WILL RETURN SHORTLY...SO THAT WE CAN CONTINUE OUR PLANS TO RESURRECT KRYPTON.

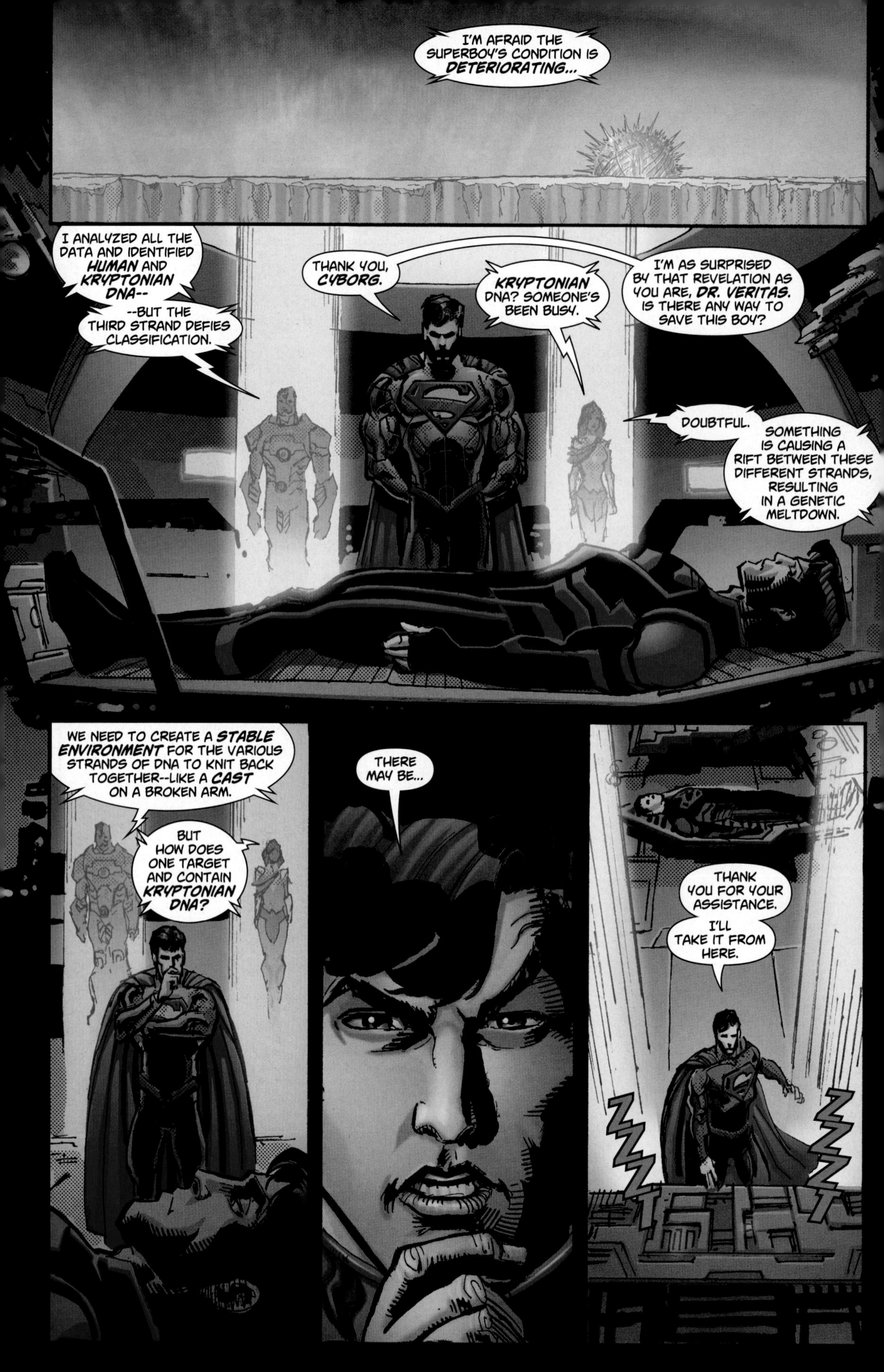
I'M AFRAID THE SUPERBOY'S CONDITION IS DETERIORATING...
I ANALYZED ALL THE DATA AND IDENTIFIED HUMAN AND KRYPTONIAN DNA--
--BUT THE THIRD STRAND DEFIES CLASSIFICATION.
THANK YOU, CYBORG.
KRYPTONIAN DNA? SOMEONE'S BEEN BUSY.
I'M AS SURPRISED BY THAT REVELATION AS YOU ARE, DR. VERITAS. IS THERE ANY WAY TO SAVE THIS BOY?
DOUBTFUL.
SOMETHING IS CAUSING A RIFT BETWEEN THESE DIFFERENT STRANDS, RESULTING IN A GENETIC MELTDOWN.
WE NEED TO CREATE A STABLE ENVIRONMENT FOR THE VARIOUS STRANDS OF DNA TO KNIT BACK TOGETHER--LIKE A CAST ON A BROKEN ARM.
BUT HOW DOES ONE TARGET AND CONTAIN KRYPTONIAN DNA?
THERE MAY BE...
THANK YOU FOR YOUR ASSISTANCE.
I'LL TAKE IT FROM HERE.
ZZZ
ZZZ

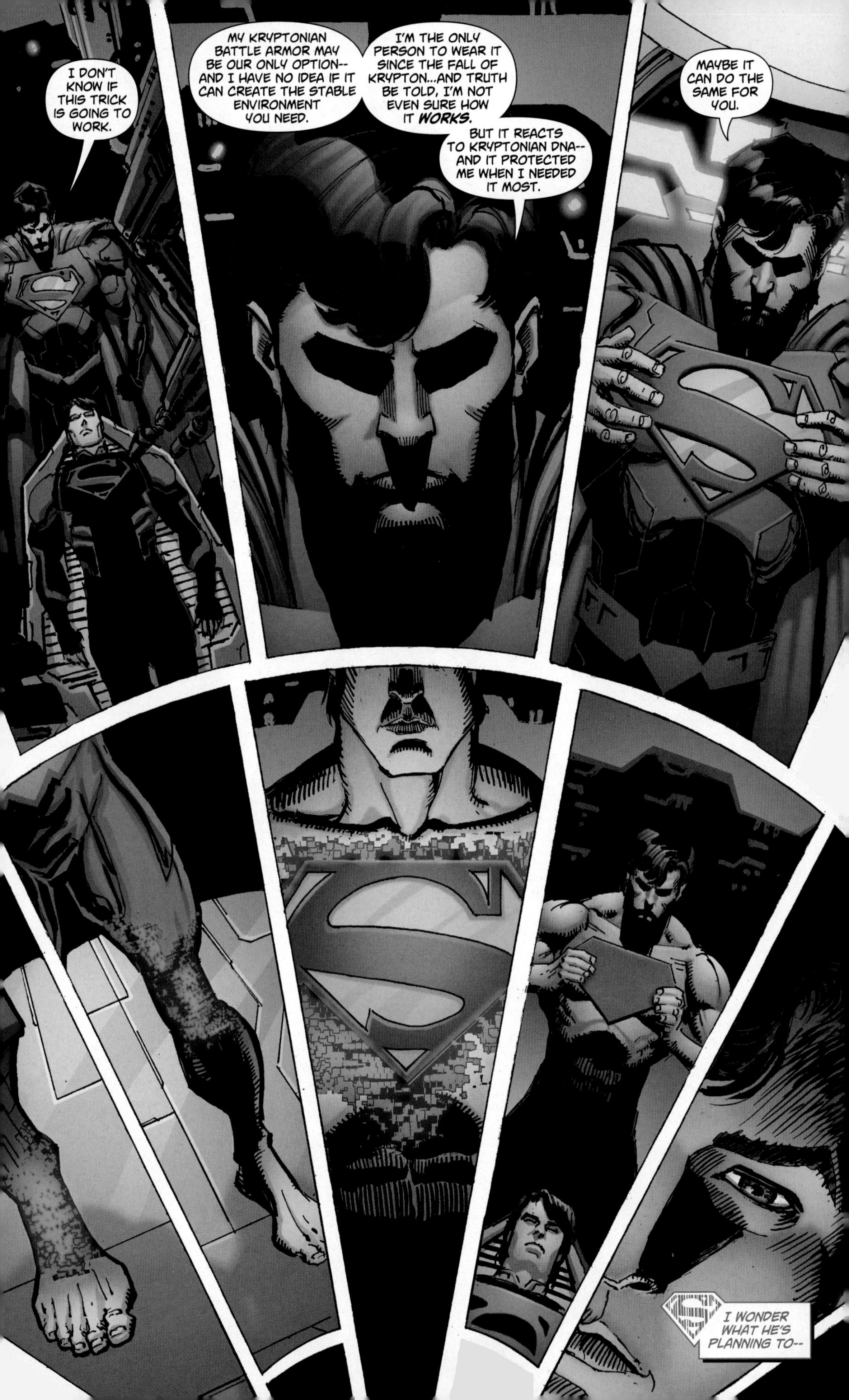
I DON'T KNOW IF THIS TRICK IS GOING TO WORK.
MY KRYPTONIAN BATTLE ARMOR MAY BE OUR ONLY OPTION-- AND I HAVE NO IDEA IF IT CAN CREATE THE STABLE ENVIRONMENT YOU NEED.
I'M THE ONLY PERSON TO WEAR IT SINCE THE FALL OF KRYPTON...AND TRUTH BE TOLD, I'M NOT EVEN SURE HOW IT **WORKS.**
BUT IT REACTS TO KRYPTONIAN DNA-- AND IT PROTECTED ME WHEN I NEEDED IT MOST.
MAYBE IT CAN DO THE SAME FOR YOU.
I WONDER WHAT HE'S PLANNING TO--

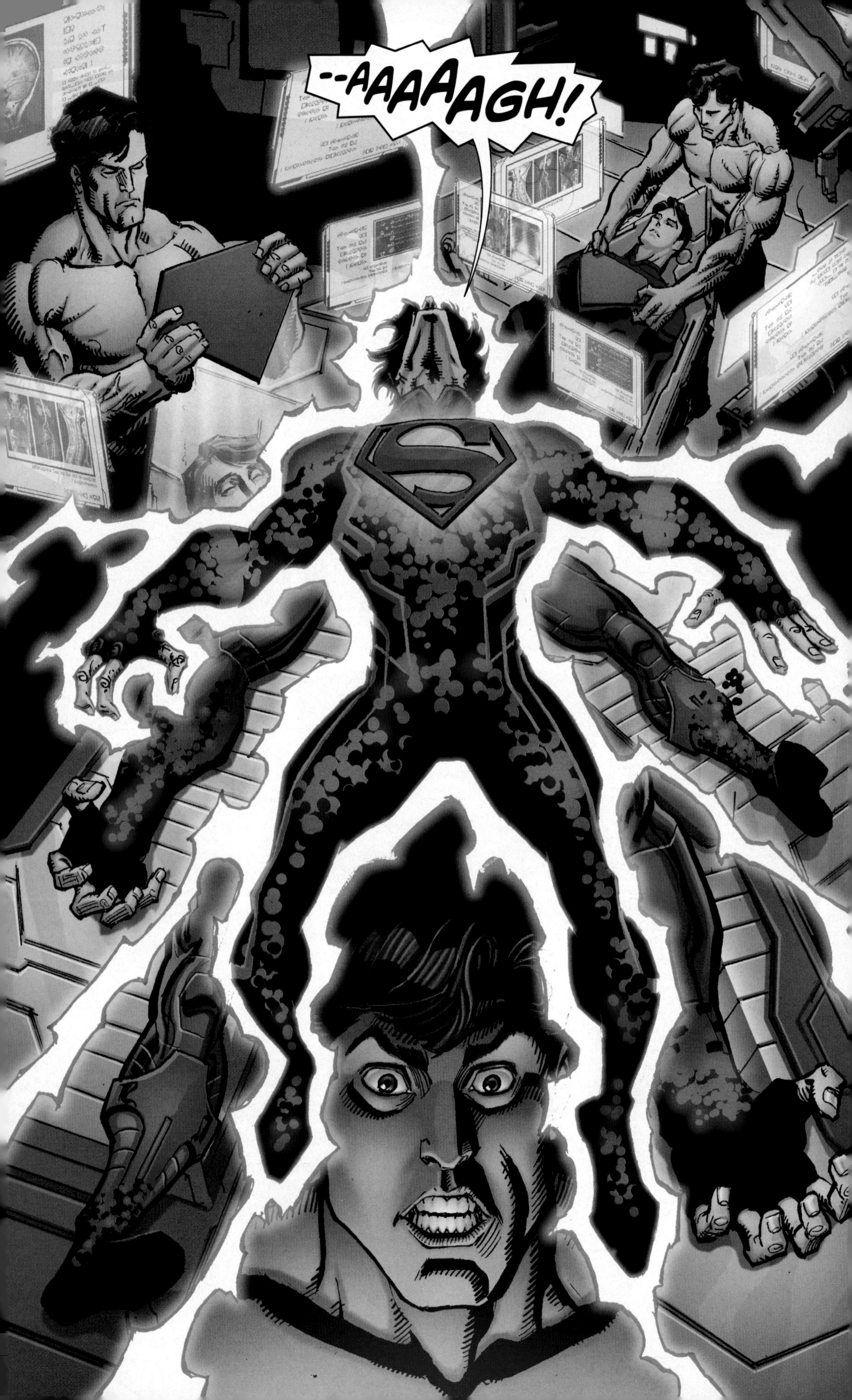
--AAAAAGH!

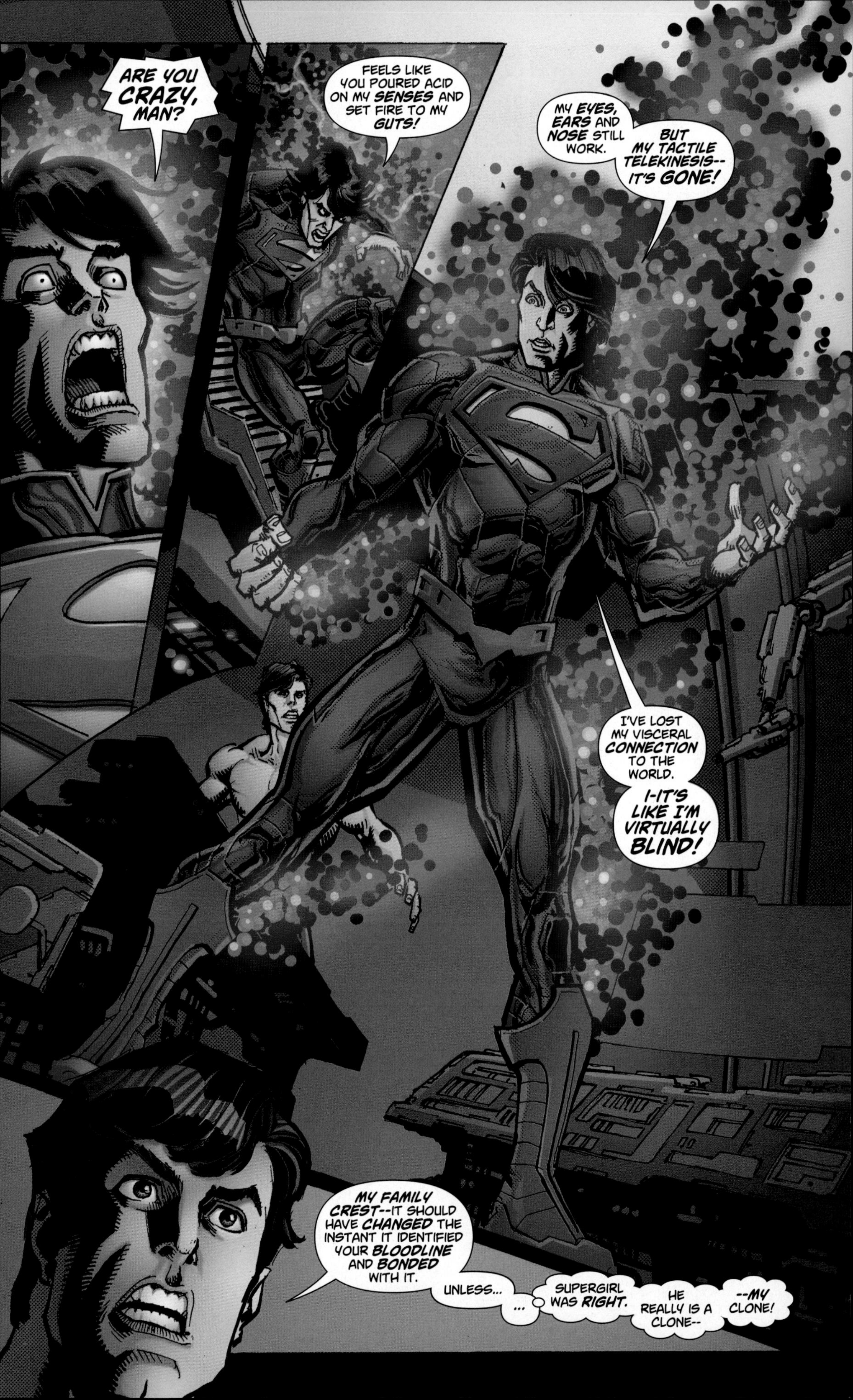
ARE YOU CRAZY, MAN?
FEELS LIKE YOU POURED ACID ON MY SENSES AND SET FIRE TO MY GUTS!
MY EYES, EARS AND NOSE STILL WORK.
BUT MY TACTILE TELEKINESIS--IT'S GONE!
I'VE LOST MY VISCERAL CONNECTION TO THE WORLD.
I-IT'S LIKE I'M VIRTUALLY BLIND!
MY FAMILY CREST--IT SHOULD HAVE CHANGED THE INSTANT IT IDENTIFIED YOUR BLOODLINE AND BONDED WITH IT.
UNLESS...
...
SUPERGIRL WAS RIGHT.
HE REALLY IS A CLONE--
--MY CLONE!

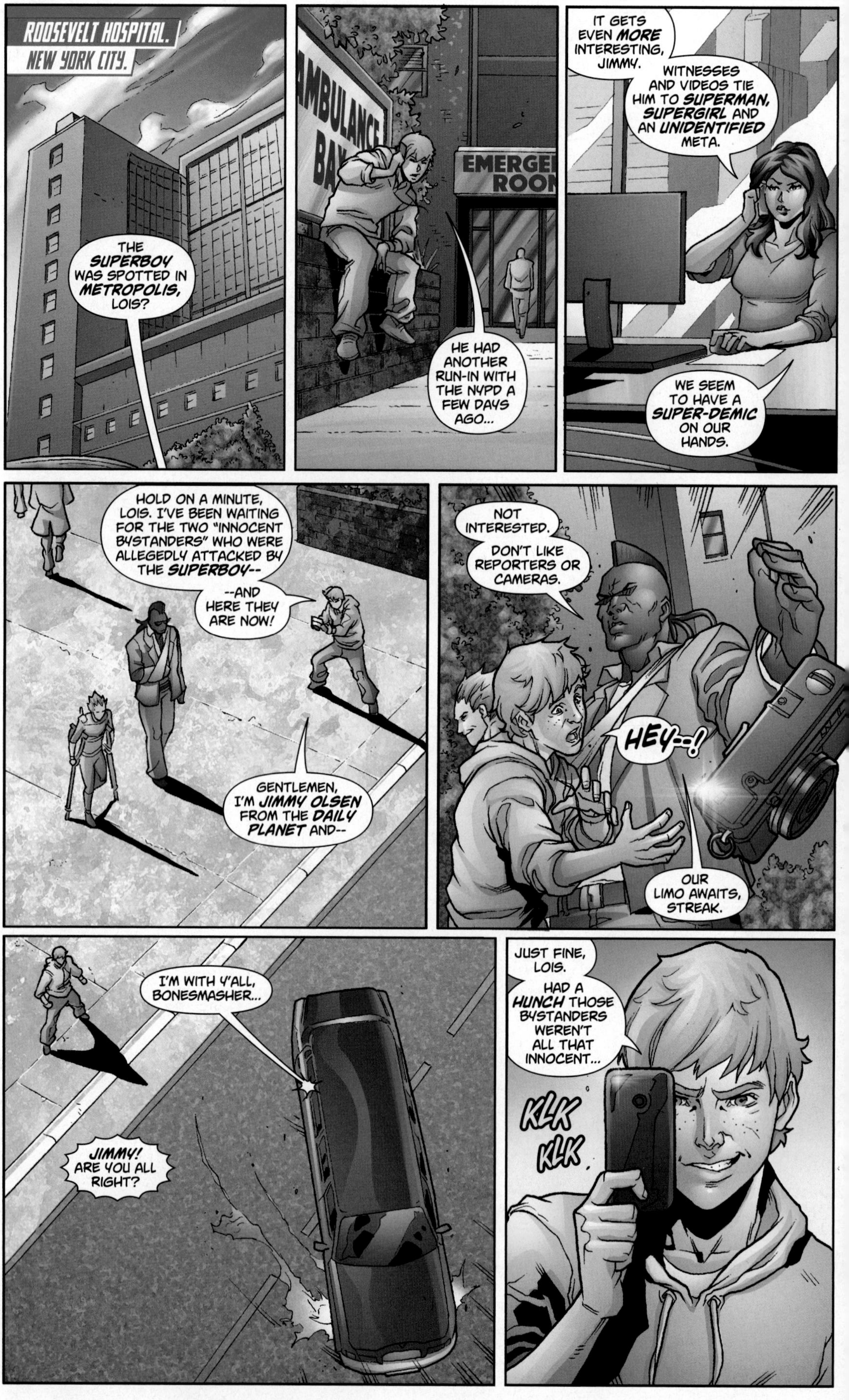
ROOSEVELT HOSPITAL.
NEW YORK CITY.
AMBULANCE BAY
EMERGE ROOM
THE SUPERBOY WAS SPOTTED IN METROPOLIS, LOIS?
HE HAD ANOTHER RUN-IN WITH THE NYPD A FEW DAYS AGO...
IT GETS EVEN MORE INTERESTING, JIMMY.
WITNESSES AND VIDEOS TIE HIM TO SUPERMAN, SUPERGIRL AND AN UNIDENTIFIED META.
WE SEEM TO HAVE A SUPER-DEMIC ON OUR HANDS.
HOLD ON A MINUTE, LOIS. I'VE BEEN WAITING FOR THE TWO "INNOCENT BYSTANDERS" WHO WERE ALLEGEDLY ATTACKED BY THE SUPERBOY--
--AND HERE THEY ARE NOW!
GENTLEMEN, I'M JIMMY OLSEN FROM THE DAILY PLANET AND--
NOT INTERESTED.
DON'T LIKE REPORTERS OR CAMERAS.
HEY--!
OUR LIMO AWAITS, STREAK.
I'M WITH Y'ALL, BONESMASHER...
JIMMY! ARE YOU ALL RIGHT?
JUST FINE, LOIS.
HAD A HUNCH THOSE BYSTANDERS WEREN'T ALL THAT INNOCENT...
KLK
KLK

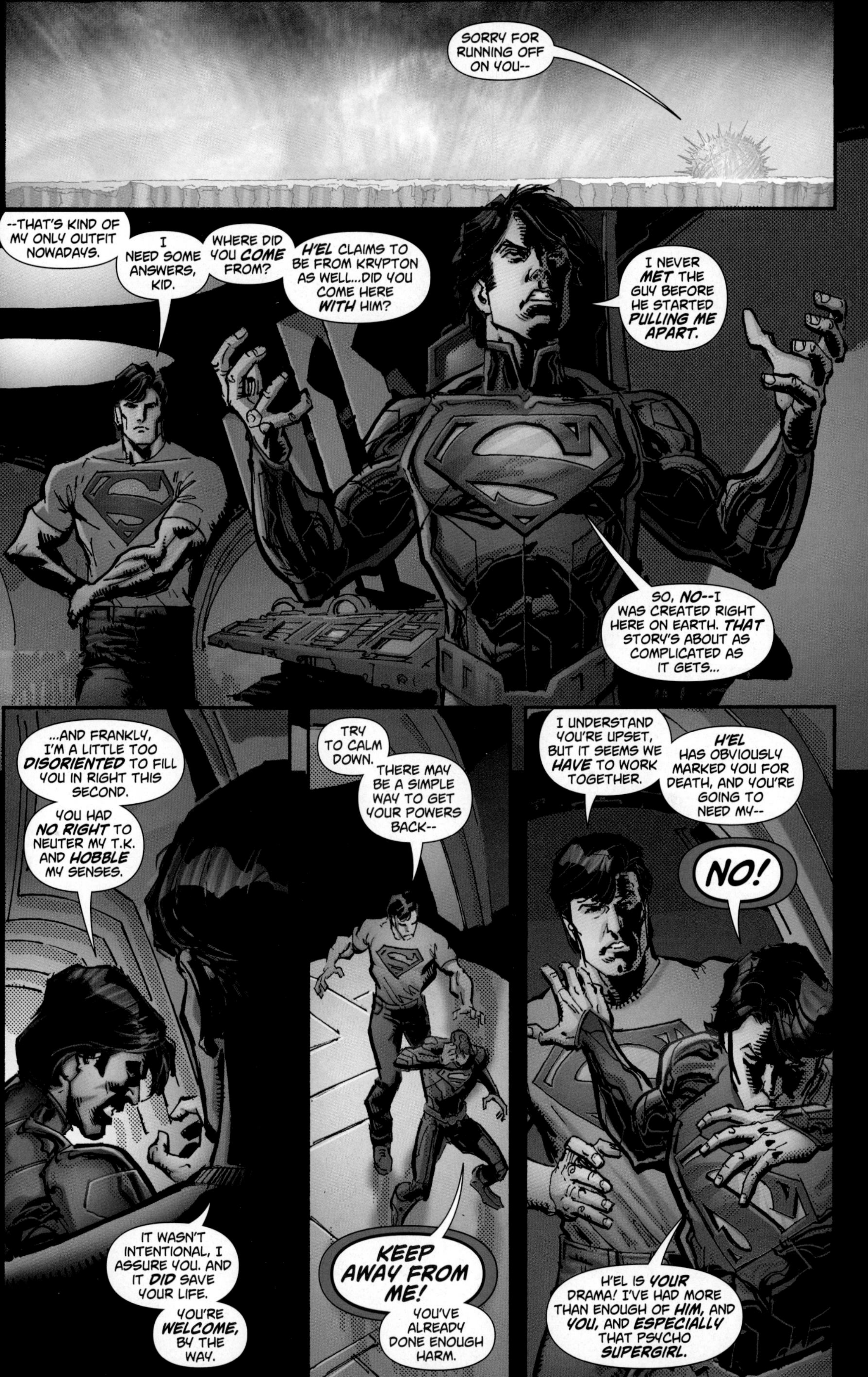
SORRY FOR RUNNING OFF ON YOU--
--THAT'S KIND OF MY ONLY OUTFIT NOWADAYS.
I NEED SOME ANSWERS, KID.
WHERE DID YOU COME FROM?
H'EL CLAIMS TO BE FROM KRYPTON AS WELL...DID YOU COME HERE WITH HIM?
I NEVER MET THE GUY BEFORE HE STARTED PULLING ME APART.
SO, NO--I WAS CREATED RIGHT HERE ON EARTH. THAT STORY'S ABOUT AS COMPLICATED AS IT GETS...
...AND FRANKLY, I'M A LITTLE TOO DISORIENTED TO FILL YOU IN RIGHT THIS SECOND.
YOU HAD NO RIGHT TO NEUTER MY T.K. AND HOBBLE MY SENSES.
IT WASN'T INTENTIONAL, I ASSURE YOU. AND IT DID SAVE YOUR LIFE.
YOU'RE WELCOME, BY THE WAY.
TRY TO CALM DOWN.
THERE MAY BE A SIMPLE WAY TO GET YOUR POWERS BACK--
KEEP AWAY FROM ME!
YOU'VE ALREADY DONE ENOUGH HARM.
I UNDERSTAND YOU'RE UPSET, BUT IT SEEMS WE HAVE TO WORK TOGETHER.
H'EL HAS OBVIOUSLY MARKED YOU FOR DEATH, AND YOU'RE GOING TO NEED MY--
NO!
H'EL IS YOUR DRAMA! I'VE HAD MORE THAN ENOUGH OF HIM, AND YOU, AND ESPECIALLY THAT PSYCHO SUPERGIRL.

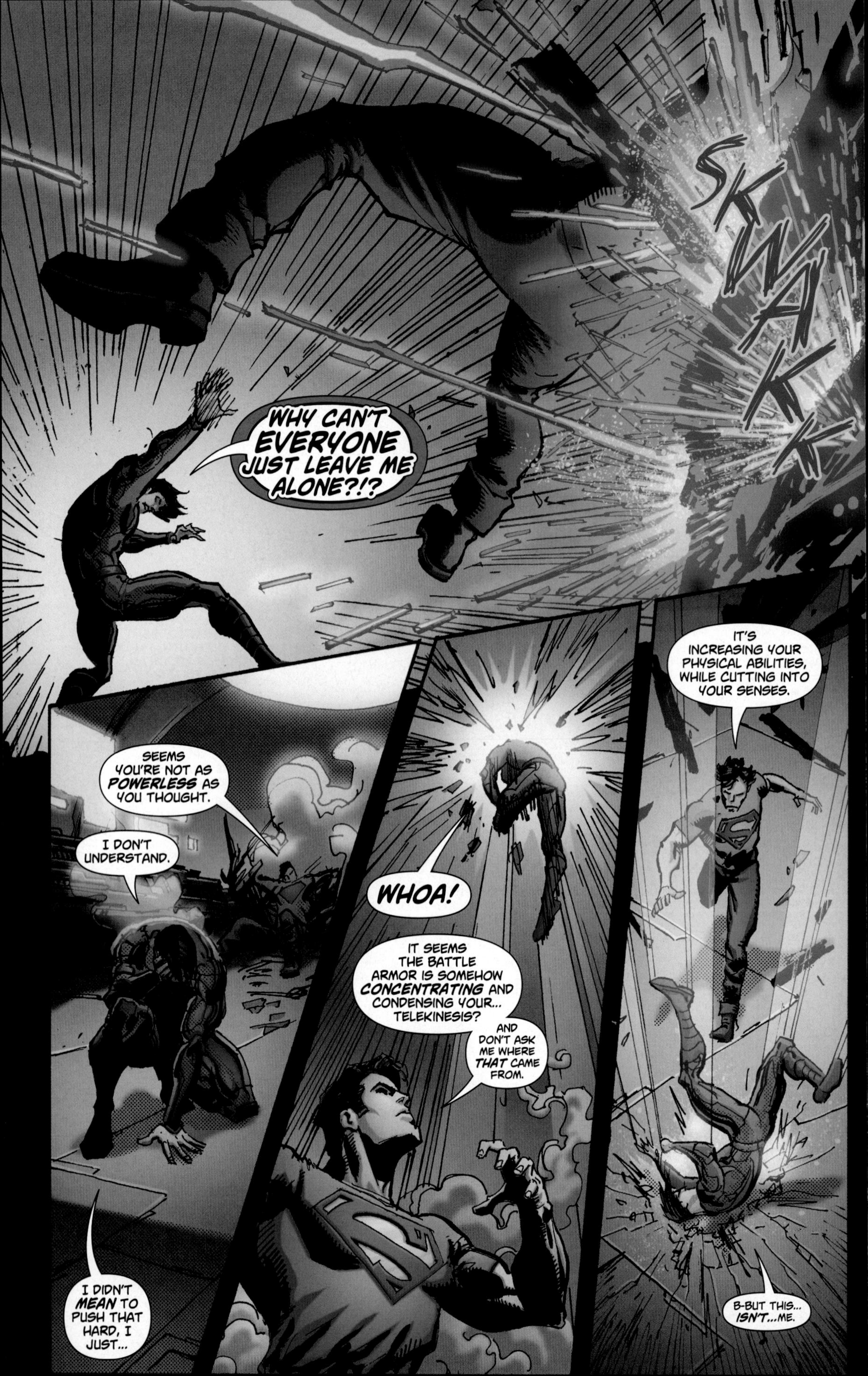

SKWAKKK
WHY CAN'T EVERYONE JUST LEAVE ME ALONE?!?
SEEMS YOU'RE NOT AS POWERLESS AS YOU THOUGHT.
I DON'T UNDERSTAND.
I DIDN'T MEAN TO PUSH THAT HARD, I JUST...
WHOA!
IT SEEMS THE BATTLE ARMOR IS SOMEHOW CONCENTRATING AND CONDENSING YOUR... TELEKINESIS?
AND DON'T ASK ME WHERE THAT CAME FROM.
IT'S INCREASING YOUR PHYSICAL ABILITIES, WHILE CUTTING INTO YOUR SENSES.
B-BUT THIS... ISN'T...ME.

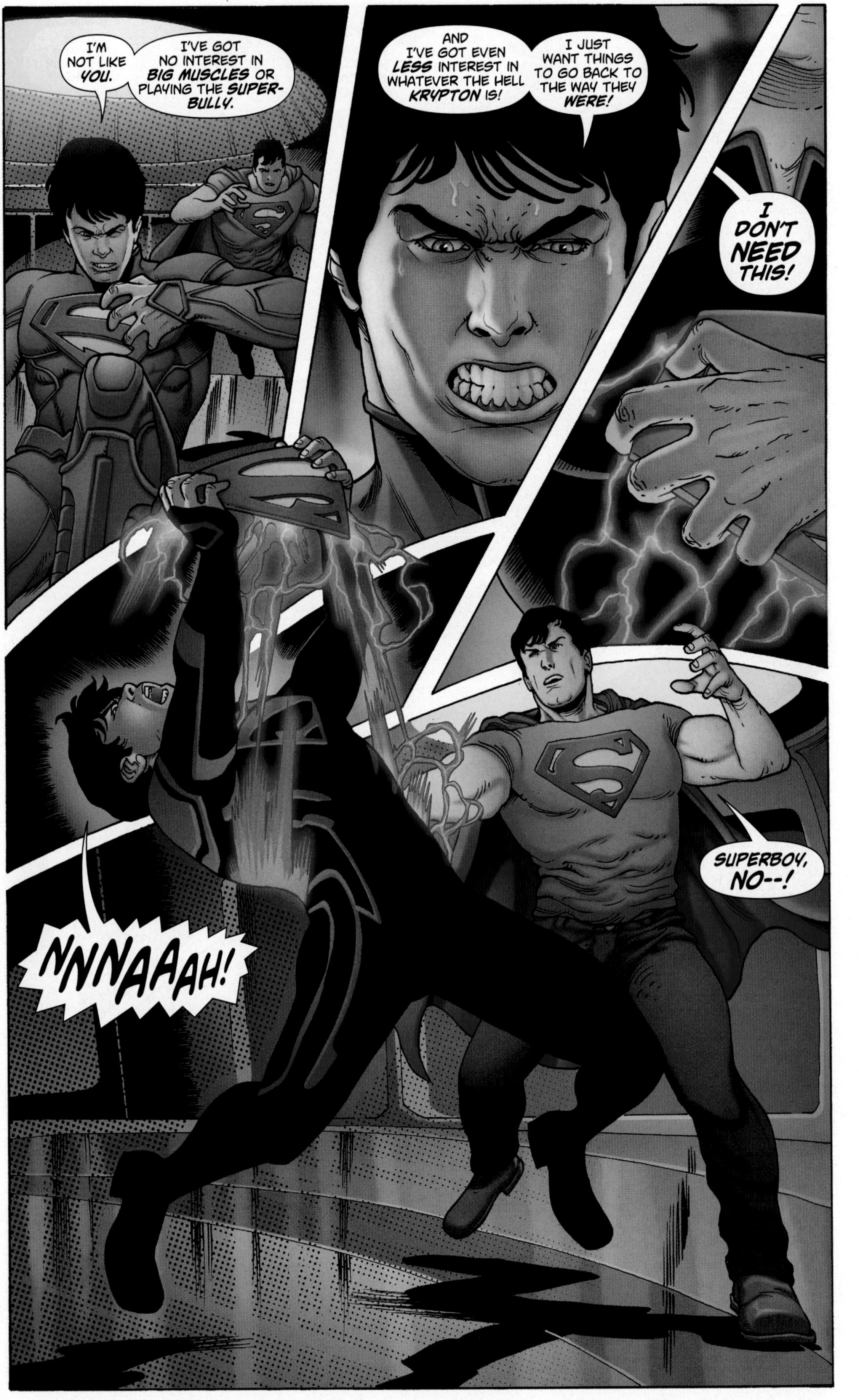
I'M NOT LIKE YOU.
I'VE GOT NO INTEREST IN BIG MUSCLES OR PLAYING THE SUPER-BULLY.
AND I'VE GOT EVEN LESS INTEREST IN WHATEVER THE HELL KRYPTON IS!
I JUST WANT THINGS TO GO BACK TO THE WAY THEY WERE!
I DON'T NEED THIS!
SUPERBOY, NO--!
NNNAAAH!

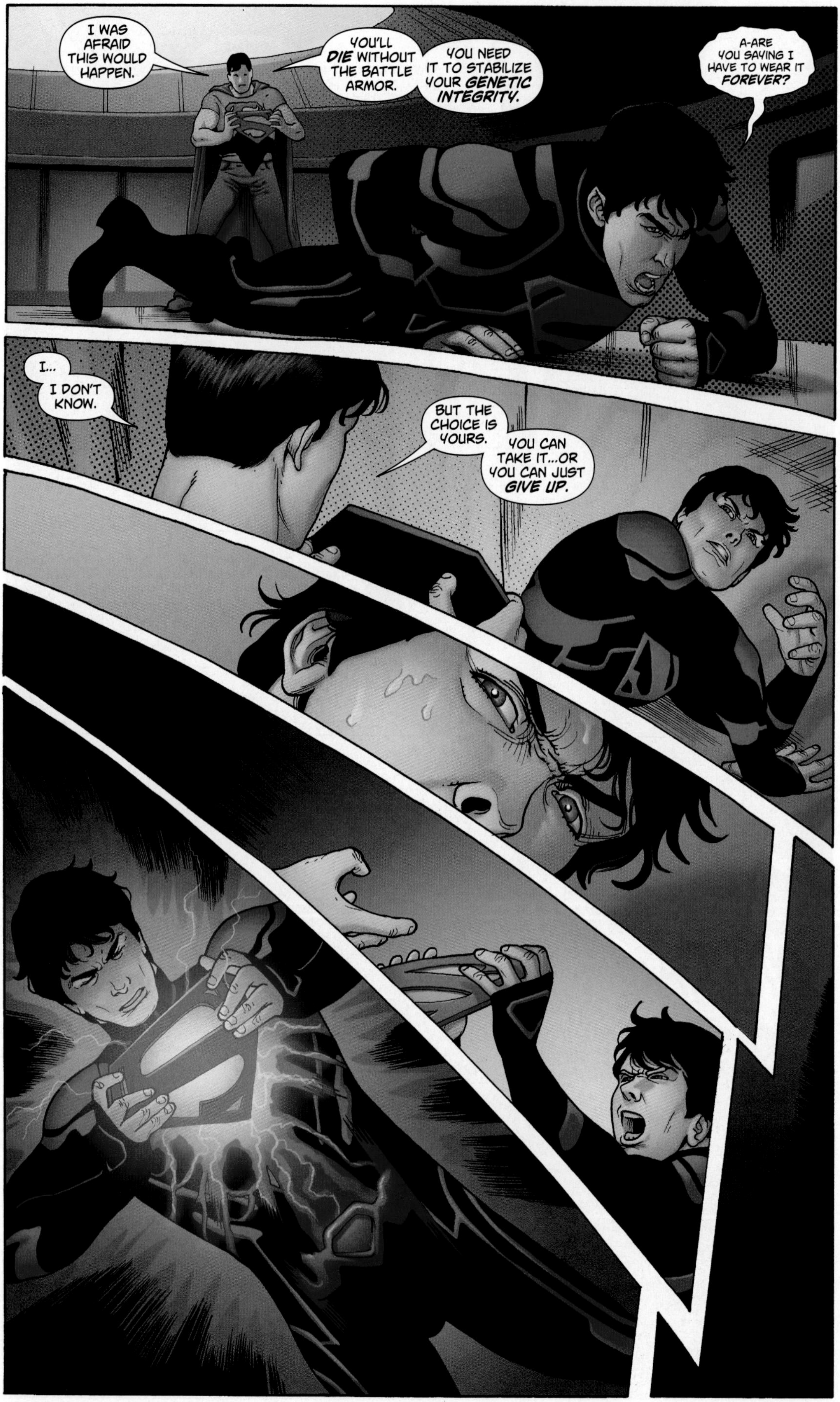
I WAS AFRAID THIS WOULD HAPPEN.
YOU'LL DIE WITHOUT THE BATTLE ARMOR.
YOU NEED IT TO STABILIZE YOUR GENETIC INTEGRITY.
A-ARE YOU SAYING I HAVE TO WEAR IT FOREVER?
I... I DON'T KNOW.
BUT THE CHOICE IS YOURS.
YOU CAN TAKE IT...OR YOU CAN JUST GIVE UP.

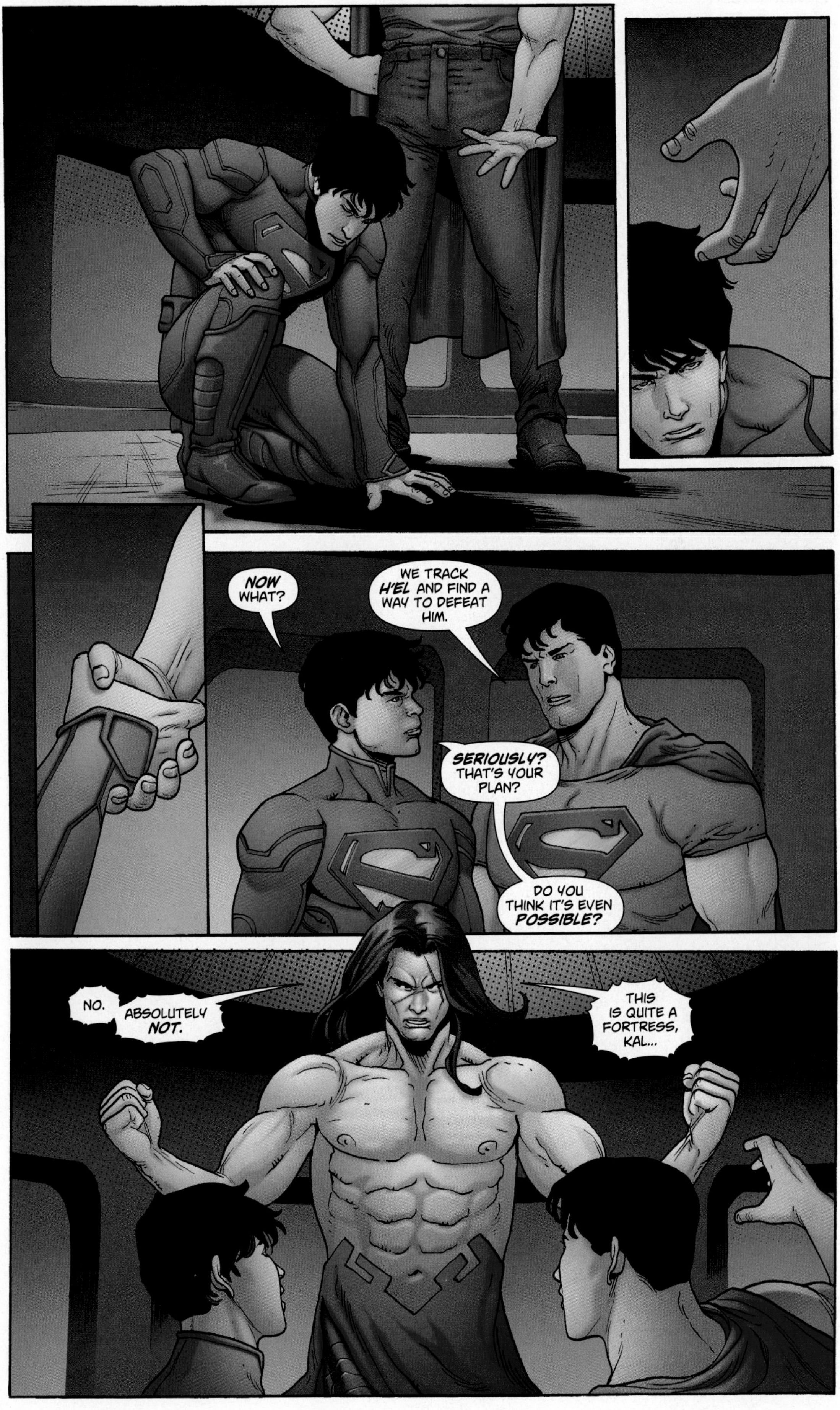
NOW WHAT?
WE TRACK H'EL AND FIND A WAY TO DEFEAT HIM.
SERIOUSLY? THAT'S YOUR PLAN?
DO YOU THINK IT'S EVEN POSSIBLE?
NO.
ABSOLUTELY NOT.
THIS IS QUITE A FORTRESS, KAL...

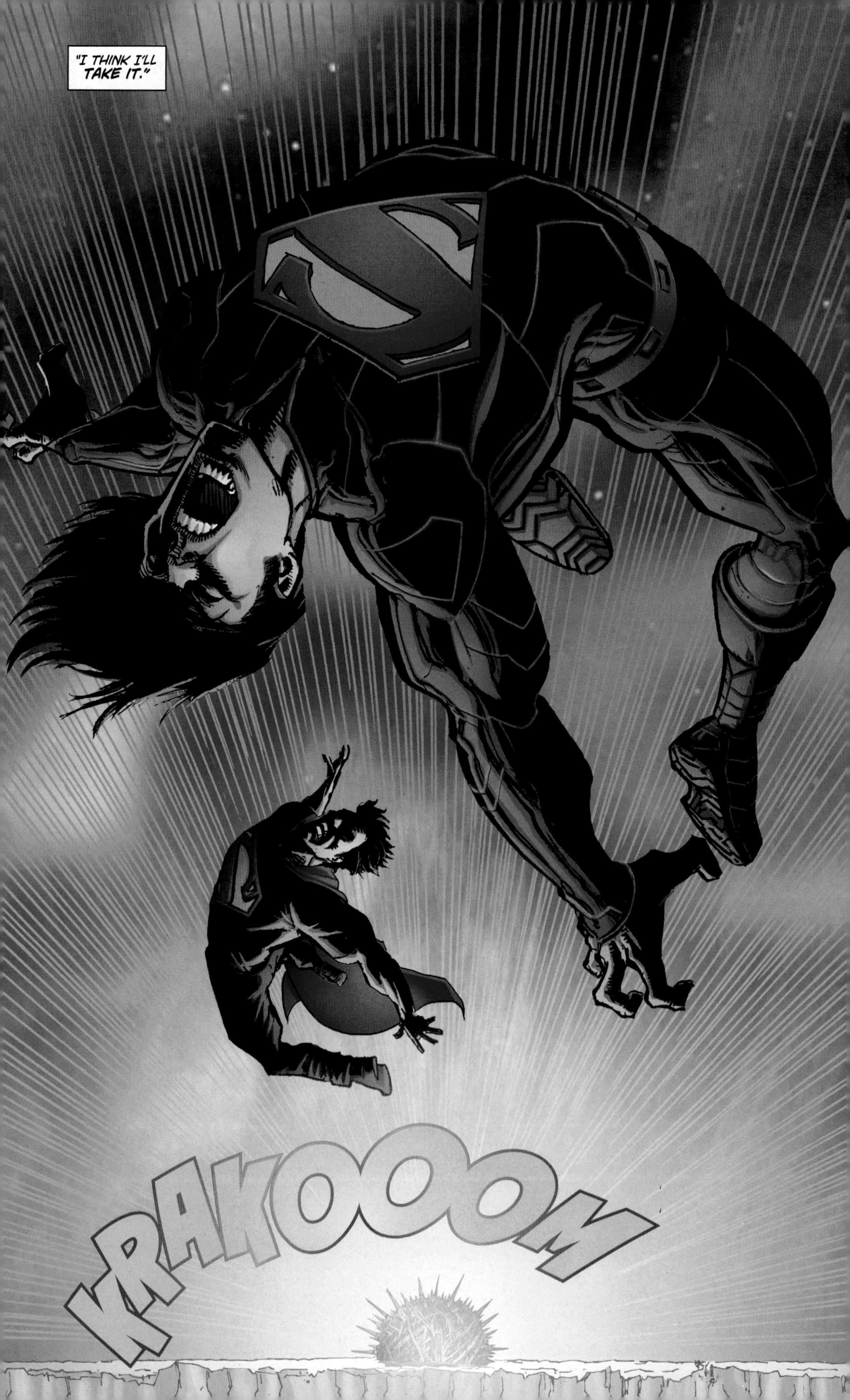
"I THINK I'LL TAKE IT."
KRAKOOOM

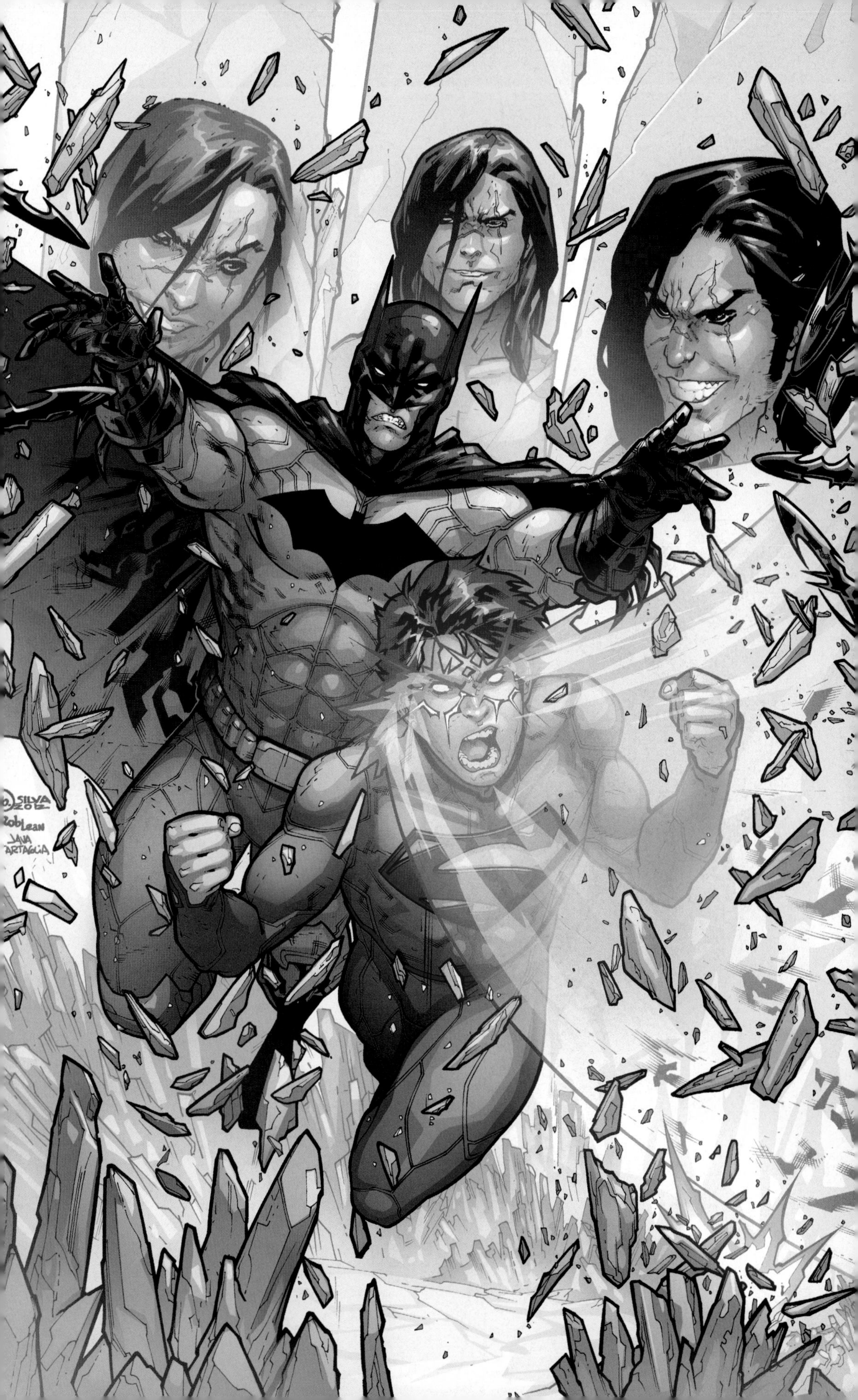

SILVA 2012
Rob Lean

TRIGGERS!

TOM DeFALCO writer **RON FRENZ** thumbnails **AMILCAR PINNA** artist **IBAN COELLO** penciller **ROB LEAN** inker
cover art by **R.B. SILVA, ROB LEAN & JAVA TARTAGLIA**

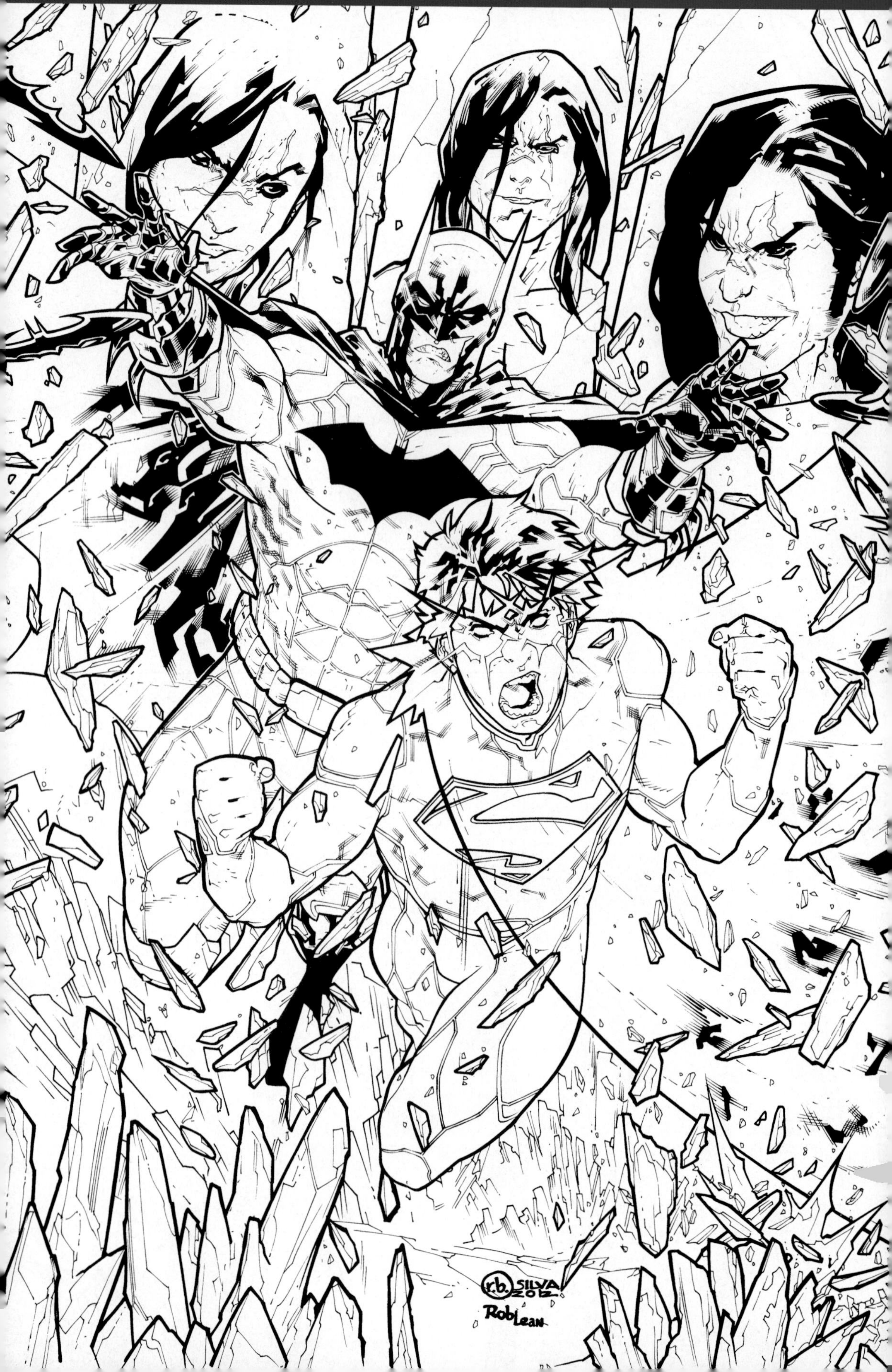
r.b. SILVA 2012
Rob Lean

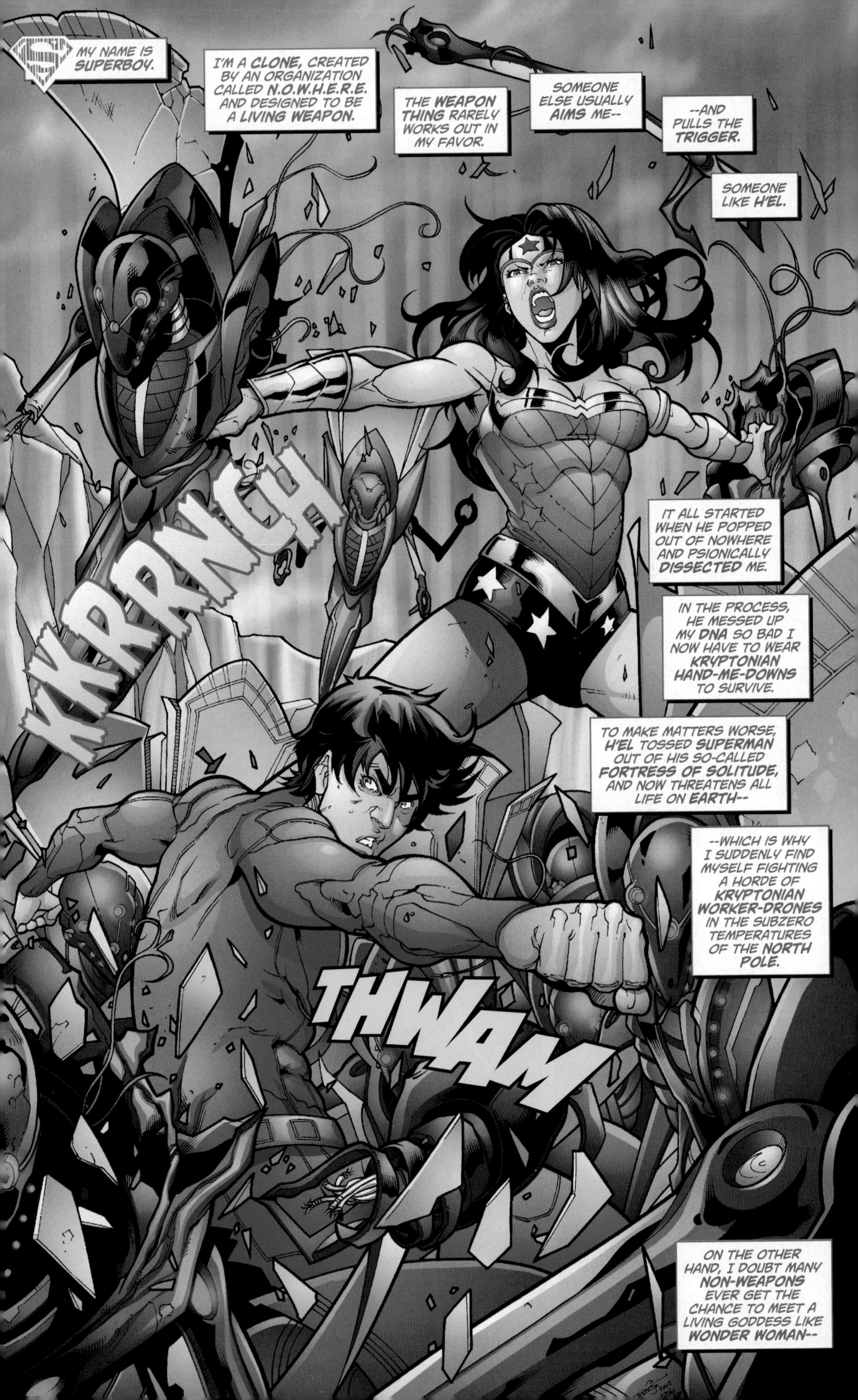

MY NAME IS SUPERBOY.
I'M A CLONE, CREATED BY AN ORGANIZATION CALLED N.O.W.H.E.R.E. AND DESIGNED TO BE A LIVING WEAPON.
THE WEAPON THING RARELY WORKS OUT IN MY FAVOR.
SOMEONE ELSE USUALLY AIMS ME--
--AND PULLS THE TRIGGER.
SOMEONE LIKE H'EL.
KKRRNCH
IT ALL STARTED WHEN HE POPPED OUT OF NOWHERE AND PSIONICALLY DISSECTED ME.
IN THE PROCESS, HE MESSED UP MY DNA SO BAD I NOW HAVE TO WEAR KRYPTONIAN HAND-ME-DOWNS TO SURVIVE.
TO MAKE MATTERS WORSE, H'EL TOSSED SUPERMAN OUT OF HIS SO-CALLED FORTRESS OF SOLITUDE, AND NOW THREATENS ALL LIFE ON EARTH--
--WHICH IS WHY I SUDDENLY FIND MYSELF FIGHTING A HORDE OF KRYPTONIAN WORKER-DRONES IN THE SUBZERO TEMPERATURES OF THE NORTH POLE.
THWAM
ON THE OTHER HAND, I DOUBT MANY NON-WEAPONS EVER GET THE CHANCE TO MEET A LIVING GODDESS LIKE WONDER WOMAN--

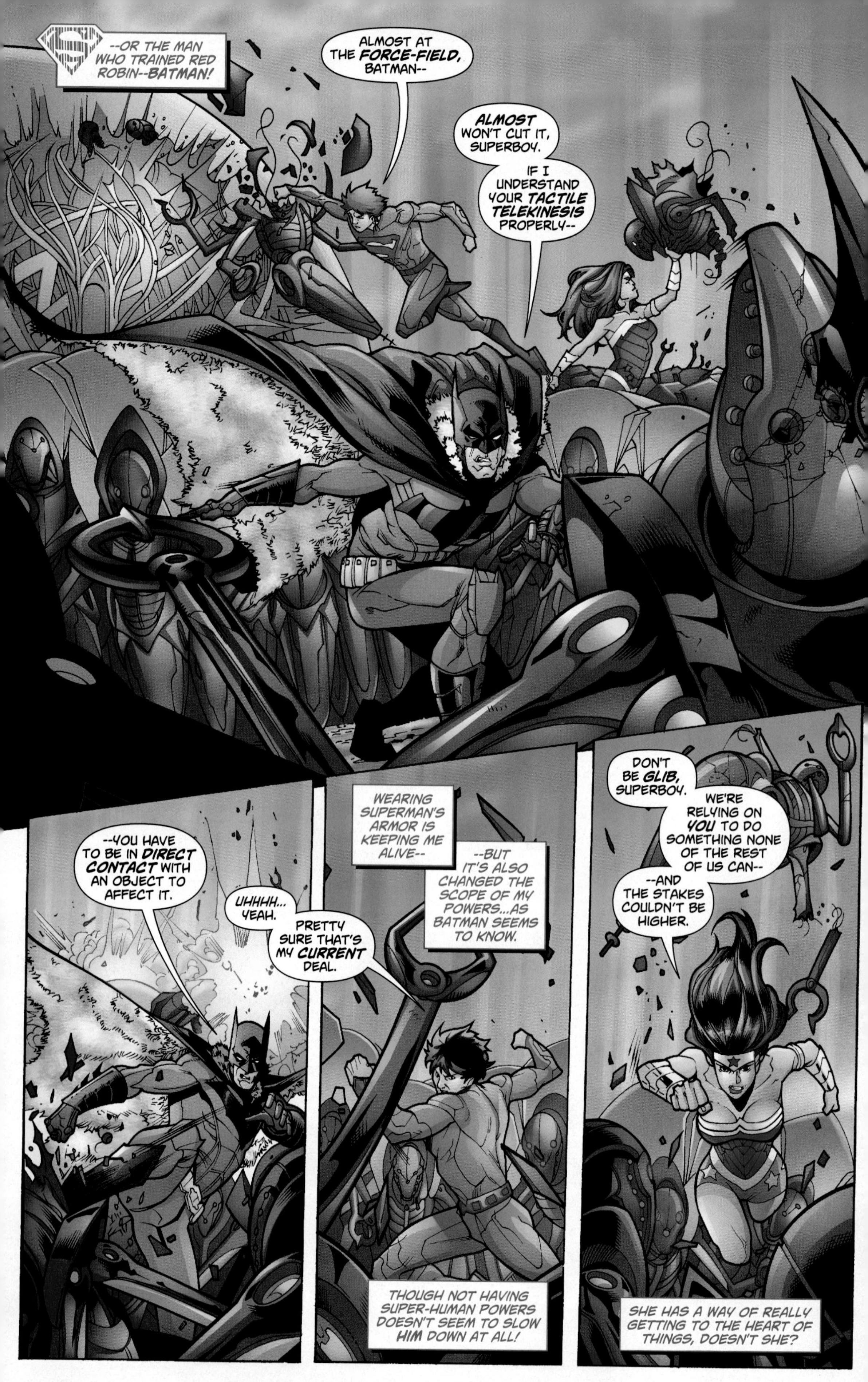

--OR THE MAN WHO TRAINED RED ROBIN--BATMAN!
ALMOST AT THE FORCE-FIELD, BATMAN--
ALMOST WON'T CUT IT, SUPERBOY.
IF I UNDERSTAND YOUR TACTILE TELEKINESIS PROPERLY--
--YOU HAVE TO BE IN DIRECT CONTACT WITH AN OBJECT TO AFFECT IT.
UHHHH... YEAH.
PRETTY SURE THAT'S MY CURRENT DEAL.
WEARING SUPERMAN'S ARMOR IS KEEPING ME ALIVE--
--BUT IT'S ALSO CHANGED THE SCOPE OF MY POWERS...AS BATMAN SEEMS TO KNOW.
THOUGH NOT HAVING SUPER-HUMAN POWERS DOESN'T SEEM TO SLOW HIM DOWN AT ALL!
DON'T BE GLIB, SUPERBOY.
WE'RE RELYING ON YOU TO DO SOMETHING NONE OF THE REST OF US CAN--
--AND THE STAKES COULDN'T BE HIGHER.
SHE HAS A WAY OF REALLY GETTING TO THE HEART OF THINGS, DOESN'T SHE?

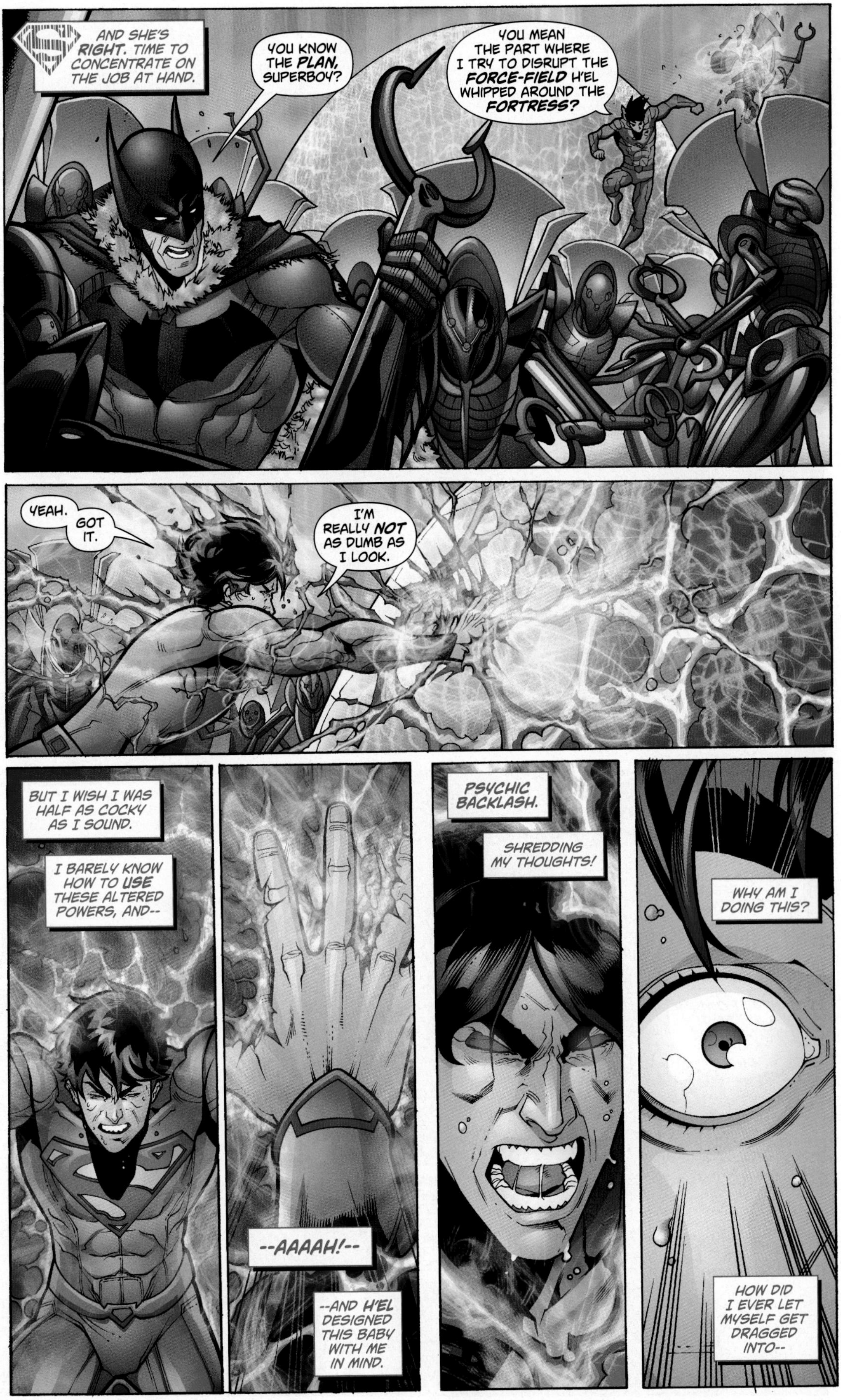
AND SHE'S RIGHT. TIME TO CONCENTRATE ON THE JOB AT HAND.
YOU KNOW THE PLAN, SUPERBOY?
YOU MEAN THE PART WHERE I TRY TO DISRUPT THE FORCE-FIELD H'EL WHIPPED AROUND THE FORTRESS?
YEAH. GOT IT.
I'M REALLY NOT AS DUMB AS I LOOK.
BUT I WISH I WAS HALF AS COCKY AS I SOUND.
I BARELY KNOW HOW TO USE THESE ALTERED POWERS, AND--
--AAAAH!--
--AND H'EL DESIGNED THIS BABY WITH ME IN MIND.
PSYCHIC BACKLASH.
SHREDDING MY THOUGHTS!
WHY AM I DOING THIS?
HOW DID I EVER LET MYSELF GET DRAGGED INTO--

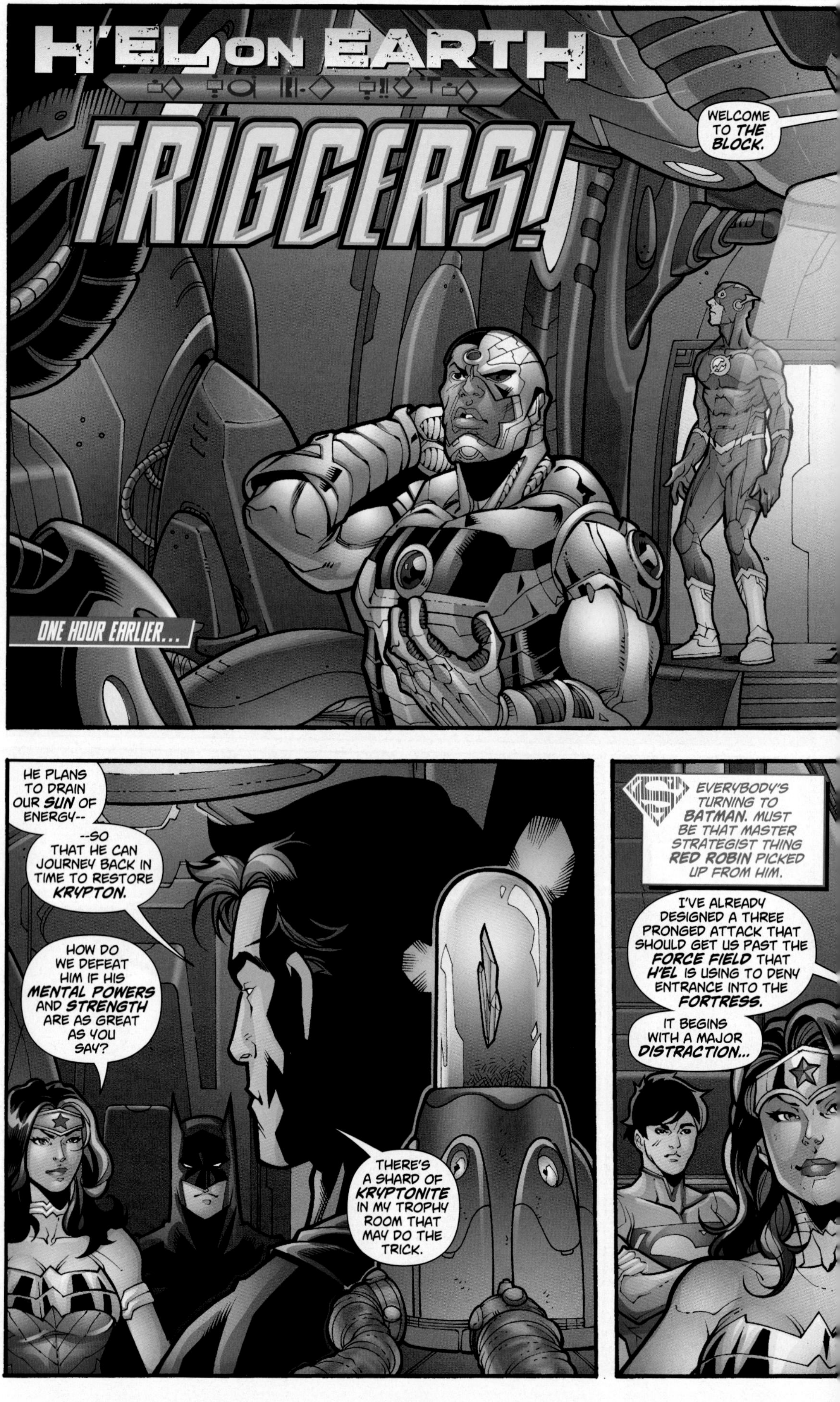
H'EL ON EARTH
TRIGGERS!
WELCOME TO THE BLOCK.
ONE HOUR EARLIER...
HE PLANS TO DRAIN OUR SUN OF ENERGY--
--SO THAT HE CAN JOURNEY BACK IN TIME TO RESTORE KRYPTON.
HOW DO WE DEFEAT HIM IF HIS MENTAL POWERS AND STRENGTH ARE AS GREAT AS YOU SAY?
THERE'S A SHARD OF KRYPTONITE IN MY TROPHY ROOM THAT MAY DO THE TRICK.
EVERYBODY'S TURNING TO BATMAN. MUST BE THAT MASTER STRATEGIST THING RED ROBIN PICKED UP FROM HIM.
I'VE ALREADY DESIGNED A THREE PRONGED ATTACK THAT SHOULD GET US PAST THE FORCE FIELD THAT H'EL IS USING TO DENY ENTRANCE INTO THE FORTRESS.
IT BEGINS WITH A MAJOR DISTRACTION...

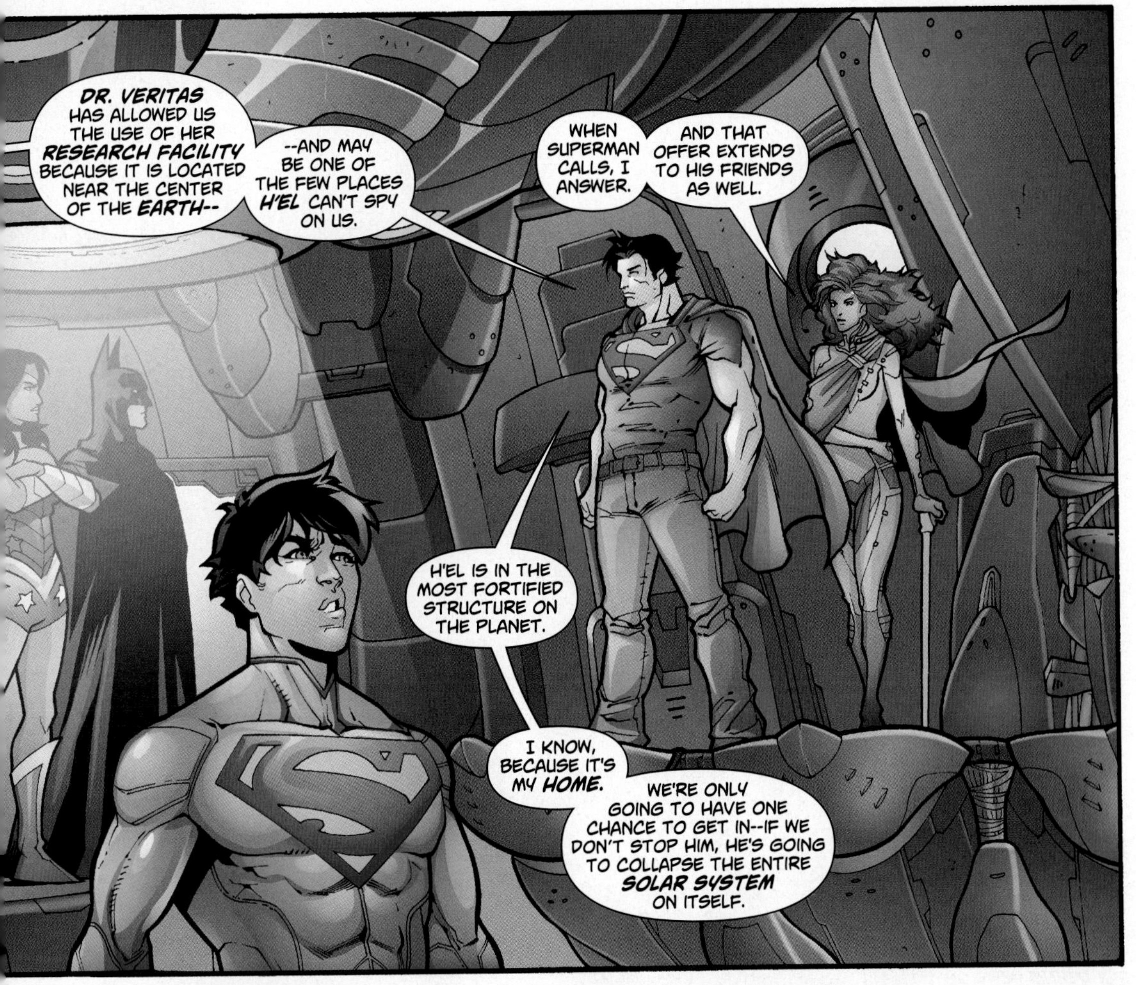
DR. VERITAS HAS ALLOWED US THE USE OF HER RESEARCH FACILITY BECAUSE IT IS LOCATED NEAR THE CENTER OF THE EARTH--
--AND MAY BE ONE OF THE FEW PLACES H'EL CAN'T SPY ON US.
WHEN SUPERMAN CALLS, I ANSWER.
AND THAT OFFER EXTENDS TO HIS FRIENDS AS WELL.
H'EL IS IN THE MOST FORTIFIED STRUCTURE ON THE PLANET.
I KNOW, BECAUSE IT'S MY HOME.
WE'RE ONLY GOING TO HAVE ONE CHANCE TO GET IN--IF WE DON'T STOP HIM, HE'S GOING TO COLLAPSE THE ENTIRE SOLAR SYSTEM ON ITSELF.

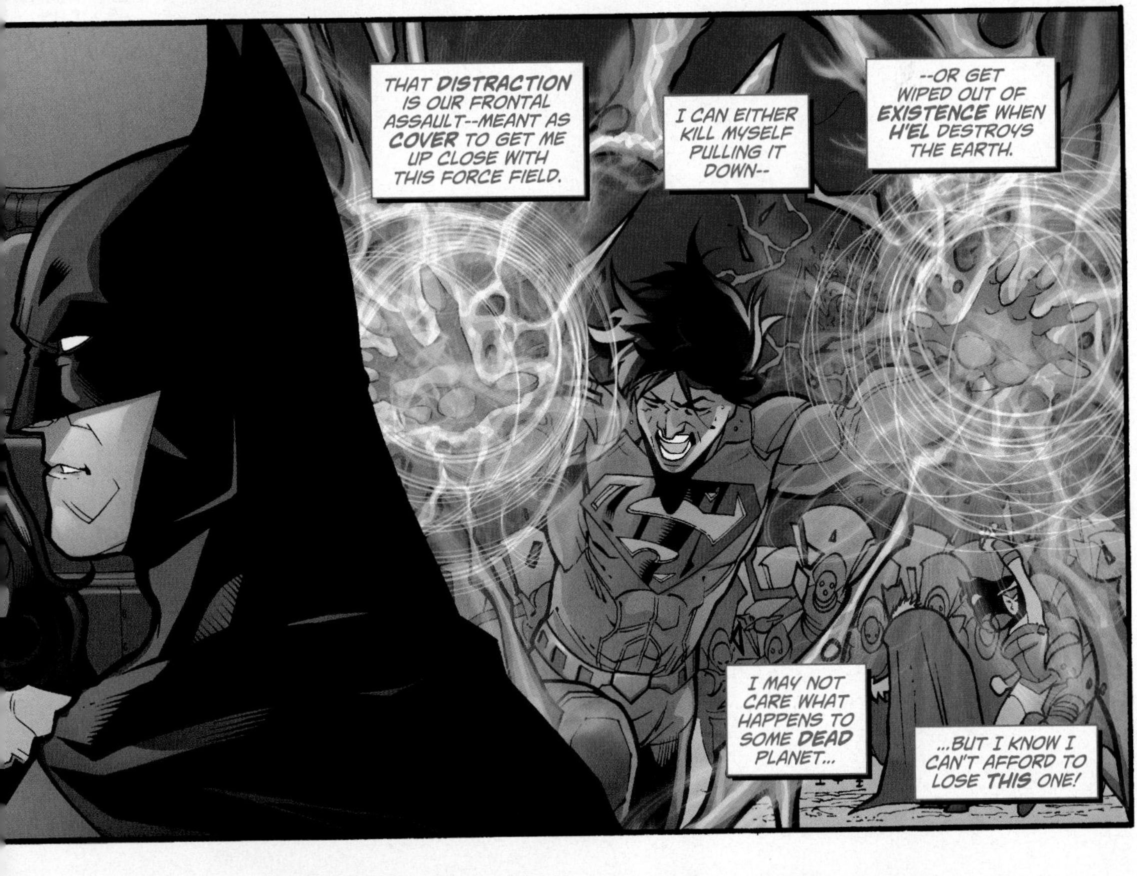
THAT DISTRACTION IS OUR FRONTAL ASSAULT--MEANT AS COVER TO GET ME UP CLOSE WITH THIS FORCE FIELD.
I CAN EITHER KILL MYSELF PULLING IT DOWN--
--OR GET WIPED OUT OF EXISTENCE WHEN H'EL DESTROYS THE EARTH.
I MAY NOT CARE WHAT HAPPENS TO SOME DEAD PLANET...
...BUT I KNOW I CAN'T AFFORD TO LOSE THIS ONE!

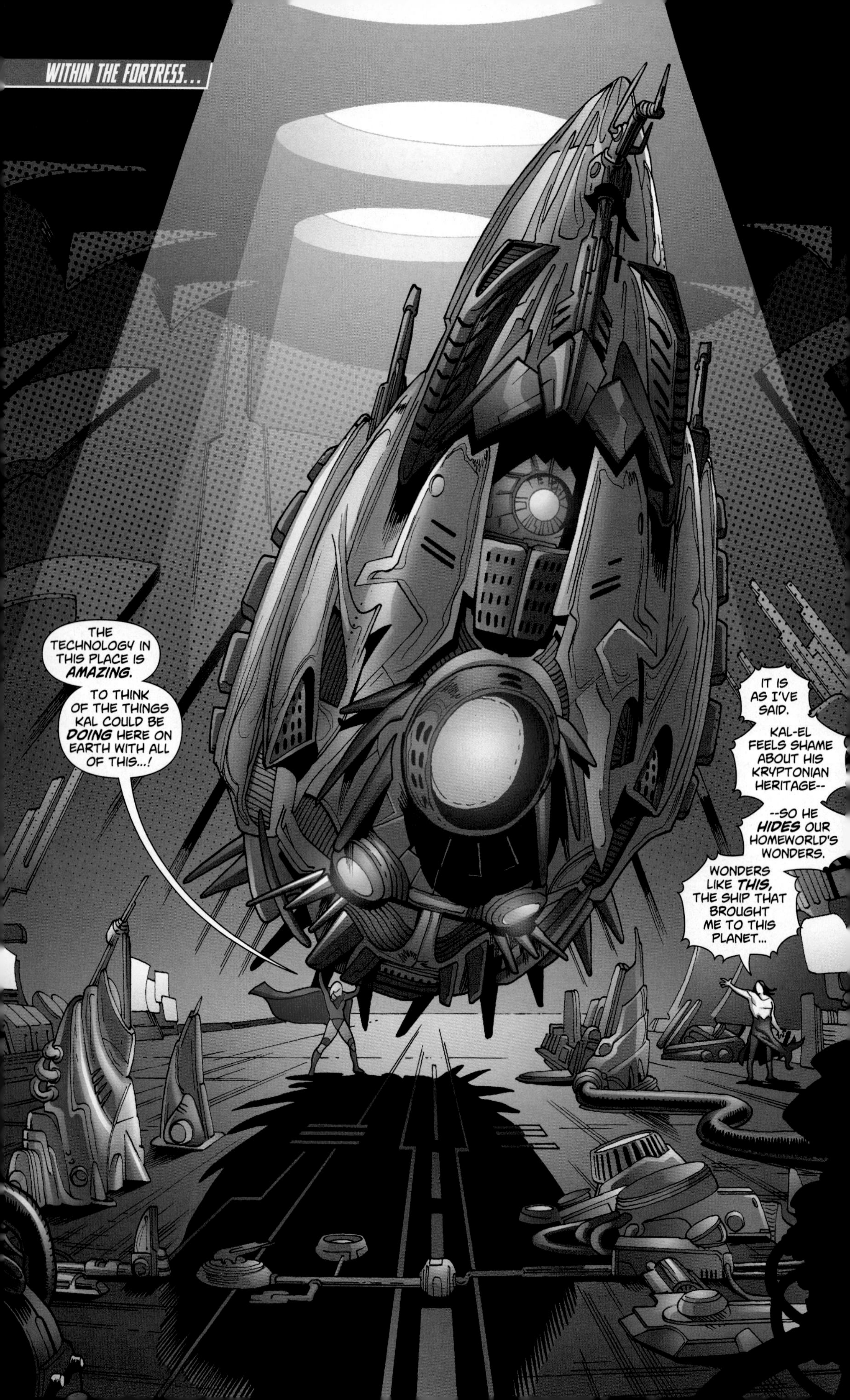
WITHIN THE FORTRESS...
THE TECHNOLOGY IN THIS PLACE IS AMAZING.
TO THINK OF THE THINGS KAL COULD BE DOING HERE ON EARTH WITH ALL OF THIS...!
IT IS AS I'VE SAID.
KAL-EL FEELS SHAME ABOUT HIS KRYPTONIAN HERITAGE--
--SO HE HIDES OUR HOMEWORLD'S WONDERS.
WONDERS LIKE THIS, THE SHIP THAT BROUGHT ME TO THIS PLANET...

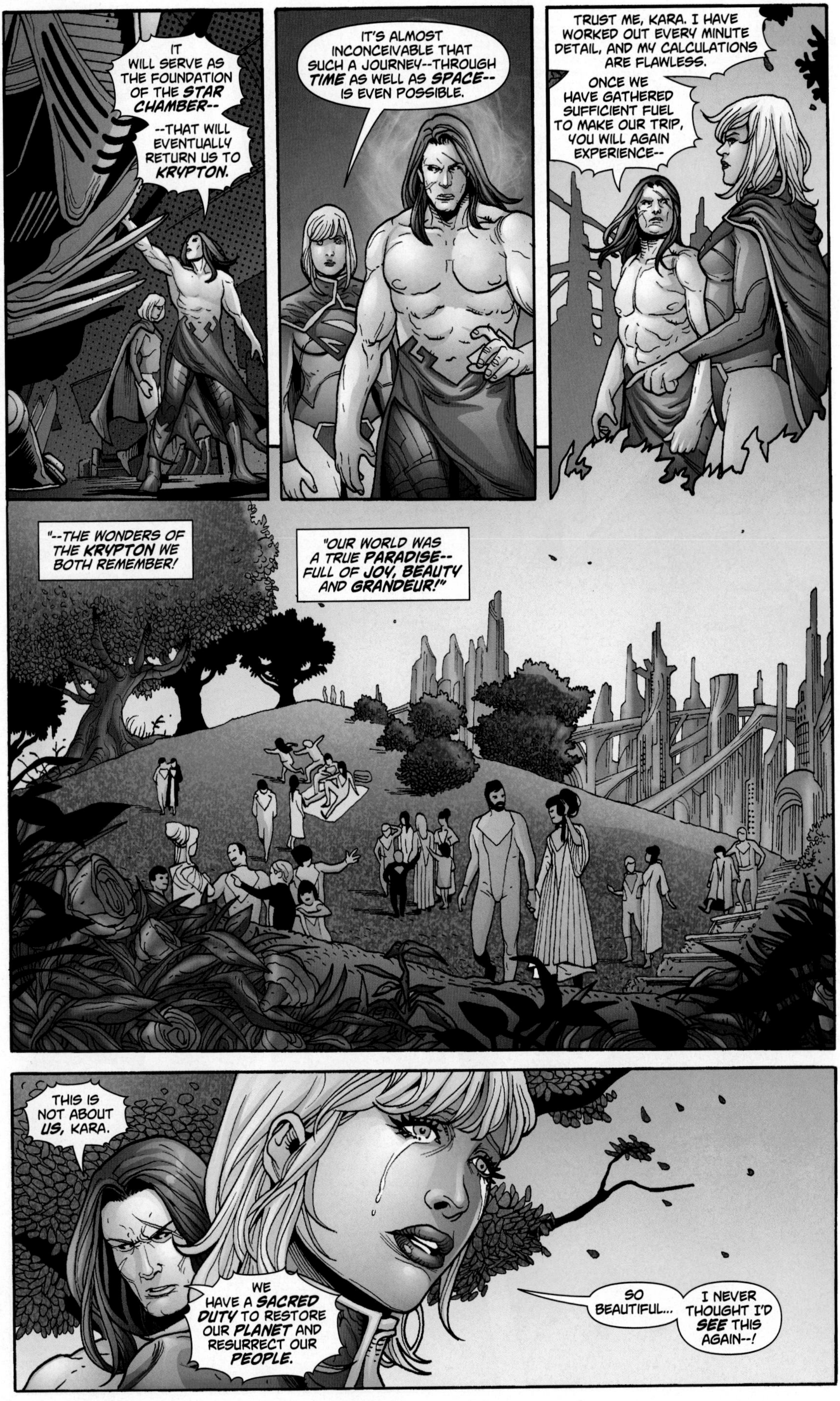
IT WILL SERVE AS THE FOUNDATION OF THE STAR CHAMBER--
--THAT WILL EVENTUALLY RETURN US TO KRYPTON.
IT'S ALMOST INCONCEIVABLE THAT SUCH A JOURNEY--THROUGH TIME AS WELL AS SPACE--IS EVEN POSSIBLE.
TRUST ME, KARA. I HAVE WORKED OUT EVERY MINUTE DETAIL, AND MY CALCULATIONS ARE FLAWLESS.
ONCE WE HAVE GATHERED SUFFICIENT FUEL TO MAKE OUR TRIP, YOU WILL AGAIN EXPERIENCE--
"--THE WONDERS OF THE KRYPTON WE BOTH REMEMBER!
"OUR WORLD WAS A TRUE PARADISE--FULL OF JOY, BEAUTY AND GRANDEUR!"
SO BEAUTIFUL...
I NEVER THOUGHT I'D SEE THIS AGAIN--!
THIS IS NOT ABOUT US, KARA.
WE HAVE A SACRED DUTY TO RESTORE OUR PLANET AND RESURRECT OUR PEOPLE.

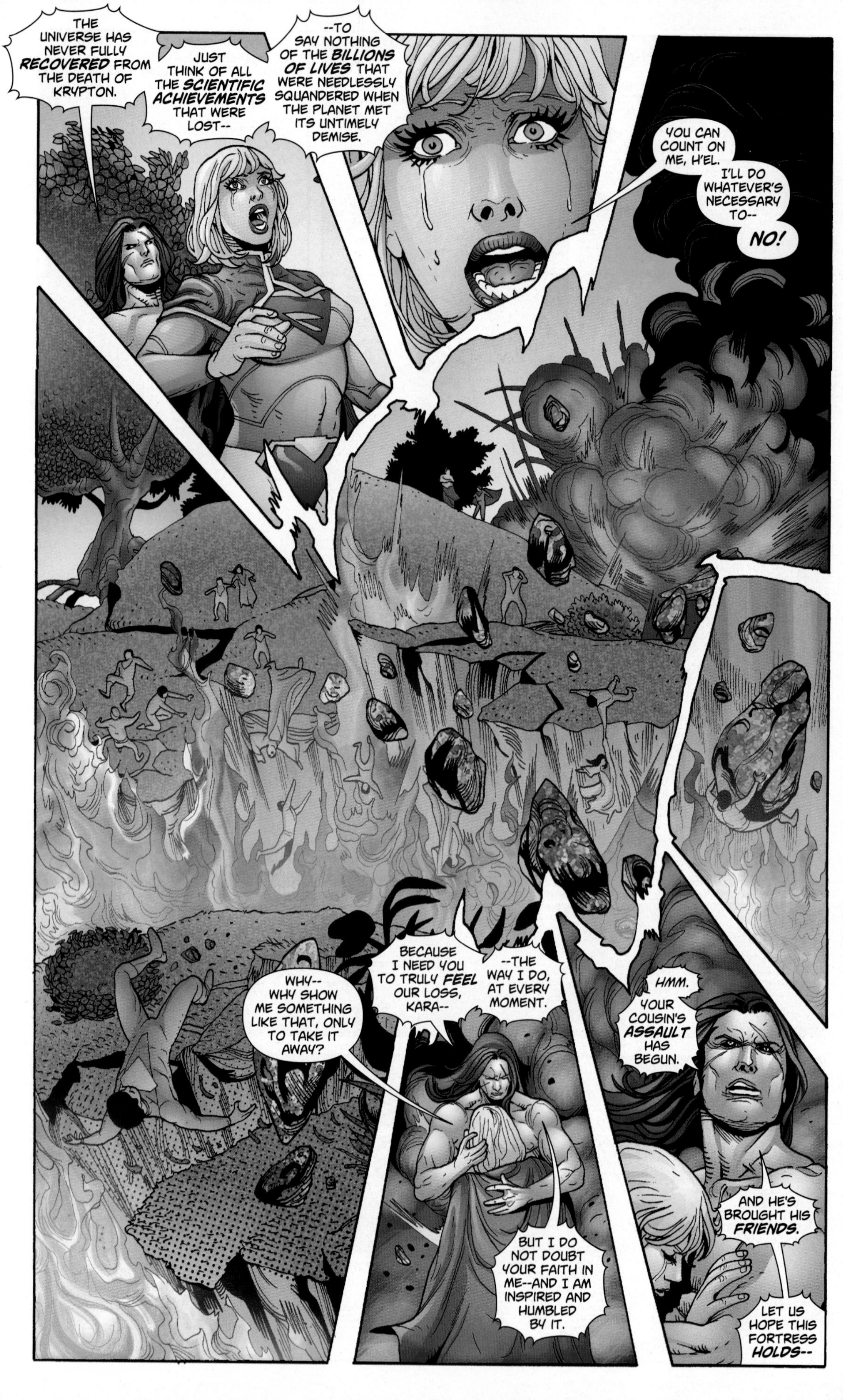
THE UNIVERSE HAS NEVER FULLY RECOVERED FROM THE DEATH OF KRYPTON.
JUST THINK OF ALL THE SCIENTIFIC ACHIEVEMENTS THAT WERE LOST--
--TO SAY NOTHING OF THE BILLIONS OF LIVES THAT WERE NEEDLESSLY SQUANDERED WHEN THE PLANET MET ITS UNTIMELY DEMISE.
YOU CAN COUNT ON ME, H'EL.
I'LL DO WHATEVER'S NECESSARY TO--
NO!
WHY-- WHY SHOW ME SOMETHING LIKE THAT, ONLY TO TAKE IT AWAY?
BECAUSE I NEED YOU TO TRULY FEEL OUR LOSS, KARA--
--THE WAY I DO, AT EVERY MOMENT.
BUT I DO NOT DOUBT YOUR FAITH IN ME--AND I AM INSPIRED AND HUMBLED BY IT.
HMM.
YOUR COUSIN'S ASSAULT HAS BEGUN.
AND HE'S BROUGHT HIS FRIENDS.
LET US HOPE THIS FORTRESS HOLDS--

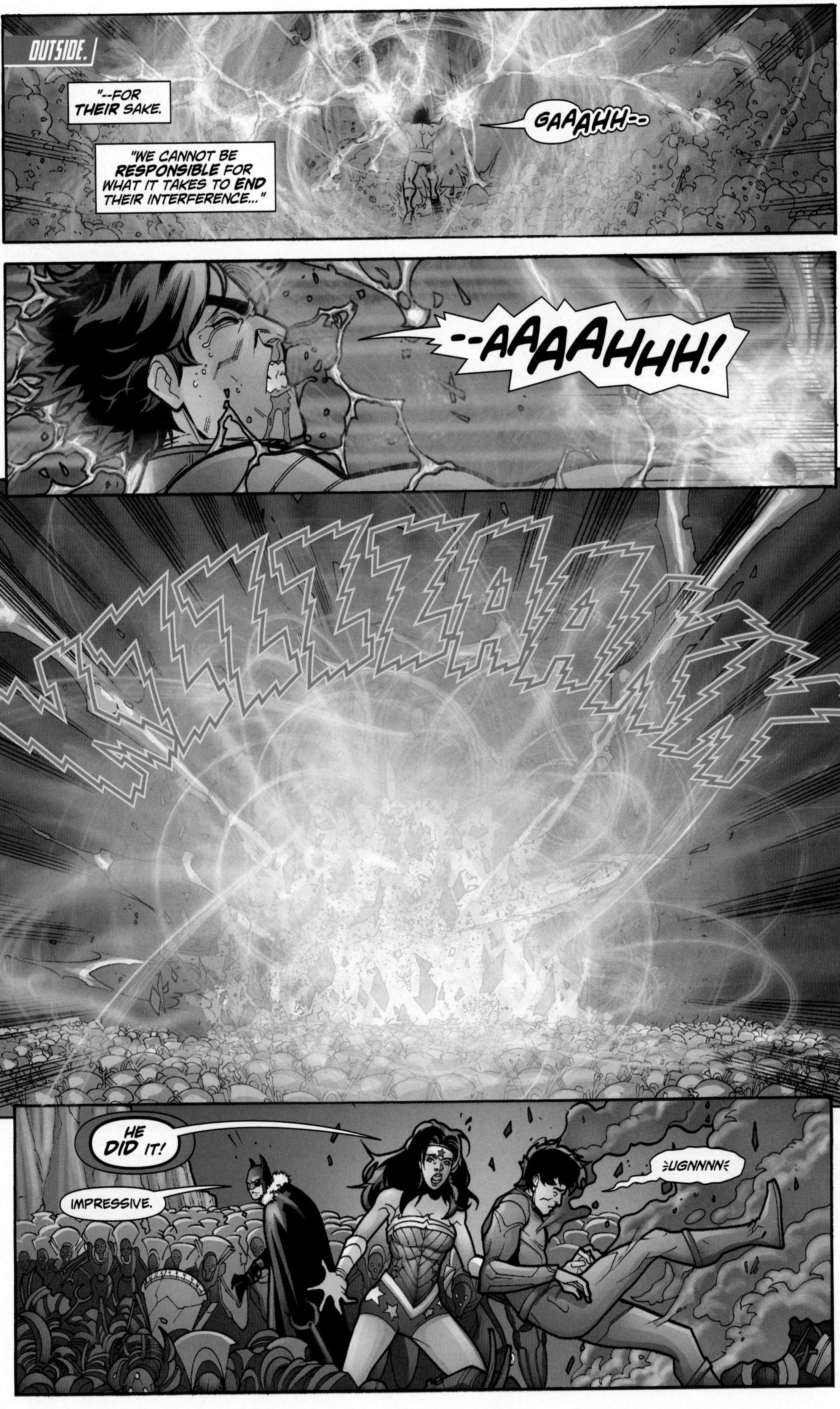
OUTSIDE.
"--FOR THEIR SAKE.
"WE CANNOT BE RESPONSIBLE FOR WHAT IT TAKES TO END THEIR INTERFERENCE..."
GAAAHH--
--AAAAAHHH!
HE DID IT!
IMPRESSIVE.
UGNNNN

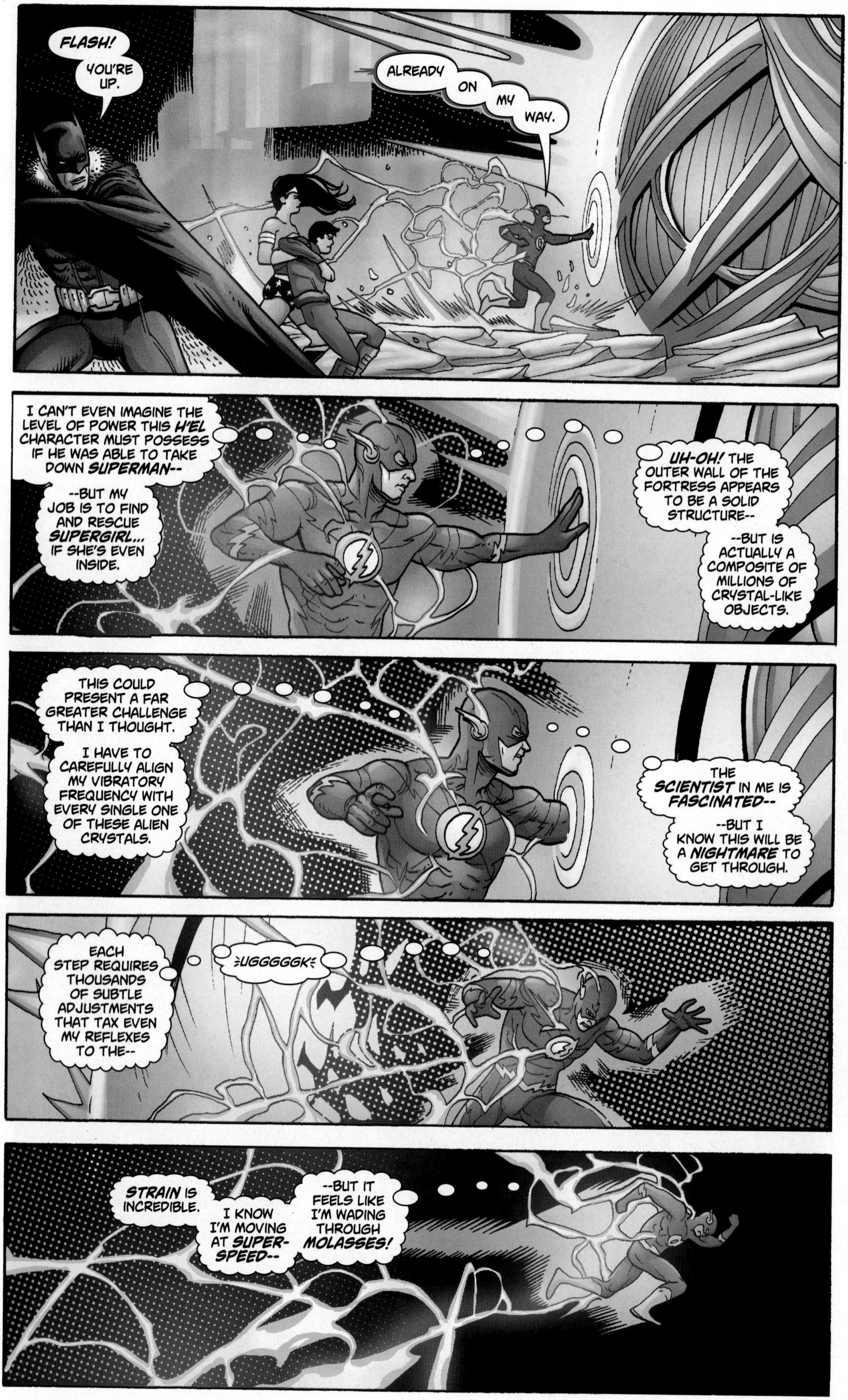
FLASH!
YOU'RE UP.
ALREADY ON MY WAY.
I CAN'T EVEN IMAGINE THE LEVEL OF POWER THIS H'EL CHARACTER MUST POSSESS IF HE WAS ABLE TO TAKE DOWN SUPERMAN--
--BUT MY JOB IS TO FIND AND RESCUE SUPERGIRL... IF SHE'S EVEN INSIDE.
UH-OH! THE OUTER WALL OF THE FORTRESS APPEARS TO BE A SOLID STRUCTURE--
--BUT IS ACTUALLY A COMPOSITE OF MILLIONS OF CRYSTAL-LIKE OBJECTS.
THIS COULD PRESENT A FAR GREATER CHALLENGE THAN I THOUGHT.
I HAVE TO CAREFULLY ALIGN MY VIBRATORY FREQUENCY WITH EVERY SINGLE ONE OF THESE ALIEN CRYSTALS.
THE SCIENTIST IN ME IS FASCINATED--
--BUT I KNOW THIS WILL BE A NIGHTMARE TO GET THROUGH.
EACH STEP REQUIRES THOUSANDS OF SUBTLE ADJUSTMENTS THAT TAX EVEN MY REFLEXES TO THE--
UGGGGGK
STRAIN IS INCREDIBLE.
I KNOW I'M MOVING AT SUPER-SPEED--
--BUT IT FEELS LIKE I'M WADING THROUGH MOLASSES!

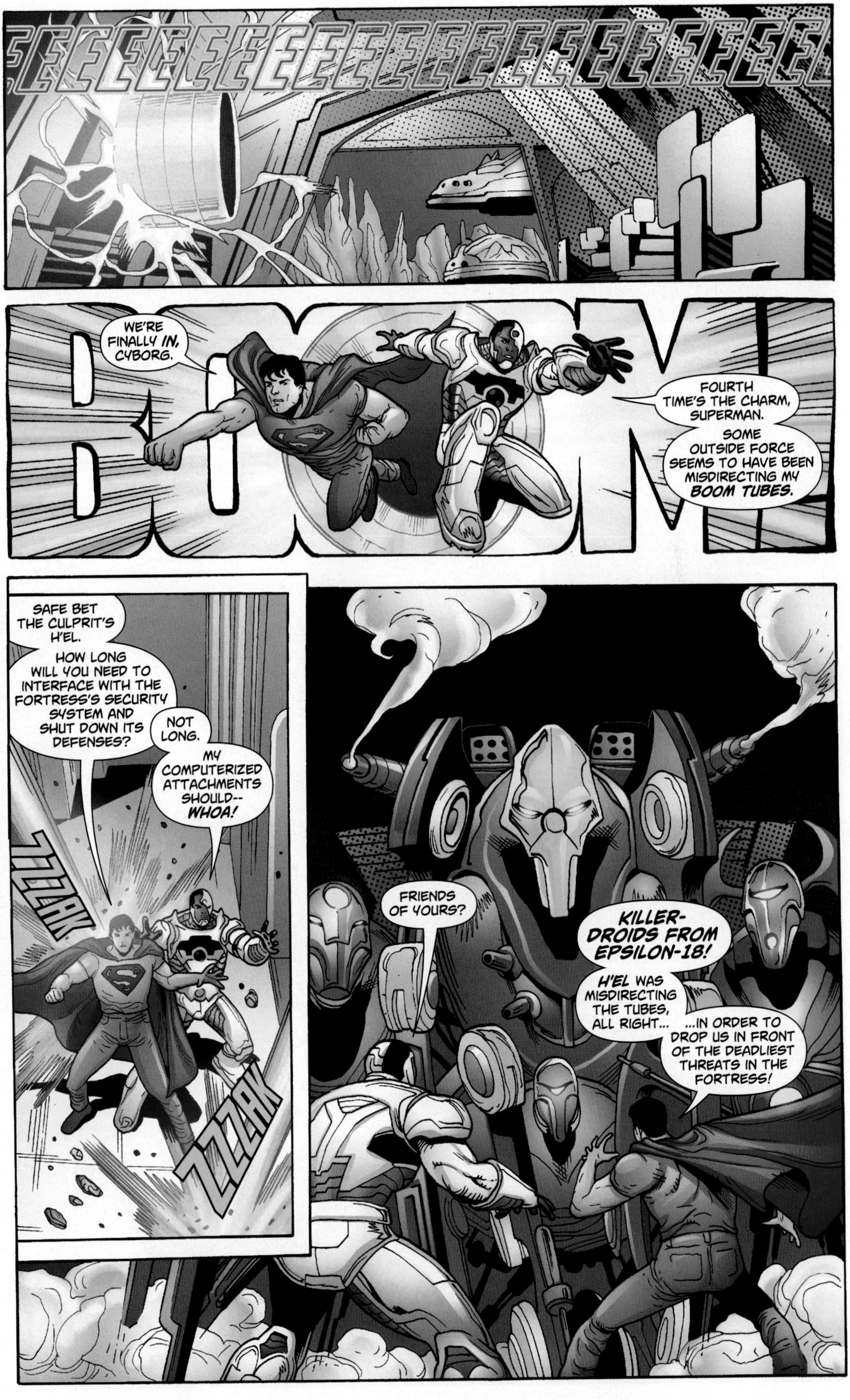
EEEEEEEEEEEEEEEEEEEEEEEEEL
BOOM!
WE'RE FINALLY IN, CYBORG.
FOURTH TIME'S THE CHARM, SUPERMAN.
SOME OUTSIDE FORCE SEEMS TO HAVE BEEN MISDIRECTING MY BOOM TUBES.
SAFE BET THE CULPRIT'S H'EL.
HOW LONG WILL YOU NEED TO INTERFACE WITH THE FORTRESS'S SECURITY SYSTEM AND SHUT DOWN ITS DEFENSES?
NOT LONG.
MY COMPUTERIZED ATTACHMENTS SHOULD-- WHOA!
ZZZAK
ZZZAK
FRIENDS OF YOURS?
KILLER-DROIDS FROM EPSILON-18!
H'EL WAS MISDIRECTING THE TUBES, ALL RIGHT...
...IN ORDER TO DROP US IN FRONT OF THE DEADLIEST THREATS IN THE FORTRESS!

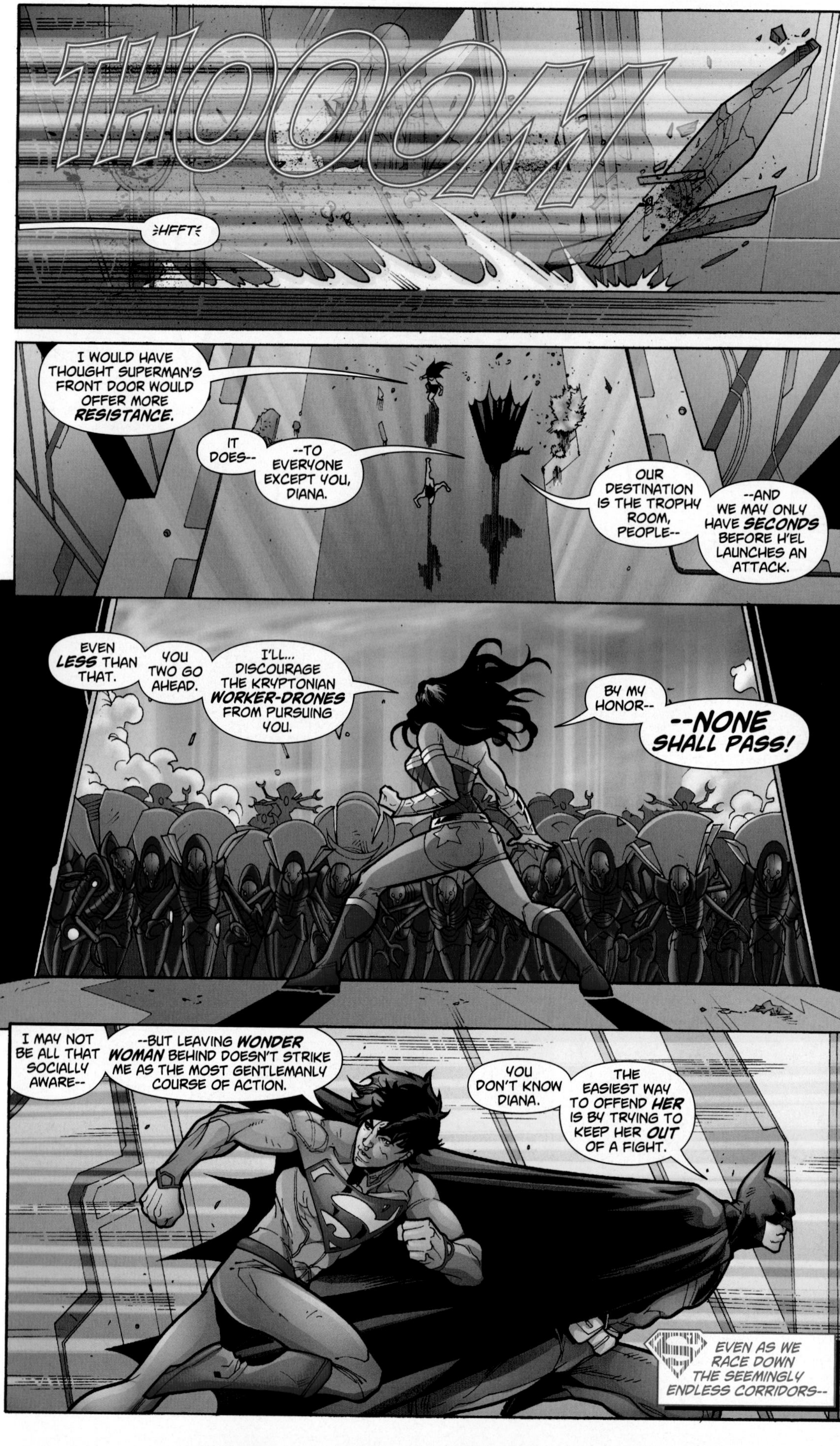
THOOOM
HFFT
I WOULD HAVE THOUGHT SUPERMAN'S FRONT DOOR WOULD OFFER MORE RESISTANCE.
IT DOES--
--TO EVERYONE EXCEPT YOU, DIANA.
OUR DESTINATION IS THE TROPHY ROOM, PEOPLE--
--AND WE MAY ONLY HAVE SECONDS BEFORE H'EL LAUNCHES AN ATTACK.
EVEN LESS THAN THAT.
YOU TWO GO AHEAD.
I'LL... DISCOURAGE THE KRYPTONIAN WORKER-DRONES FROM PURSUING YOU.
BY MY HONOR--
--NONE SHALL PASS!
I MAY NOT BE ALL THAT SOCIALLY AWARE--
--BUT LEAVING WONDER WOMAN BEHIND DOESN'T STRIKE ME AS THE MOST GENTLEMANLY COURSE OF ACTION.
YOU DON'T KNOW DIANA.
THE EASIEST WAY TO OFFEND HER IS BY TRYING TO KEEP HER OUT OF A FIGHT.
EVEN AS WE RACE DOWN THE SEEMINGLY ENDLESS CORRIDORS--

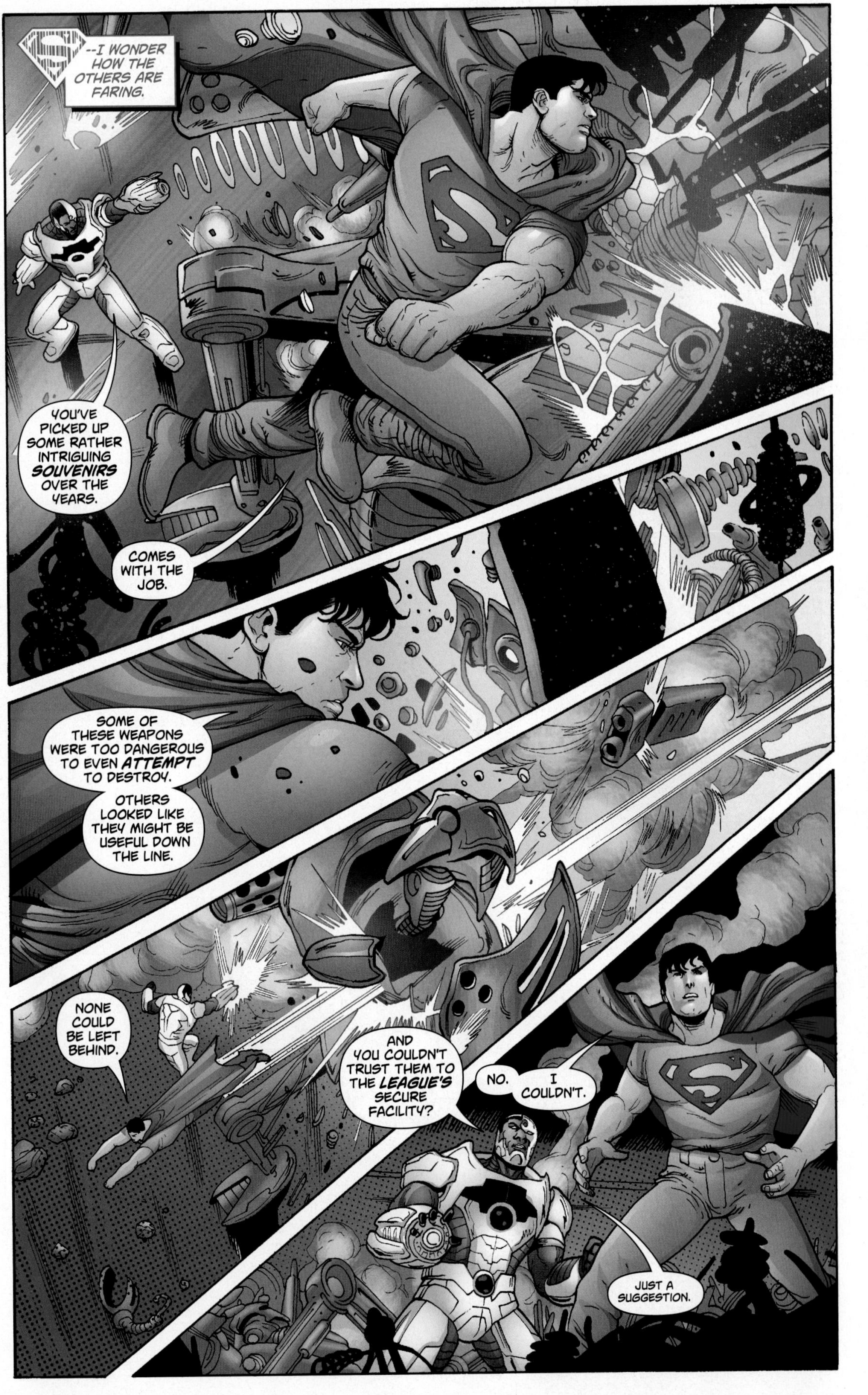
--I WONDER HOW THE OTHERS ARE FARING.
YOU'VE PICKED UP SOME RATHER INTRIGUING SOUVENIRS OVER THE YEARS.
COMES WITH THE JOB.
SOME OF THESE WEAPONS WERE TOO DANGEROUS TO EVEN ATTEMPT TO DESTROY.
OTHERS LOOKED LIKE THEY MIGHT BE USEFUL DOWN THE LINE.
NONE COULD BE LEFT BEHIND.
AND YOU COULDN'T TRUST THEM TO THE LEAGUE'S SECURE FACILITY?
NO.
I COULDN'T.
JUST A SUGGESTION.

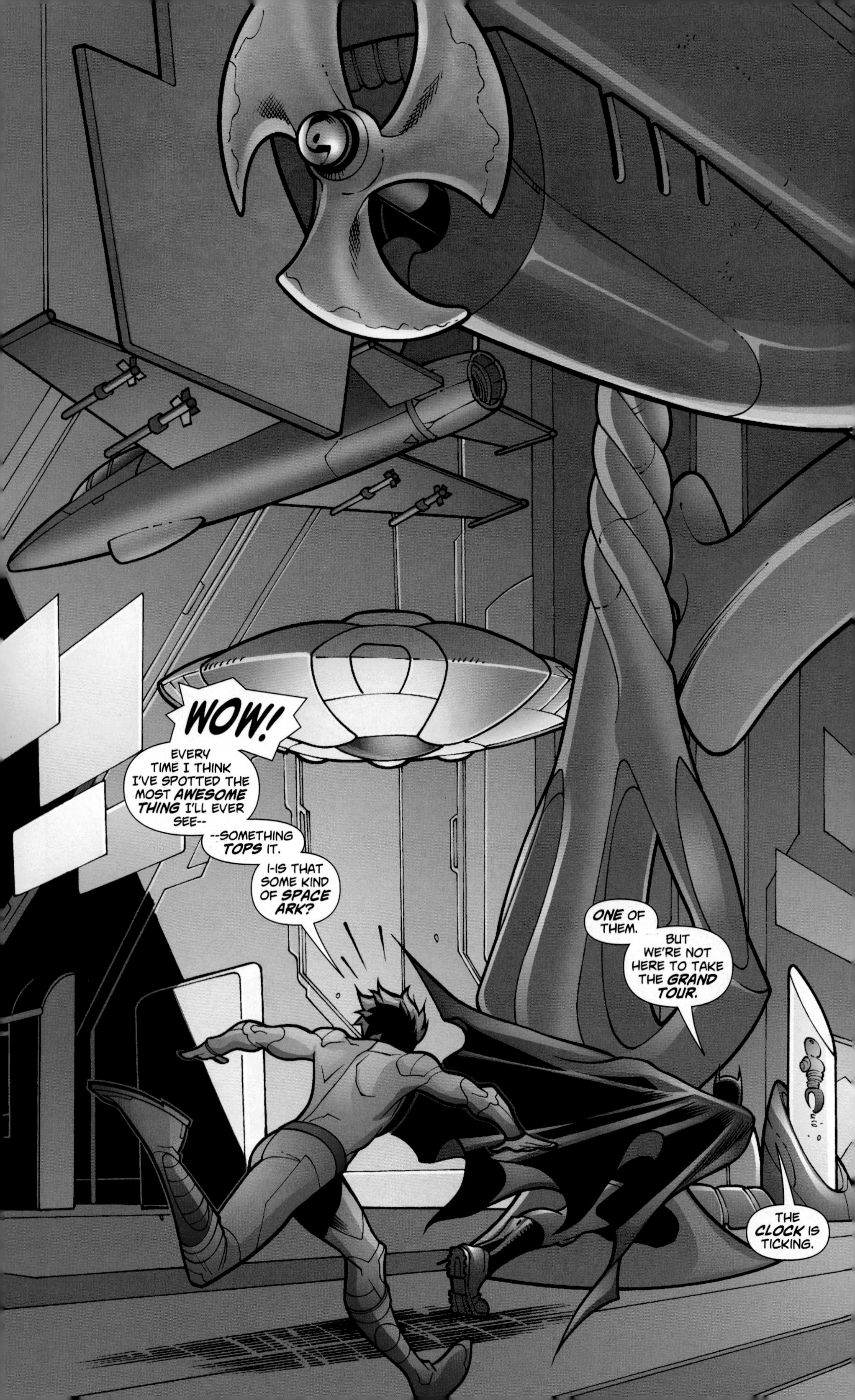
WOW!
EVERY TIME I THINK I'VE SPOTTED THE MOST AWESOME THING I'LL EVER SEE--
--SOMETHING TOPS IT.
I-IS THAT SOME KIND OF SPACE ARK?
ONE OF THEM.
BUT WE'RE NOT HERE TO TAKE THE GRAND TOUR.
THE CLOCK IS TICKING.

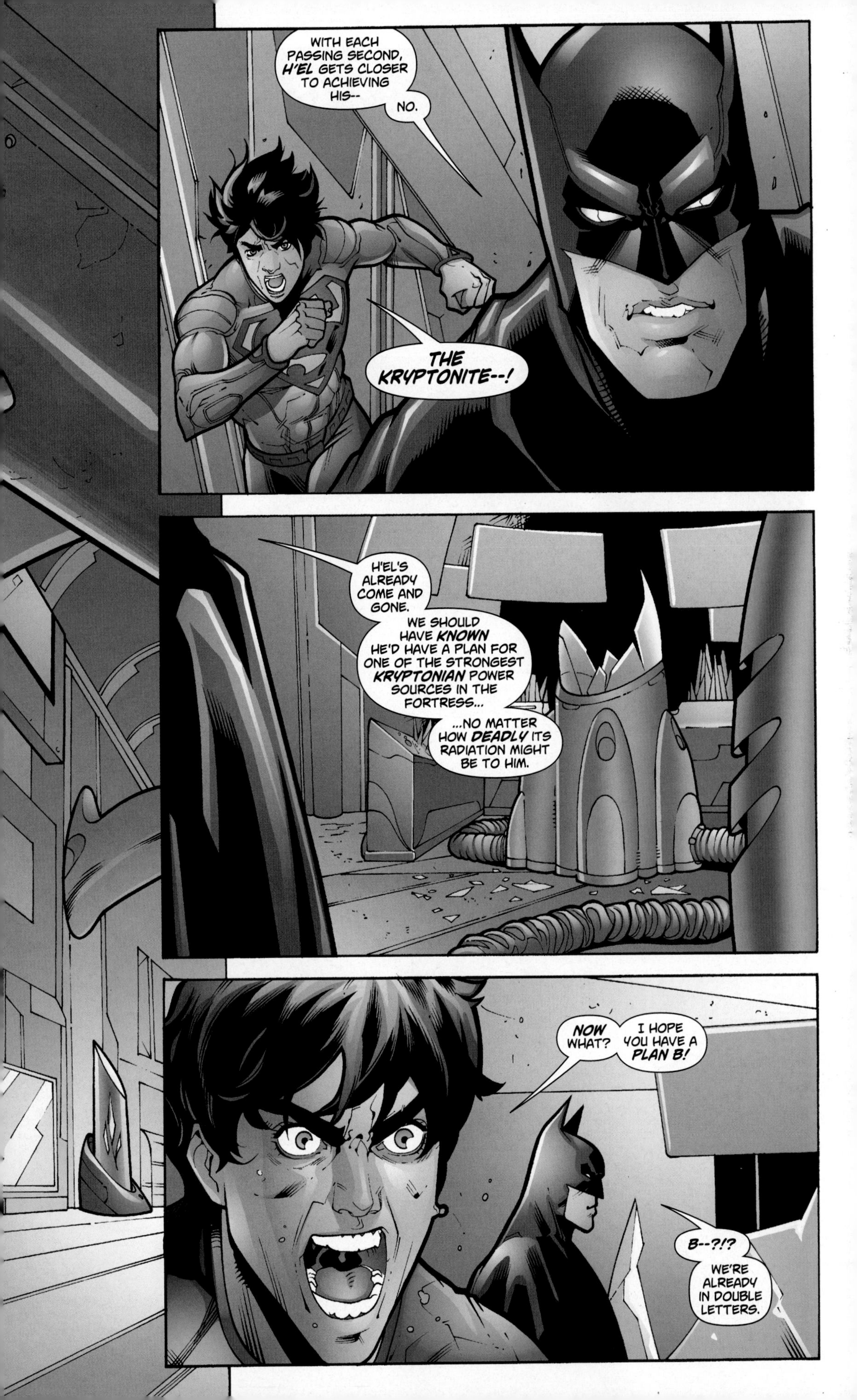
WITH EACH PASSING SECOND, H'EL GETS CLOSER TO ACHIEVING HIS--
NO.
THE KRYPTONITE--!
H'EL'S ALREADY COME AND GONE.
WE SHOULD HAVE KNOWN HE'D HAVE A PLAN FOR ONE OF THE STRONGEST KRYPTONIAN POWER SOURCES IN THE FORTRESS...
...NO MATTER HOW DEADLY ITS RADIATION MIGHT BE TO HIM.
NOW WHAT?
I HOPE YOU HAVE A PLAN B!
B--?!?
WE'RE ALREADY IN DOUBLE LETTERS.

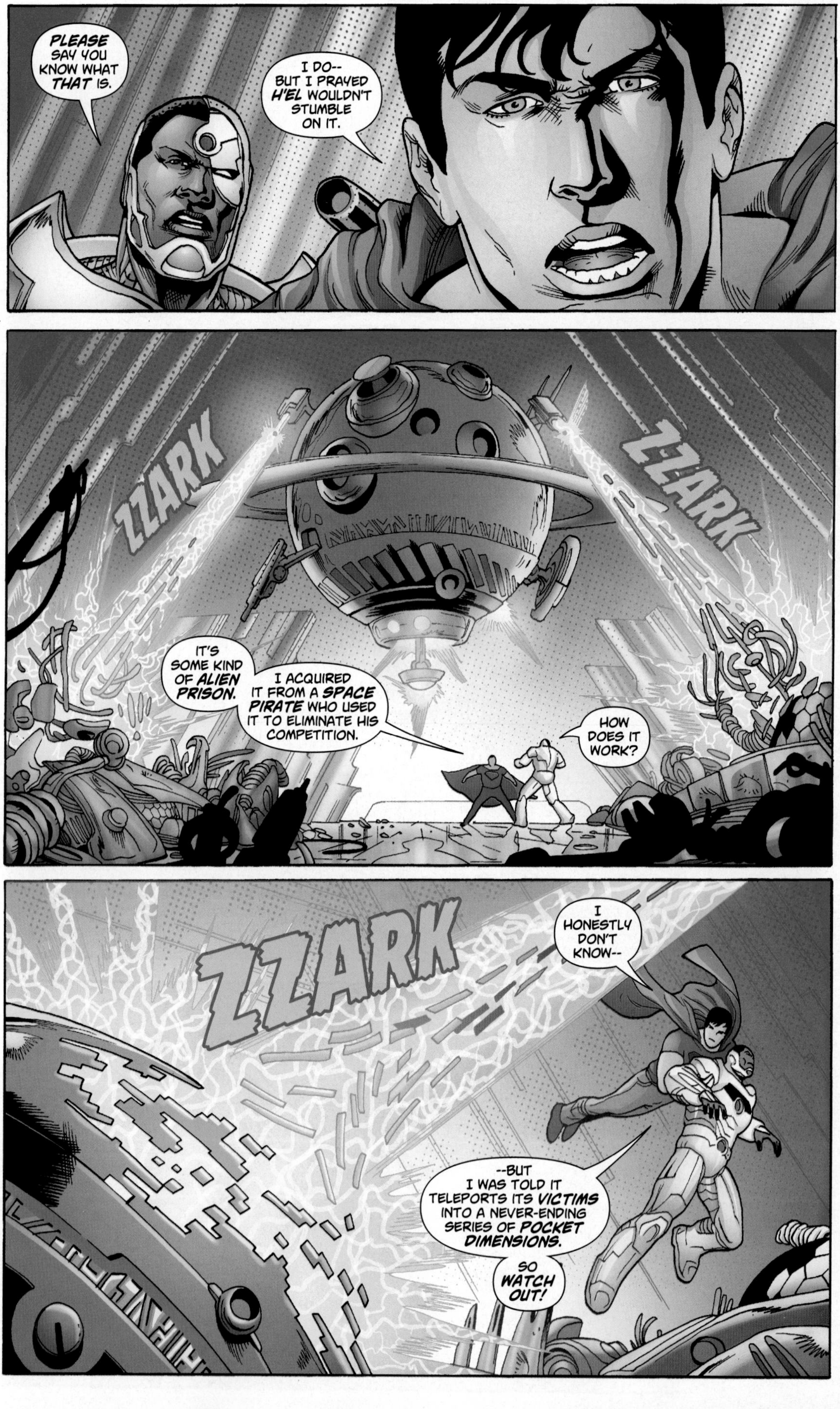
PLEASE SAY YOU KNOW WHAT THAT IS.
I DO-- BUT I PRAYED H'EL WOULDN'T STUMBLE ON IT.
ZZARK
ZZARK
IT'S SOME KIND OF ALIEN PRISON.
I ACQUIRED IT FROM A SPACE PIRATE WHO USED IT TO ELIMINATE HIS COMPETITION.
HOW DOES IT WORK?
ZZARK
I HONESTLY DON'T KNOW--
--BUT I WAS TOLD IT TELEPORTS ITS VICTIMS INTO A NEVER-ENDING SERIES OF POCKET DIMENSIONS.
SO WATCH OUT!

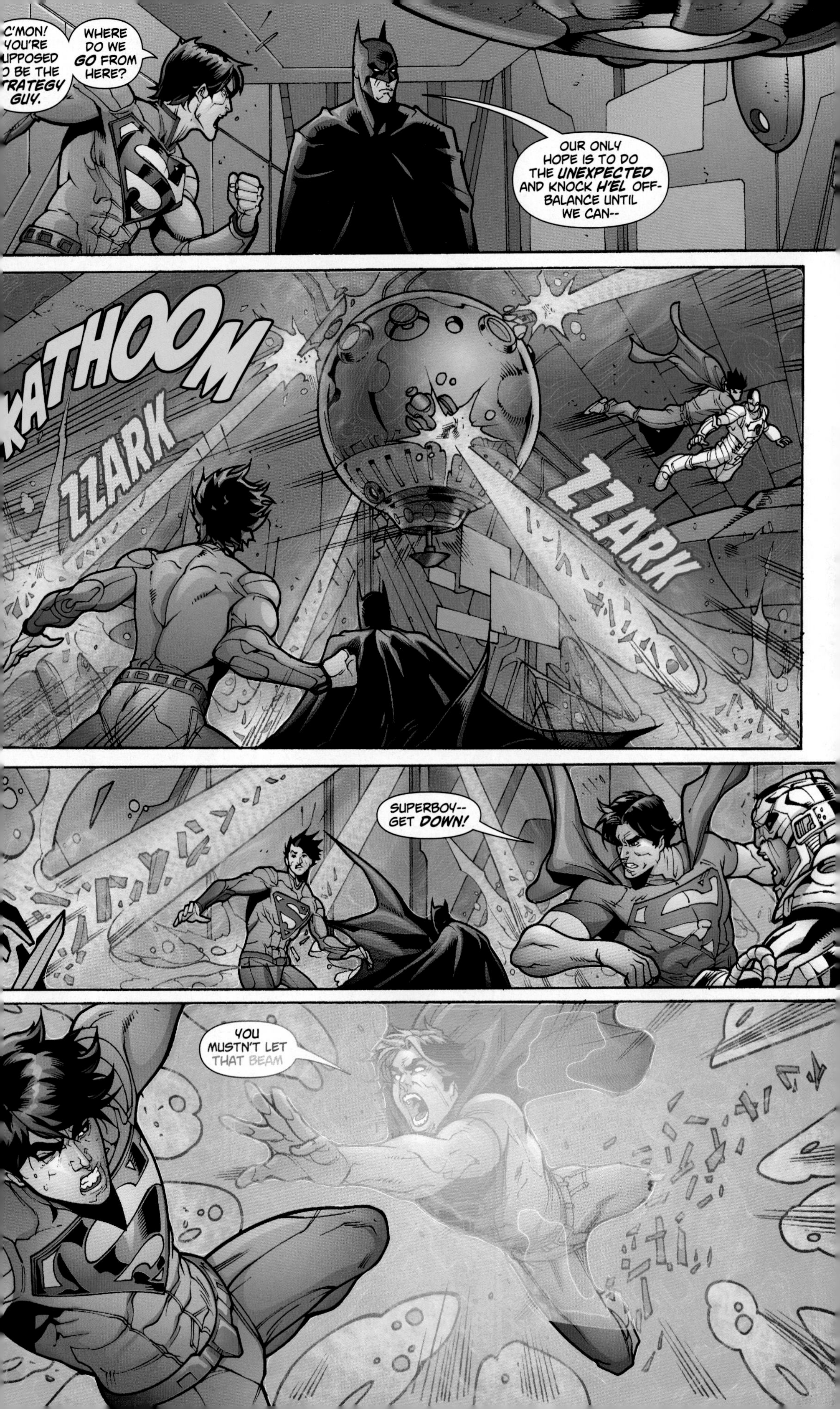

C'MON! YOU'RE SUPPOSED TO BE THE STRATEGY GUY.
WHERE DO WE GO FROM HERE?
OUR ONLY HOPE IS TO DO THE UNEXPECTED AND KNOCK H'EL OFF-BALANCE UNTIL WE CAN--
KATHOOM
ZZARK
ZZARK
SUPERBOY-- GET DOWN!
YOU MUSTN'T LET THAT BEAM

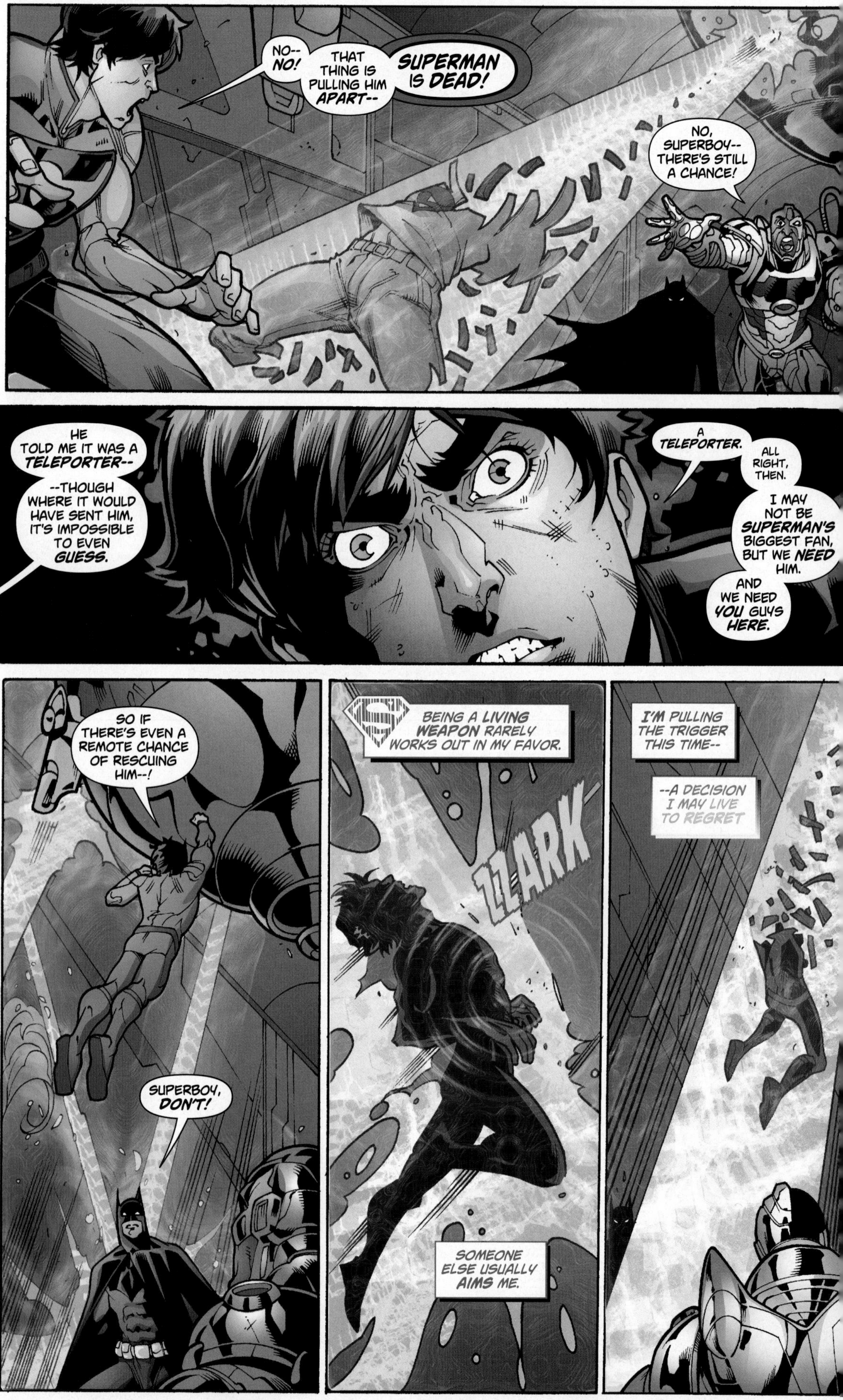
NO-- NO!
THAT THING IS PULLING HIM APART--
SUPERMAN IS DEAD!
NO, SUPERBOY-- THERE'S STILL A CHANCE!
HE TOLD ME IT WAS A TELEPORTER--
--THOUGH WHERE IT WOULD HAVE SENT HIM, IT'S IMPOSSIBLE TO EVEN GUESS.
A TELEPORTER.
ALL RIGHT, THEN.
I MAY NOT BE SUPERMAN'S BIGGEST FAN, BUT WE NEED HIM.
AND WE NEED YOU GUYS HERE.
SO IF THERE'S EVEN A REMOTE CHANCE OF RESCUING HIM--!
SUPERBOY, DON'T!
BEING A LIVING WEAPON RARELY WORKS OUT IN MY FAVOR.
ZZARK
SOMEONE ELSE USUALLY AIMS ME.
I'M PULLING THE TRIGGER THIS TIME--
--A DECISION I MAY LIVE TO REGRET

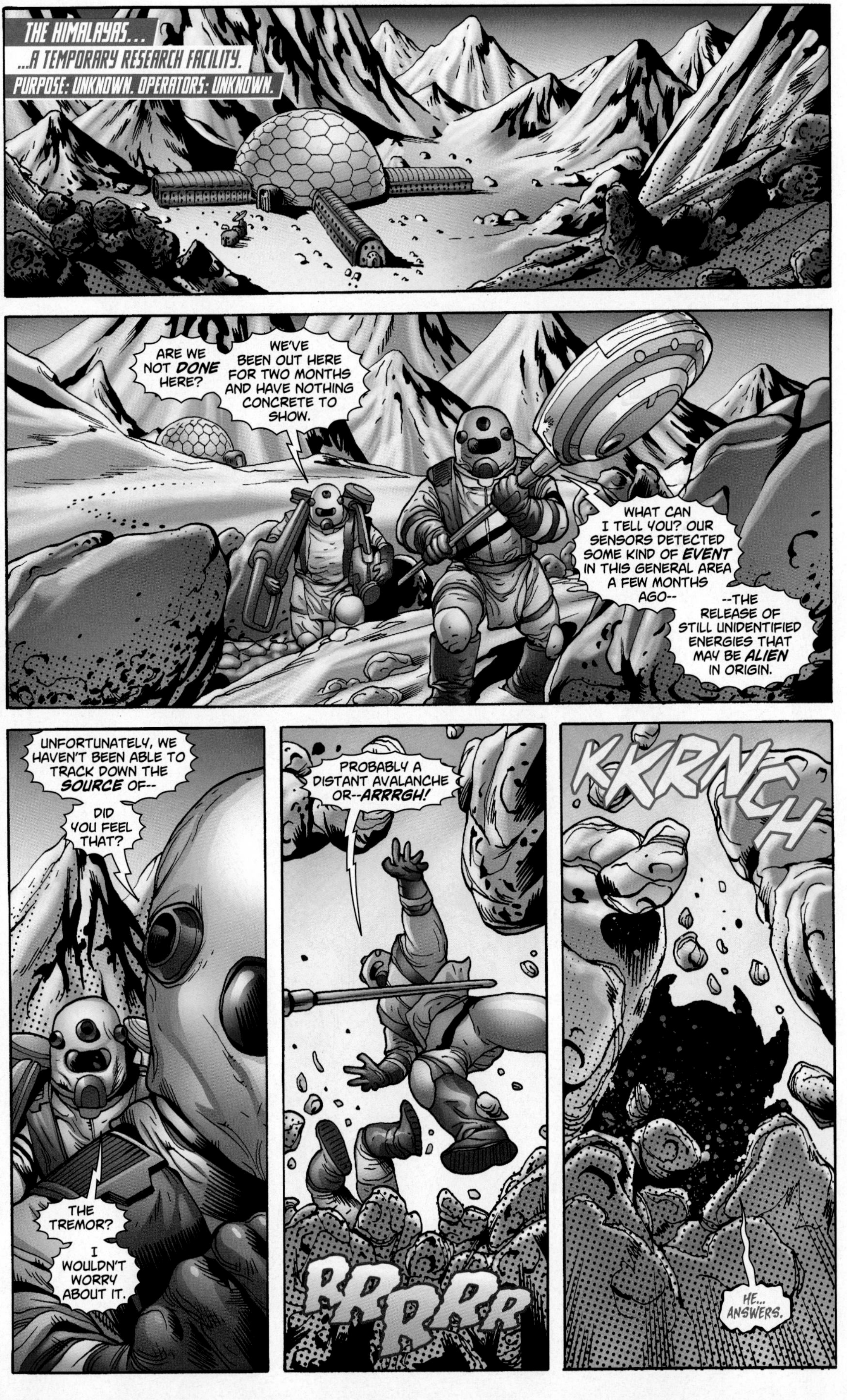
THE HIMALAYAS...
...A TEMPORARY RESEARCH FACILITY.
PURPOSE: UNKNOWN. OPERATORS: UNKNOWN.
ARE WE NOT DONE HERE?
WE'VE BEEN OUT HERE FOR TWO MONTHS AND HAVE NOTHING CONCRETE TO SHOW.
WHAT CAN I TELL YOU? OUR SENSORS DETECTED SOME KIND OF EVENT IN THIS GENERAL AREA A FEW MONTHS AGO--
--THE RELEASE OF STILL UNIDENTIFIED ENERGIES THAT MAY BE ALIEN IN ORIGIN.
UNFORTUNATELY, WE HAVEN'T BEEN ABLE TO TRACK DOWN THE SOURCE OF--
DID YOU FEEL THAT?
THE TREMOR?
I WOULDN'T WORRY ABOUT IT.
PROBABLY A DISTANT AVALANCHE OR--ARRRGH!
RRRRR
KKRNCH
HE... ANSWERS.

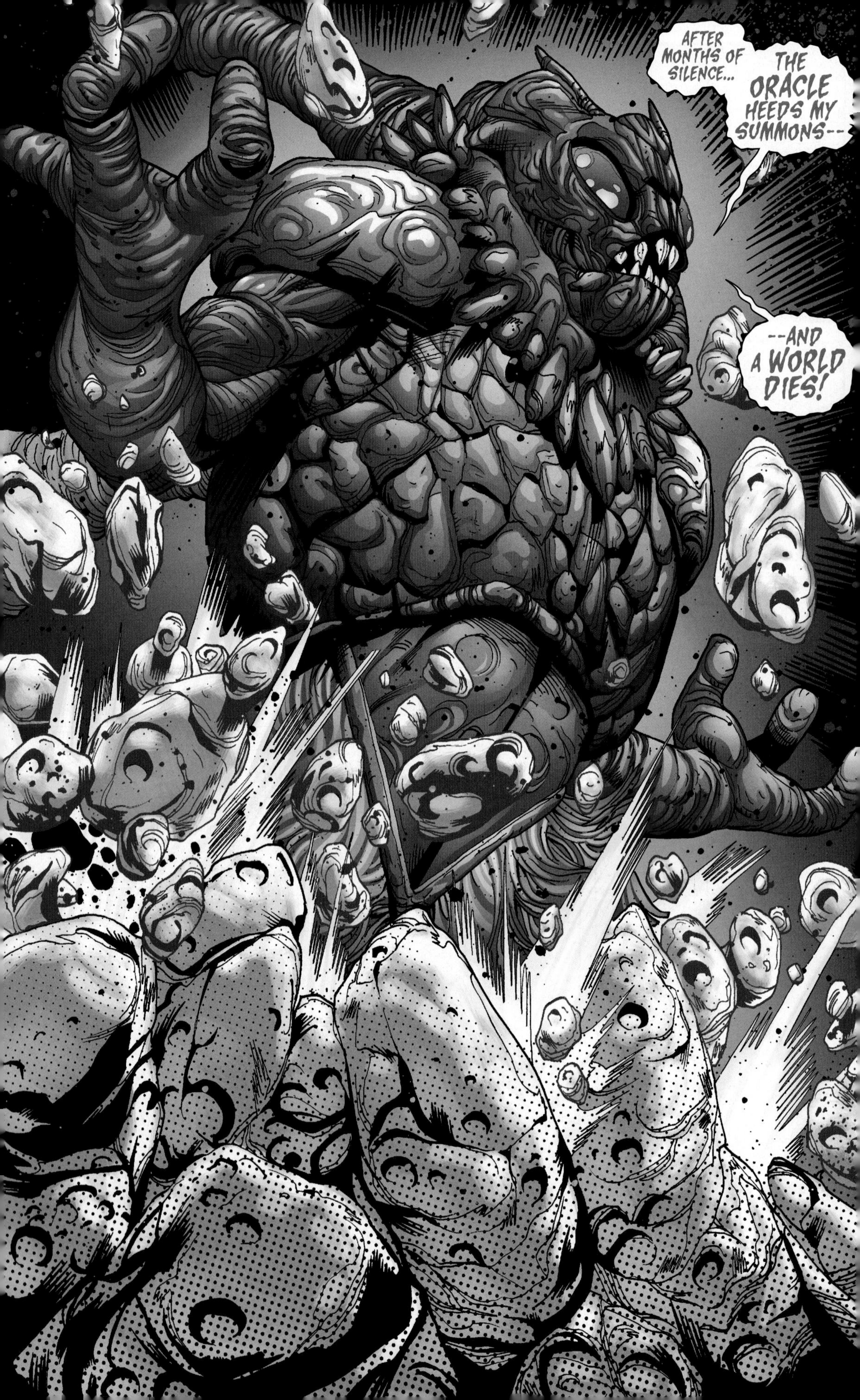
AFTER MONTHS OF SILENCE... THE ORACLE HEEDS MY SUMMONS--
--AND A WORLD DIES!

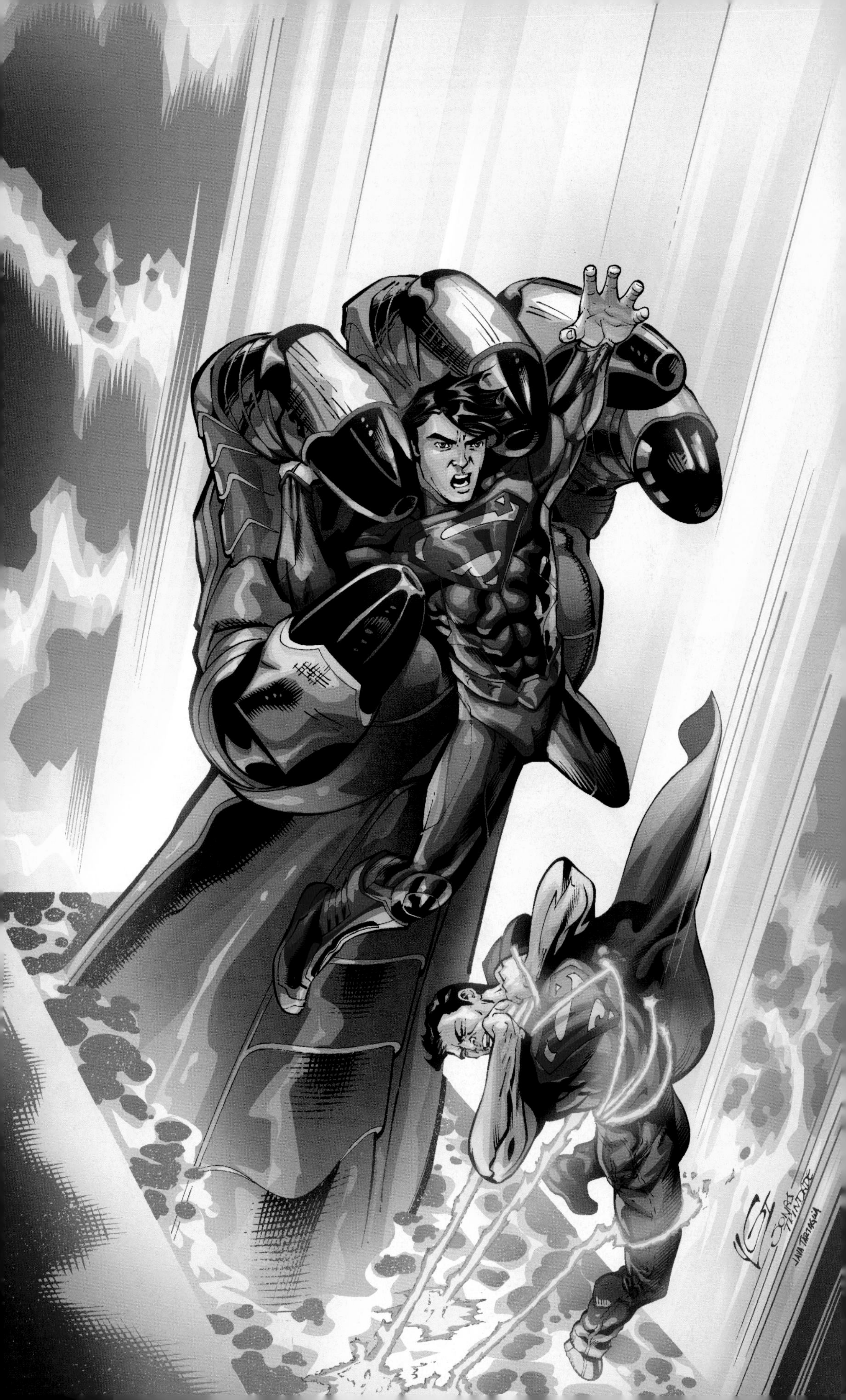
JONAS TRINDADE
JAVA TARTAGLIA

LOST HORIZONS!

TOM DeFALCO writer **TOM DERENICK** artist **YVEL GUICHET & IBAN COELLO** pencillers **JONAS TRINDADE & ROB LEAN** inkers
cover art by **YVEL GUICHET, JONAS TRINDADE & JAVA TARTAGLIA**

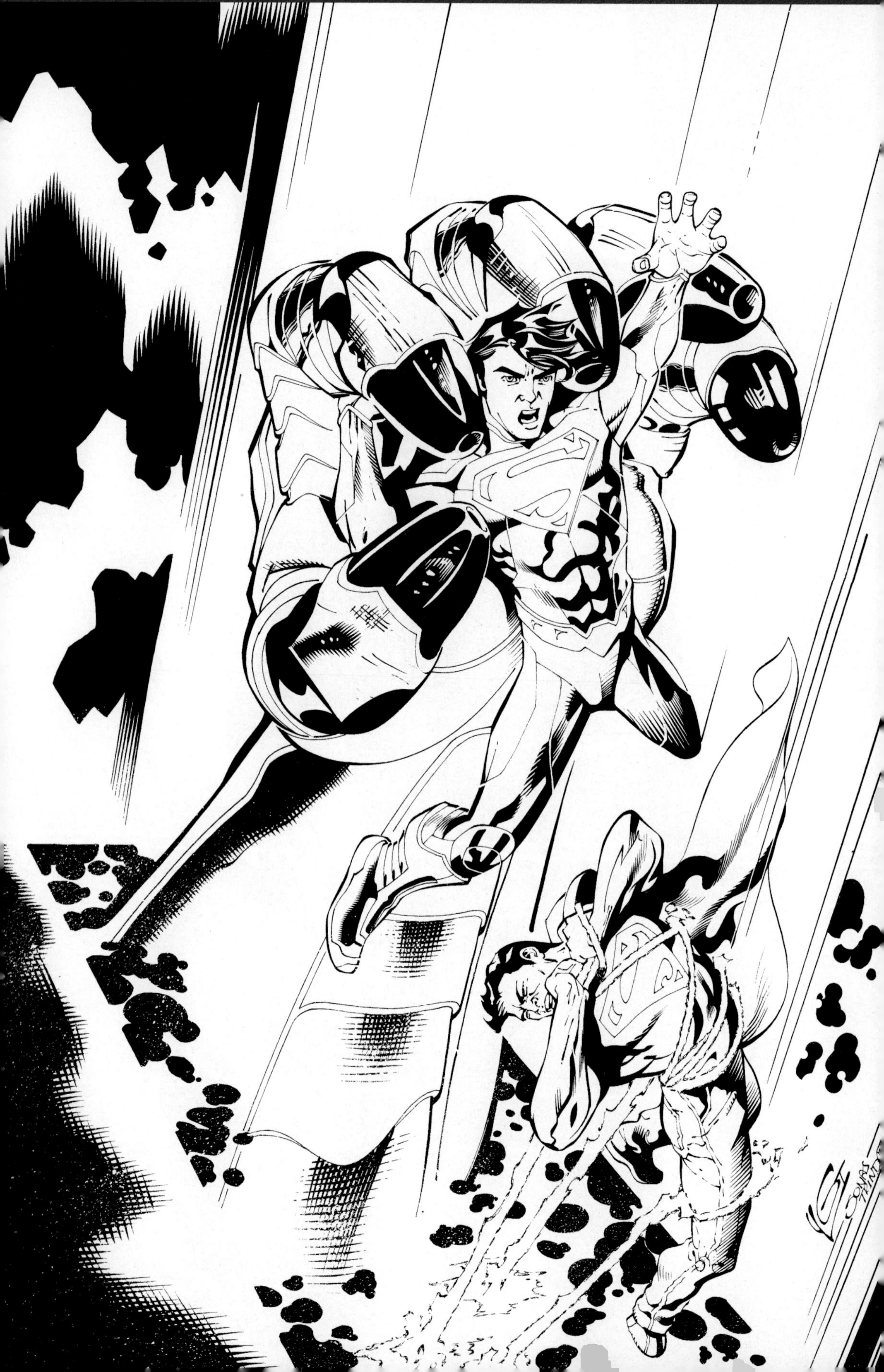

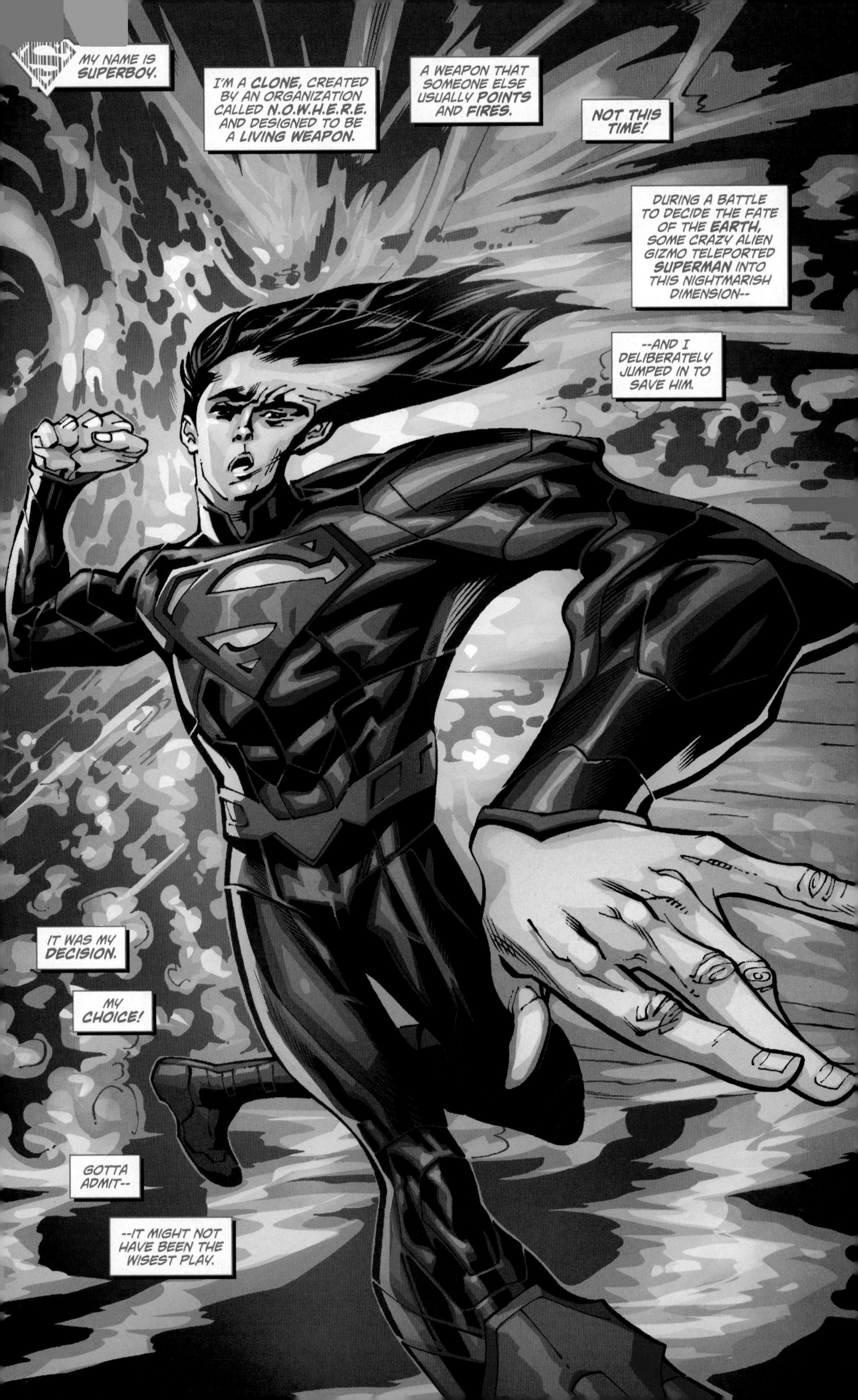
MY NAME IS SUPERBOY.
I'M A CLONE, CREATED BY AN ORGANIZATION CALLED N.O.W.H.E.R.E. AND DESIGNED TO BE A LIVING WEAPON.
A WEAPON THAT SOMEONE ELSE USUALLY POINTS AND FIRES.
NOT THIS TIME!
DURING A BATTLE TO DECIDE THE FATE OF THE EARTH, SOME CRAZY ALIEN GIZMO TELEPORTED SUPERMAN INTO THIS NIGHTMARISH DIMENSION--
--AND I DELIBERATELY JUMPED IN TO SAVE HIM.
IT WAS MY DECISION.
MY CHOICE!
GOTTA ADMIT--
--IT MIGHT NOT HAVE BEEN THE WISEST PLAY.

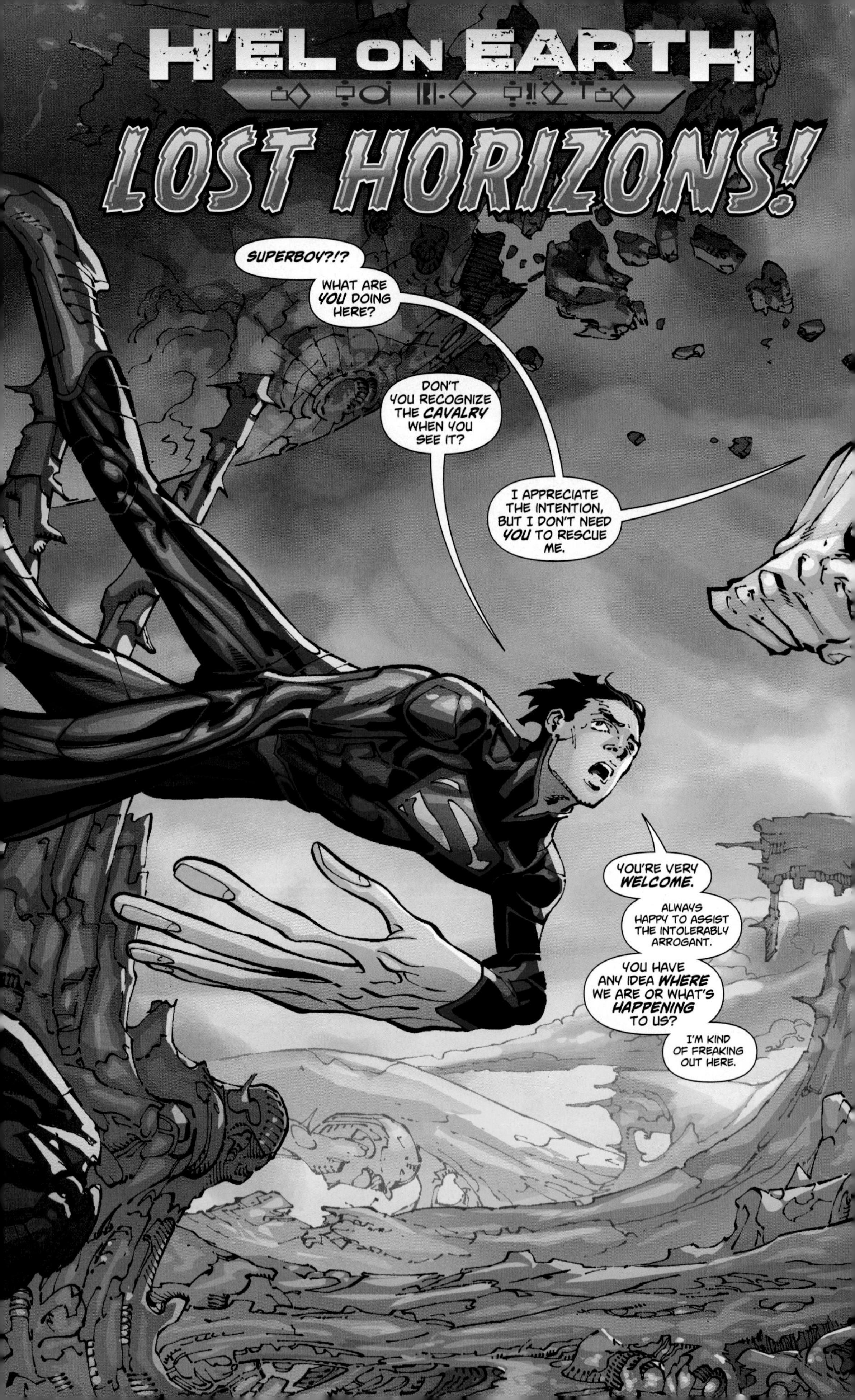
H'EL ON EARTH
LOST HORIZONS!
SUPERBOY?!?
WHAT ARE YOU DOING HERE?
DON'T YOU RECOGNIZE THE CAVALRY WHEN YOU SEE IT?
I APPRECIATE THE INTENTION, BUT I DON'T NEED YOU TO RESCUE ME.
YOU'RE VERY WELCOME.
ALWAYS HAPPY TO ASSIST THE INTOLERABLY ARROGANT.
YOU HAVE ANY IDEA WHERE WE ARE OR WHAT'S HAPPENING TO US?
I'M KIND OF FREAKING OUT HERE.

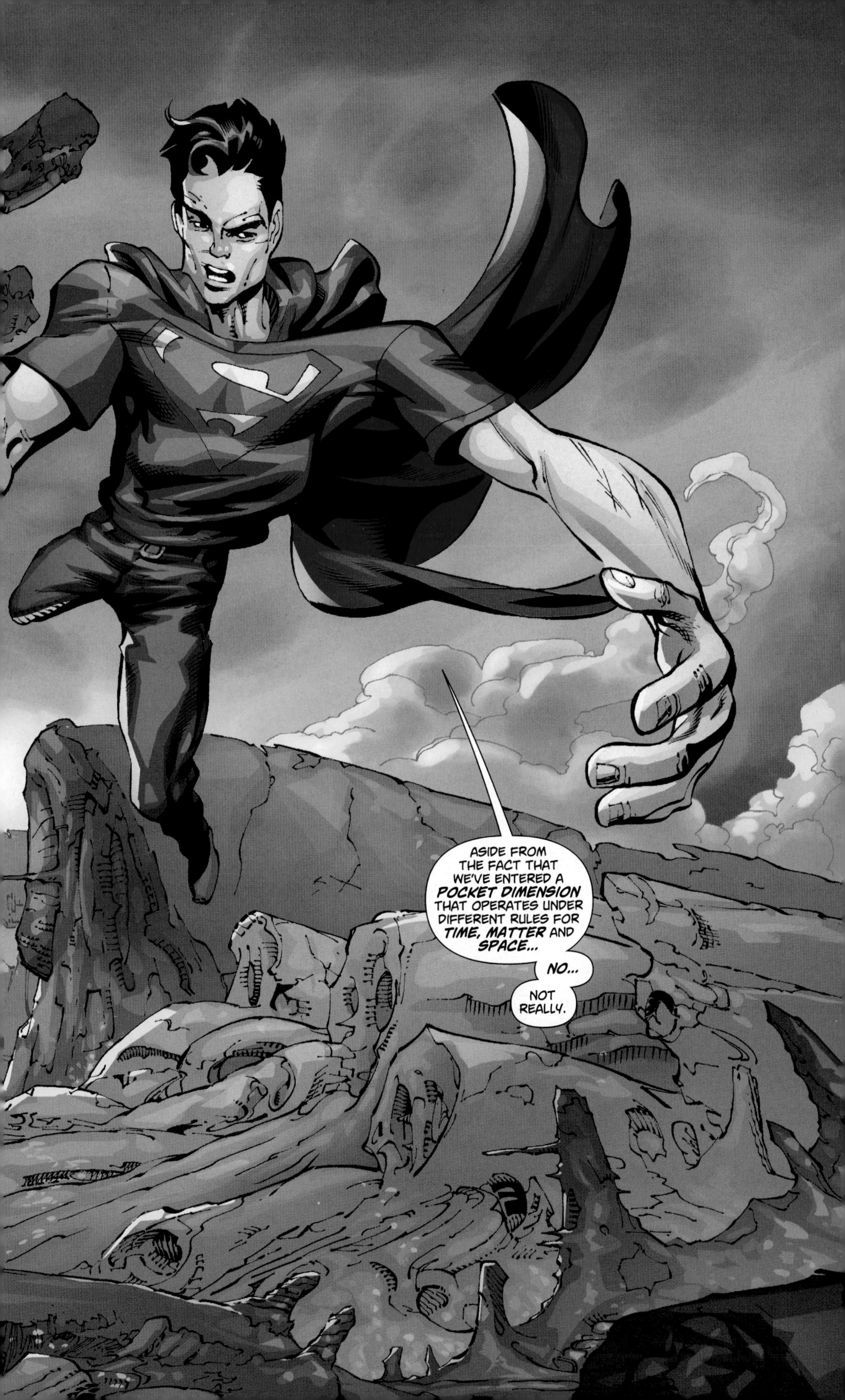
ASIDE FROM THE FACT THAT WE'VE ENTERED A POCKET DIMENSION THAT OPERATES UNDER DIFFERENT RULES FOR TIME, MATTER AND SPACE...
NO...
NOT REALLY.

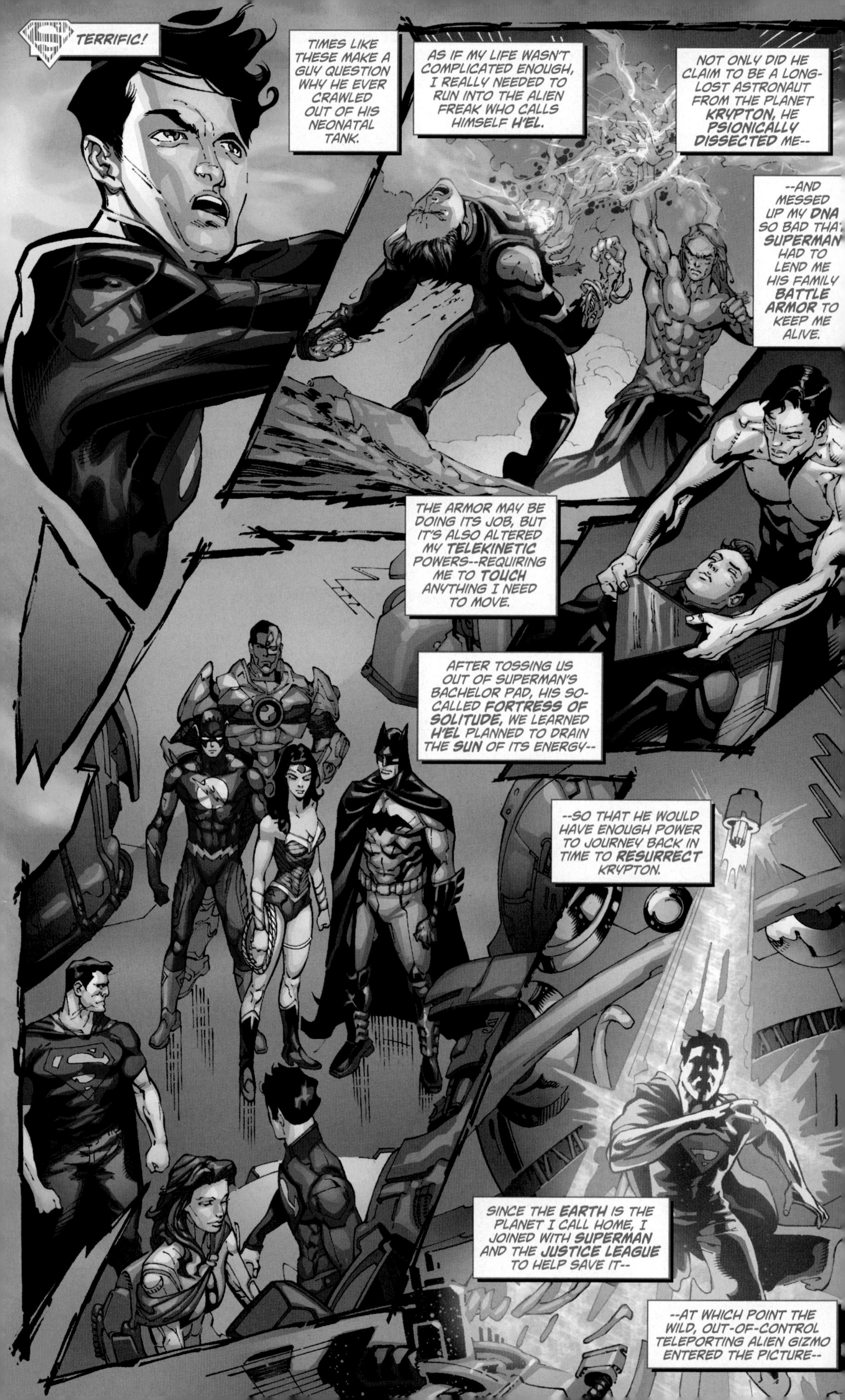
TERRIFIC!
TIMES LIKE THESE MAKE A GUY QUESTION WHY HE EVER CRAWLED OUT OF HIS NEONATAL TANK.
AS IF MY LIFE WASN'T COMPLICATED ENOUGH, I REALLY NEEDED TO RUN INTO THE ALIEN FREAK WHO CALLS HIMSELF H'EL.
NOT ONLY DID HE CLAIM TO BE A LONG-LOST ASTRONAUT FROM THE PLANET KRYPTON, HE PSIONICALLY DISSECTED ME--
--AND MESSED UP MY DNA SO BAD THAT SUPERMAN HAD TO LEND ME HIS FAMILY BATTLE ARMOR TO KEEP ME ALIVE.
THE ARMOR MAY BE DOING ITS JOB, BUT IT'S ALSO ALTERED MY TELEKINETIC POWERS--REQUIRING ME TO TOUCH ANYTHING I NEED TO MOVE.
AFTER TOSSING US OUT OF SUPERMAN'S BACHELOR PAD, HIS SO-CALLED FORTRESS OF SOLITUDE, WE LEARNED H'EL PLANNED TO DRAIN THE SUN OF ITS ENERGY--
--SO THAT HE WOULD HAVE ENOUGH POWER TO JOURNEY BACK IN TIME TO RESURRECT KRYPTON.
SINCE THE EARTH IS THE PLANET I CALL HOME, I JOINED WITH SUPERMAN AND THE JUSTICE LEAGUE TO HELP SAVE IT--
--AT WHICH POINT THE WILD, OUT-OF-CONTROL TELEPORTING ALIEN GIZMO ENTERED THE PICTURE--

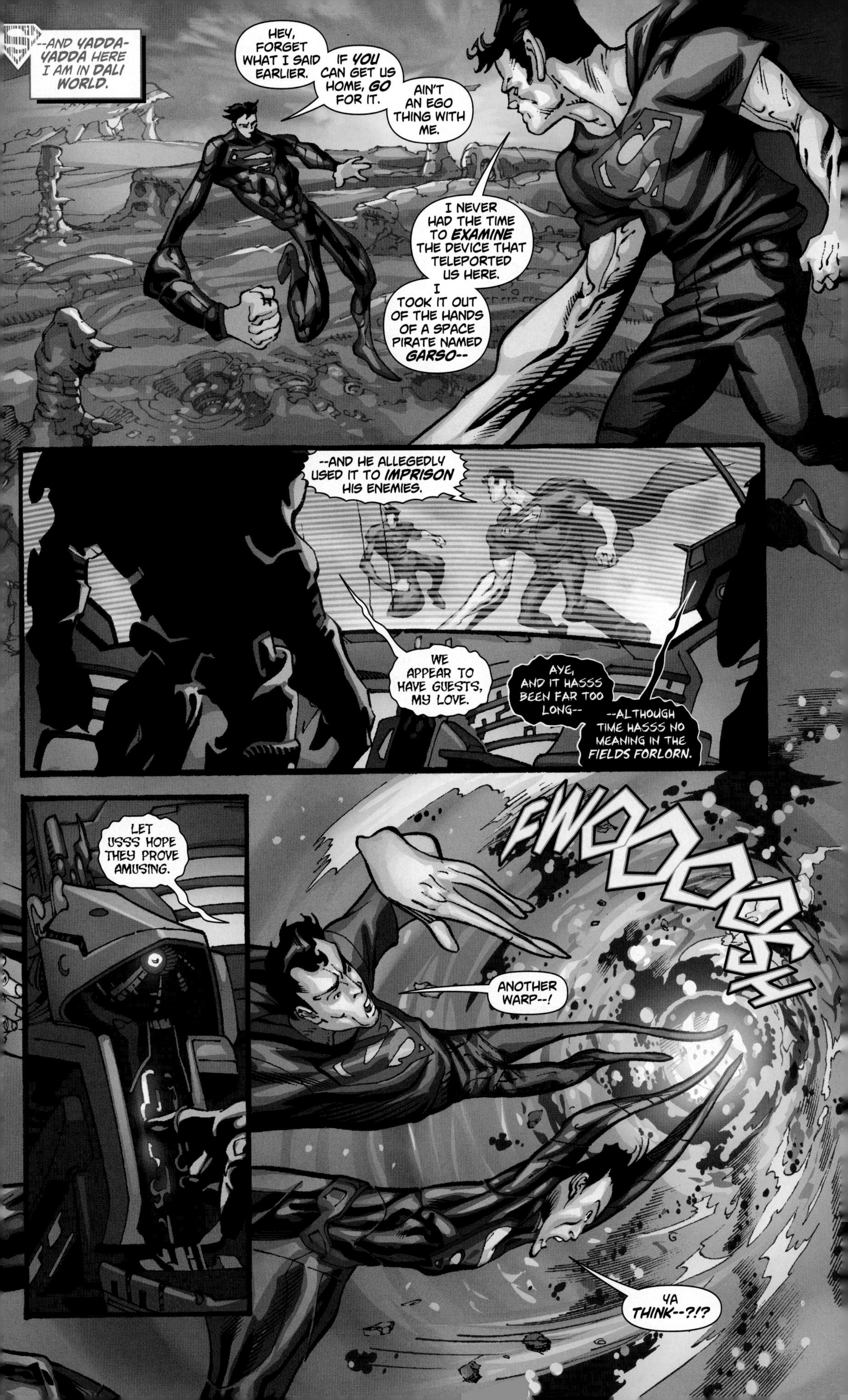
--AND YADDA-YADDA HERE I AM IN DALI WORLD.
HEY, FORGET WHAT I SAID EARLIER.
IF YOU CAN GET US HOME, GO FOR IT.
AIN'T AN EGO THING WITH ME.
I NEVER HAD THE TIME TO EXAMINE THE DEVICE THAT TELEPORTED US HERE.
I TOOK IT OUT OF THE HANDS OF A SPACE PIRATE NAMED GARSO--
--AND HE ALLEGEDLY USED IT TO IMPRISON HIS ENEMIES.
WE APPEAR TO HAVE GUESTS, MY LOVE.
AYE, AND IT HASSS BEEN FAR TOO LONG--
--ALTHOUGH TIME HASSS NO MEANING IN THE FIELDS FORLORN.
LET USSS HOPE THEY PROVE AMUSING.
FWOOOOSH
ANOTHER WARP--!
YA THINK--?!?

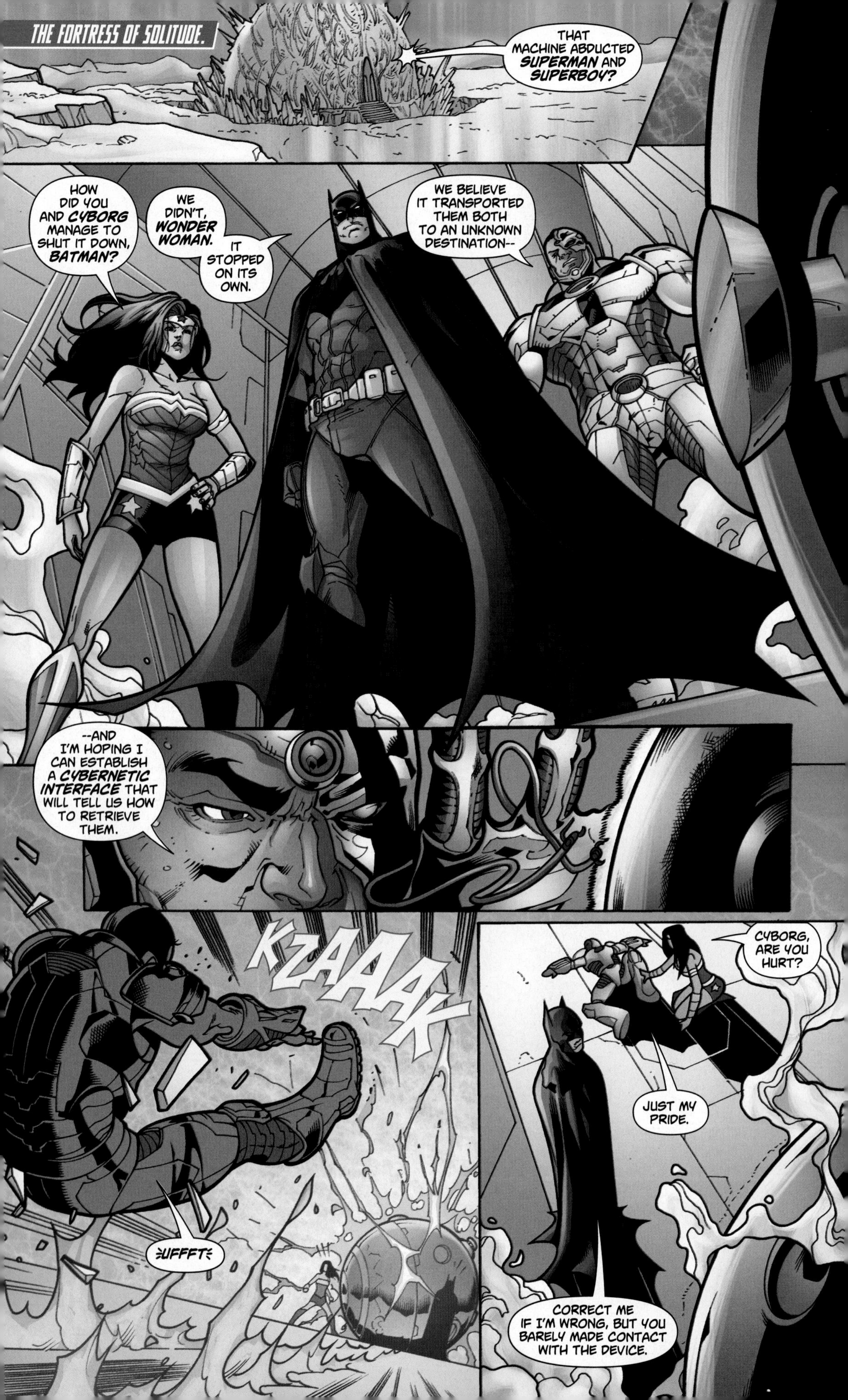
THE FORTRESS OF SOLITUDE.
THAT MACHINE ABDUCTED SUPERMAN AND SUPERBOY?
HOW DID YOU AND CYBORG MANAGE TO SHUT IT DOWN, BATMAN?
WE DIDN'T, WONDER WOMAN.
IT STOPPED ON ITS OWN.
WE BELIEVE IT TRANSPORTED THEM BOTH TO AN UNKNOWN DESTINATION--
--AND I'M HOPING I CAN ESTABLISH A CYBERNETIC INTERFACE THAT WILL TELL US HOW TO RETRIEVE THEM.
KZAAAK
UFFFT
CYBORG, ARE YOU HURT?
JUST MY PRIDE.
CORRECT ME IF I'M WRONG, BUT YOU BARELY MADE CONTACT WITH THE DEVICE.

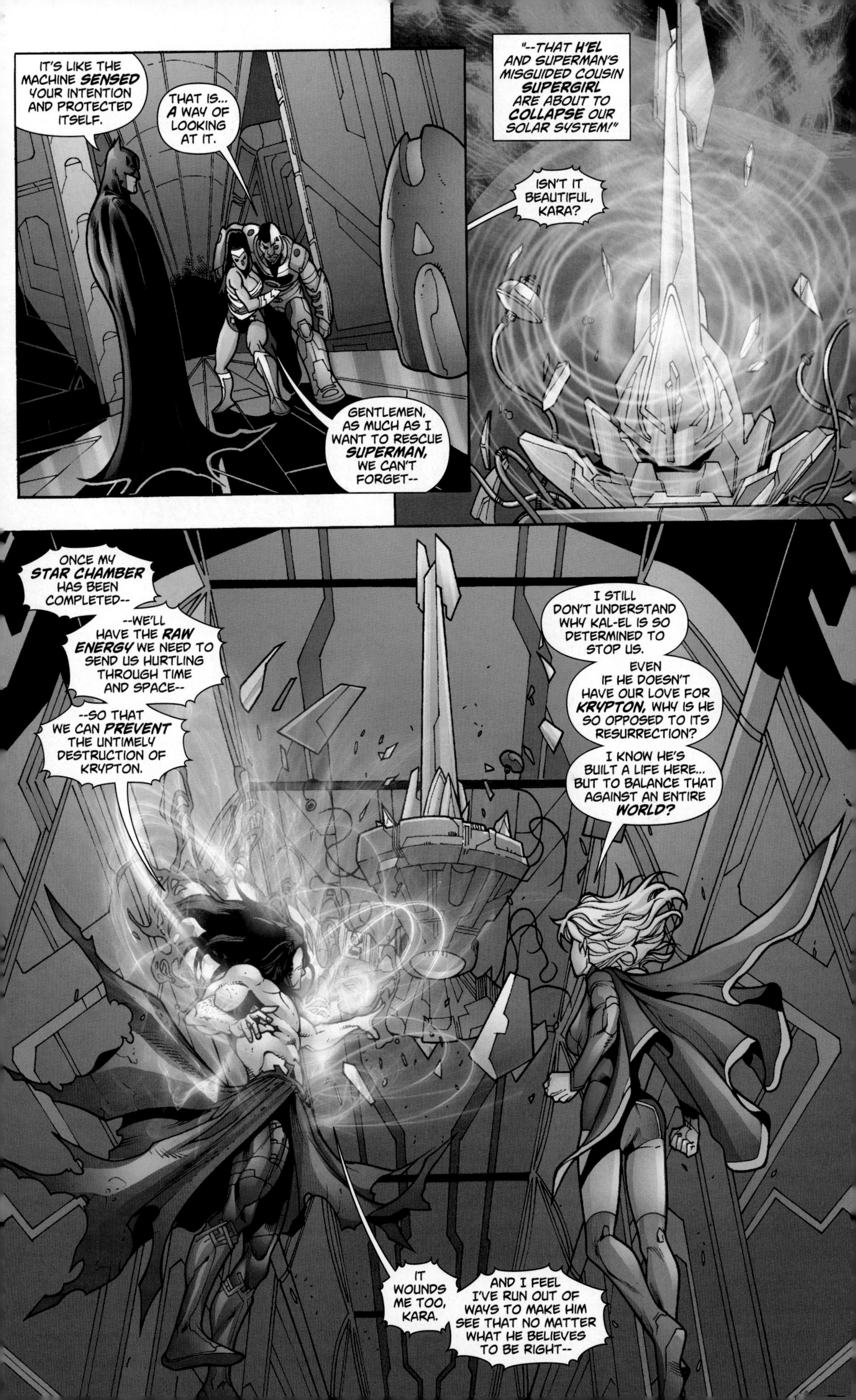
IT'S LIKE THE MACHINE SENSED YOUR INTENTION AND PROTECTED ITSELF.
THAT IS... A WAY OF LOOKING AT IT.
GENTLEMEN, AS MUCH AS I WANT TO RESCUE SUPERMAN, WE CAN'T FORGET--
"--THAT H'EL AND SUPERMAN'S MISGUIDED COUSIN SUPERGIRL ARE ABOUT TO COLLAPSE OUR SOLAR SYSTEM!"
ISN'T IT BEAUTIFUL, KARA?
ONCE MY STAR CHAMBER HAS BEEN COMPLETED--
--WE'LL HAVE THE RAW ENERGY WE NEED TO SEND US HURTLING THROUGH TIME AND SPACE--
--SO THAT WE CAN PREVENT THE UNTIMELY DESTRUCTION OF KRYPTON.
I STILL DON'T UNDERSTAND WHY KAL-EL IS SO DETERMINED TO STOP US.
EVEN IF HE DOESN'T HAVE OUR LOVE FOR KRYPTON, WHY IS HE SO OPPOSED TO ITS RESURRECTION?
I KNOW HE'S BUILT A LIFE HERE... BUT TO BALANCE THAT AGAINST AN ENTIRE WORLD?
IT WOUNDS ME TOO, KARA.
AND I FEEL I'VE RUN OUT OF WAYS TO MAKE HIM SEE THAT NO MATTER WHAT HE BELIEVES TO BE RIGHT--

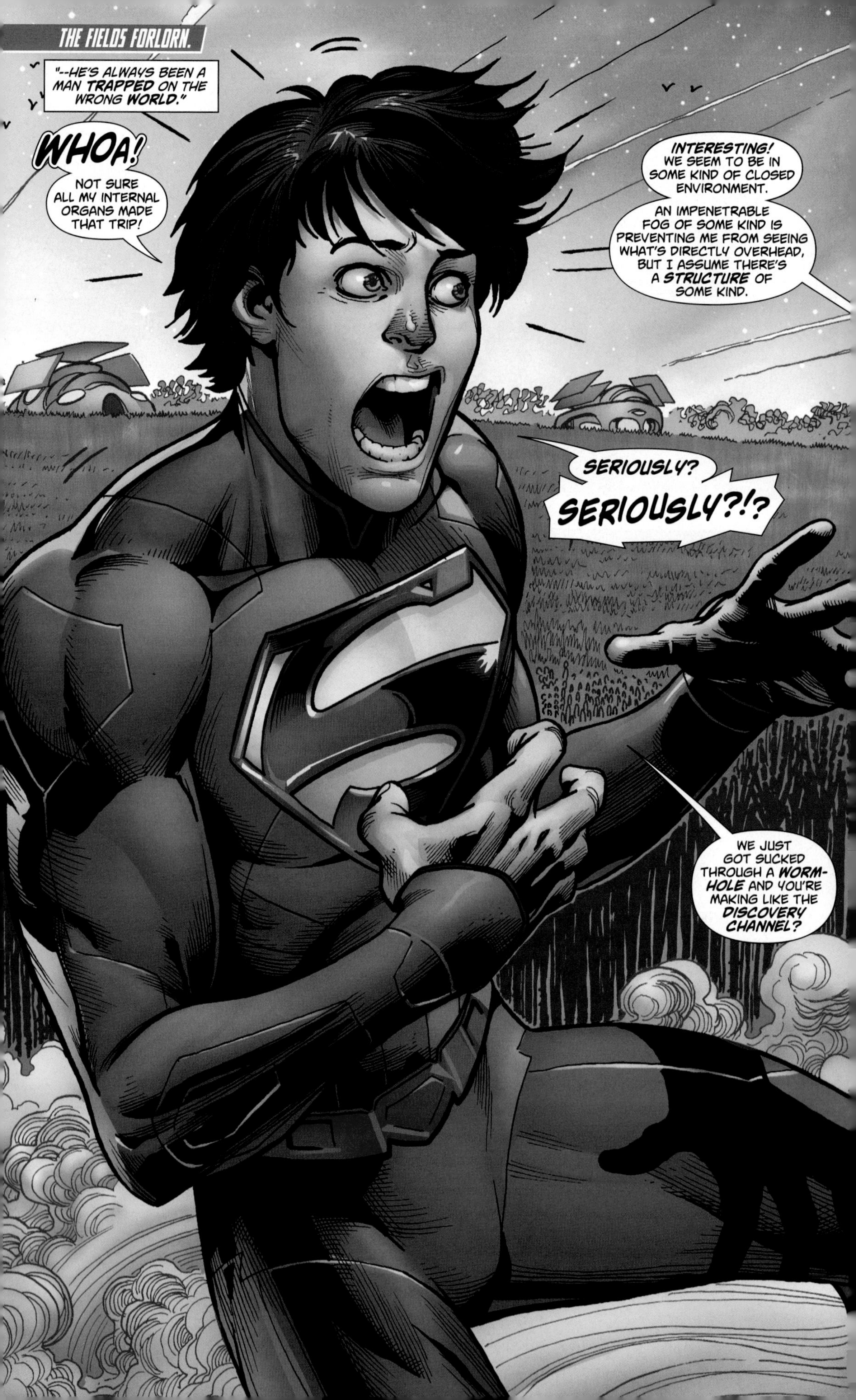
THE FIELDS FORLORN.
"--HE'S ALWAYS BEEN A MAN TRAPPED ON THE WRONG WORLD."
WHOA!
NOT SURE ALL MY INTERNAL ORGANS MADE THAT TRIP!
INTERESTING! WE SEEM TO BE IN SOME KIND OF CLOSED ENVIRONMENT.
AN IMPENETRABLE FOG OF SOME KIND IS PREVENTING ME FROM SEEING WHAT'S DIRECTLY OVERHEAD, BUT I ASSUME THERE'S A STRUCTURE OF SOME KIND.
SERIOUSLY?
SERIOUSLY?!?
WE JUST GOT SUCKED THROUGH A WORM-HOLE AND YOU'RE MAKING LIKE THE DISCOVERY CHANNEL?

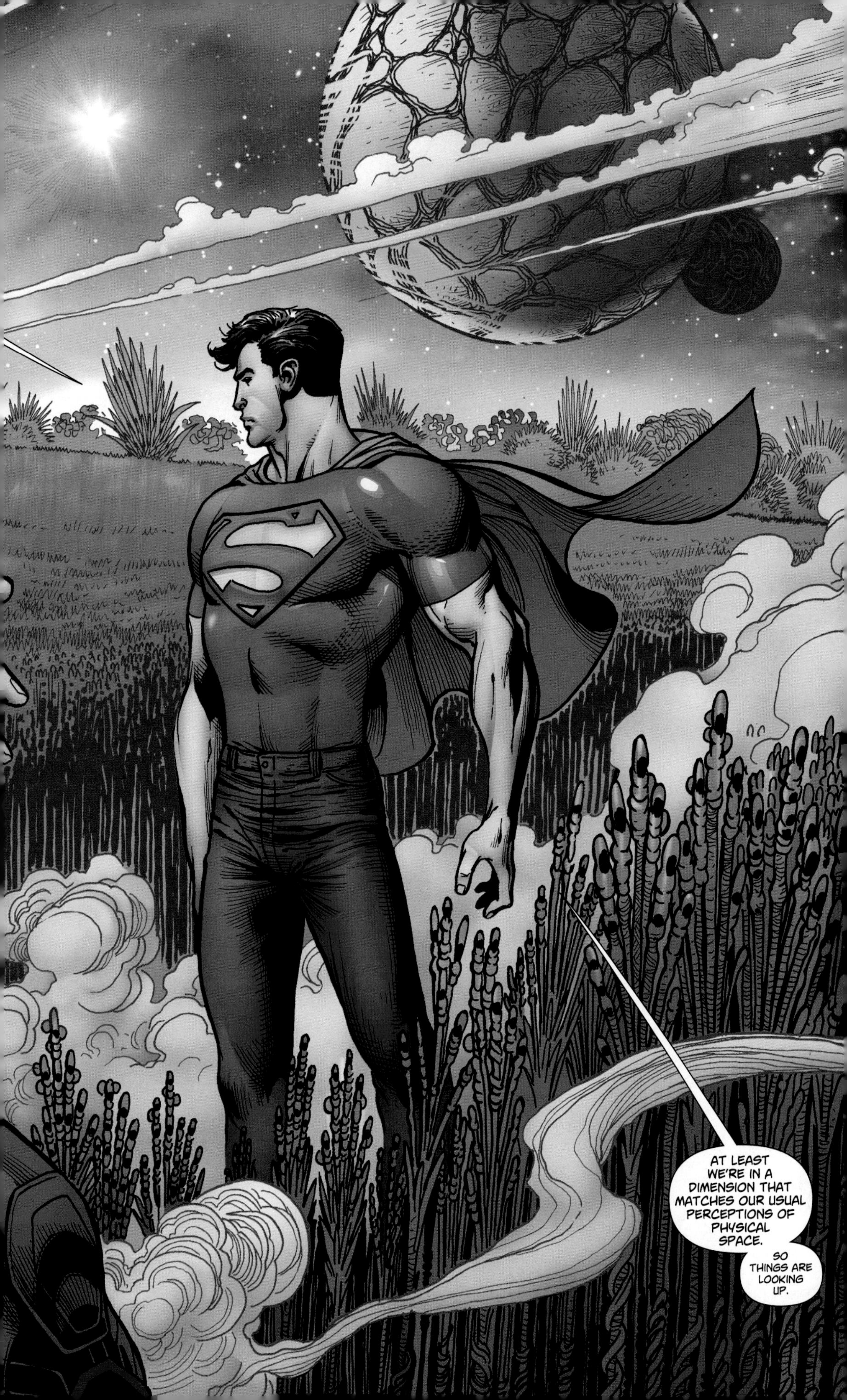

AT LEAST WE'RE IN A DIMENSION THAT MATCHES OUR USUAL PERCEPTIONS OF PHYSICAL SPACE.
SO THINGS ARE LOOKING UP.

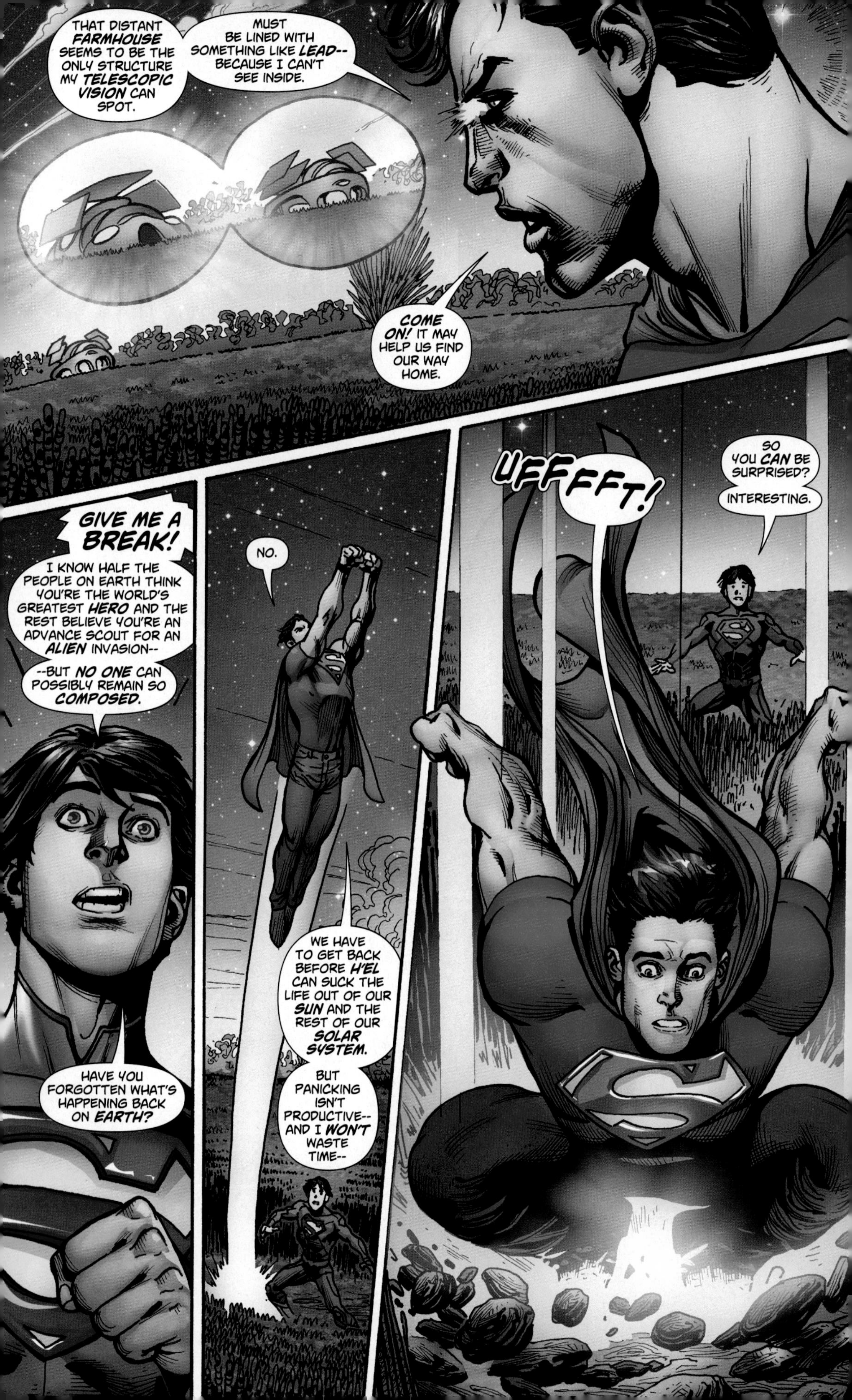
THAT DISTANT FARMHOUSE SEEMS TO BE THE ONLY STRUCTURE MY TELESCOPIC VISION CAN SPOT.
MUST BE LINED WITH SOMETHING LIKE LEAD-- BECAUSE I CAN'T SEE INSIDE.
COME ON! IT MAY HELP US FIND OUR WAY HOME.
GIVE ME A BREAK!
I KNOW HALF THE PEOPLE ON EARTH THINK YOU'RE THE WORLD'S GREATEST HERO AND THE REST BELIEVE YOU'RE AN ADVANCE SCOUT FOR AN ALIEN INVASION--
--BUT NO ONE CAN POSSIBLY REMAIN SO COMPOSED.
HAVE YOU FORGOTTEN WHAT'S HAPPENING BACK ON EARTH?
NO.
WE HAVE TO GET BACK BEFORE H'EL CAN SUCK THE LIFE OUT OF OUR SUN AND THE REST OF OUR SOLAR SYSTEM.
BUT PANICKING ISN'T PRODUCTIVE-- AND I WON'T WASTE TIME--
UFFFFT!
SO YOU CAN BE SURPRISED?
INTERESTING.

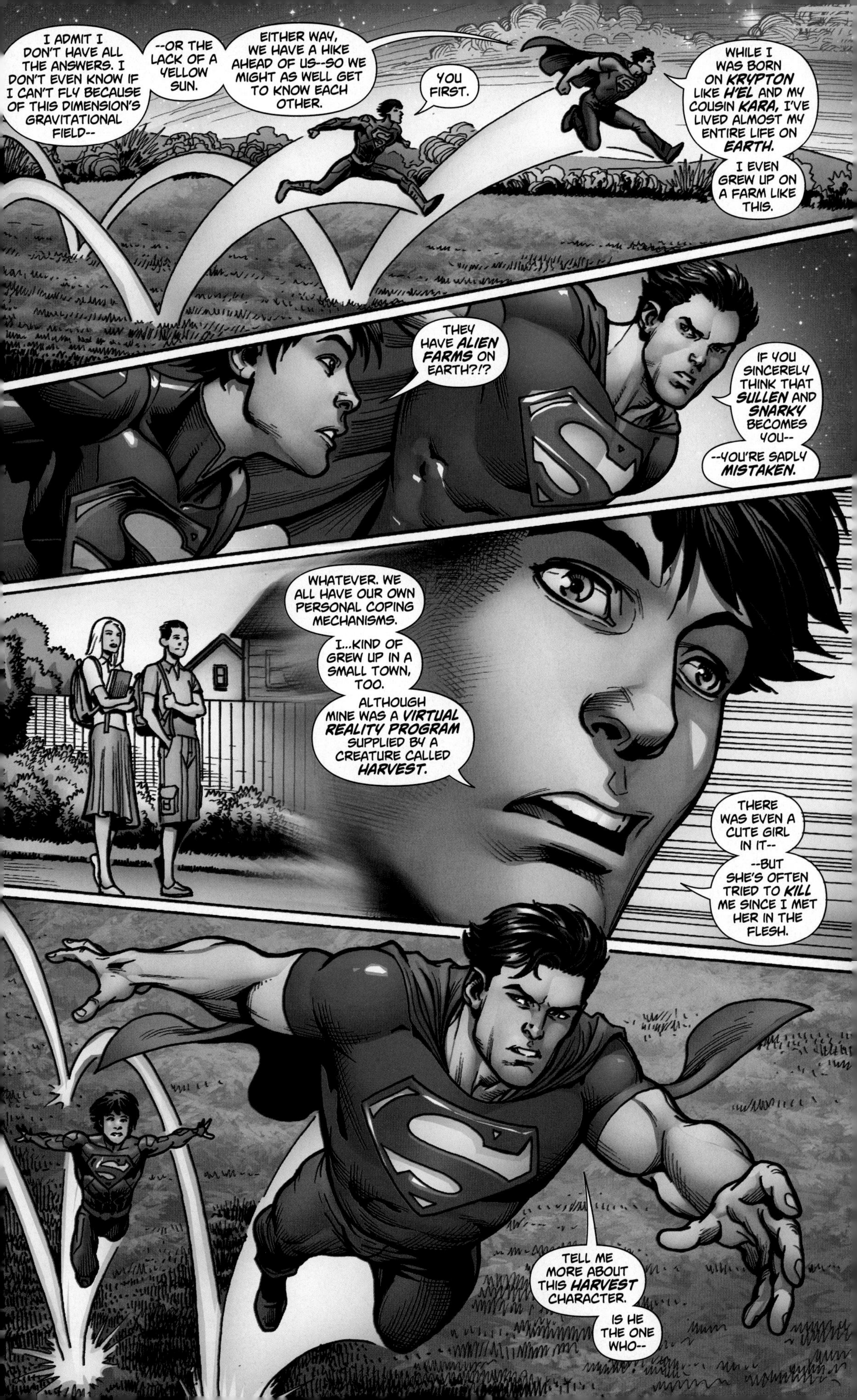
I ADMIT I DON'T HAVE ALL THE ANSWERS. I DON'T EVEN KNOW IF I CAN'T FLY BECAUSE OF THIS DIMENSION'S GRAVITATIONAL FIELD--
--OR THE LACK OF A YELLOW SUN.
EITHER WAY, WE HAVE A HIKE AHEAD OF US--SO WE MIGHT AS WELL GET TO KNOW EACH OTHER.
YOU FIRST.
WHILE I WAS BORN ON KRYPTON LIKE H'EL AND MY COUSIN KARA, I'VE LIVED ALMOST MY ENTIRE LIFE ON EARTH.
I EVEN GREW UP ON A FARM LIKE THIS.
THEY HAVE ALIEN FARMS ON EARTH?!?
IF YOU SINCERELY THINK THAT SULLEN AND SNARKY BECOMES YOU--
--YOU'RE SADLY MISTAKEN.
WHATEVER. WE ALL HAVE OUR OWN PERSONAL COPING MECHANISMS.
I...KIND OF GREW UP IN A SMALL TOWN, TOO.
ALTHOUGH MINE WAS A VIRTUAL REALITY PROGRAM SUPPLIED BY A CREATURE CALLED HARVEST.
THERE WAS EVEN A CUTE GIRL IN IT--
--BUT SHE'S OFTEN TRIED TO KILL ME SINCE I MET HER IN THE FLESH.
TELL ME MORE ABOUT THIS HARVEST CHARACTER.
IS HE THE ONE WHO--

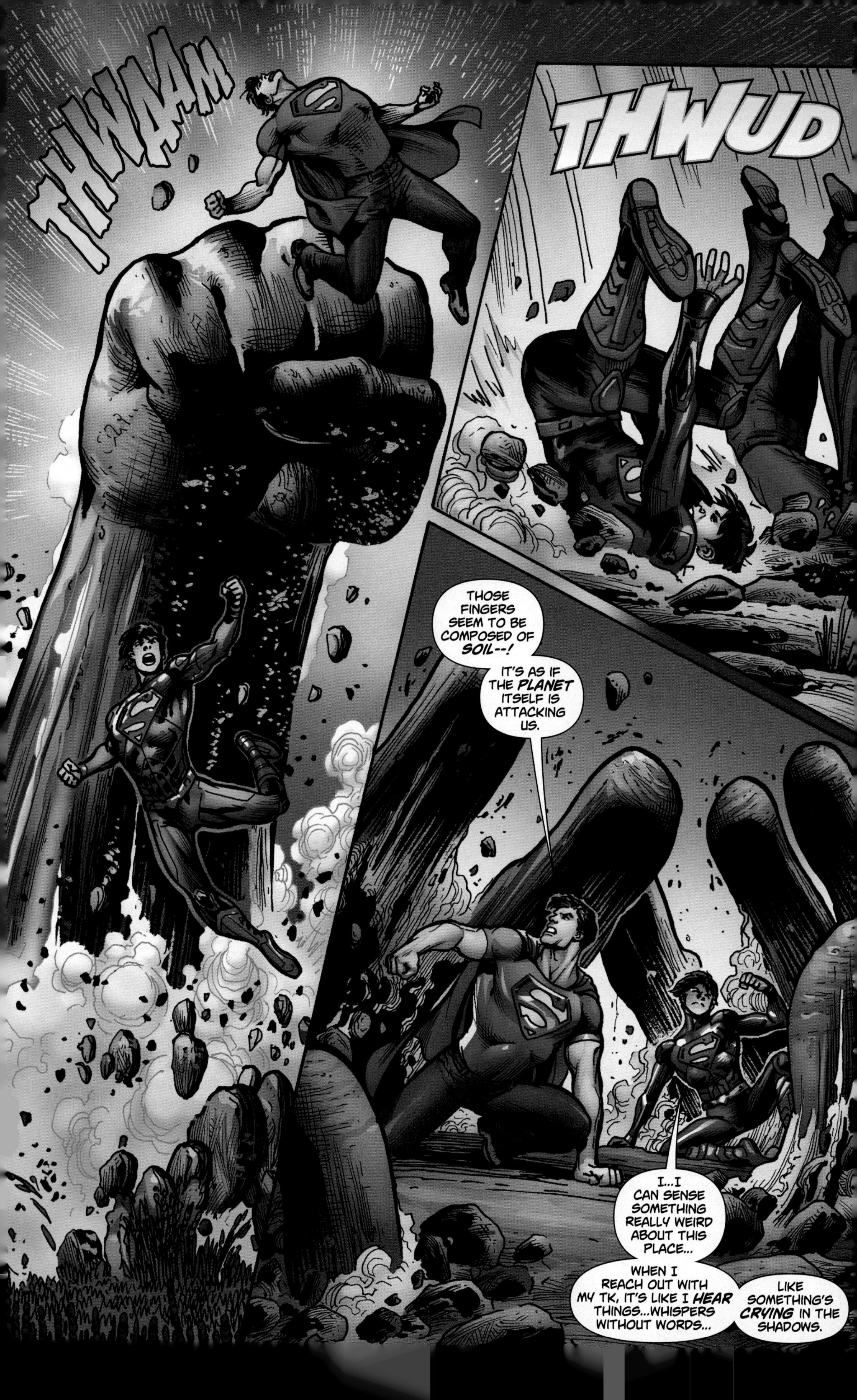
THWAAM
THWUD
THOSE FINGERS SEEM TO BE COMPOSED OF SOIL--!
IT'S AS IF THE PLANET ITSELF IS ATTACKING US.
I...I CAN SENSE SOMETHING REALLY WEIRD ABOUT THIS PLACE...
WHEN I REACH OUT WITH MY TK, IT'S LIKE I HEAR THINGS...WHISPERS WITHOUT WORDS...
LIKE SOMETHING'S CRYING IN THE SHADOWS.

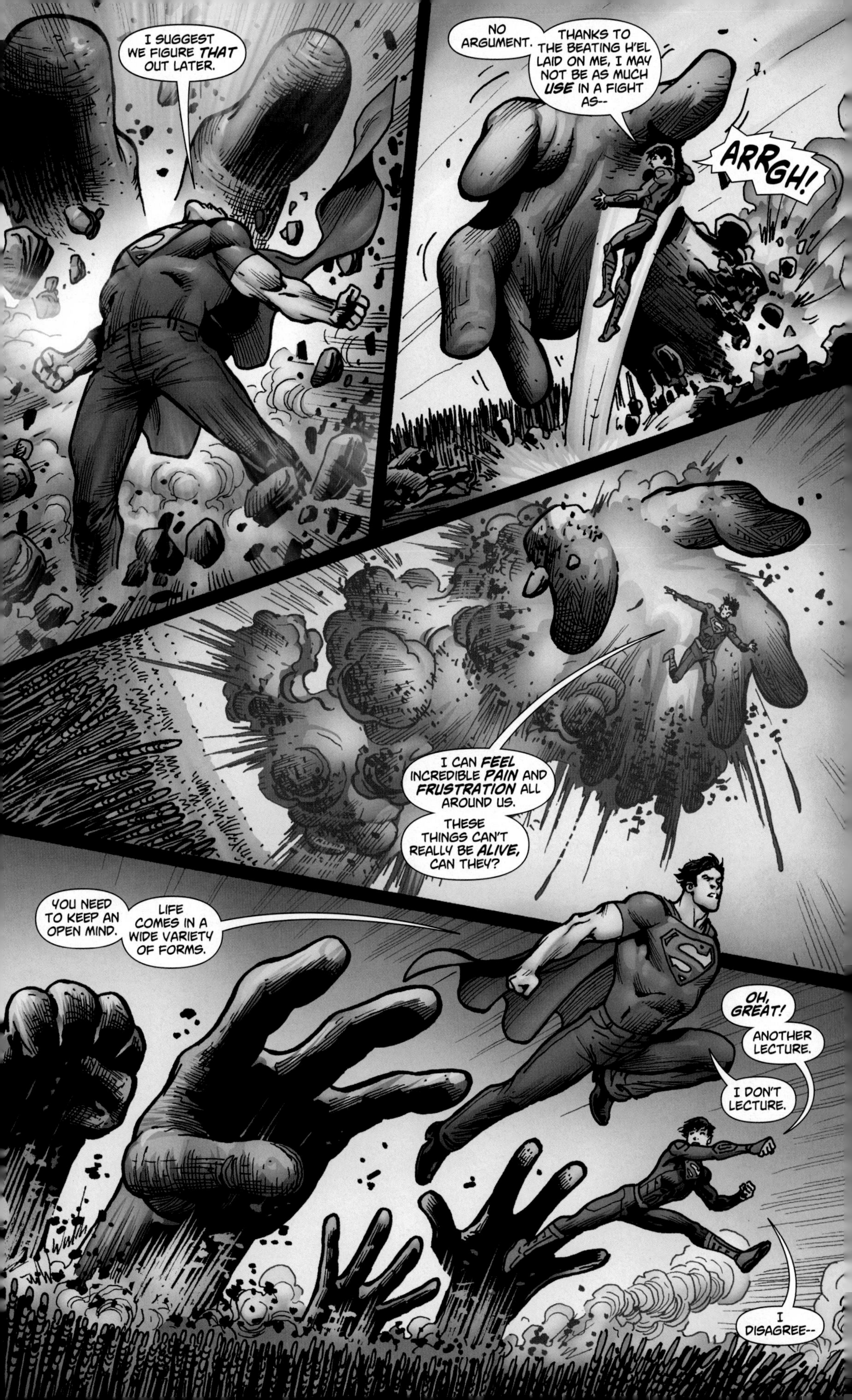
I SUGGEST WE FIGURE THAT OUT LATER.
NO ARGUMENT.
THANKS TO THE BEATING H'EL LAID ON ME, I MAY NOT BE AS MUCH USE IN A FIGHT AS--
ARRGH!
I CAN FEEL INCREDIBLE PAIN AND FRUSTRATION ALL AROUND US.
THESE THINGS CAN'T REALLY BE ALIVE, CAN THEY?
YOU NEED TO KEEP AN OPEN MIND.
LIFE COMES IN A WIDE VARIETY OF FORMS.
OH, GREAT!
ANOTHER LECTURE.
I DON'T LECTURE.
I DISAGREE--

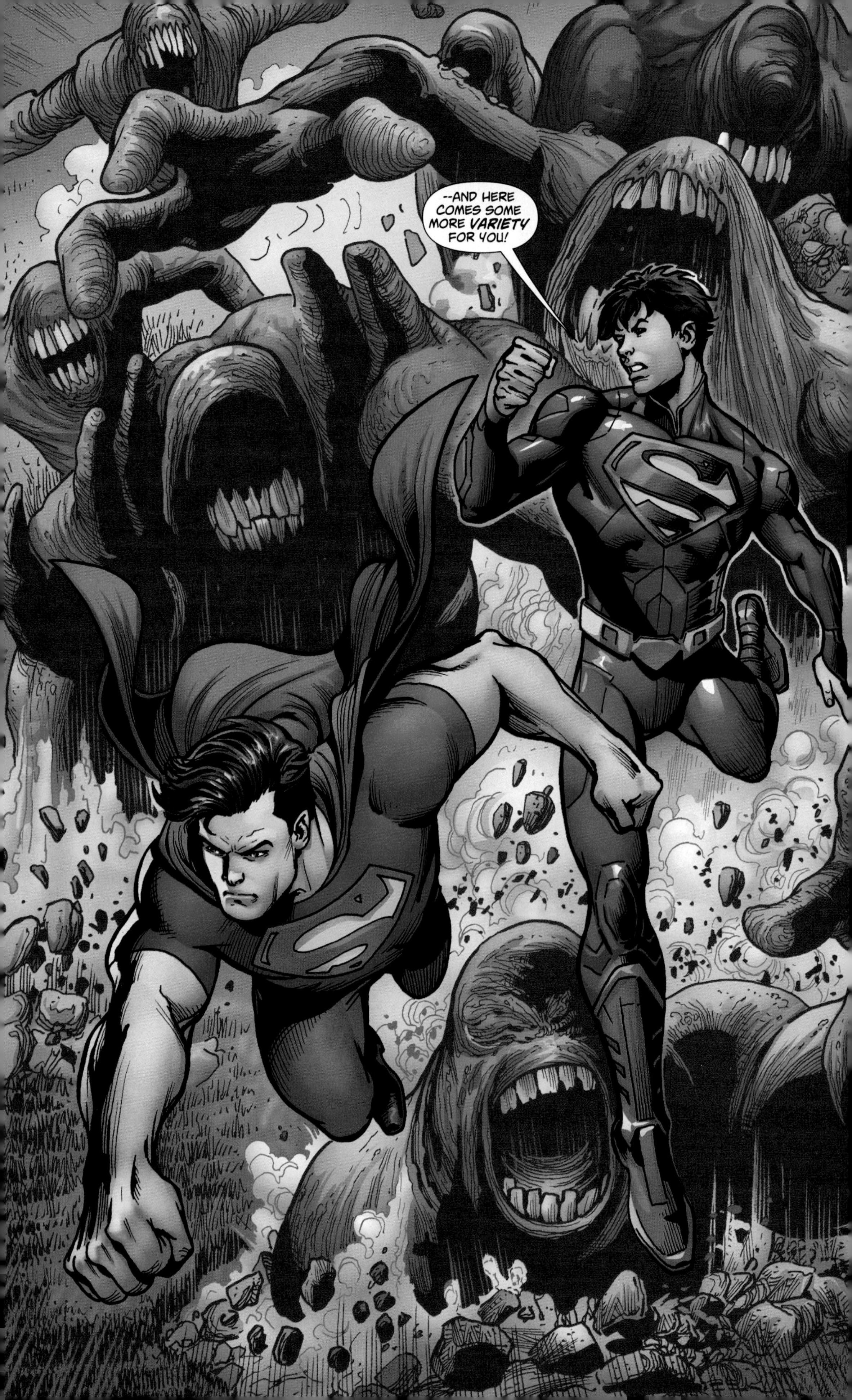
--AND HERE COMES SOME MORE VARIETY FOR YOU!

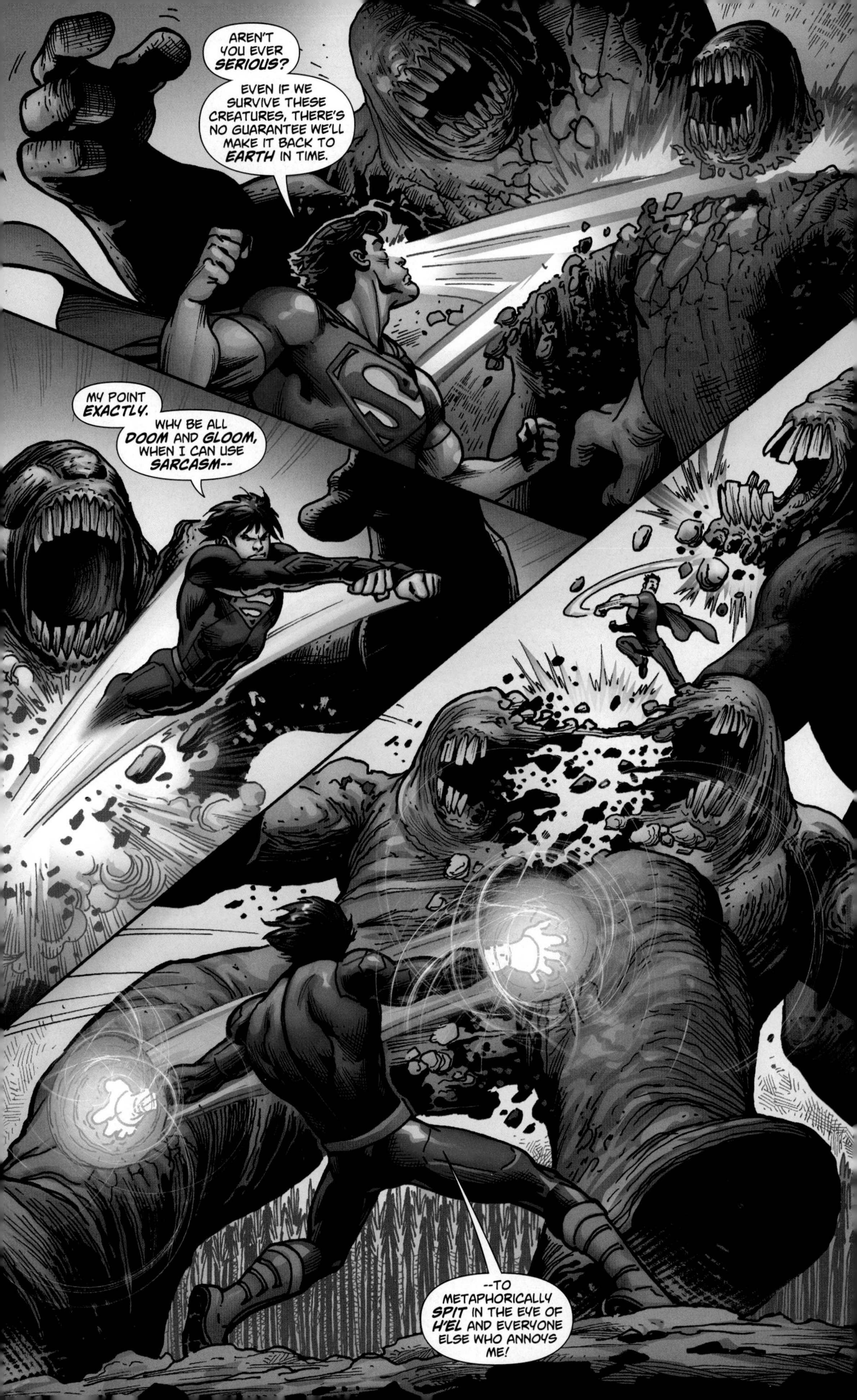
AREN'T YOU EVER SERIOUS?
EVEN IF WE SURVIVE THESE CREATURES, THERE'S NO GUARANTEE WE'LL MAKE IT BACK TO EARTH IN TIME.
MY POINT EXACTLY.
WHY BE ALL DOOM AND GLOOM, WHEN I CAN USE SARCASM--
--TO METAPHORICALLY SPIT IN THE EYE OF H'EL AND EVERYONE ELSE WHO ANNOYS ME!

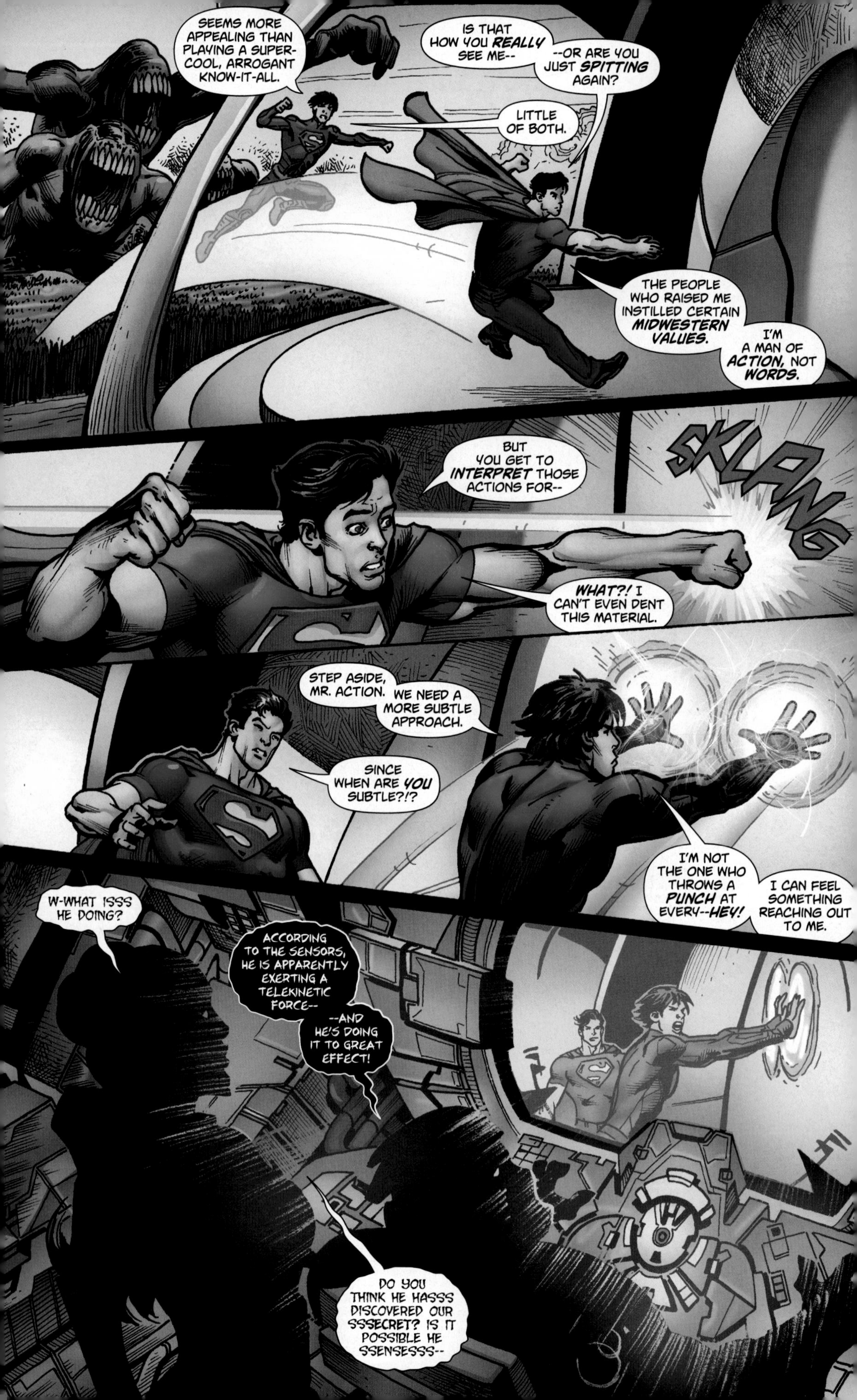
SEEMS MORE APPEALING THAN PLAYING A SUPER-COOL, ARROGANT KNOW-IT-ALL.
IS THAT HOW YOU REALLY SEE ME--
--OR ARE YOU JUST SPITTING AGAIN?
LITTLE OF BOTH.
THE PEOPLE WHO RAISED ME INSTILLED CERTAIN MIDWESTERN VALUES.
I'M A MAN OF ACTION, NOT WORDS.
BUT YOU GET TO INTERPRET THOSE ACTIONS FOR--
SKLANG
WHAT?! I CAN'T EVEN DENT THIS MATERIAL.
STEP ASIDE, MR. ACTION.
WE NEED A MORE SUBTLE APPROACH.
SINCE WHEN ARE YOU SUBTLE?!?
I'M NOT THE ONE WHO THROWS A PUNCH AT EVERY--HEY!
I CAN FEEL SOMETHING REACHING OUT TO ME.
W-WHAT ISSS HE DOING?
ACCORDING TO THE SENSORS, HE IS APPARENTLY EXERTING A TELEKINETIC FORCE--
--AND HE'S DOING IT TO GREAT EFFECT!
DO YOU THINK HE HASSS DISCOVERED OUR SSSECRET? IS IT POSSIBLE HE SSENSESSS--

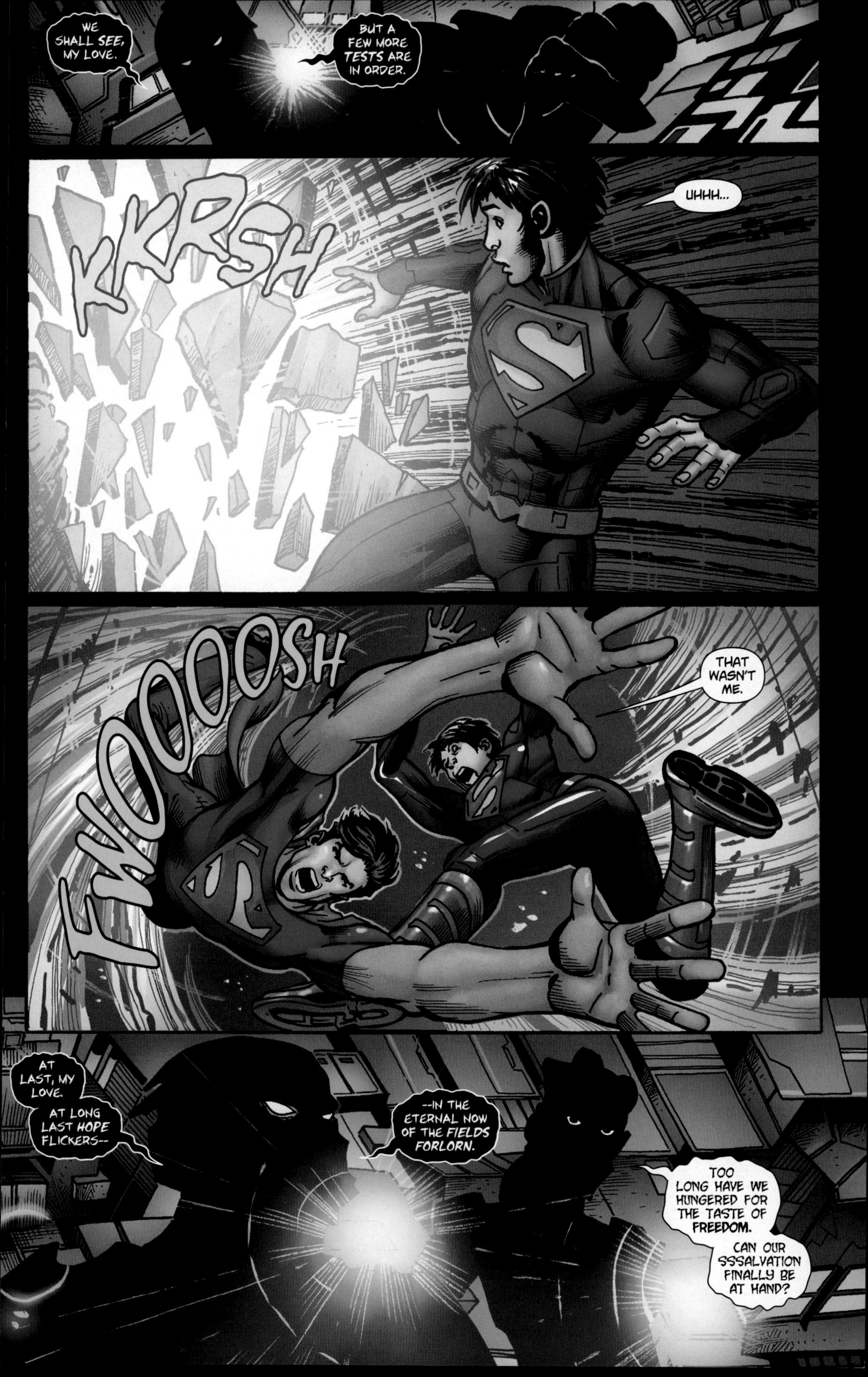
WE SHALL SEE, MY LOVE.
BUT A FEW MORE TESTS ARE IN ORDER.
KKRSH
UHHH...
FWOOOOSH
THAT WASN'T ME.
AT LAST, MY LOVE.
AT LONG LAST HOPE FLICKERS--
--IN THE ETERNAL NOW OF THE FIELDS FORLORN.
TOO LONG HAVE WE HUNGERED FOR THE TASTE OF FREEDOM.
CAN OUR SSSALVATION FINALLY BE AT HAND?

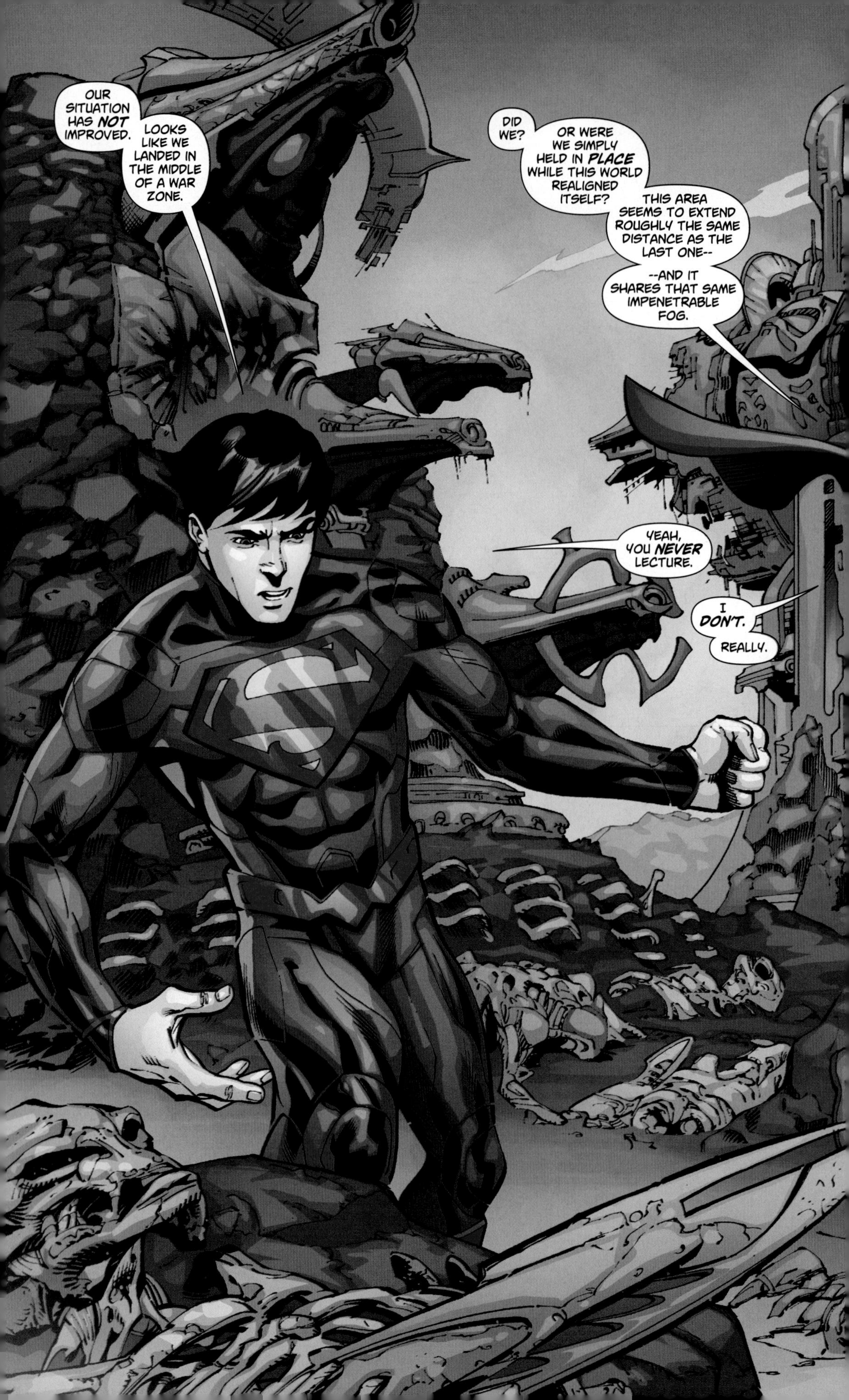
OUR SITUATION HAS NOT IMPROVED.
LOOKS LIKE WE LANDED IN THE MIDDLE OF A WAR ZONE.
DID WE?
OR WERE WE SIMPLY HELD IN PLACE WHILE THIS WORLD REALIGNED ITSELF?
THIS AREA SEEMS TO EXTEND ROUGHLY THE SAME DISTANCE AS THE LAST ONE--
--AND IT SHARES THAT SAME IMPENETRABLE FOG.
YEAH, YOU NEVER LECTURE.
I DON'T.
REALLY.

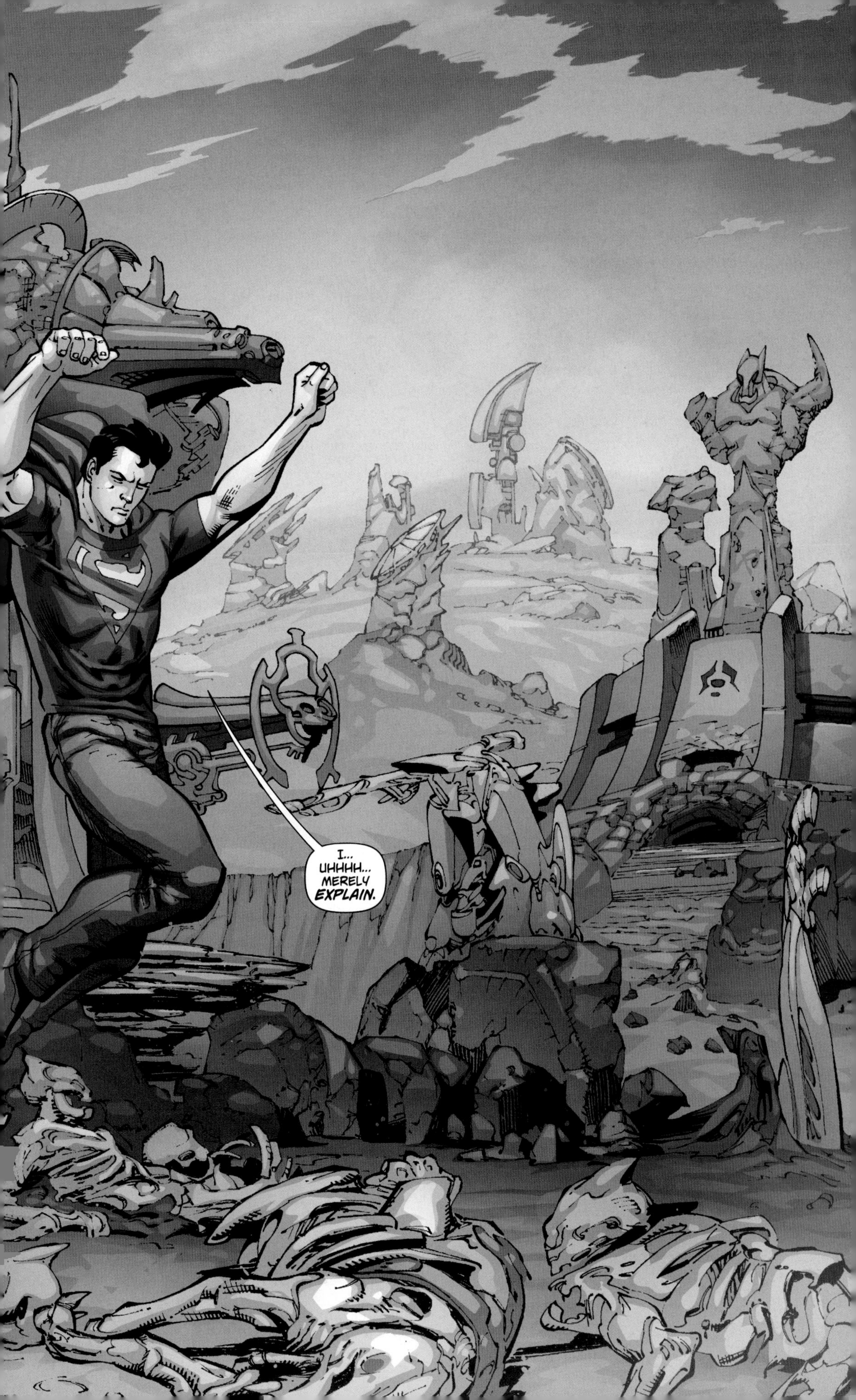
I... UHHHH... MERELY EXPLAIN.

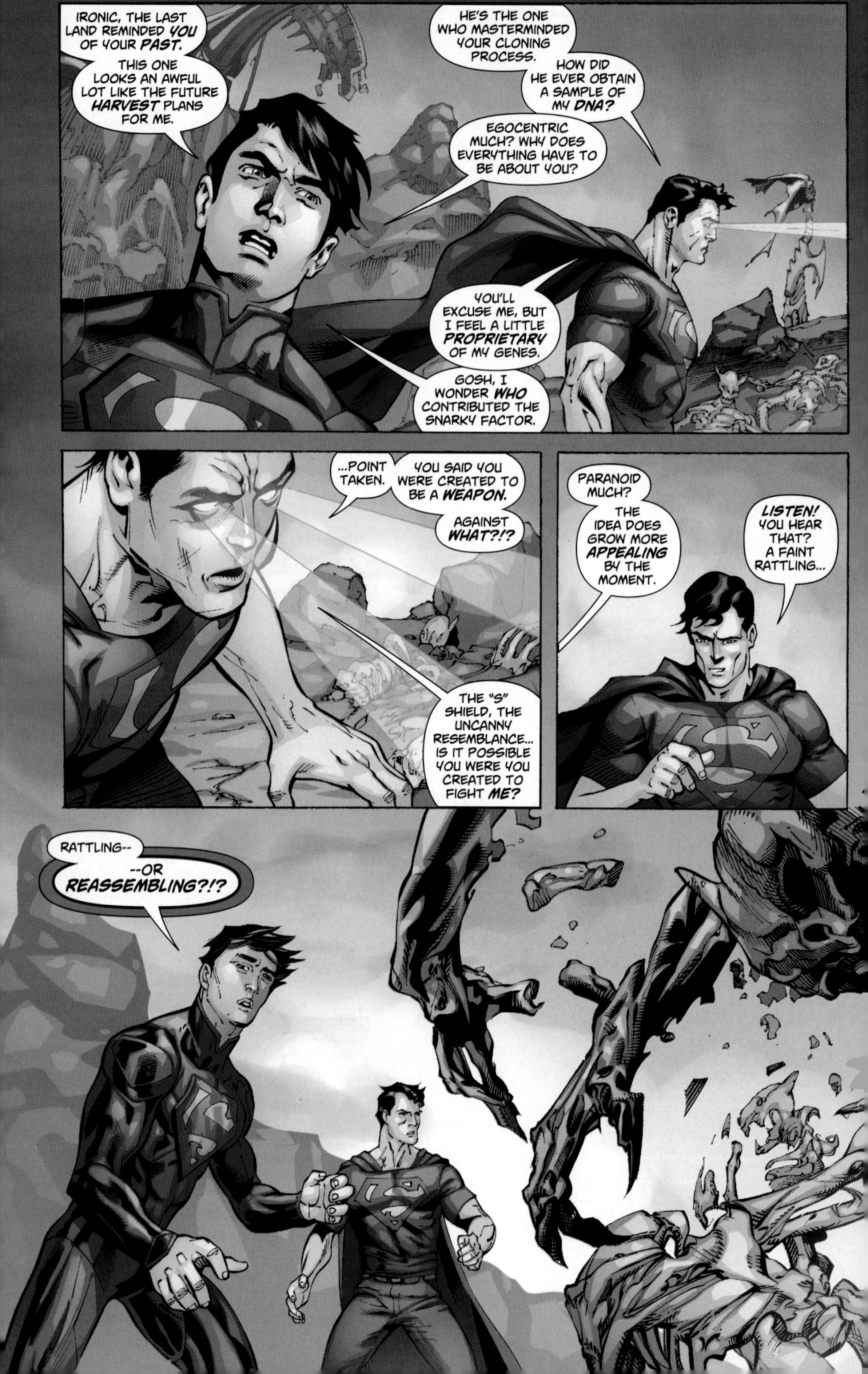
IRONIC, THE LAST LAND REMINDED YOU OF YOUR PAST.
THIS ONE LOOKS AN AWFUL LOT LIKE THE FUTURE HARVEST PLANS FOR ME.
HE'S THE ONE WHO MASTERMINDED YOUR CLONING PROCESS.
HOW DID HE EVER OBTAIN A SAMPLE OF MY DNA?
EGOCENTRIC MUCH? WHY DOES EVERYTHING HAVE TO BE ABOUT YOU?
YOU'LL EXCUSE ME, BUT I FEEL A LITTLE PROPRIETARY OF MY GENES.
GOSH, I WONDER WHO CONTRIBUTED THE SNARKY FACTOR.
...POINT TAKEN.
YOU SAID YOU WERE CREATED TO BE A WEAPON.
AGAINST WHAT?!?
THE "S" SHIELD, THE UNCANNY RESEMBLANCE... IS IT POSSIBLE YOU WERE YOU CREATED TO FIGHT ME?
PARANOID MUCH?
THE IDEA DOES GROW MORE APPEALING BY THE MOMENT.
LISTEN! YOU HEAR THAT? A FAINT RATTLING...
RATTLING--
--OR REASSEMBLING?!?

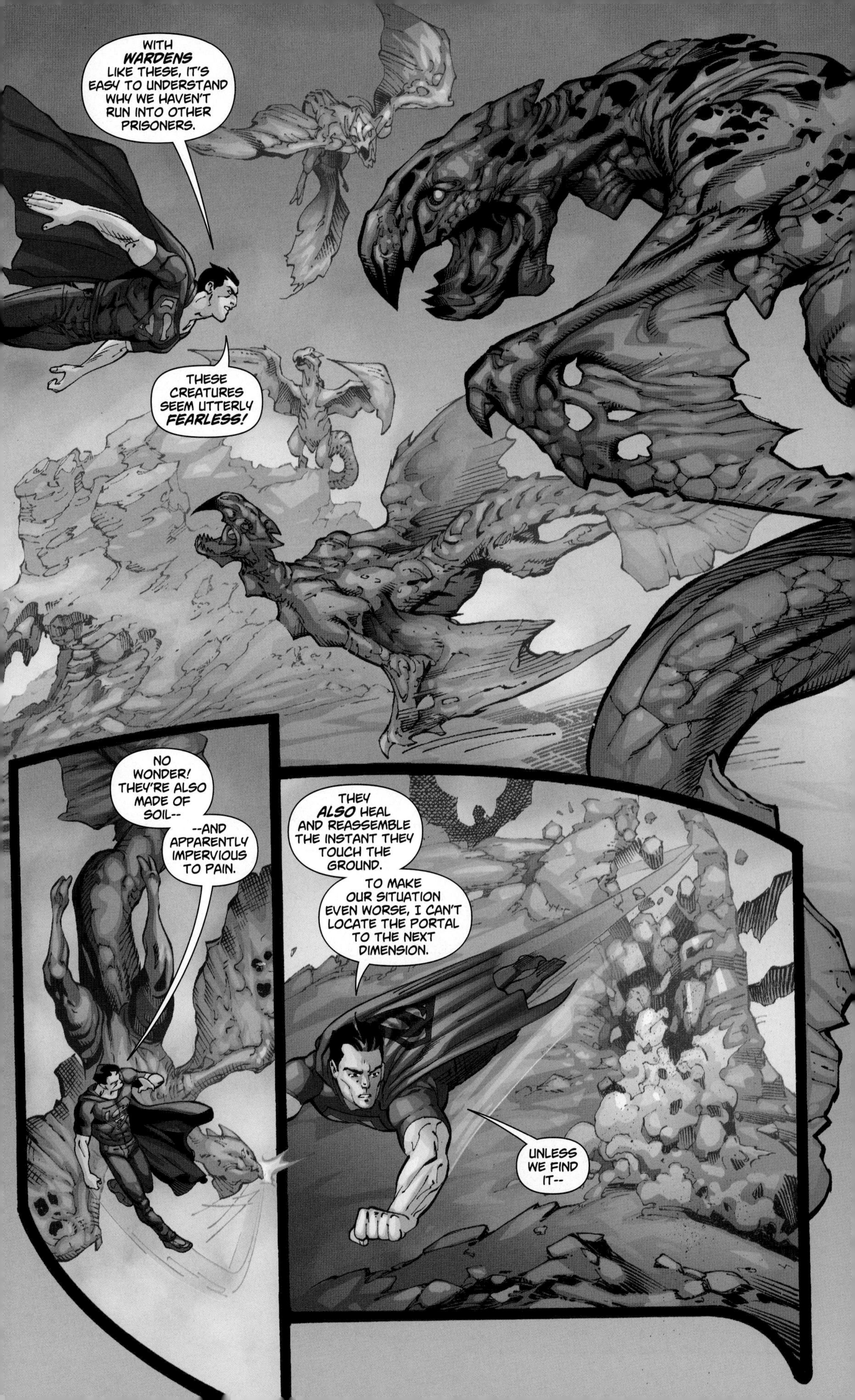
WITH WARDENS LIKE THESE, IT'S EASY TO UNDERSTAND WHY WE HAVEN'T RUN INTO OTHER PRISONERS.
THESE CREATURES SEEM UTTERLY FEARLESS!
NO WONDER! THEY'RE ALSO MADE OF SOIL--
--AND APPARENTLY IMPERVIOUS TO PAIN.
THEY ALSO HEAL AND REASSEMBLE THE INSTANT THEY TOUCH THE GROUND.
TO MAKE OUR SITUATION EVEN WORSE, I CAN'T LOCATE THE PORTAL TO THE NEXT DIMENSION.
UNLESS WE FIND IT--

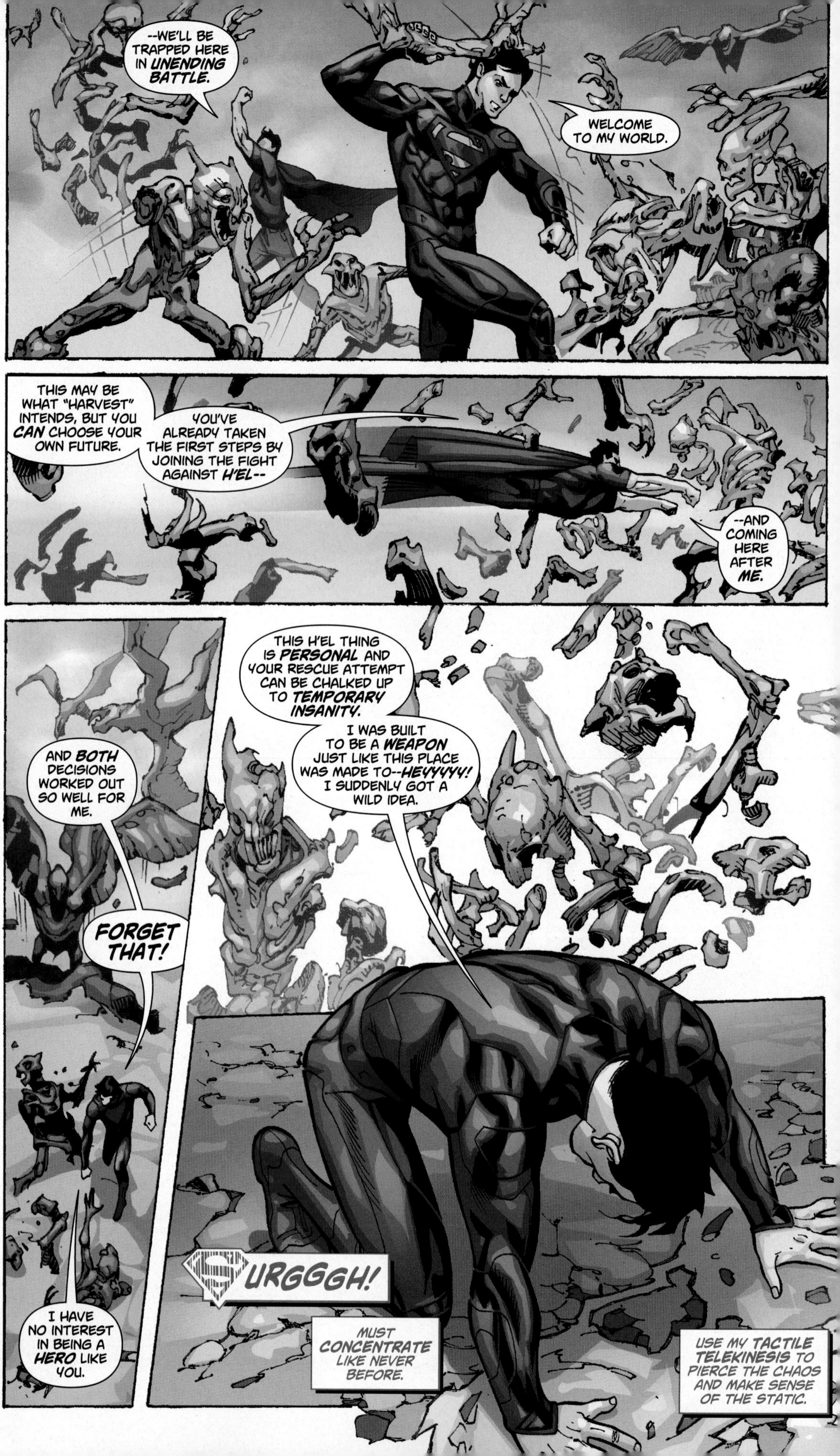
--WE'LL BE TRAPPED HERE IN UNENDING BATTLE.
WELCOME TO MY WORLD.
THIS MAY BE WHAT "HARVEST" INTENDS, BUT YOU CAN CHOOSE YOUR OWN FUTURE.
YOU'VE ALREADY TAKEN THE FIRST STEPS BY JOINING THE FIGHT AGAINST H'EL--
--AND COMING HERE AFTER ME.
AND BOTH DECISIONS WORKED OUT SO WELL FOR ME.
FORGET THAT!
I HAVE NO INTEREST IN BEING A HERO LIKE YOU.
THIS H'EL THING IS PERSONAL AND YOUR RESCUE ATTEMPT CAN BE CHALKED UP TO TEMPORARY INSANITY.
I WAS BUILT TO BE A WEAPON JUST LIKE THIS PLACE WAS MADE TO--HEYYYYY! I SUDDENLY GOT A WILD IDEA.
URGGGH!
MUST CONCENTRATE LIKE NEVER BEFORE.
USE MY TACTILE TELEKINESIS TO PIERCE THE CHAOS AND MAKE SENSE OF THE STATIC.

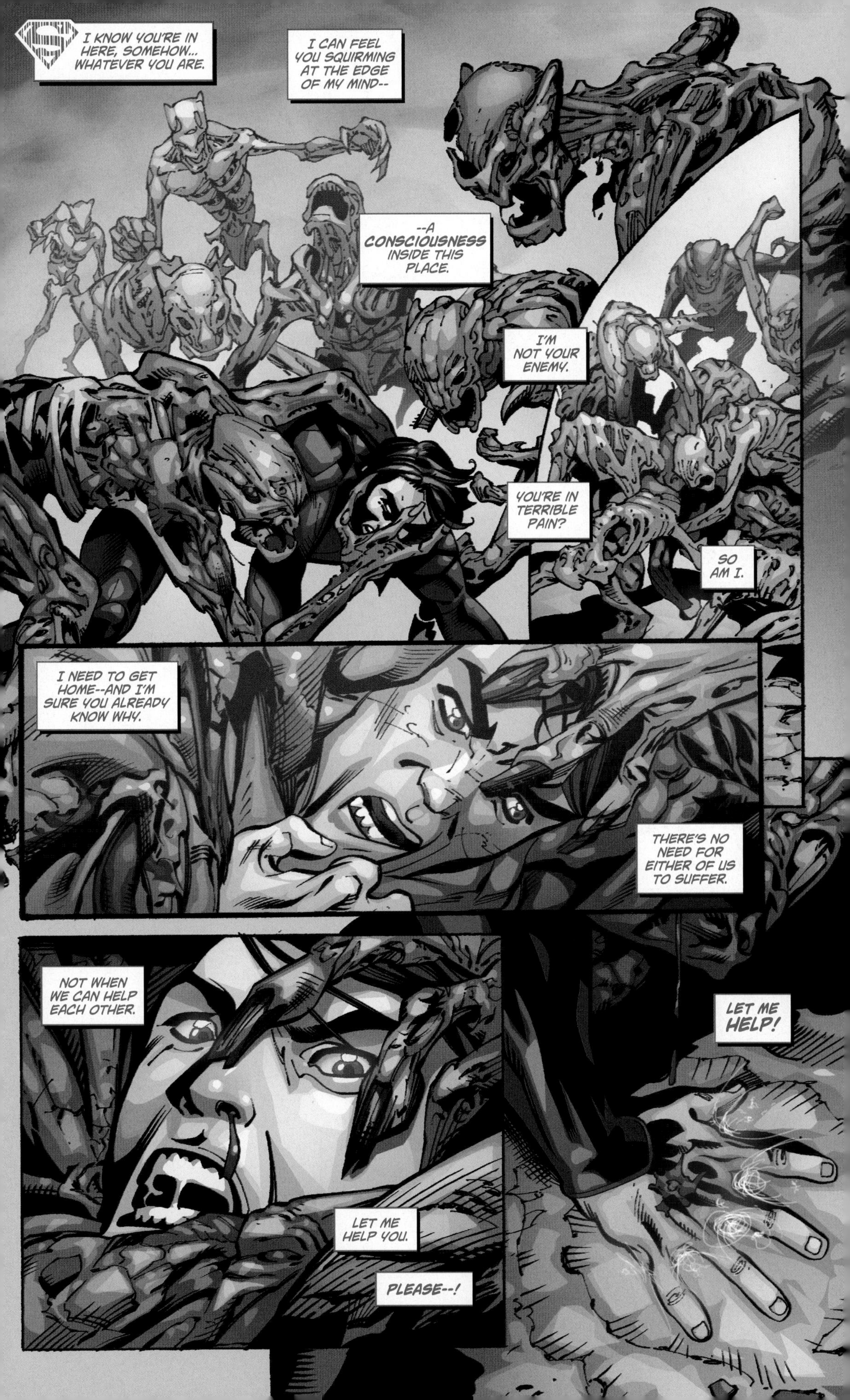

I KNOW YOU'RE IN HERE, SOMEHOW... WHATEVER YOU ARE.
I CAN FEEL YOU SQUIRMING AT THE EDGE OF MY MIND--
--A CONSCIOUSNESS INSIDE THIS PLACE.
I'M NOT YOUR ENEMY.
YOU'RE IN TERRIBLE PAIN?
SO AM I.
I NEED TO GET HOME--AND I'M SURE YOU ALREADY KNOW WHY.
THERE'S NO NEED FOR EITHER OF US TO SUFFER.
NOT WHEN WE CAN HELP EACH OTHER.
LET ME HELP YOU.
PLEASE--!
LET ME HELP!

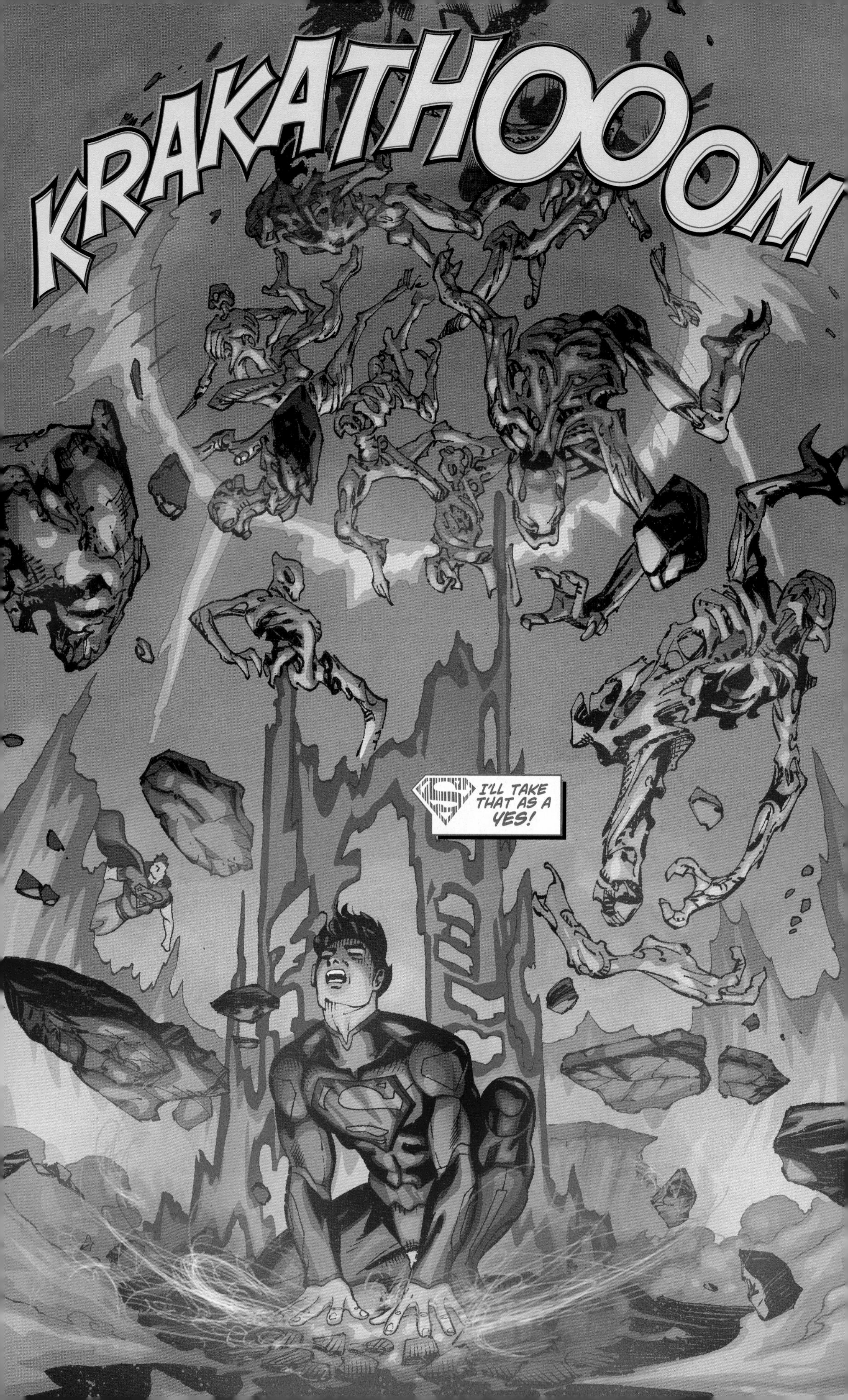
KRAKATHOOOOM
I'LL TAKE THAT AS A YES!

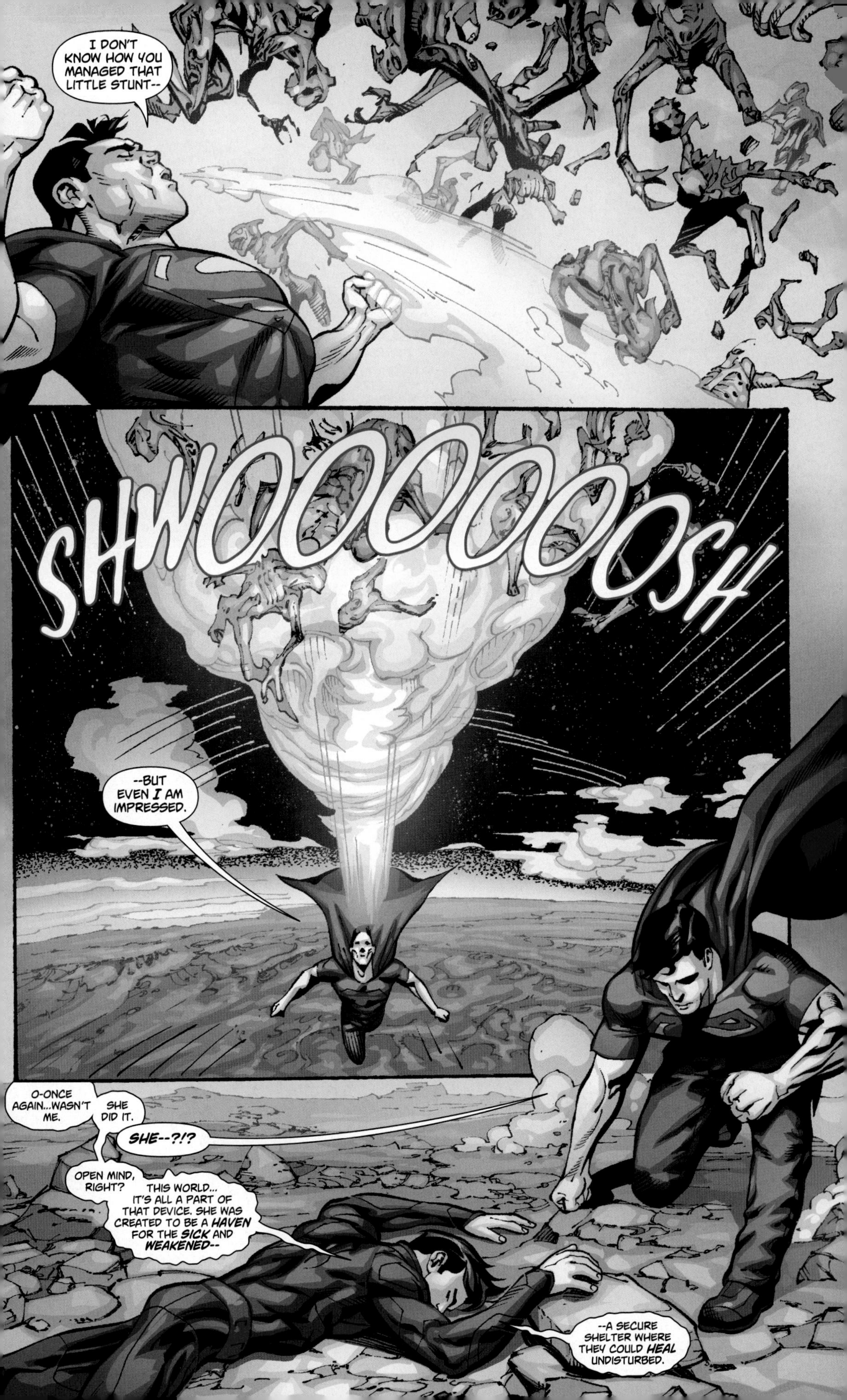
I DON'T KNOW HOW YOU MANAGED THAT LITTLE STUNT--
SHWOOOOOOOSH
--BUT EVEN I AM IMPRESSED.
O-ONCE AGAIN...WASN'T ME.
SHE DID IT.
SHE--?!?
OPEN MIND, RIGHT?
THIS WORLD... IT'S ALL A PART OF THAT DEVICE. SHE WAS CREATED TO BE A HAVEN FOR THE SICK AND WEAKENED--
--A SECURE SHELTER WHERE THEY COULD HEAL UNDISTURBED.

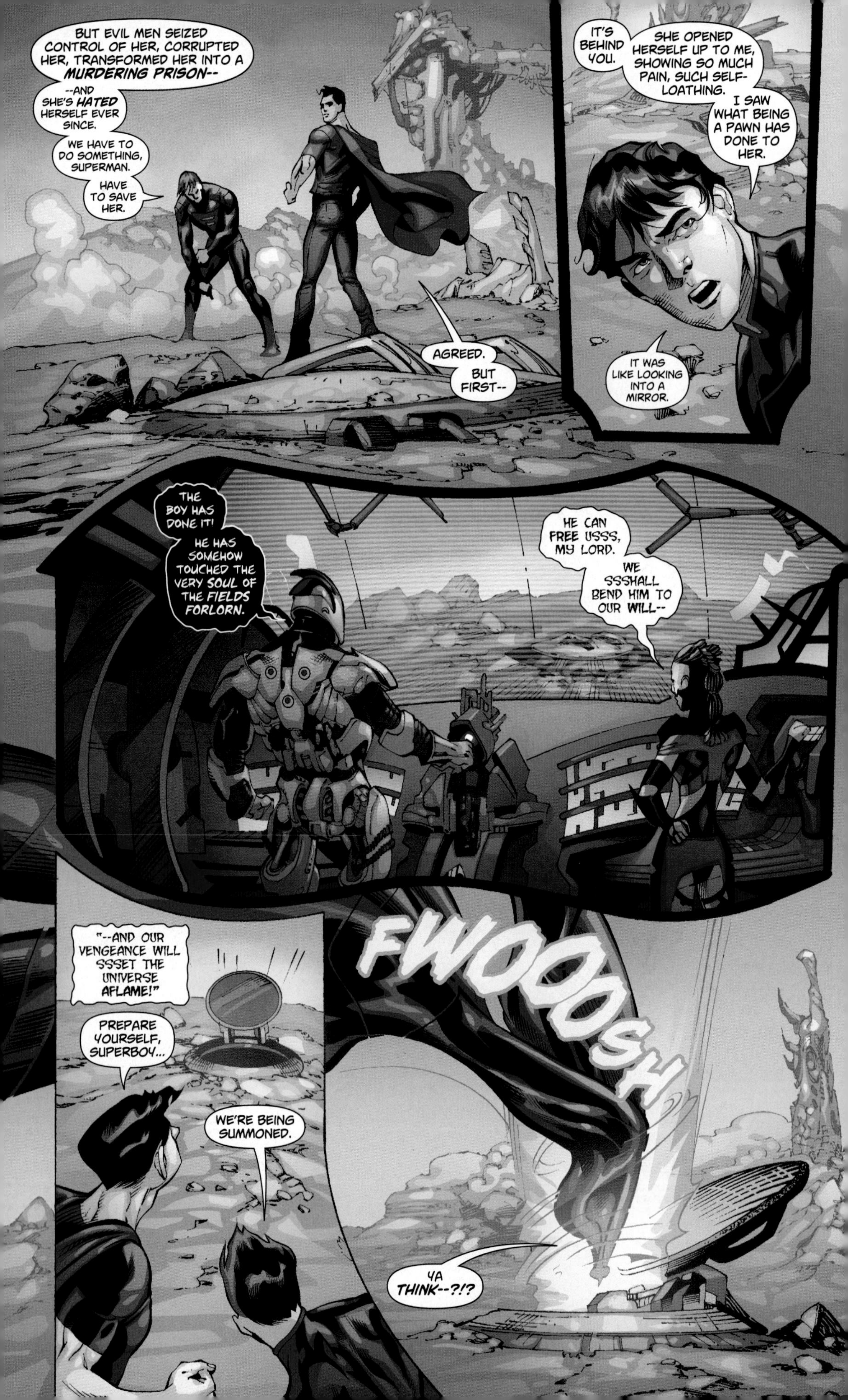
BUT EVIL MEN SEIZED CONTROL OF HER, CORRUPTED HER, TRANSFORMED HER INTO A MURDERING PRISON--
--AND SHE'S HATED HERSELF EVER SINCE.
WE HAVE TO DO SOMETHING, SUPERMAN.
HAVE TO SAVE HER.
AGREED.
BUT FIRST--
IT'S BEHIND YOU.
SHE OPENED HERSELF UP TO ME, SHOWING SO MUCH PAIN, SUCH SELF-LOATHING.
I SAW WHAT BEING A PAWN HAS DONE TO HER.
IT WAS LIKE LOOKING INTO A MIRROR.
THE BOY HAS DONE IT!
HE HAS SOMEHOW TOUCHED THE VERY SOUL OF THE FIELDS FORLORN.
HE CAN FREE USSS, MY LORD.
WE SSSHALL BEND HIM TO OUR WILL--
"--AND OUR VENGEANCE WILL SSSET THE UNIVERSE AFLAME!"
PREPARE YOURSELF, SUPERBOY...
WE'RE BEING SUMMONED.
FWOOOSH
YA THINK--?!?

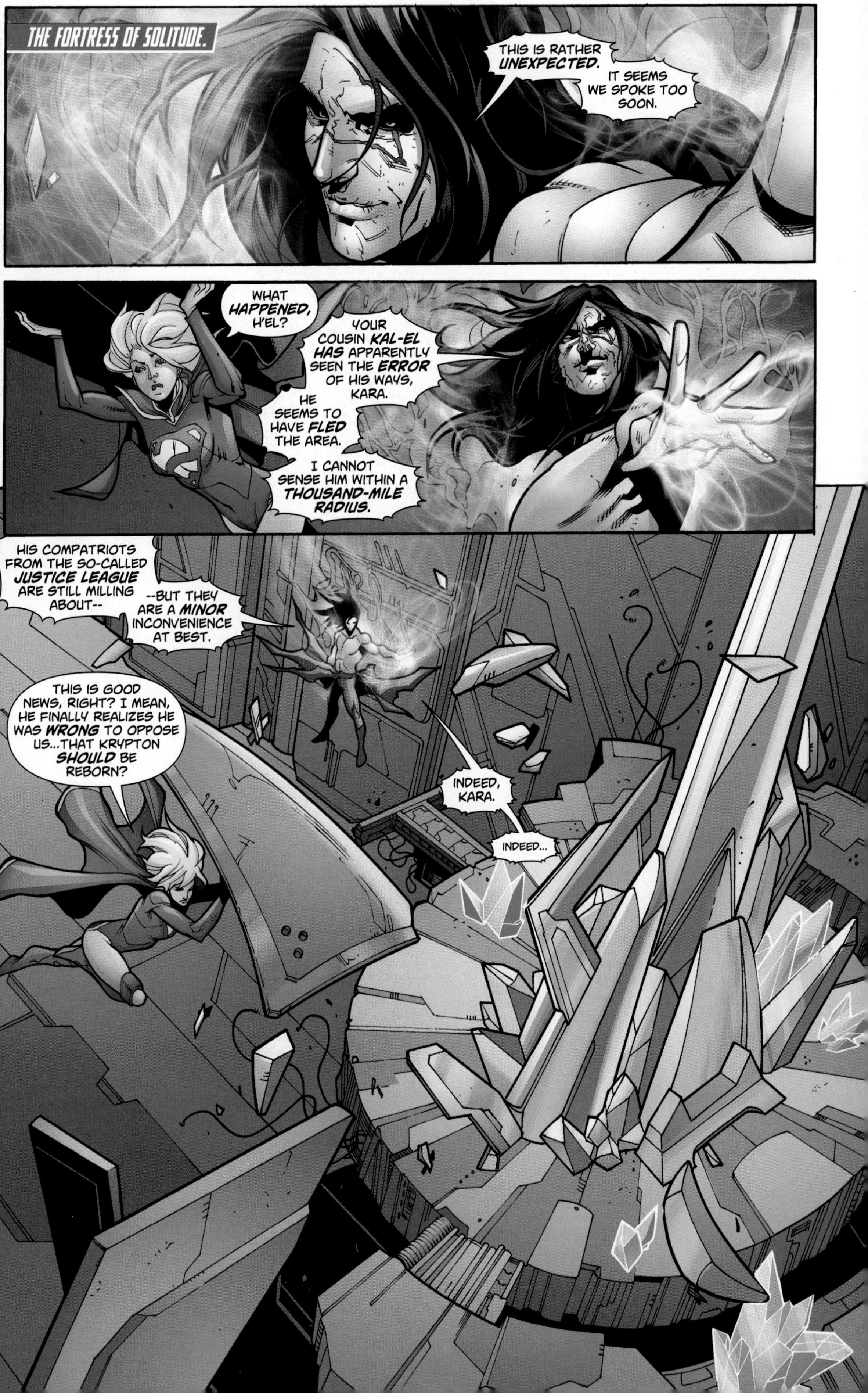
THE FORTRESS OF SOLITUDE.
THIS IS RATHER UNEXPECTED.
IT SEEMS WE SPOKE TOO SOON.
WHAT HAPPENED, H'EL?
YOUR COUSIN KAL-EL HAS APPARENTLY SEEN THE ERROR OF HIS WAYS, KARA.
HE SEEMS TO HAVE FLED THE AREA.
I CANNOT SENSE HIM WITHIN A THOUSAND-MILE RADIUS.
HIS COMPATRIOTS FROM THE SO-CALLED JUSTICE LEAGUE ARE STILL MILLING ABOUT--
--BUT THEY ARE A MINOR INCONVENIENCE AT BEST.
THIS IS GOOD NEWS, RIGHT? I MEAN, HE FINALLY REALIZES HE WAS WRONG TO OPPOSE US...THAT KRYPTON SHOULD BE REBORN?
INDEED, KARA.
INDEED...

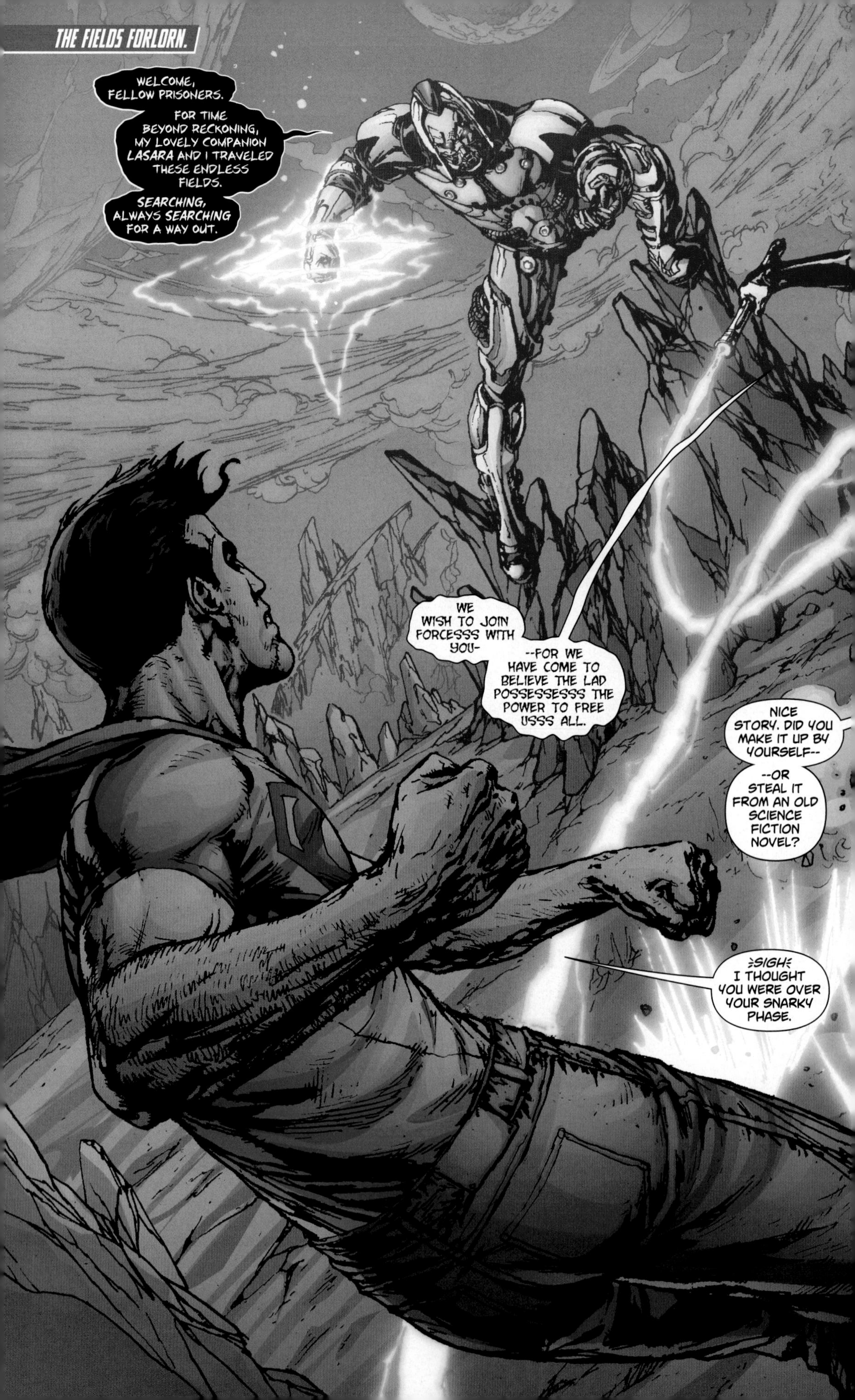
THE FIELDS FORLORN.
WELCOME, FELLOW PRISONERS.
FOR TIME BEYOND RECKONING, MY LOVELY COMPANION LASARA AND I TRAVELED THESE ENDLESS FIELDS.
SEARCHING, ALWAYS SEARCHING FOR A WAY OUT.
WE WISH TO JOIN FORCESSS WITH YOU-
--FOR WE HAVE COME TO BELIEVE THE LAD POSSESSESSS THE POWER TO FREE USSS ALL.
NICE STORY. DID YOU MAKE IT UP BY YOURSELF--
--OR STEAL IT FROM AN OLD SCIENCE FICTION NOVEL?
SIGH I THOUGHT YOU WERE OVER YOUR SNARKY PHASE.

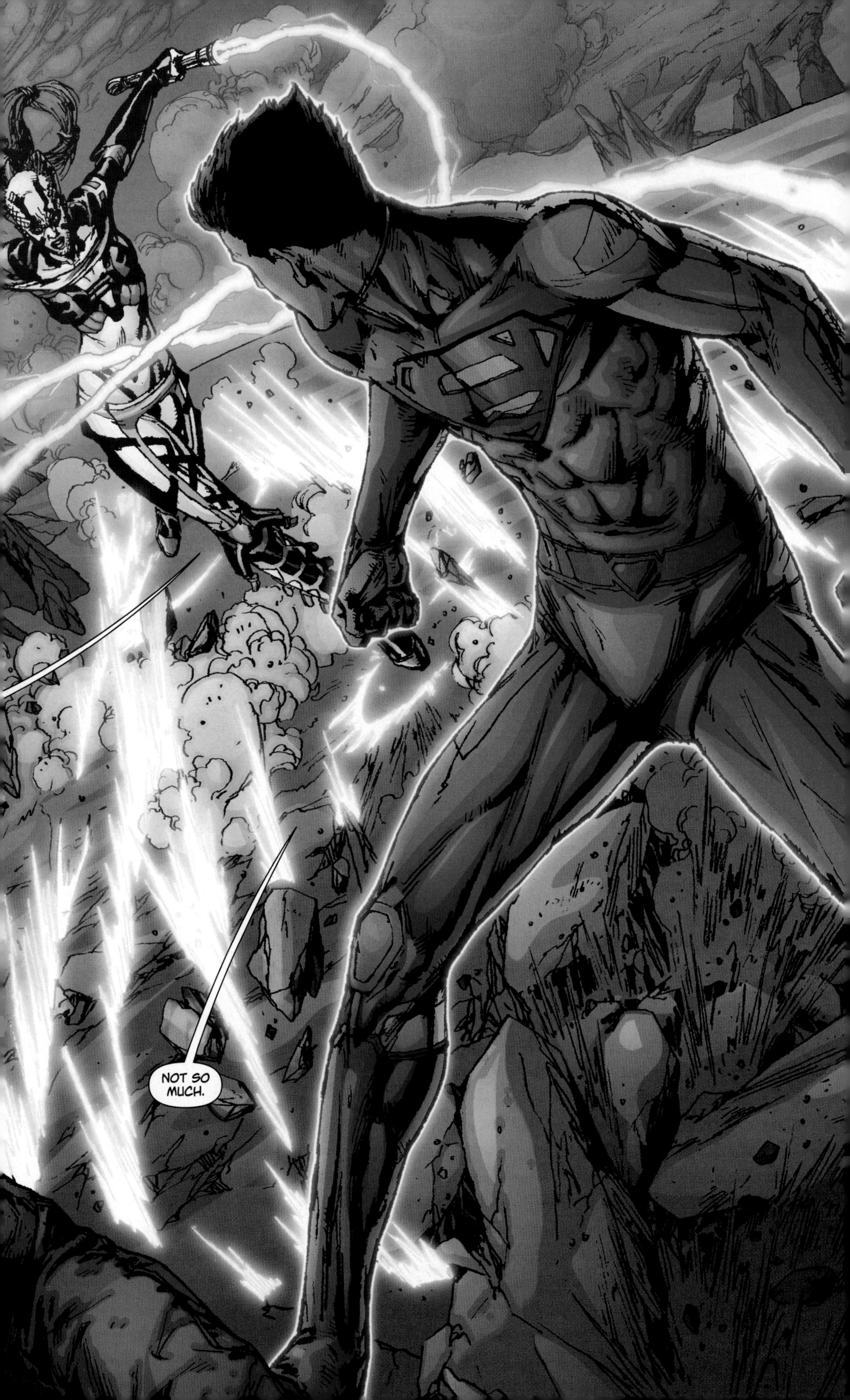
NOT SO MUCH.

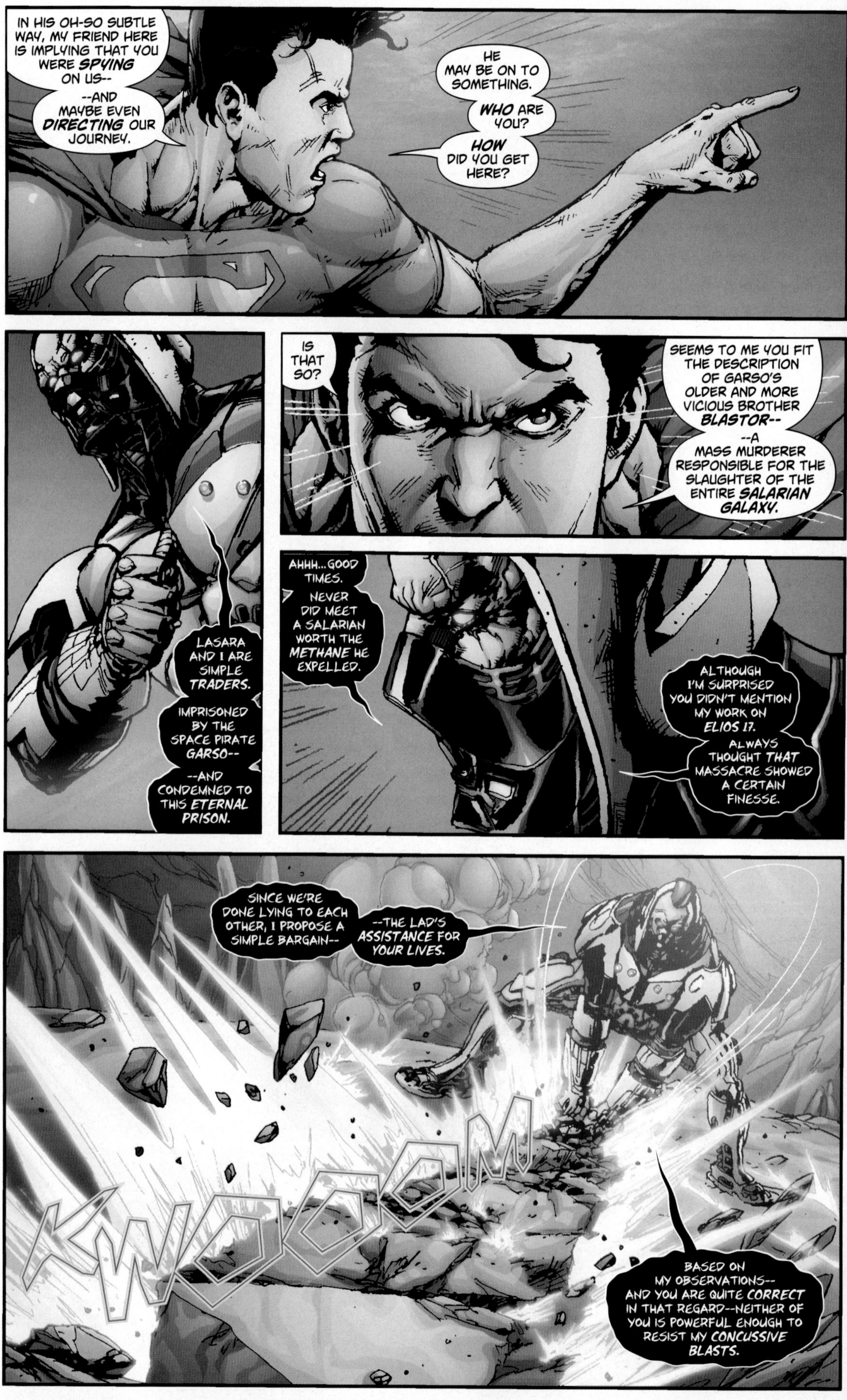
IN HIS OH-SO SUBTLE WAY, MY FRIEND HERE IS IMPLYING THAT YOU WERE SPYING ON US--
--AND MAYBE EVEN DIRECTING OUR JOURNEY.
HE MAY BE ON TO SOMETHING.
WHO ARE YOU?
HOW DID YOU GET HERE?
LASARA AND I ARE SIMPLE TRADERS.
IMPRISONED BY THE SPACE PIRATE GARSO--
--AND CONDEMNED TO THIS ETERNAL PRISON.
IS THAT SO?
SEEMS TO ME YOU FIT THE DESCRIPTION OF GARSO'S OLDER AND MORE VICIOUS BROTHER BLASTOR--
--A MASS MURDERER RESPONSIBLE FOR THE SLAUGHTER OF THE ENTIRE SALARIAN GALAXY.
AHHH...GOOD TIMES.
NEVER DID MEET A SALARIAN WORTH THE METHANE HE EXPELLED.
ALTHOUGH I'M SURPRISED YOU DIDN'T MENTION MY WORK ON ELIOS 17.
ALWAYS THOUGHT THAT MASSACRE SHOWED A CERTAIN FINESSE.
SINCE WE'RE DONE LYING TO EACH OTHER, I PROPOSE A SIMPLE BARGAIN--
--THE LAD'S ASSISTANCE FOR YOUR LIVES.
KWOOOM
BASED ON MY OBSERVATIONS-- AND YOU ARE QUITE CORRECT IN THAT REGARD--NEITHER OF YOU IS POWERFUL ENOUGH TO RESIST MY CONCUSSIVE BLASTS.

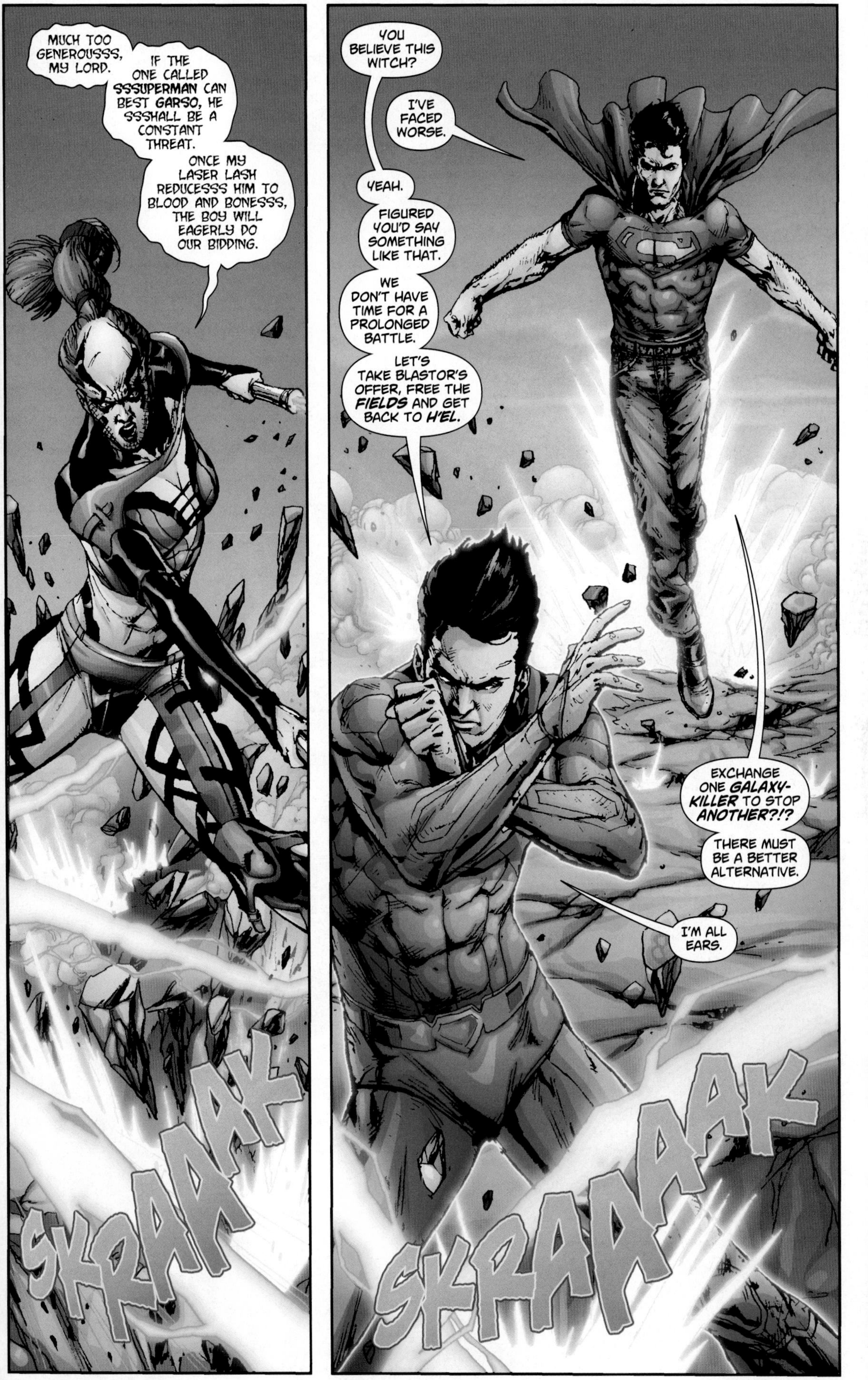
MUCH TOO GENEROUSSS, MY LORD.
IF THE ONE CALLED SSSUPERMAN CAN BEST GARSO, HE SSSHALL BE A CONSTANT THREAT.
ONCE MY LASER LASH REDUCESSS HIM TO BLOOD AND BONESSS, THE BOY WILL EAGERLY DO OUR BIDDING.
SKRAAK
YOU BELIEVE THIS WITCH?
I'VE FACED WORSE.
YEAH.
FIGURED YOU'D SAY SOMETHING LIKE THAT.
WE DON'T HAVE TIME FOR A PROLONGED BATTLE.
LET'S TAKE BLASTOR'S OFFER, FREE THE *FIELDS* AND GET BACK TO *H'EL*.
EXCHANGE ONE *GALAXY-KILLER* TO STOP *ANOTHER?!?*
THERE MUST BE A BETTER ALTERNATIVE.
I'M ALL EARS.
SKRAAAAK

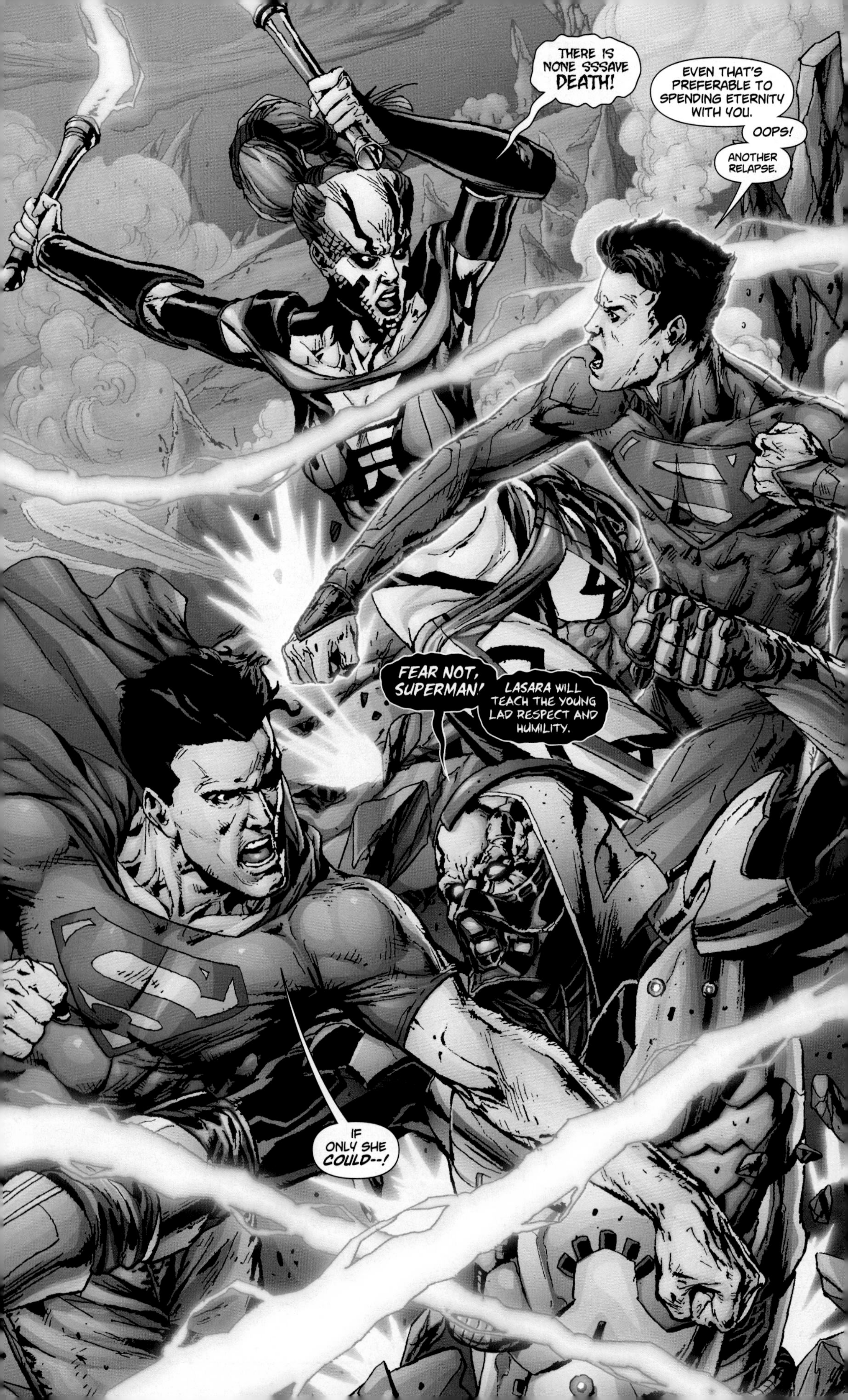
THERE IS NONE SSSAVE DEATH!
EVEN THAT'S PREFERABLE TO SPENDING ETERNITY WITH YOU.
OOPS!
ANOTHER RELAPSE.
FEAR NOT, SUPERMAN!
LASARA WILL TEACH THE YOUNG LAD RESPECT AND HUMILITY.
IF ONLY SHE COULD--!

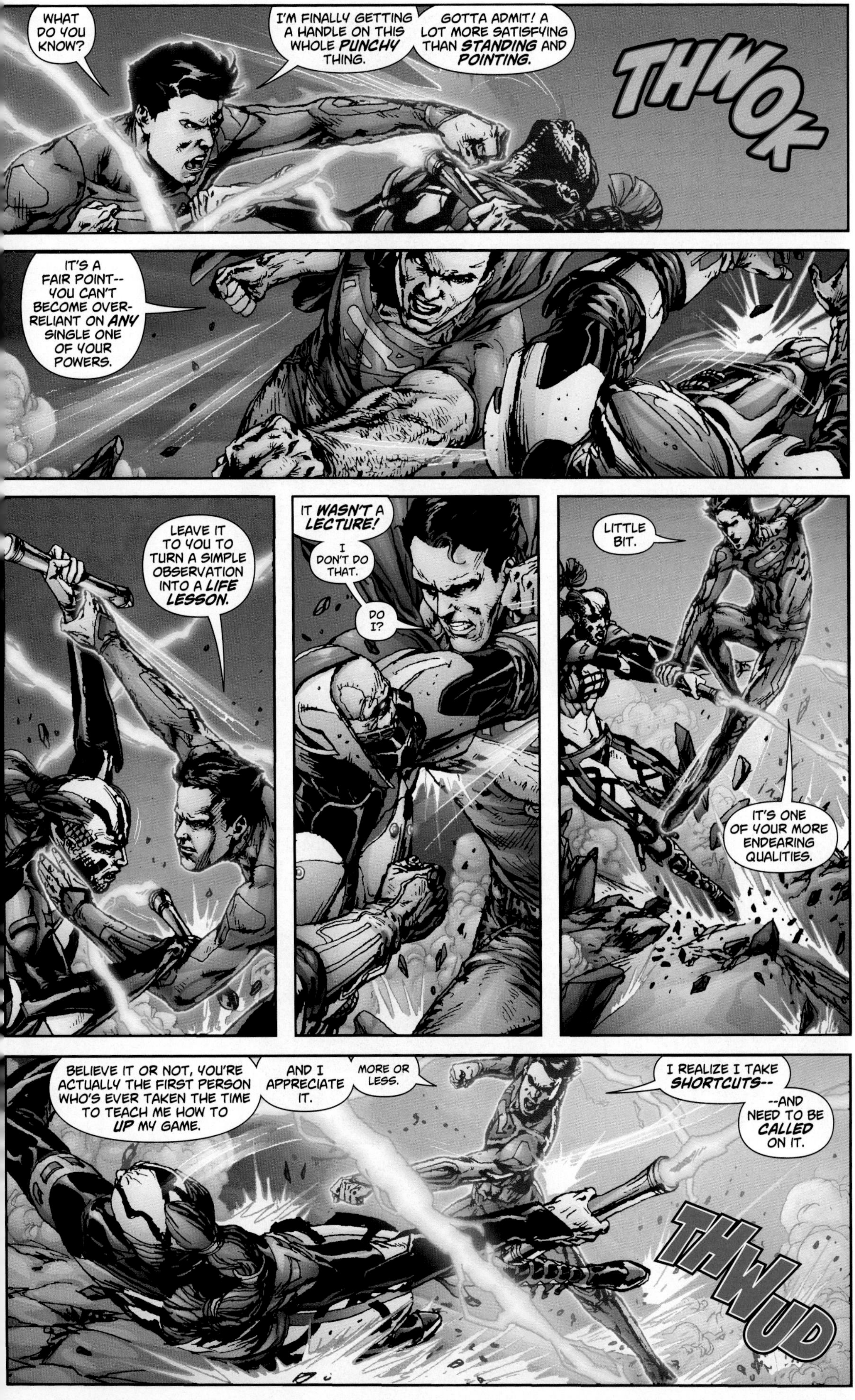
WHAT DO YOU KNOW?
I'M FINALLY GETTING A HANDLE ON THIS WHOLE PUNCHY THING.
GOTTA ADMIT! A LOT MORE SATISFYING THAN STANDING AND POINTING.
THWOK
IT'S A FAIR POINT-- YOU CAN'T BECOME OVER-RELIANT ON ANY SINGLE ONE OF YOUR POWERS.
LEAVE IT TO YOU TO TURN A SIMPLE OBSERVATION INTO A LIFE LESSON.
IT WASN'T A LECTURE!
I DON'T DO THAT.
DO I?
LITTLE BIT.
IT'S ONE OF YOUR MORE ENDEARING QUALITIES.
BELIEVE IT OR NOT, YOU'RE ACTUALLY THE FIRST PERSON WHO'S EVER TAKEN THE TIME TO TEACH ME HOW TO UP MY GAME.
AND I APPRECIATE IT.
MORE OR LESS.
I REALIZE I TAKE SHORTCUTS--
--AND NEED TO BE CALLED ON IT.
THWUD

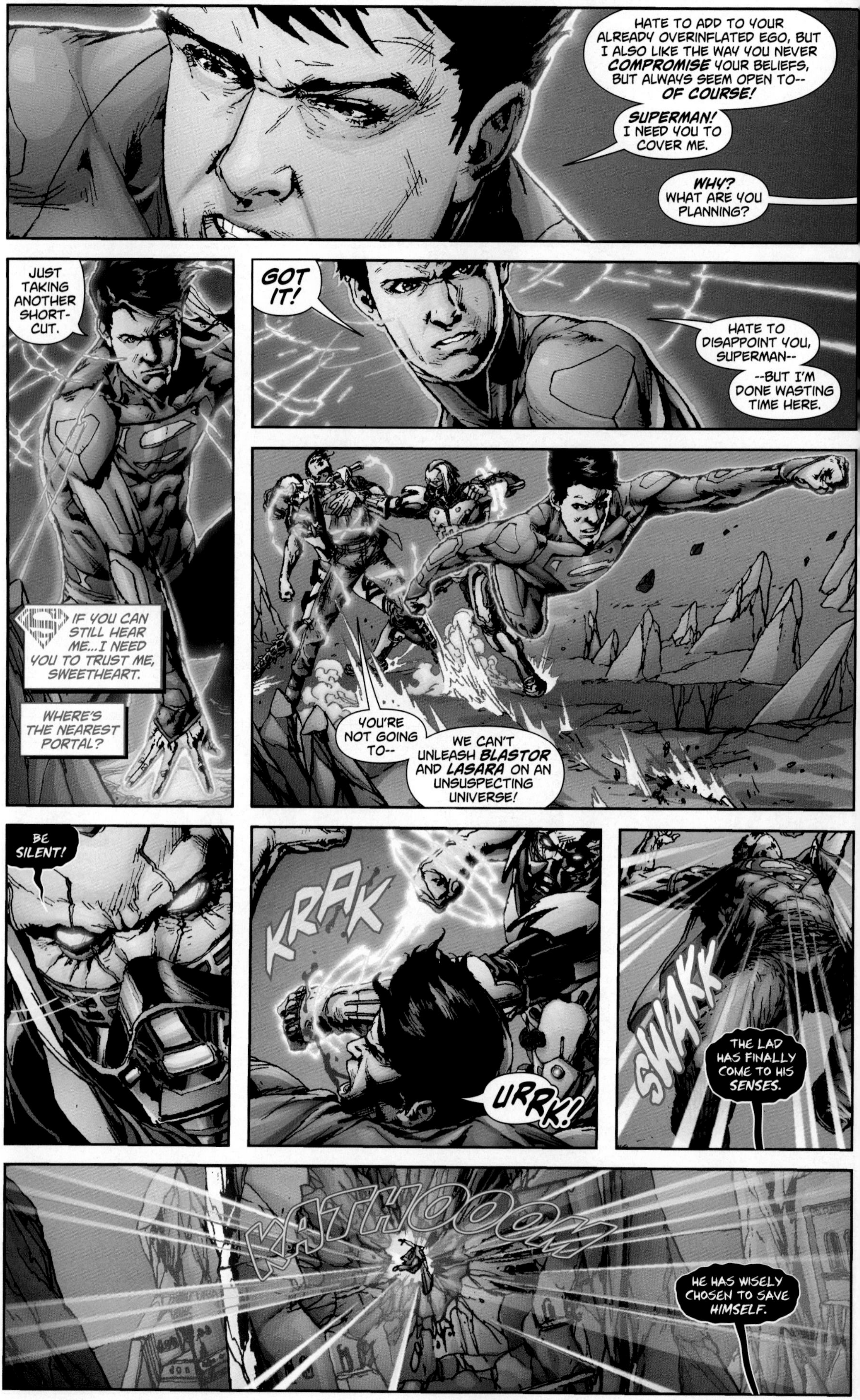

HATE TO ADD TO YOUR ALREADY OVERINFLATED EGO, BUT I ALSO LIKE THE WAY YOU NEVER COMPROMISE YOUR BELIEFS, BUT ALWAYS SEEM OPEN TO-- OF COURSE!
SUPERMAN! I NEED YOU TO COVER ME.
WHY? WHAT ARE YOU PLANNING?
JUST TAKING ANOTHER SHORT-CUT.
IF YOU CAN STILL HEAR ME...I NEED YOU TO TRUST ME, SWEETHEART.
WHERE'S THE NEAREST PORTAL?
GOT IT!
HATE TO DISAPPOINT YOU, SUPERMAN--
--BUT I'M DONE WASTING TIME HERE.
YOU'RE NOT GOING TO--
WE CAN'T UNLEASH BLASTOR AND LASARA ON AN UNSUSPECTING UNIVERSE!
BE SILENT!
KRAK
URRK!
SWAKK
THE LAD HAS FINALLY COME TO HIS SENSES.
KATHOOOM
HE HAS WISELY CHOSEN TO SAVE HIMSELF.

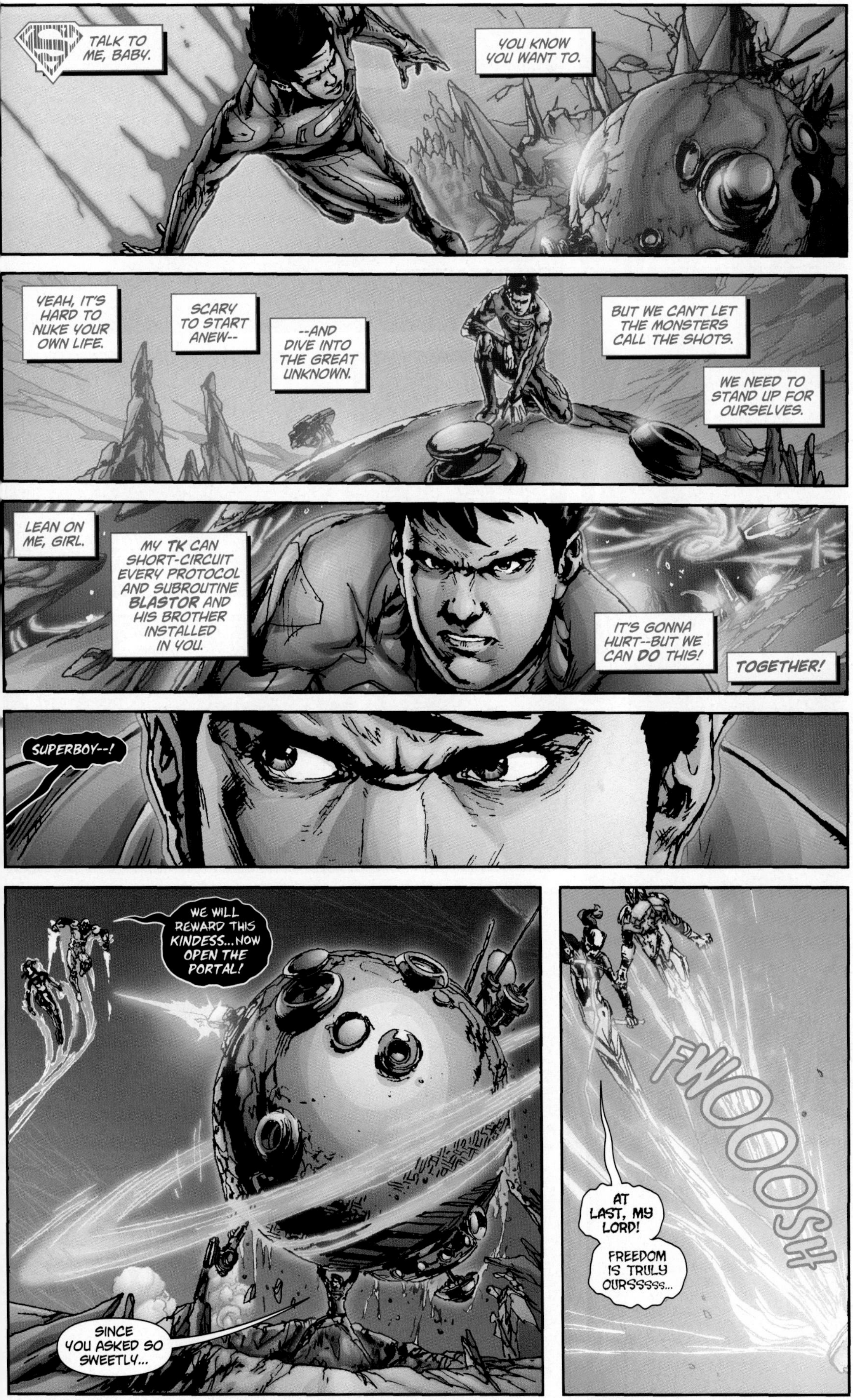
TALK TO ME, BABY.
YOU KNOW YOU WANT TO.
YEAH, IT'S HARD TO NUKE YOUR OWN LIFE.
SCARY TO START ANEW--
--AND DIVE INTO THE GREAT UNKNOWN.
BUT WE CAN'T LET THE MONSTERS CALL THE SHOTS.
WE NEED TO STAND UP FOR OURSELVES.
LEAN ON ME, GIRL.
MY TK CAN SHORT-CIRCUIT EVERY PROTOCOL AND SUBROUTINE BLASTOR AND HIS BROTHER INSTALLED IN YOU.
IT'S GONNA HURT--BUT WE CAN DO THIS!
TOGETHER!
SUPERBOY--!
WE WILL REWARD THIS KINDESS...NOW OPEN THE PORTAL!
SINCE YOU ASKED SO SWEETLY...
FWOOOSH
AT LAST, MY LORD!
FREEDOM IS TRULY OURSSSSS...

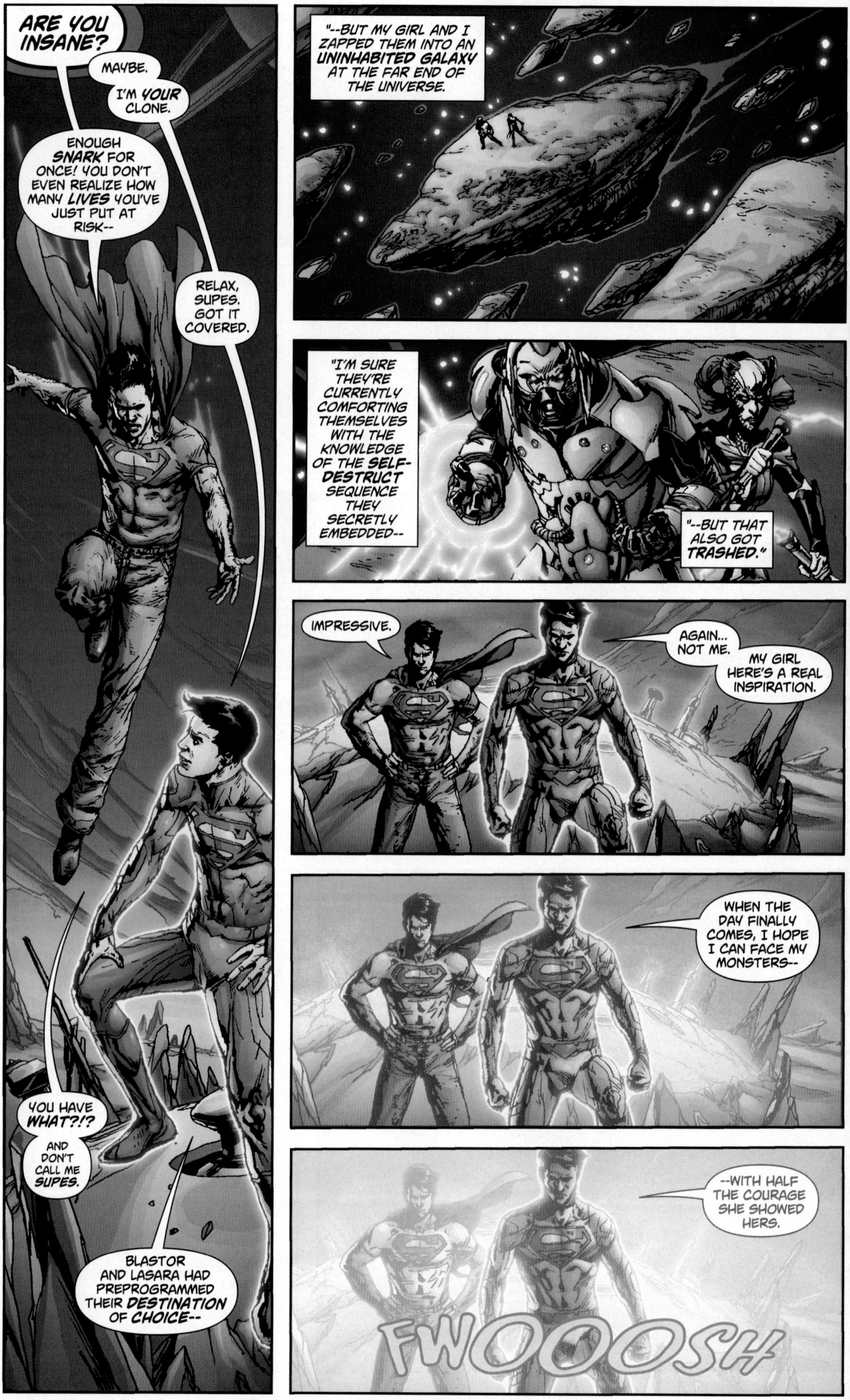
ARE YOU INSANE?
MAYBE.
I'M YOUR CLONE.
ENOUGH SNARK FOR ONCE! YOU DON'T EVEN REALIZE HOW MANY LIVES YOU'VE JUST PUT AT RISK--
RELAX, SUPES. GOT IT COVERED.
YOU HAVE WHAT?!?
AND DON'T CALL ME SUPES.
BLASTOR AND LASARA HAD PREPROGRAMMED THEIR DESTINATION OF CHOICE--
"--BUT MY GIRL AND I ZAPPED THEM INTO AN UNINHABITED GALAXY AT THE FAR END OF THE UNIVERSE.
"I'M SURE THEY'RE CURRENTLY COMFORTING THEMSELVES WITH THE KNOWLEDGE OF THE SELF-DESTRUCT SEQUENCE THEY SECRETLY EMBEDDED--
"--BUT THAT ALSO GOT TRASHED."
IMPRESSIVE.
AGAIN... NOT ME.
MY GIRL HERE'S A REAL INSPIRATION.
WHEN THE DAY FINALLY COMES, I HOPE I CAN FACE MY MONSTERS--
--WITH HALF THE COURAGE SHE SHOWED HERS.
FWOOOSH

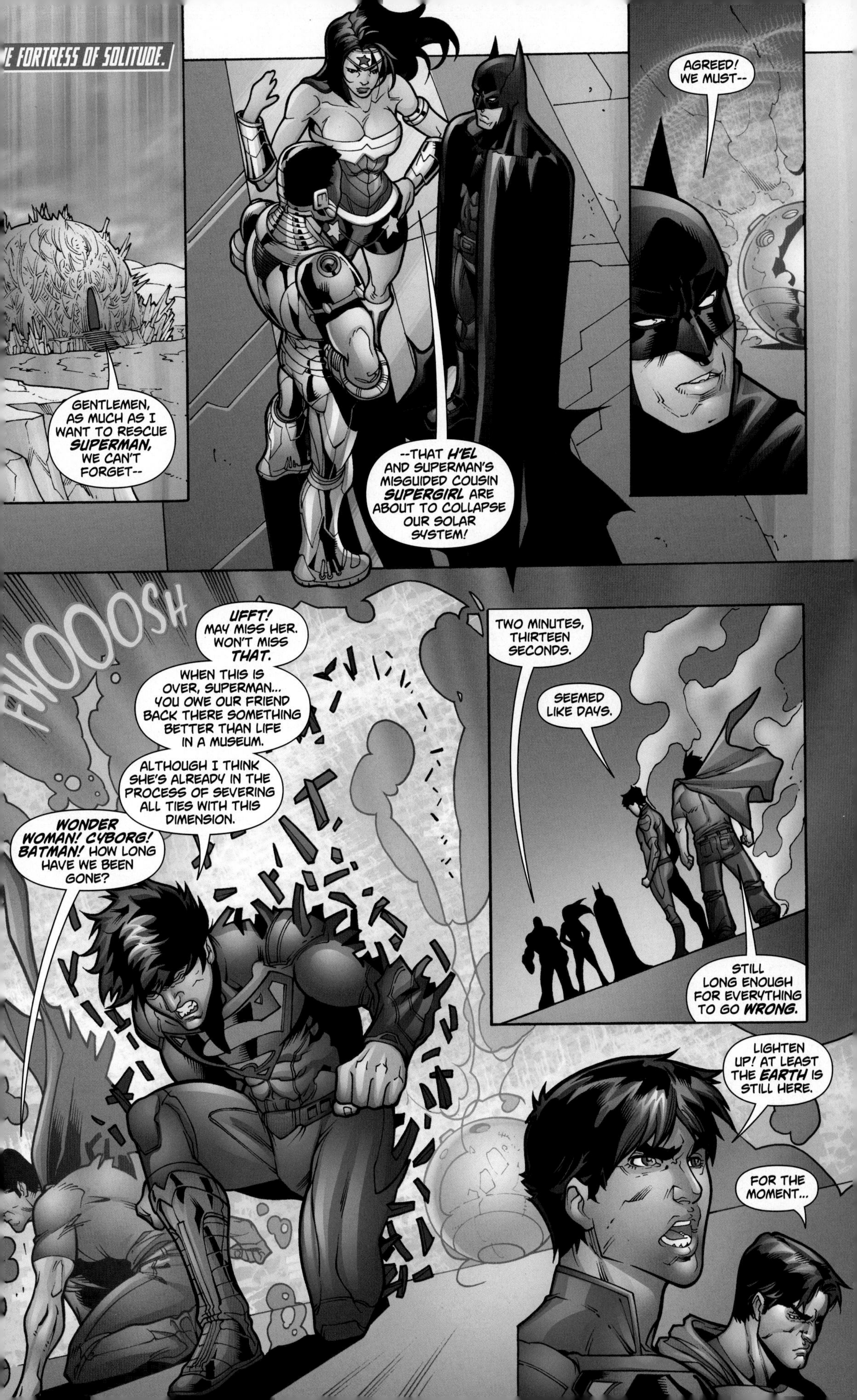

E FORTRESS OF SOLITUDE.
GENTLEMEN, AS MUCH AS I WANT TO RESCUE SUPERMAN, WE CAN'T FORGET--
--THAT H'EL AND SUPERMAN'S MISGUIDED COUSIN SUPERGIRL ARE ABOUT TO COLLAPSE OUR SOLAR SYSTEM!
AGREED! WE MUST--
FWOOOSH
UFFT! MAY MISS HER. WON'T MISS THAT.
WHEN THIS IS OVER, SUPERMAN... YOU OWE OUR FRIEND BACK THERE SOMETHING BETTER THAN LIFE IN A MUSEUM.
ALTHOUGH I THINK SHE'S ALREADY IN THE PROCESS OF SEVERING ALL TIES WITH THIS DIMENSION.
WONDER WOMAN! CYBORG! BATMAN! HOW LONG HAVE WE BEEN GONE?
TWO MINUTES, THIRTEEN SECONDS.
SEEMED LIKE DAYS.
STILL LONG ENOUGH FOR EVERYTHING TO GO WRONG.
LIGHTEN UP! AT LEAST THE EARTH IS STILL HERE.
FOR THE MOMENT...

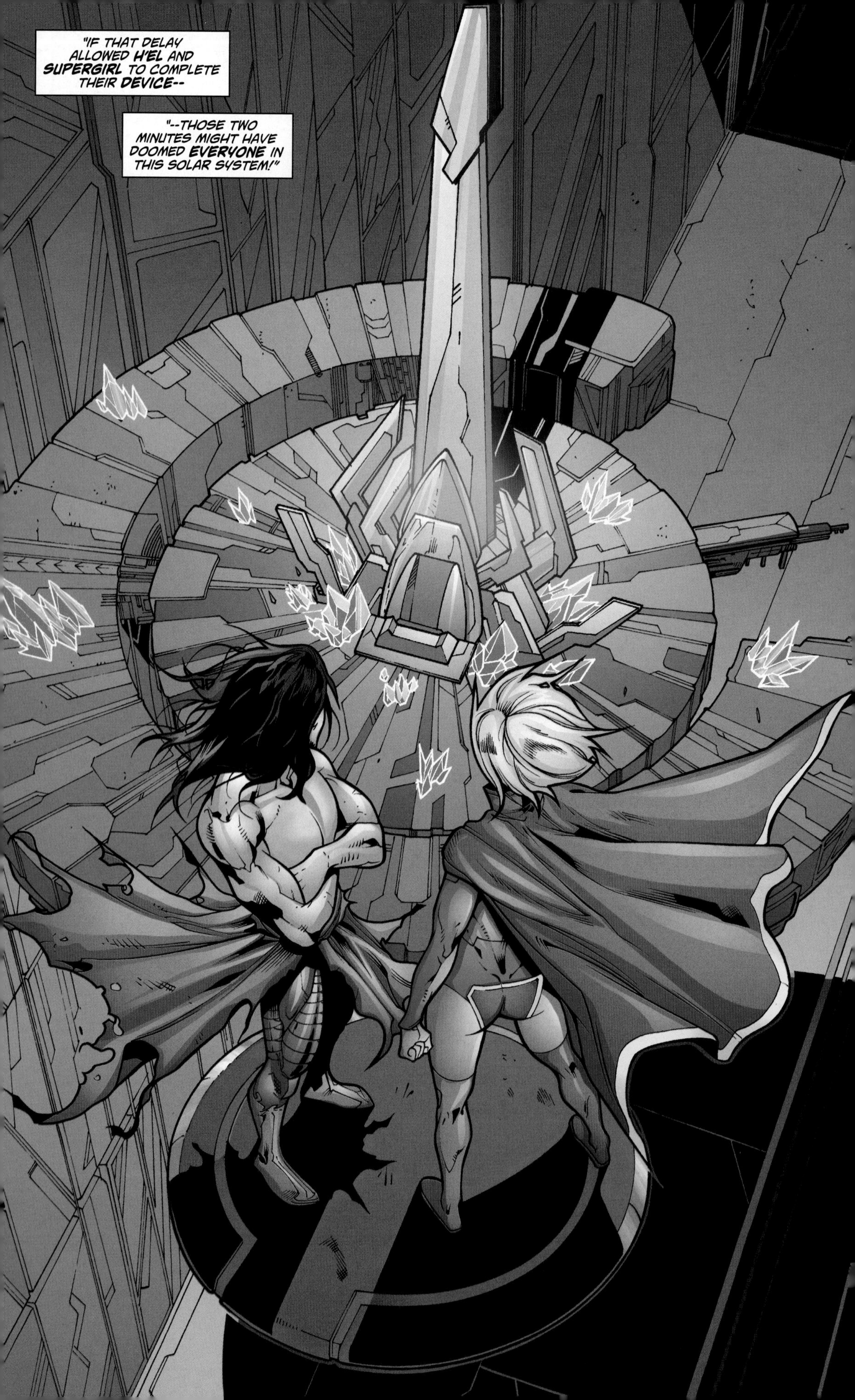
"IF THAT DELAY ALLOWED H'EL AND SUPERGIRL TO COMPLETE THEIR DEVICE--
"--THOSE TWO MINUTES MIGHT HAVE DOOMED EVERYONE IN THIS SOLAR SYSTEM!"

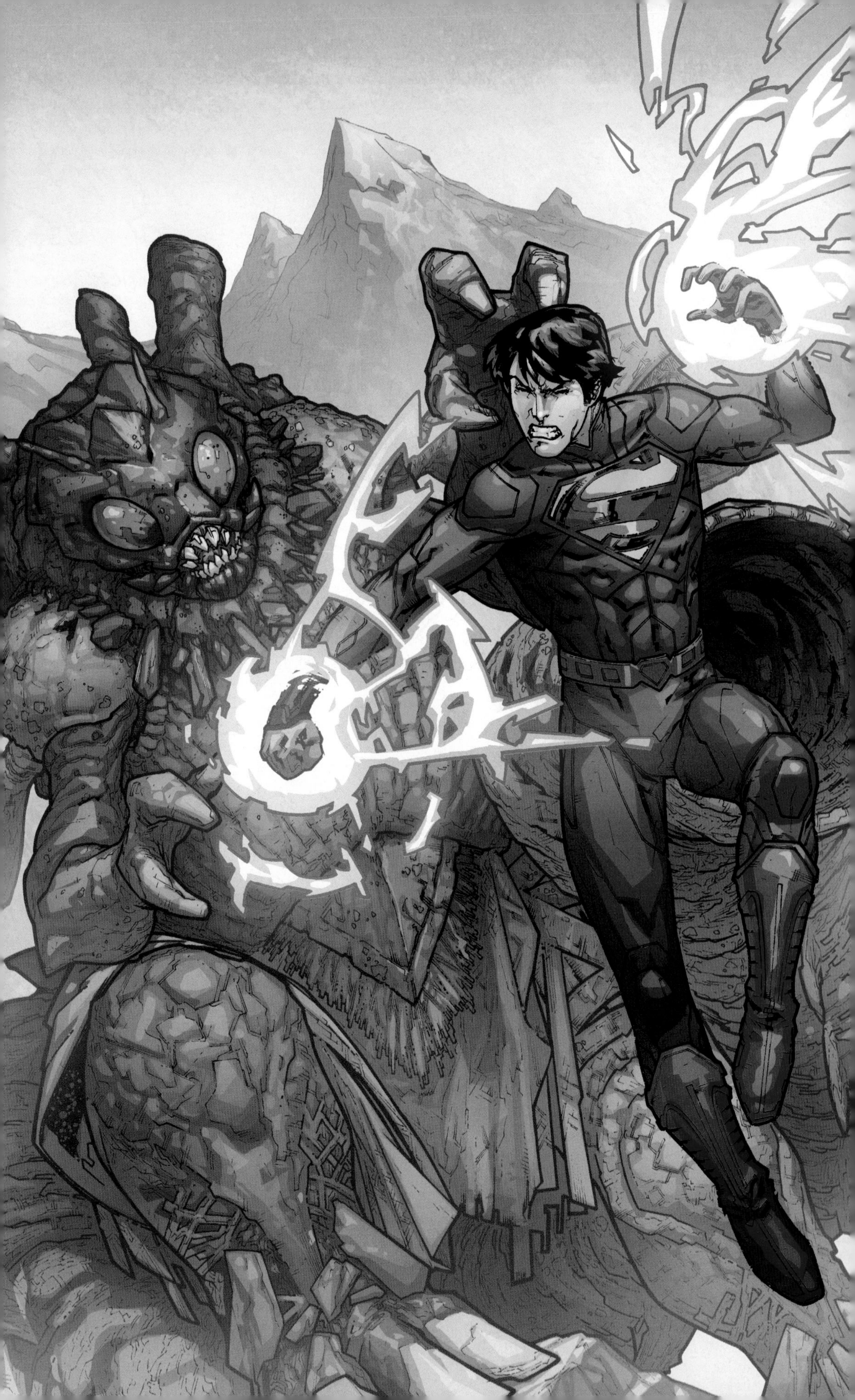

LOST CAUSE!

TOM DeFALCO writer R.B. SILVA penciller ROB LEAN inker cover art by R.B. SILVA & JAVA TARTAGLIA

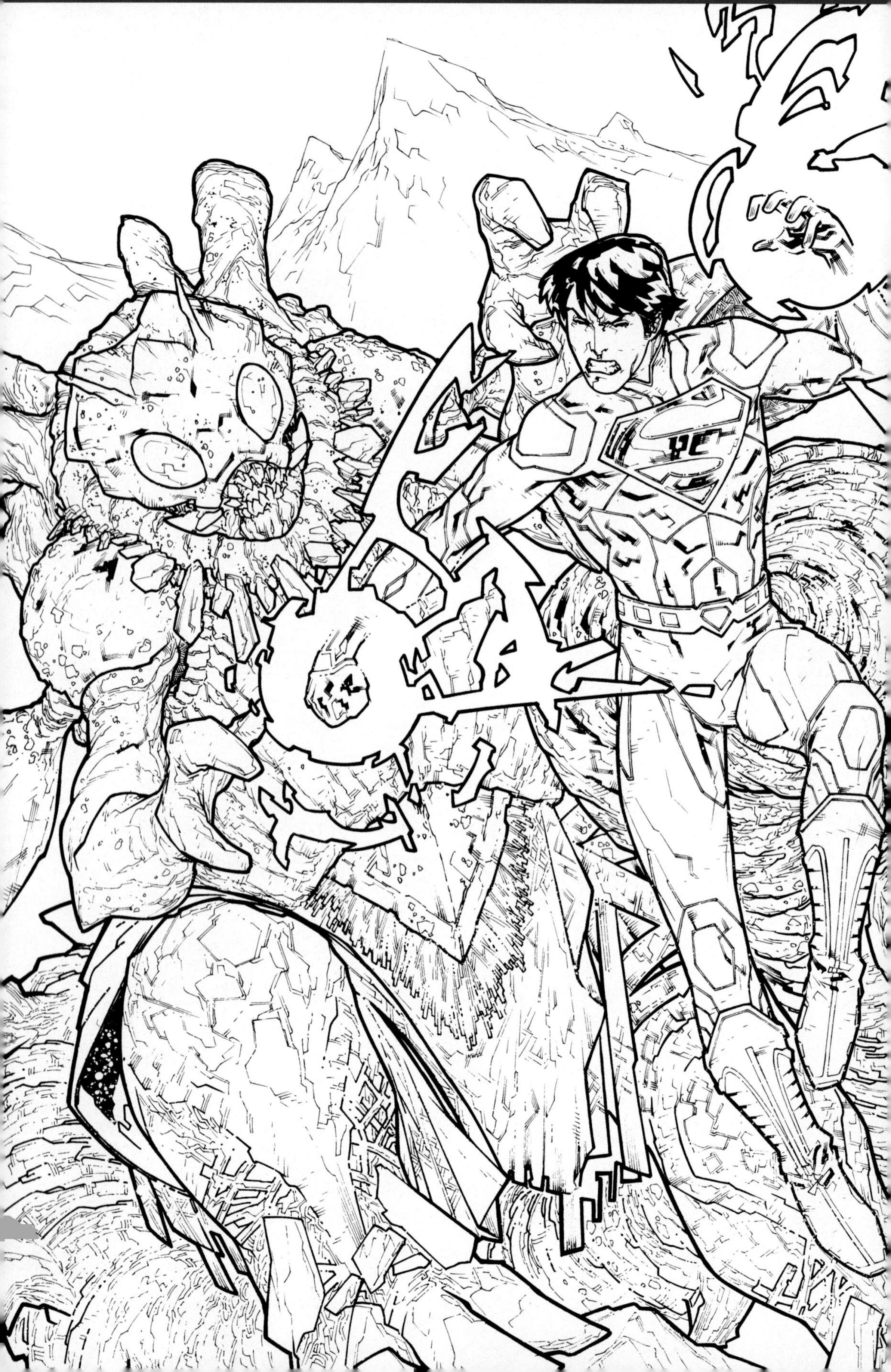

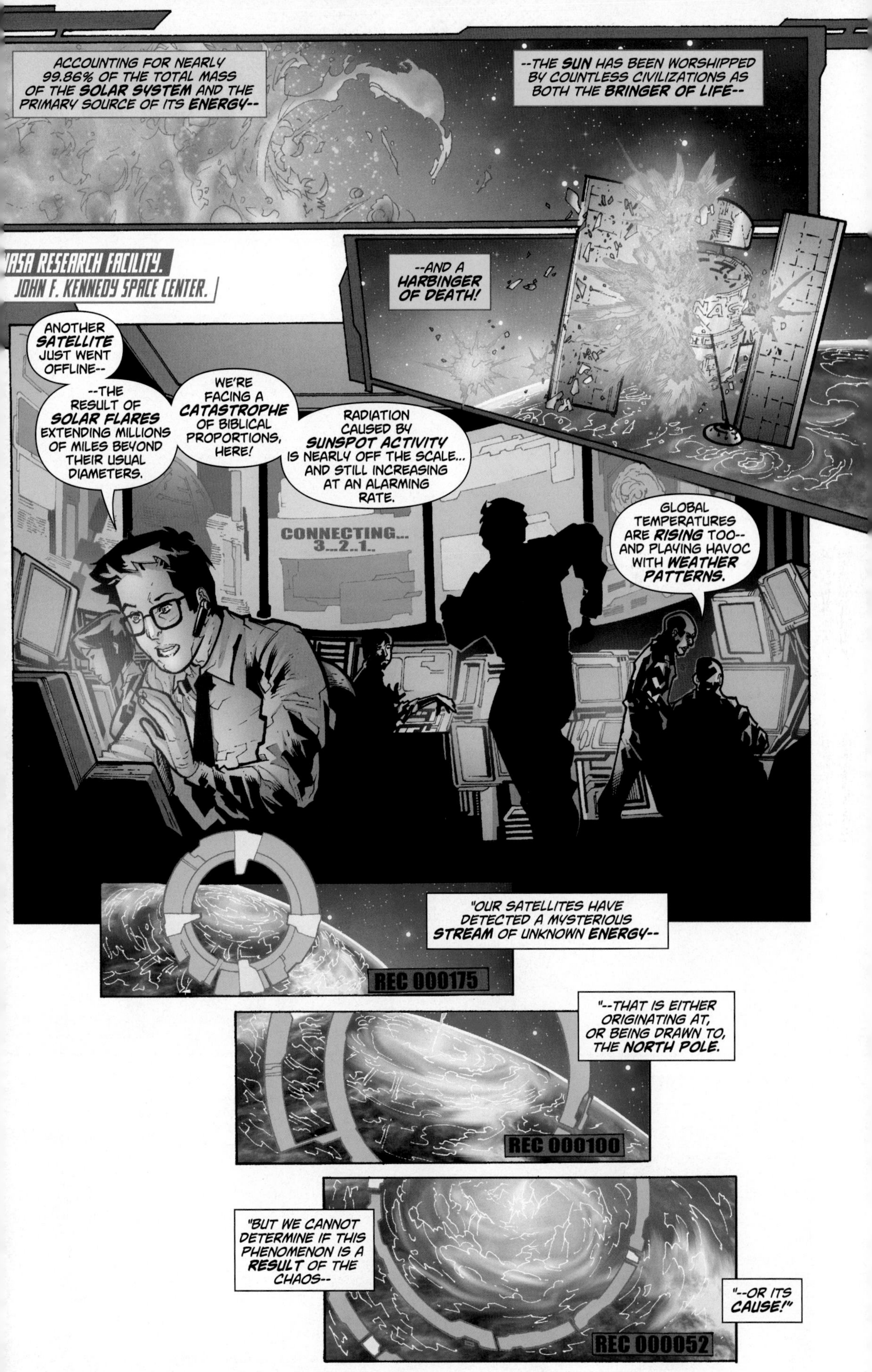
ACCOUNTING FOR NEARLY 99.86% OF THE TOTAL MASS OF THE SOLAR SYSTEM AND THE PRIMARY SOURCE OF ITS ENERGY--
--THE SUN HAS BEEN WORSHIPPED BY COUNTLESS CIVILIZATIONS AS BOTH THE BRINGER OF LIFE--
NASA RESEARCH FACILITY. JOHN F. KENNEDY SPACE CENTER.
--AND A HARBINGER OF DEATH!
ANOTHER SATELLITE JUST WENT OFFLINE--
--THE RESULT OF SOLAR FLARES EXTENDING MILLIONS OF MILES BEYOND THEIR USUAL DIAMETERS.
WE'RE FACING A CATASTROPHE OF BIBLICAL PROPORTIONS, HERE!
RADIATION CAUSED BY SUNSPOT ACTIVITY IS NEARLY OFF THE SCALE... AND STILL INCREASING AT AN ALARMING RATE.
CONNECTING... 3...2...1...
GLOBAL TEMPERATURES ARE RISING TOO--AND PLAYING HAVOC WITH WEATHER PATTERNS.
"OUR SATELLITES HAVE DETECTED A MYSTERIOUS STREAM OF UNKNOWN ENERGY--
REC 000175
"--THAT IS EITHER ORIGINATING AT, OR BEING DRAWN TO, THE NORTH POLE.
REC 000100
"BUT WE CANNOT DETERMINE IF THIS PHENOMENON IS A RESULT OF THE CHAOS--
"--OR ITS CAUSE!"
REC 000052

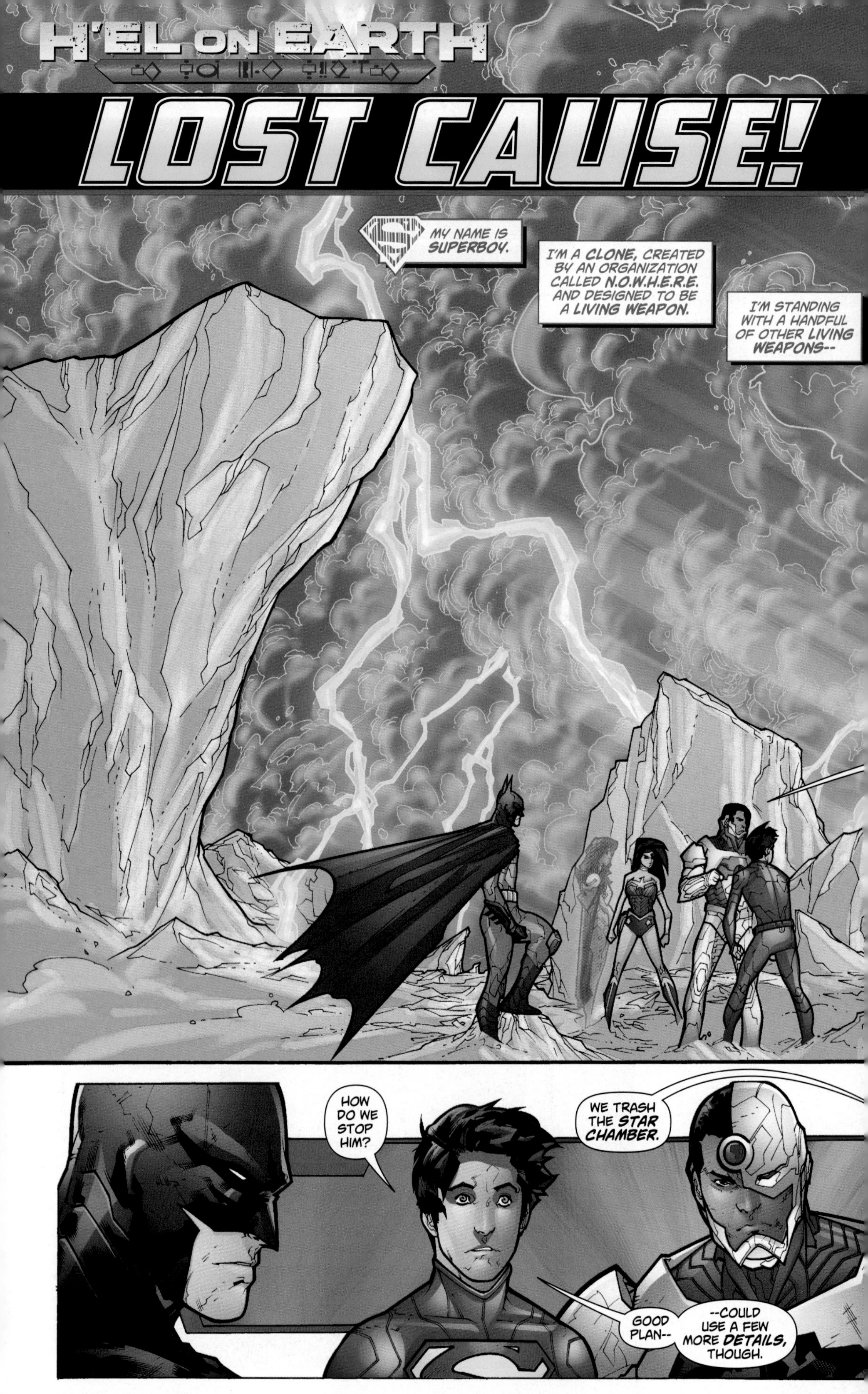
H'EL ON EARTH
LOST CAUSE!
MY NAME IS SUPERBOY.
I'M A CLONE, CREATED BY AN ORGANIZATION CALLED N.O.W.H.E.R.E. AND DESIGNED TO BE A LIVING WEAPON.
I'M STANDING WITH A HANDFUL OF OTHER LIVING WEAPONS--
HOW DO WE STOP HIM?
WE TRASH THE STAR CHAMBER.
GOOD PLAN--
--COULD USE A FEW MORE DETAILS, THOUGH.

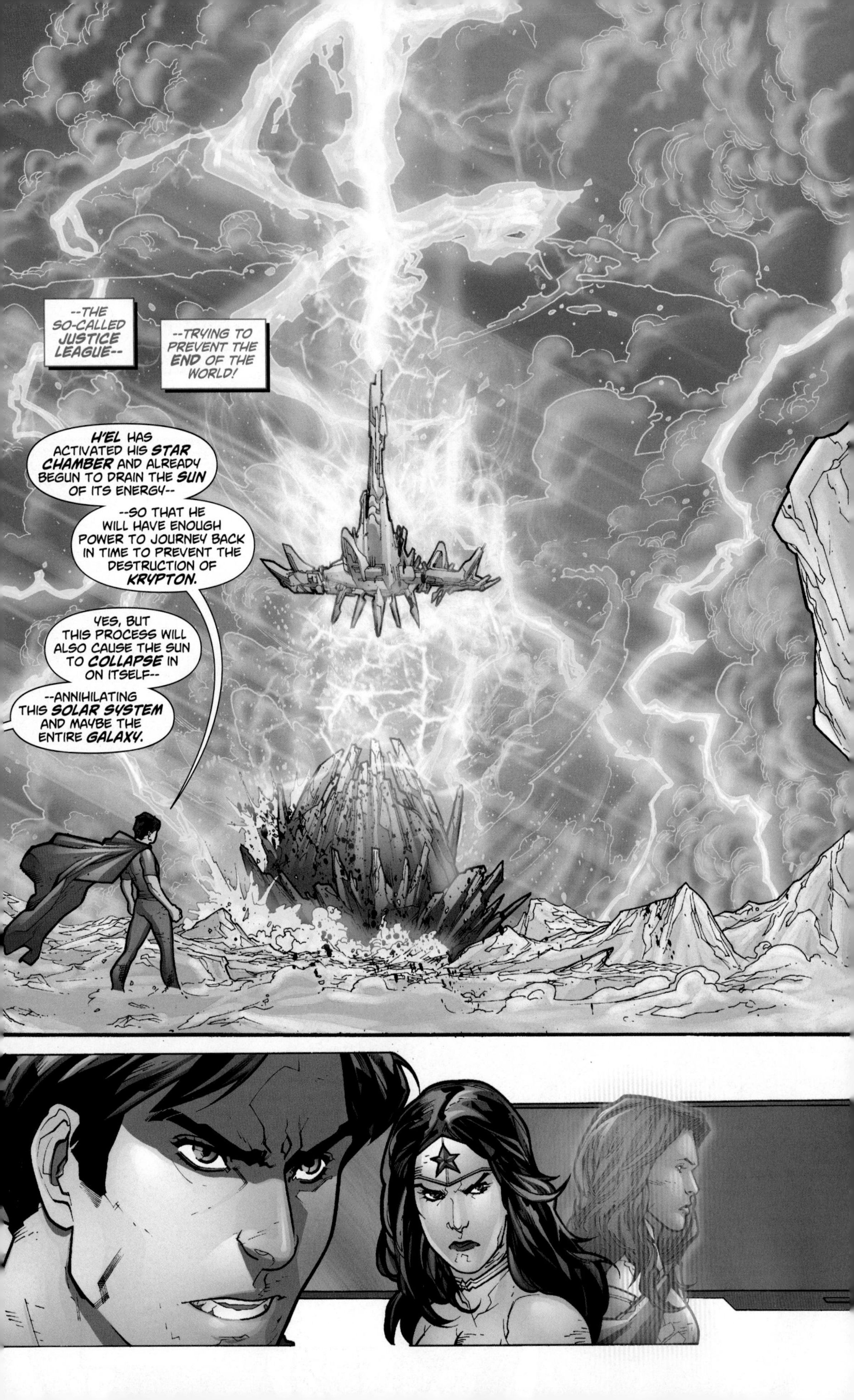
--THE SO-CALLED JUSTICE LEAGUE--
--TRYING TO PREVENT THE END OF THE WORLD!
H'EL HAS ACTIVATED HIS STAR CHAMBER AND ALREADY BEGUN TO DRAIN THE SUN OF ITS ENERGY--
--SO THAT HE WILL HAVE ENOUGH POWER TO JOURNEY BACK IN TIME TO PREVENT THE DESTRUCTION OF KRYPTON.
YES, BUT THIS PROCESS WILL ALSO CAUSE THE SUN TO COLLAPSE IN ON ITSELF--
--ANNIHILATING THIS SOLAR SYSTEM AND MAYBE THE ENTIRE GALAXY.

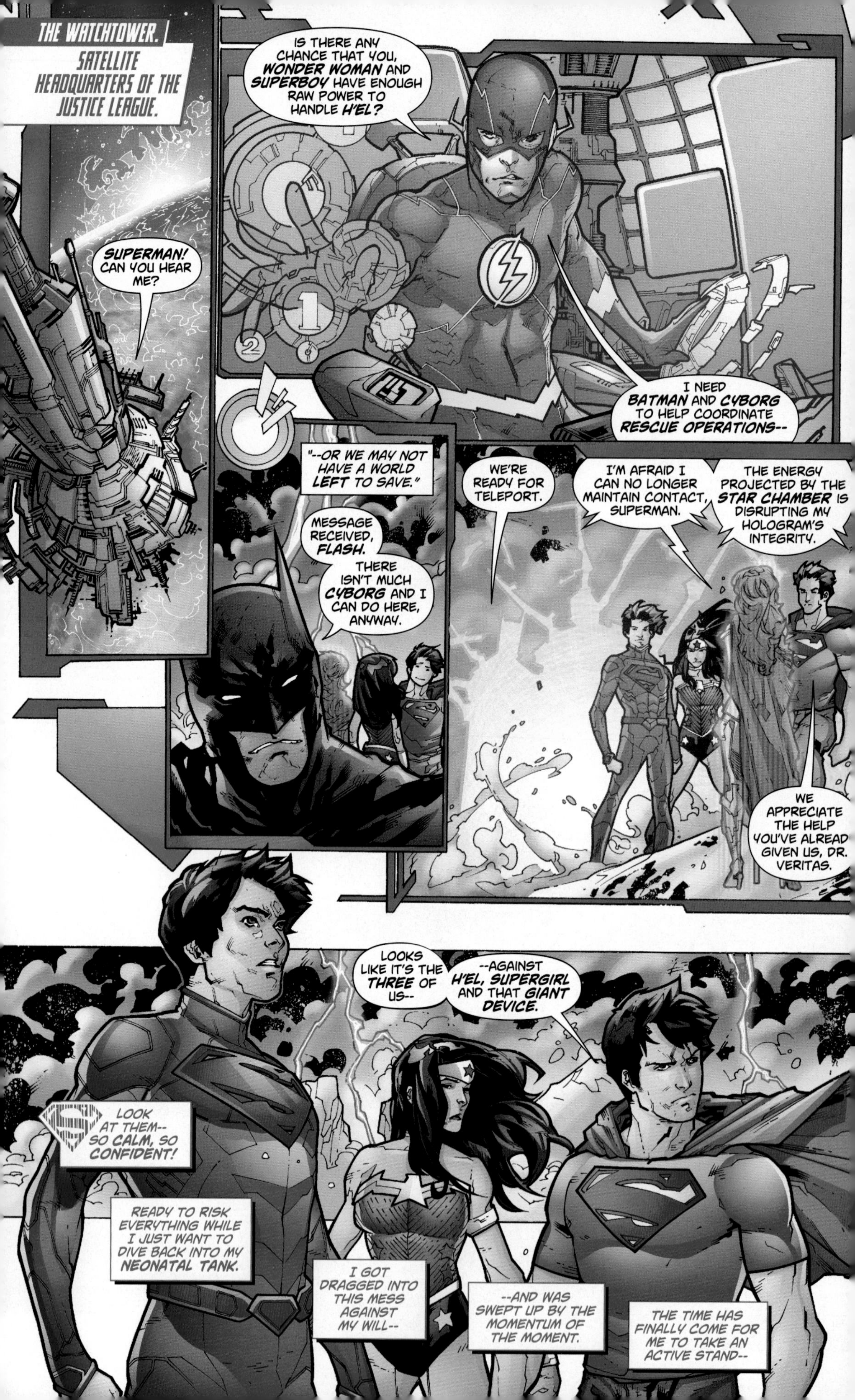
THE WATCHTOWER.
SATELLITE HEADQUARTERS OF THE JUSTICE LEAGUE.
SUPERMAN! CAN YOU HEAR ME?
IS THERE ANY CHANCE THAT YOU, WONDER WOMAN AND SUPERBOY HAVE ENOUGH RAW POWER TO HANDLE H'EL?
I NEED BATMAN AND CYBORG TO HELP COORDINATE RESCUE OPERATIONS--
"--OR WE MAY NOT HAVE A WORLD LEFT TO SAVE."
MESSAGE RECEIVED, FLASH.
THERE ISN'T MUCH CYBORG AND I CAN DO HERE, ANYWAY.
WE'RE READY FOR TELEPORT.
I'M AFRAID I CAN NO LONGER MAINTAIN CONTACT, SUPERMAN.
THE ENERGY PROJECTED BY THE STAR CHAMBER IS DISRUPTING MY HOLOGRAM'S INTEGRITY.
WE APPRECIATE THE HELP YOU'VE ALREAD GIVEN US, DR. VERITAS.
LOOKS LIKE IT'S THE THREE OF US--
--AGAINST H'EL, SUPERGIRL AND THAT GIANT DEVICE.
LOOK AT THEM-- SO CALM, SO CONFIDENT!
READY TO RISK EVERYTHING WHILE I JUST WANT TO DIVE BACK INTO MY NEONATAL TANK.
I GOT DRAGGED INTO THIS MESS AGAINST MY WILL--
--AND WAS SWEPT UP BY THE MOMENTUM OF THE MOMENT.
THE TIME HAS FINALLY COME FOR ME TO TAKE AN ACTIVE STAND--

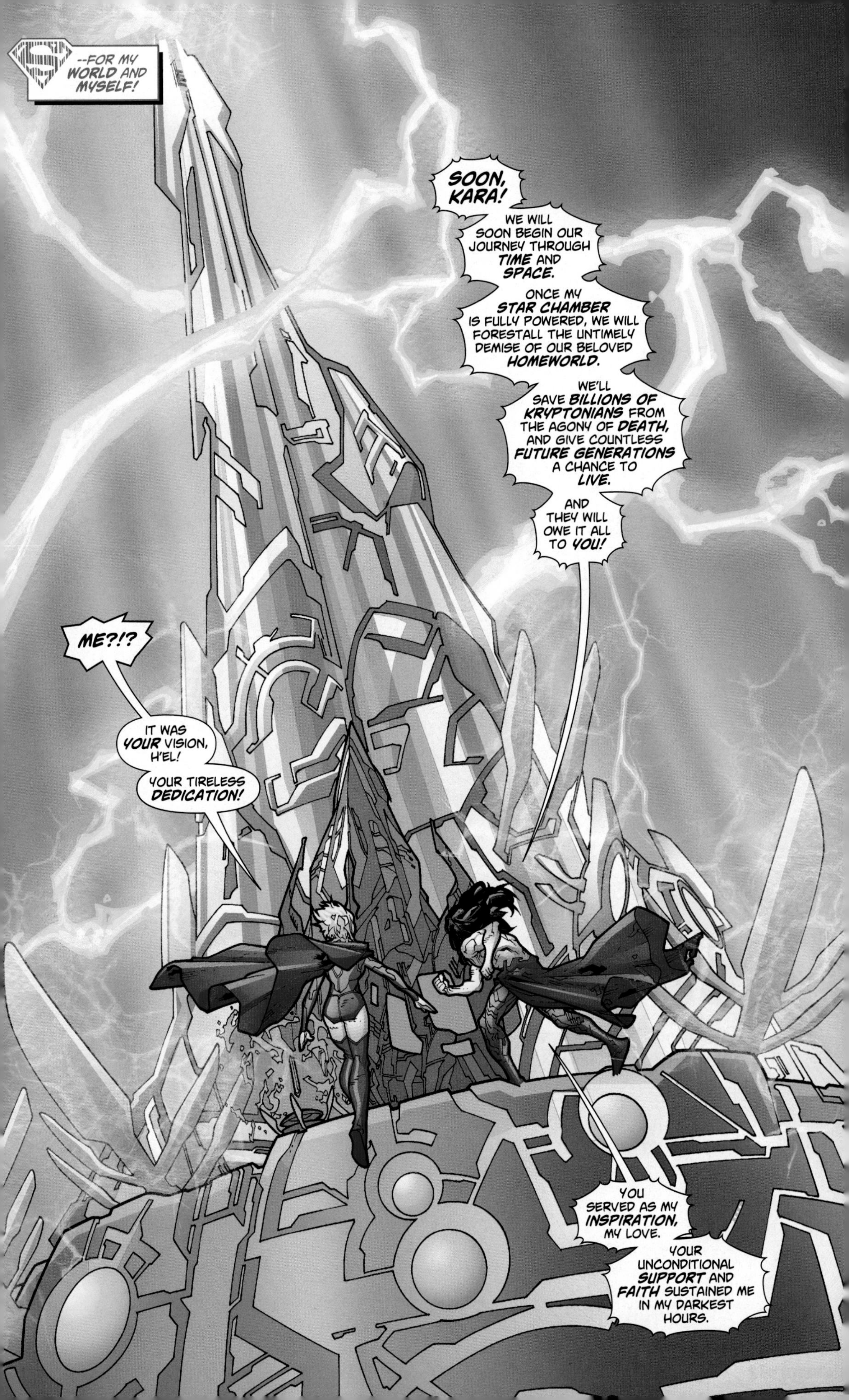
--FOR MY WORLD AND MYSELF!
SOON, KARA!
WE WILL SOON BEGIN OUR JOURNEY THROUGH TIME AND SPACE.
ONCE MY STAR CHAMBER IS FULLY POWERED, WE WILL FORESTALL THE UNTIMELY DEMISE OF OUR BELOVED HOMEWORLD.
WE'LL SAVE BILLIONS OF KRYPTONIANS FROM THE AGONY OF DEATH, AND GIVE COUNTLESS FUTURE GENERATIONS A CHANCE TO LIVE.
AND THEY WILL OWE IT ALL TO YOU!
ME?!?
IT WAS YOUR VISION, H'EL!
YOUR TIRELESS DEDICATION!
YOU SERVED AS MY INSPIRATION, MY LOVE.
YOUR UNCONDITIONAL SUPPORT AND FAITH SUSTAINED ME IN MY DARKEST HOURS.

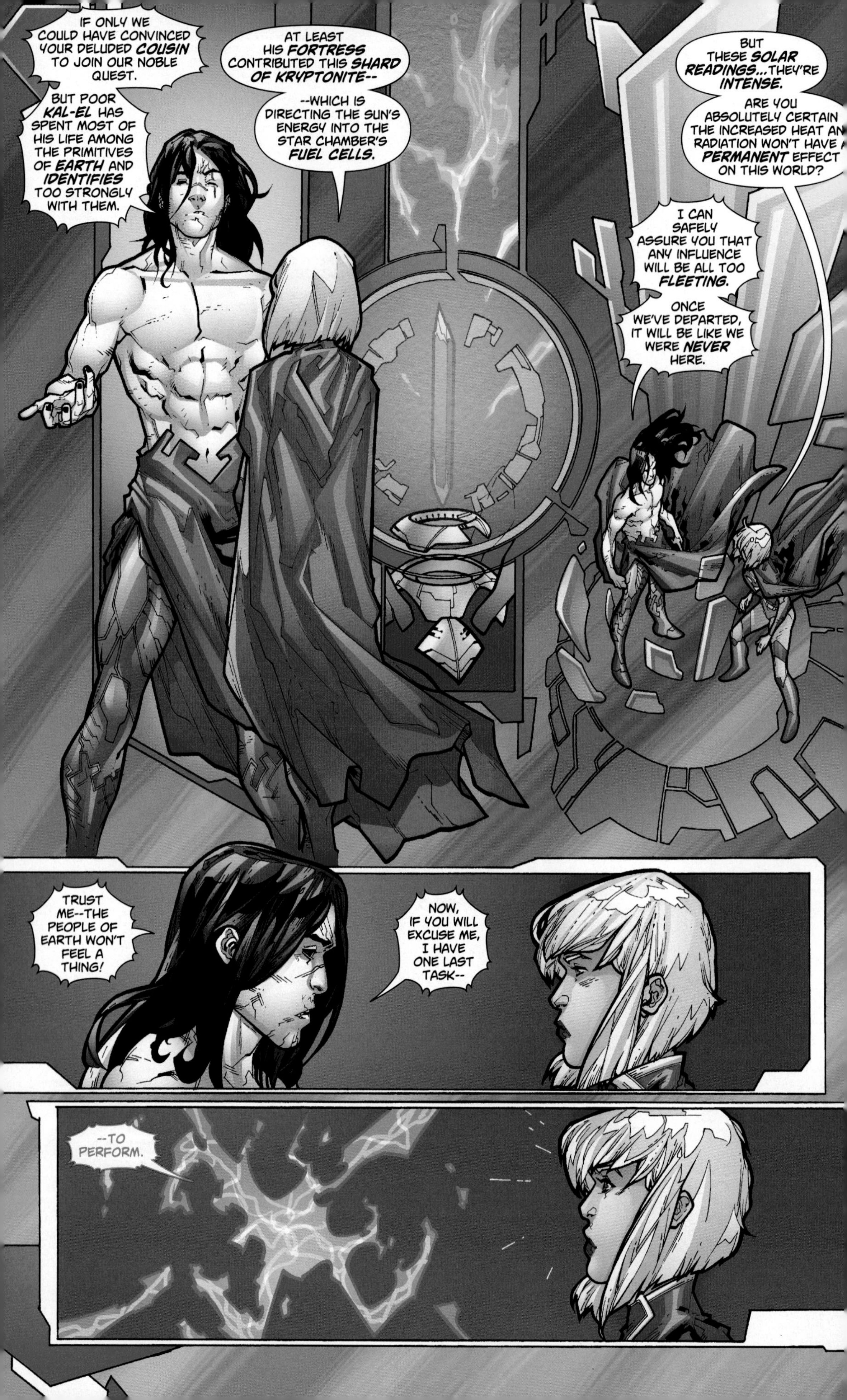
IF ONLY WE COULD HAVE CONVINCED YOUR DELUDED COUSIN TO JOIN OUR NOBLE QUEST.
BUT POOR KAL-EL HAS SPENT MOST OF HIS LIFE AMONG THE PRIMITIVES OF EARTH AND IDENTIFIES TOO STRONGLY WITH THEM.
AT LEAST HIS FORTRESS CONTRIBUTED THIS SHARD OF KRYPTONITE--
--WHICH IS DIRECTING THE SUN'S ENERGY INTO THE STAR CHAMBER'S FUEL CELLS.
BUT THESE SOLAR READINGS...THEY'RE INTENSE.
ARE YOU ABSOLUTELY CERTAIN THE INCREASED HEAT AN RADIATION WON'T HAVE PERMANENT EFFECT ON THIS WORLD?
I CAN SAFELY ASSURE YOU THAT ANY INFLUENCE WILL BE ALL TOO FLEETING.
ONCE WE'VE DEPARTED, IT WILL BE LIKE WE WERE NEVER HERE.
TRUST ME--THE PEOPLE OF EARTH WON'T FEEL A THING!
NOW, IF YOU WILL EXCUSE ME, I HAVE ONE LAST TASK--
--TO PERFORM.

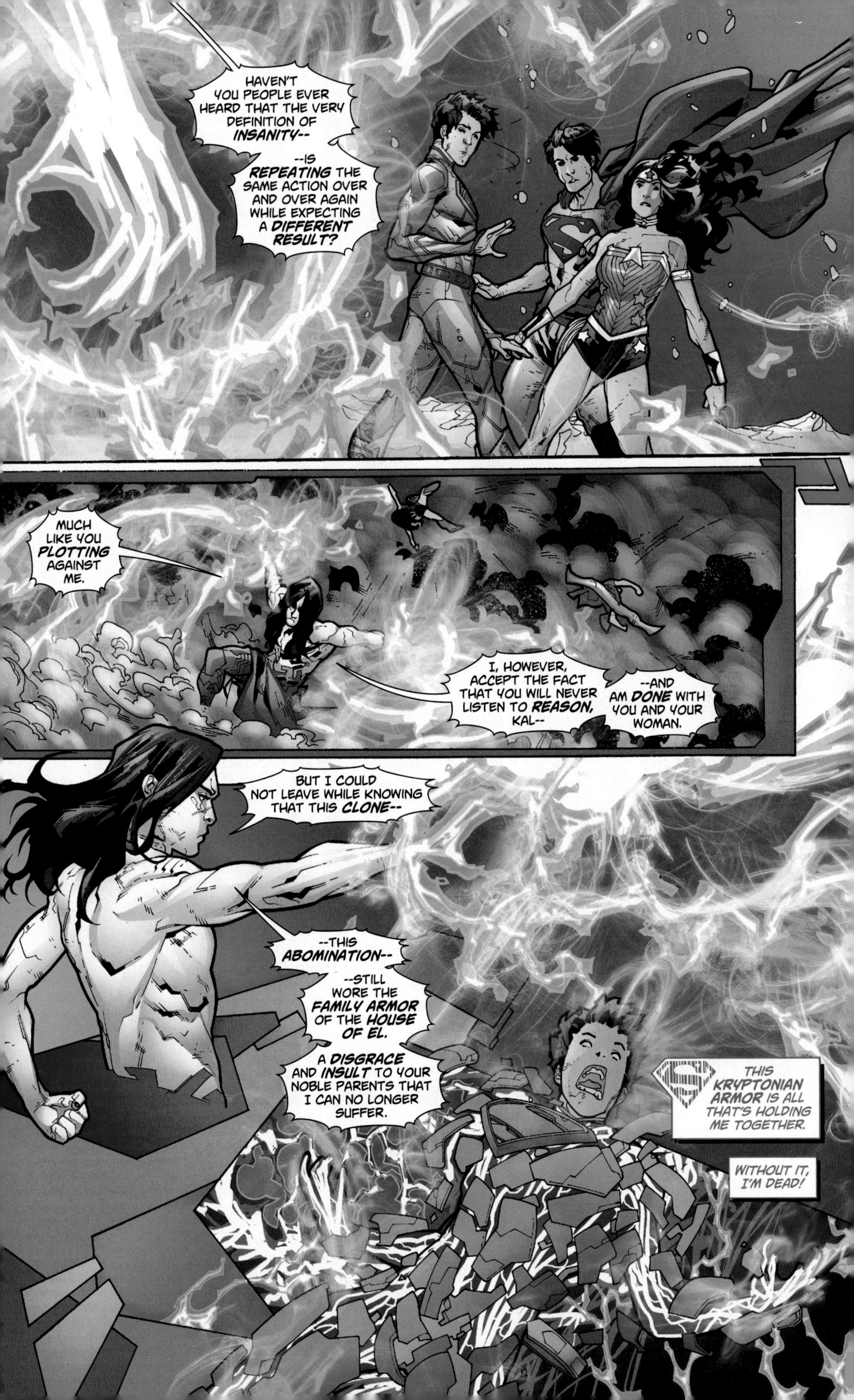
HAVEN'T YOU PEOPLE EVER HEARD THAT THE VERY DEFINITION OF INSANITY--
--IS REPEATING THE SAME ACTION OVER AND OVER AGAIN WHILE EXPECTING A DIFFERENT RESULT?
MUCH LIKE YOU PLOTTING AGAINST ME.
I, HOWEVER, ACCEPT THE FACT THAT YOU WILL NEVER LISTEN TO REASON, KAL--
--AND AM DONE WITH YOU AND YOUR WOMAN.
BUT I COULD NOT LEAVE WHILE KNOWING THAT THIS CLONE--
--THIS ABOMINATION--
--STILL WORE THE FAMILY ARMOR OF THE HOUSE OF EL.
A DISGRACE AND INSULT TO YOUR NOBLE PARENTS THAT I CAN NO LONGER SUFFER.
THIS KRYPTONIAN ARMOR IS ALL THAT'S HOLDING ME TOGETHER.
WITHOUT IT, I'M DEAD!

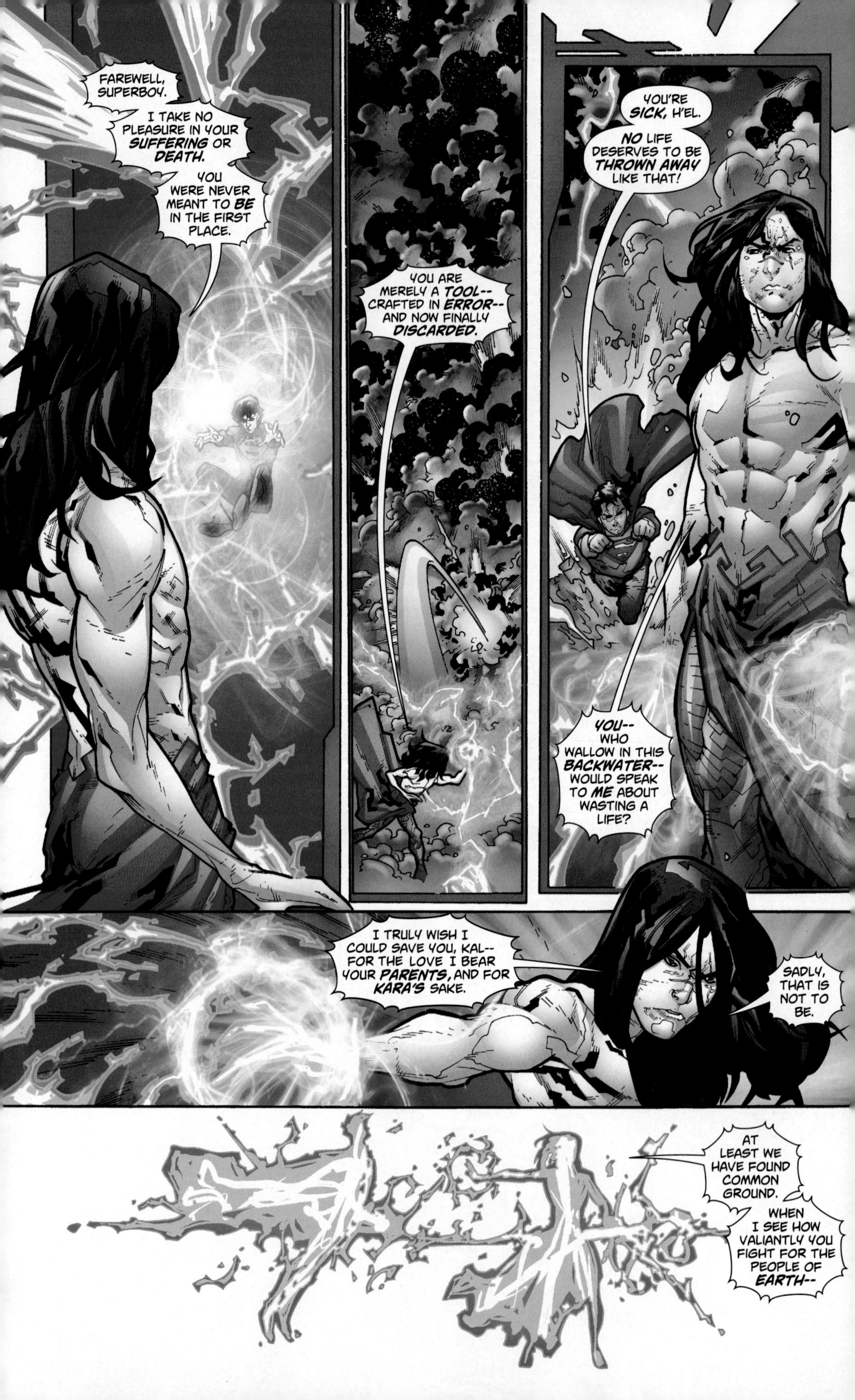
FAREWELL, SUPERBOY.
I TAKE NO PLEASURE IN YOUR SUFFERING OR DEATH.
YOU WERE NEVER MEANT TO BE IN THE FIRST PLACE.
YOU ARE MERELY A TOOL--CRAFTED IN ERROR--AND NOW FINALLY DISCARDED.
YOU'RE SICK, H'EL.
NO LIFE DESERVES TO BE THROWN AWAY LIKE THAT!
YOU--WHO WALLOW IN THIS BACKWATER--WOULD SPEAK TO ME ABOUT WASTING A LIFE?
I TRULY WISH I COULD SAVE YOU, KAL--FOR THE LOVE I BEAR YOUR PARENTS, AND FOR KARA'S SAKE.
SADLY, THAT IS NOT TO BE.
AT LEAST WE HAVE FOUND COMMON GROUND.
WHEN I SEE HOW VALIANTLY YOU FIGHT FOR THE PEOPLE OF EARTH--

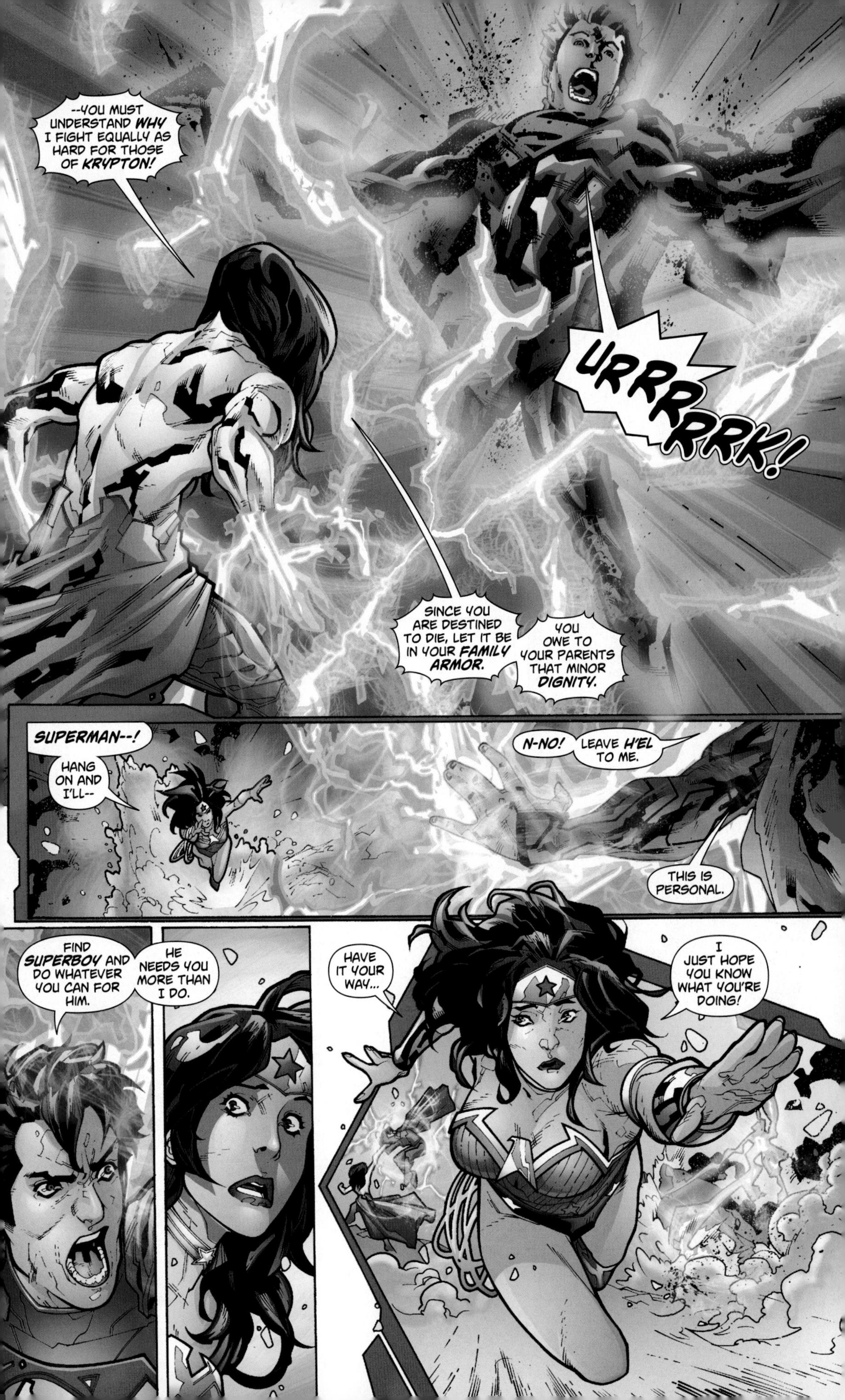
--YOU MUST UNDERSTAND WHY I FIGHT EQUALLY AS HARD FOR THOSE OF KRYPTON!
URRRRRK!
SINCE YOU ARE DESTINED TO DIE, LET IT BE IN YOUR FAMILY ARMOR.
YOU OWE TO YOUR PARENTS THAT MINOR DIGNITY.
SUPERMAN--!
HANG ON AND I'LL--
N-NO!
LEAVE H'EL TO ME.
THIS IS PERSONAL.
FIND SUPERBOY AND DO WHATEVER YOU CAN FOR HIM.
HE NEEDS YOU MORE THAN I DO.
HAVE IT YOUR WAY...
I JUST HOPE YOU KNOW WHAT YOU'RE DOING!

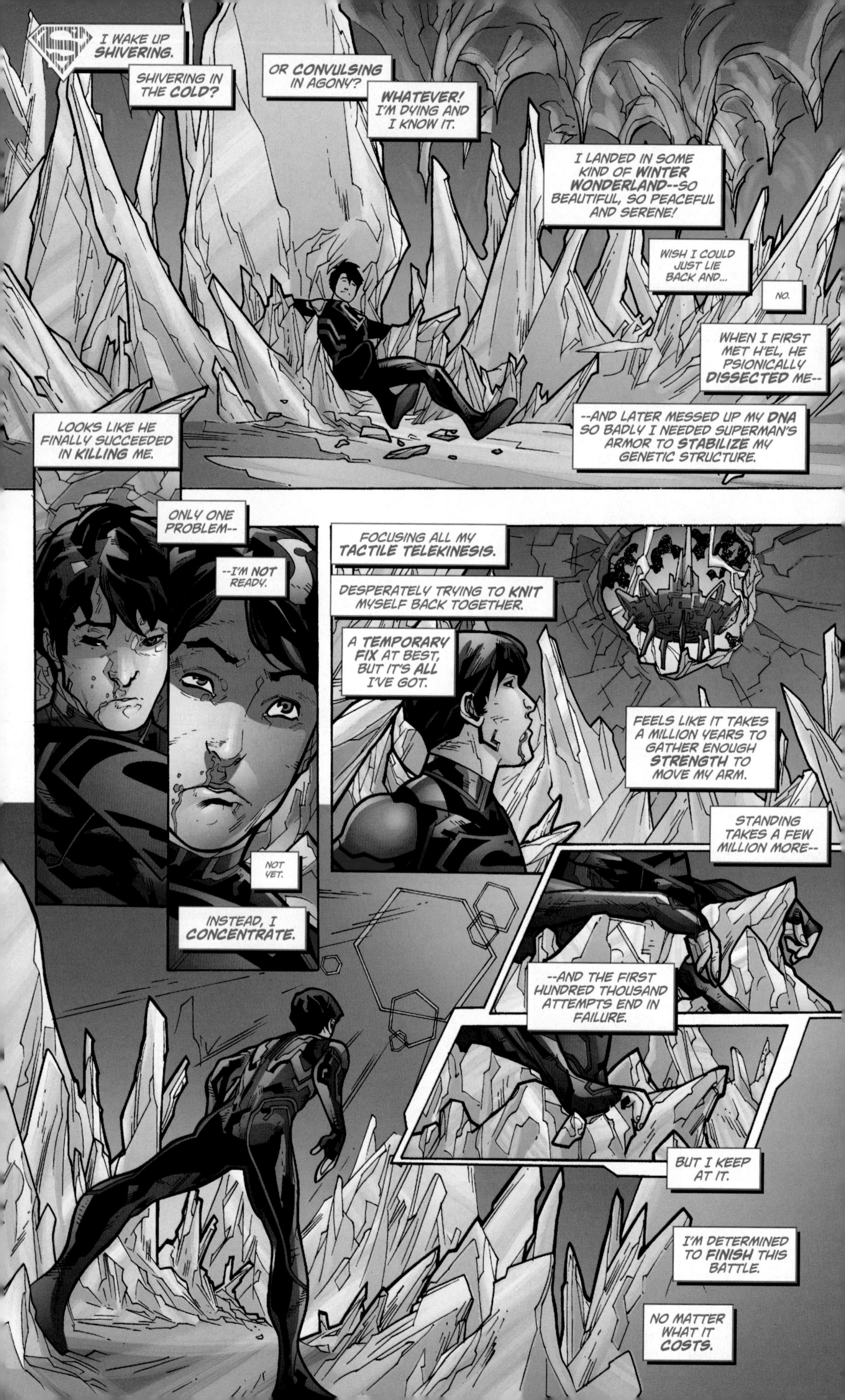

I WAKE UP SHIVERING.
SHIVERING IN THE COLD?
OR CONVULSING IN AGONY?
WHATEVER! I'M DYING AND I KNOW IT.
I LANDED IN SOME KIND OF WINTER WONDERLAND--SO BEAUTIFUL, SO PEACEFUL AND SERENE!
WISH I COULD JUST LIE BACK AND...
NO.
WHEN I FIRST MET H'EL, HE PSIONICALLY DISSECTED ME--
--AND LATER MESSED UP MY DNA SO BADLY I NEEDED SUPERMAN'S ARMOR TO STABILIZE MY GENETIC STRUCTURE.
LOOKS LIKE HE FINALLY SUCCEEDED IN KILLING ME.
ONLY ONE PROBLEM--
--I'M NOT READY.
NOT YET.
INSTEAD, I CONCENTRATE.
FOCUSING ALL MY TACTILE TELEKINESIS.
DESPERATELY TRYING TO KNIT MYSELF BACK TOGETHER.
A TEMPORARY FIX AT BEST, BUT IT'S ALL I'VE GOT.
FEELS LIKE IT TAKES A MILLION YEARS TO GATHER ENOUGH STRENGTH TO MOVE MY ARM.
STANDING TAKES A FEW MILLION MORE--
--AND THE FIRST HUNDRED THOUSAND ATTEMPTS END IN FAILURE.
BUT I KEEP AT IT.
I'M DETERMINED TO FINISH THIS BATTLE.
NO MATTER WHAT IT COSTS.

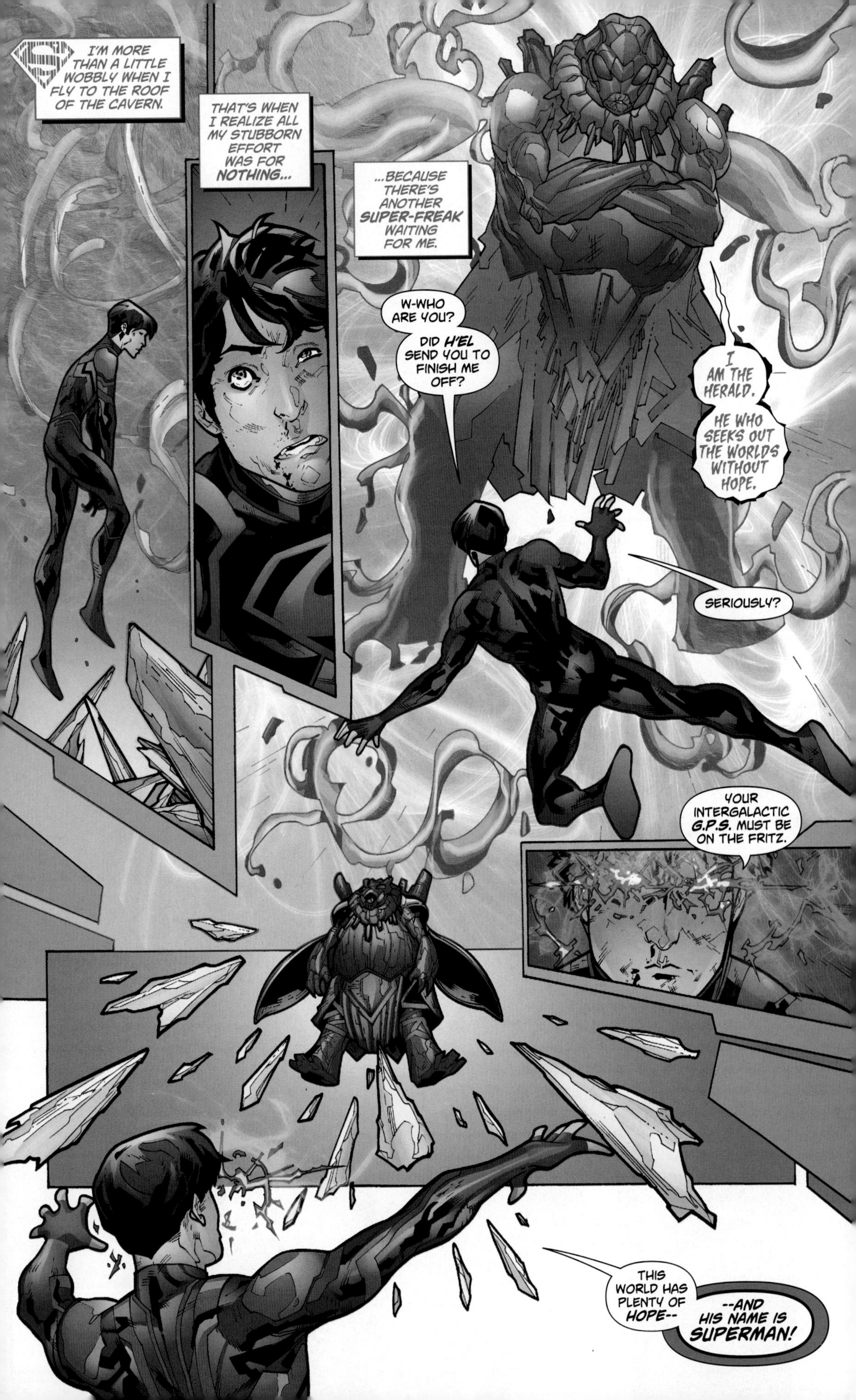
I'M MORE THAN A LITTLE WOBBLY WHEN I FLY TO THE ROOF OF THE CAVERN.
THAT'S WHEN I REALIZE ALL MY STUBBORN EFFORT WAS FOR NOTHING...
...BECAUSE THERE'S ANOTHER SUPER-FREAK WAITING FOR ME.
W-WHO ARE YOU?
DID H'EL SEND YOU TO FINISH ME OFF?
I AM THE HERALD.
HE WHO SEEKS OUT THE WORLDS WITHOUT HOPE.
SERIOUSLY?
YOUR INTERGALACTIC G.P.S. MUST BE ON THE FRITZ.
THIS WORLD HAS PLENTY OF HOPE--
--AND HIS NAME IS SUPERMAN!

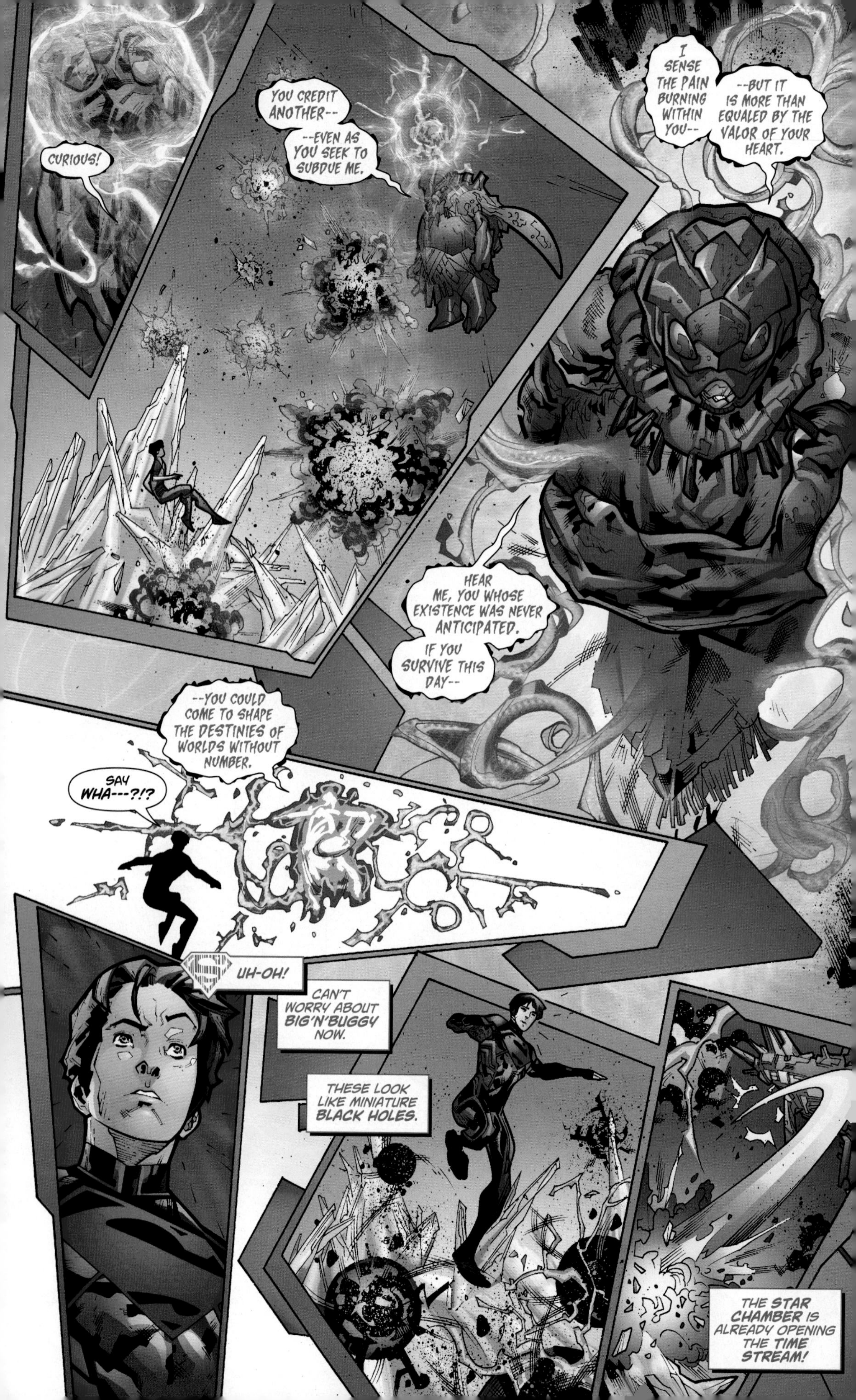
CURIOUS!
YOU CREDIT ANOTHER--
--EVEN AS YOU SEEK TO SUBDUE ME.
I SENSE THE PAIN BURNING WITHIN YOU--
--BUT IT IS MORE THAN EQUALED BY THE VALOR OF YOUR HEART.
HEAR ME, YOU WHOSE EXISTENCE WAS NEVER ANTICIPATED.
IF YOU SURVIVE THIS DAY--
--YOU COULD COME TO SHAPE THE DESTINIES OF WORLDS WITHOUT NUMBER.
SAY WHA---?!?
UH-OH!
CAN'T WORRY ABOUT BIG'N'BUGGY NOW.
THESE LOOK LIKE MINIATURE BLACK HOLES.
THE STAR CHAMBER IS ALREADY OPENING THE TIME STREAM!

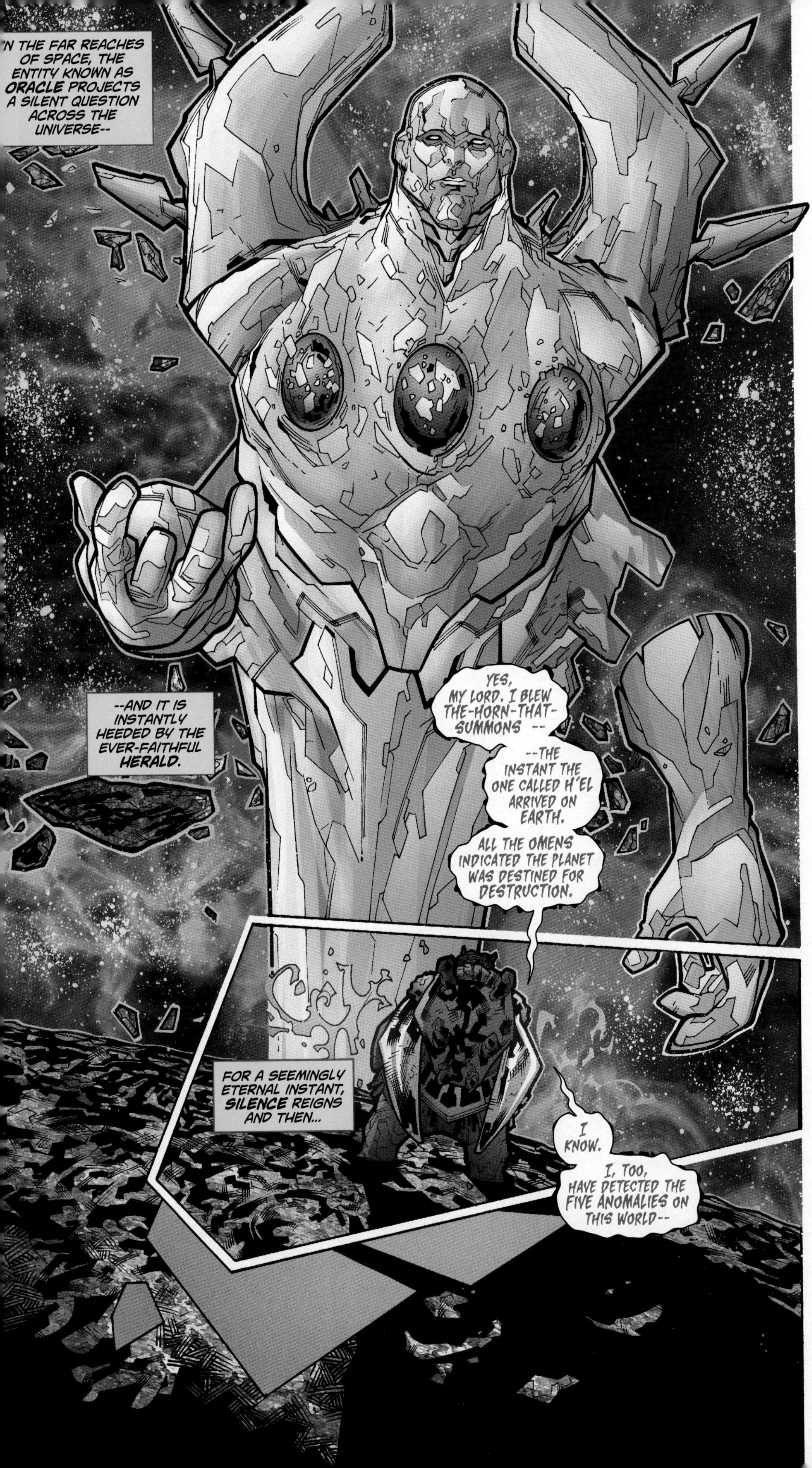
'N THE FAR REACHES OF SPACE, THE ENTITY KNOWN AS ORACLE PROJECTS A SILENT QUESTION ACROSS THE UNIVERSE--
--AND IT IS INSTANTLY HEEDED BY THE EVER-FAITHFUL HERALD.
YES, MY LORD. I BLEW THE-HORN-THAT-SUMMONS --
--THE INSTANT THE ONE CALLED H'EL ARRIVED ON EARTH.
ALL THE OMENS INDICATED THE PLANET WAS DESTINED FOR DESTRUCTION.
FOR A SEEMINGLY ETERNAL INSTANT, SILENCE REIGNS AND THEN...
I KNOW.
I, TOO, HAVE DETECTED THE FIVE ANOMALIES ON THIS WORLD--

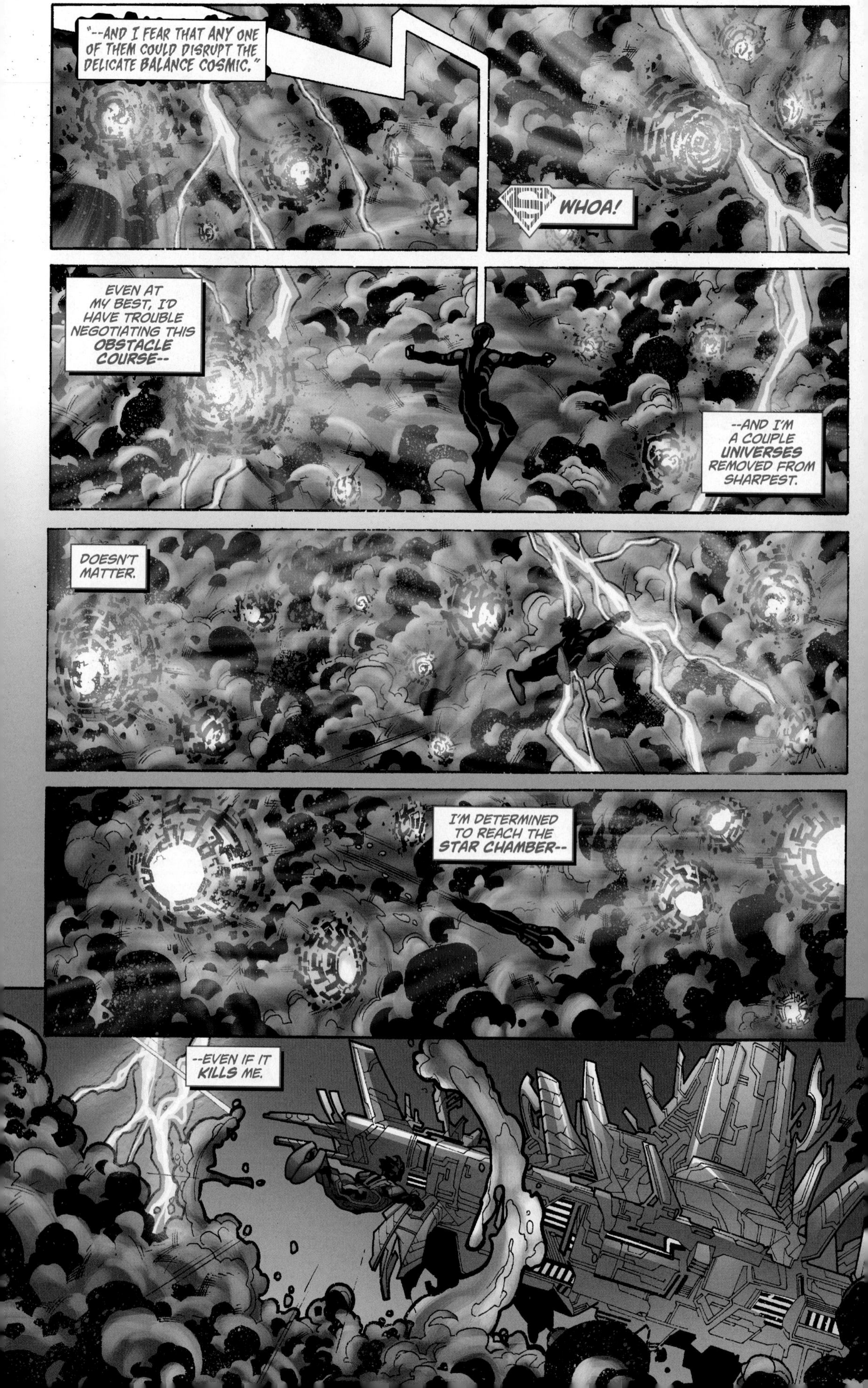
"--AND I FEAR THAT ANY ONE OF THEM COULD DISRUPT THE DELICATE BALANCE COSMIC."
WHOA!
EVEN AT MY BEST, I'D HAVE TROUBLE NEGOTIATING THIS OBSTACLE COURSE--
--AND I'M A COUPLE UNIVERSES REMOVED FROM SHARPEST.
DOESN'T MATTER.
I'M DETERMINED TO REACH THE STAR CHAMBER--
--EVEN IF IT KILLS ME.

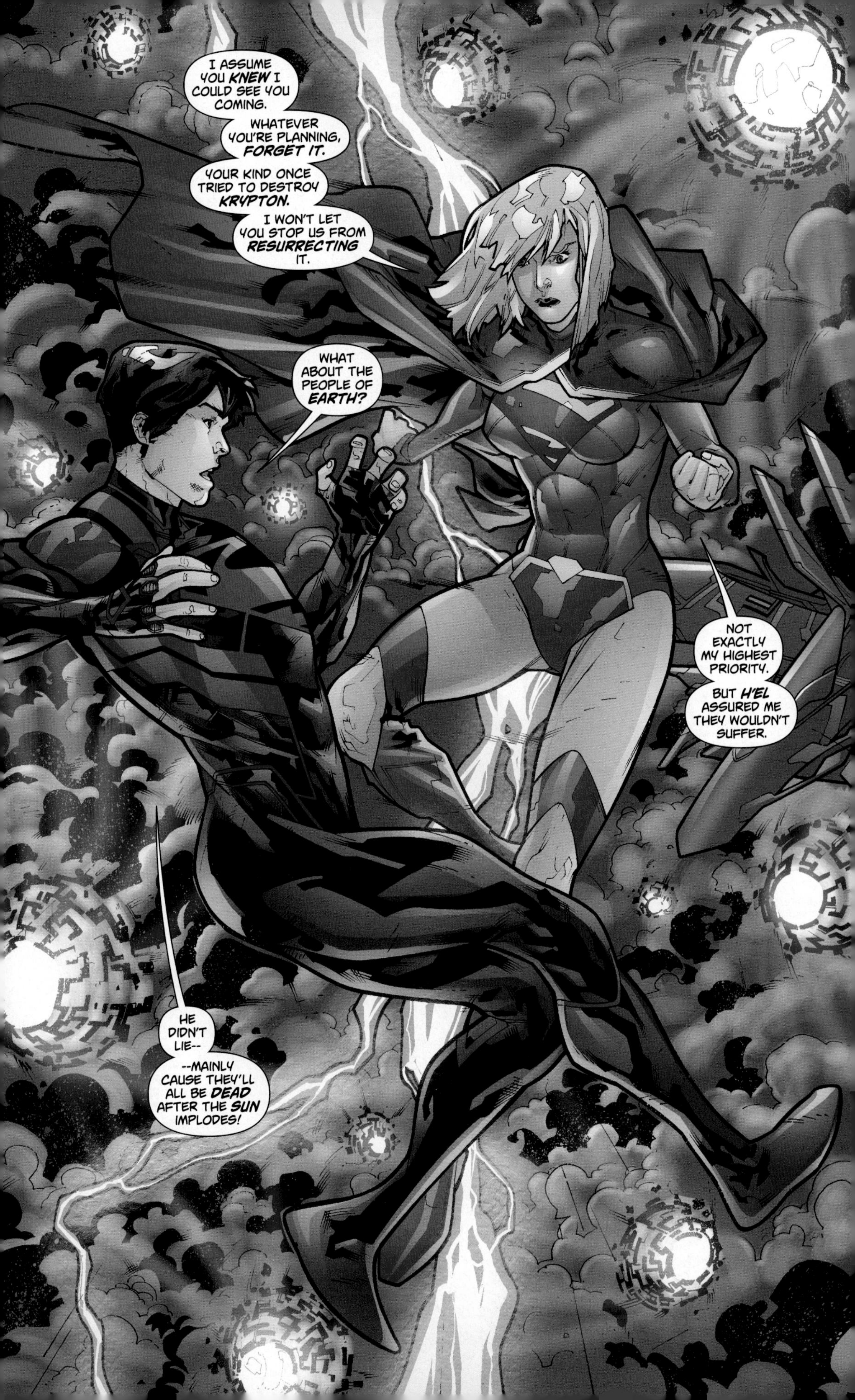
I ASSUME YOU KNEW I COULD SEE YOU COMING.
WHATEVER YOU'RE PLANNING, FORGET IT.
YOUR KIND ONCE TRIED TO DESTROY KRYPTON.
I WON'T LET YOU STOP US FROM RESURRECTING IT.
WHAT ABOUT THE PEOPLE OF EARTH?
NOT EXACTLY MY HIGHEST PRIORITY.
BUT H'EL ASSURED ME THEY WOULDN'T SUFFER.
HE DIDN'T LIE--
--MAINLY CAUSE THEY'LL ALL BE DEAD AFTER THE SUN IMPLODES!

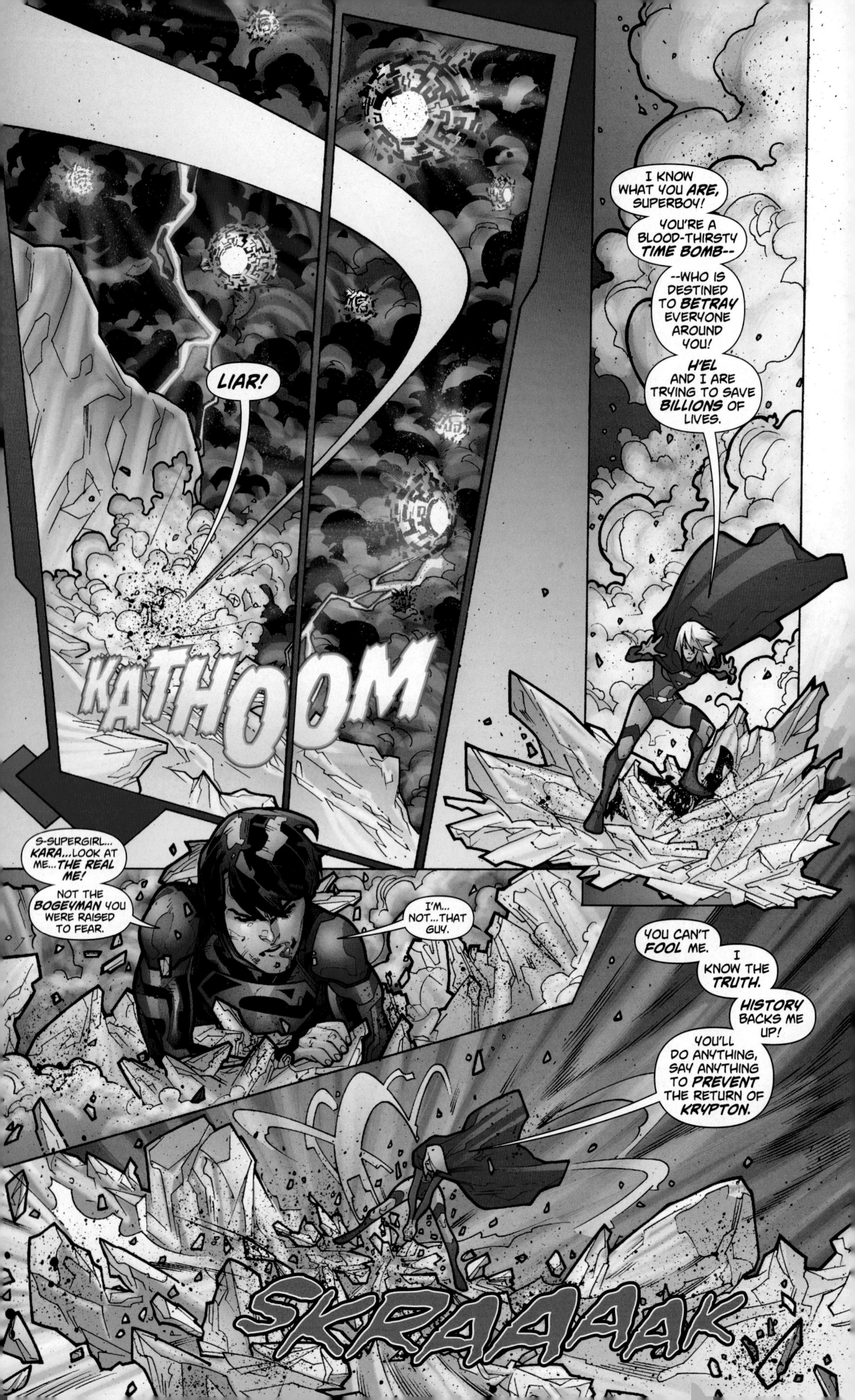
LIAR!
KATHOOM
I KNOW WHAT YOU ARE, SUPERBOY!
YOU'RE A BLOOD-THIRSTY TIME BOMB--
--WHO IS DESTINED TO BETRAY EVERYONE AROUND YOU!
H'EL AND I ARE TRYING TO SAVE BILLIONS OF LIVES.
S-SUPERGIRL... KARA...LOOK AT ME...THE REAL ME!
NOT THE BOGEYMAN YOU WERE RAISED TO FEAR.
I'M... NOT...THAT GUY.
YOU CAN'T FOOL ME.
I KNOW THE TRUTH.
HISTORY BACKS ME UP!
YOU'LL DO ANYTHING, SAY ANYTHING TO PREVENT THE RETURN OF KRYPTON.
SKRAAAAAK

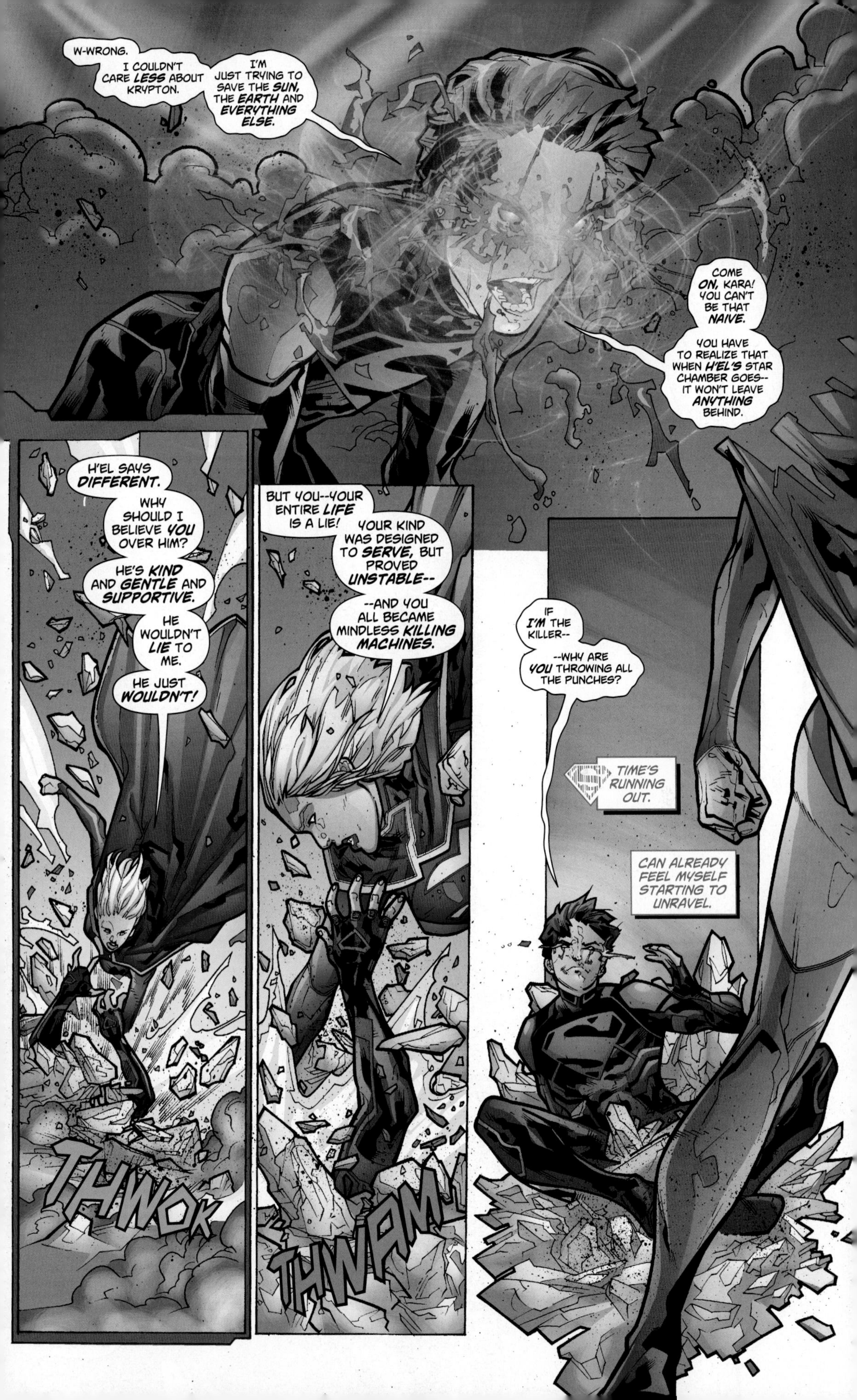
W-WRONG.
I COULDN'T CARE LESS ABOUT KRYPTON.
I'M JUST TRYING TO SAVE THE SUN, THE EARTH AND EVERYTHING ELSE.
COME ON, KARA! YOU CAN'T BE THAT NAIVE.
YOU HAVE TO REALIZE THAT WHEN H'EL'S STAR CHAMBER GOES-- IT WON'T LEAVE ANYTHING BEHIND.
H'EL SAYS DIFFERENT.
WHY SHOULD I BELIEVE YOU OVER HIM?
HE'S KIND AND GENTLE AND SUPPORTIVE.
HE WOULDN'T LIE TO ME.
HE JUST WOULDN'T!
THWOK
BUT YOU--YOUR ENTIRE LIFE IS A LIE!
YOUR KIND WAS DESIGNED TO SERVE, BUT PROVED UNSTABLE--
--AND YOU ALL BECAME MINDLESS KILLING MACHINES.
THWAM
IF I'M THE KILLER--
--WHY ARE YOU THROWING ALL THE PUNCHES?
TIME'S RUNNING OUT.
CAN ALREADY FEEL MYSELF STARTING TO UNRAVEL.

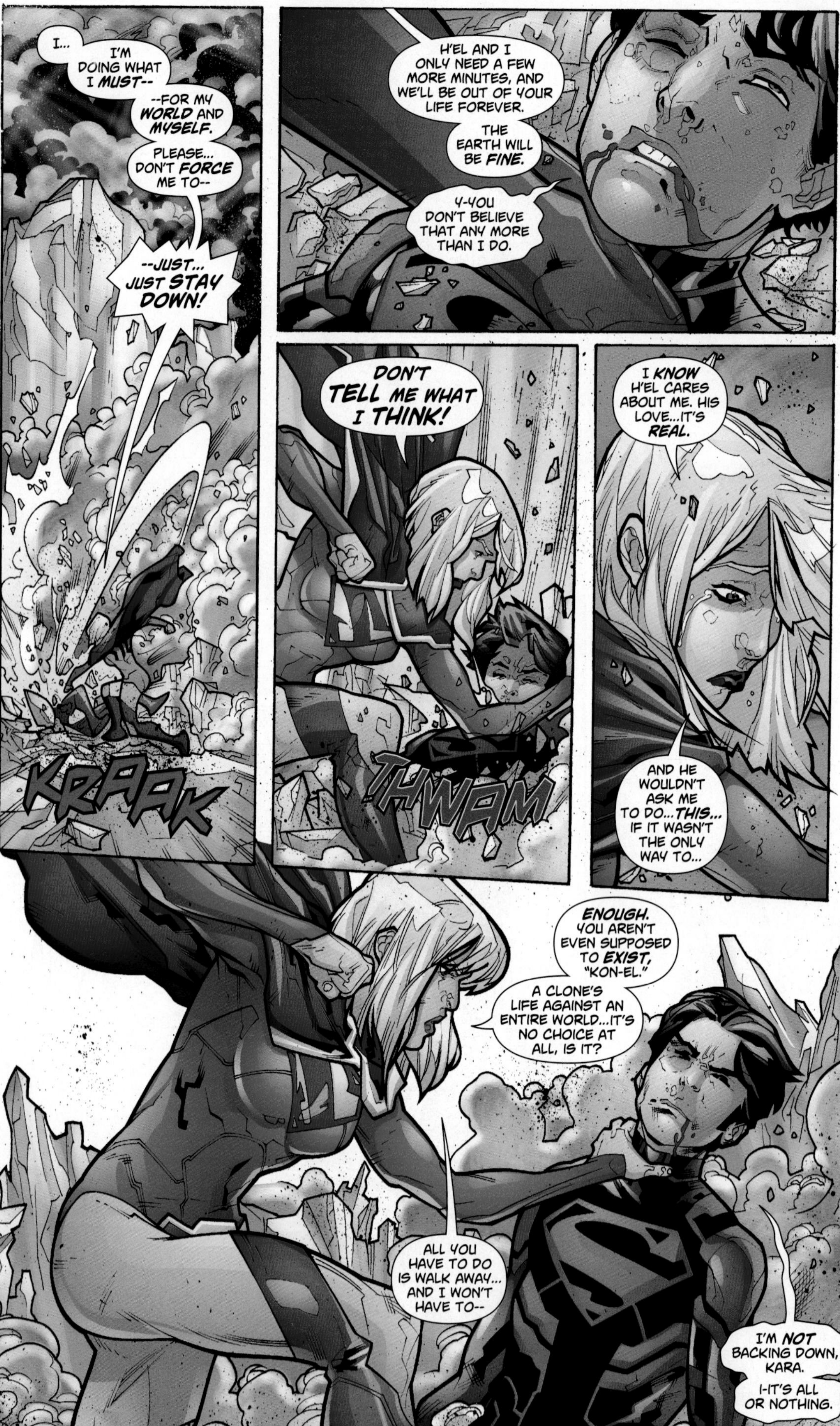
I...
I'M DOING WHAT I MUST--
--FOR MY WORLD AND MYSELF.
PLEASE... DON'T FORCE ME TO--
--JUST... JUST STAY DOWN!
KRAAAK
H'EL AND I ONLY NEED A FEW MORE MINUTES, AND WE'LL BE OUT OF YOUR LIFE FOREVER.
THE EARTH WILL BE FINE.
Y-YOU DON'T BELIEVE THAT ANY MORE THAN I DO.
DON'T TELL ME WHAT I THINK!
THWAM
I KNOW H'EL CARES ABOUT ME. HIS LOVE...IT'S REAL.
AND HE WOULDN'T ASK ME TO DO...THIS... IF IT WASN'T THE ONLY WAY TO...
ENOUGH. YOU AREN'T EVEN SUPPOSED TO EXIST, "KON-EL."
A CLONE'S LIFE AGAINST AN ENTIRE WORLD...IT'S NO CHOICE AT ALL, IS IT?
ALL YOU HAVE TO DO IS WALK AWAY... AND I WON'T HAVE TO--
I'M NOT BACKING DOWN, KARA.
I-IT'S ALL OR NOTHING.

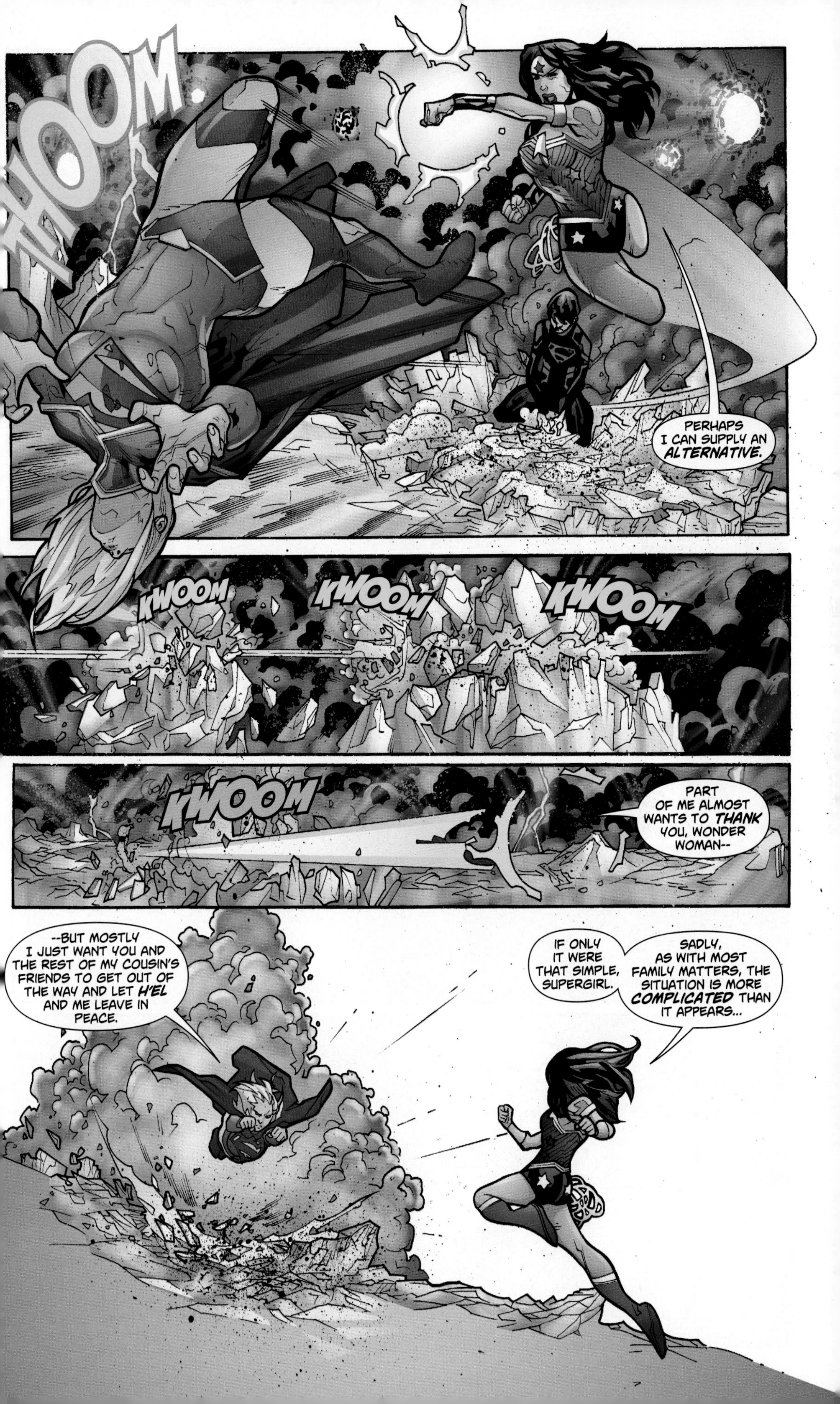
THOOM
PERHAPS I CAN SUPPLY AN ALTERNATIVE.
KWOOM
KWOOM
KWOOM
KWOOM
PART OF ME ALMOST WANTS TO THANK YOU, WONDER WOMAN--
--BUT MOSTLY I JUST WANT YOU AND THE REST OF MY COUSIN'S FRIENDS TO GET OUT OF THE WAY AND LET H'EL AND ME LEAVE IN PEACE.
IF ONLY IT WERE THAT SIMPLE, SUPERGIRL.
SADLY, AS WITH MOST FAMILY MATTERS, THE SITUATION IS MORE COMPLICATED THAN IT APPEARS...

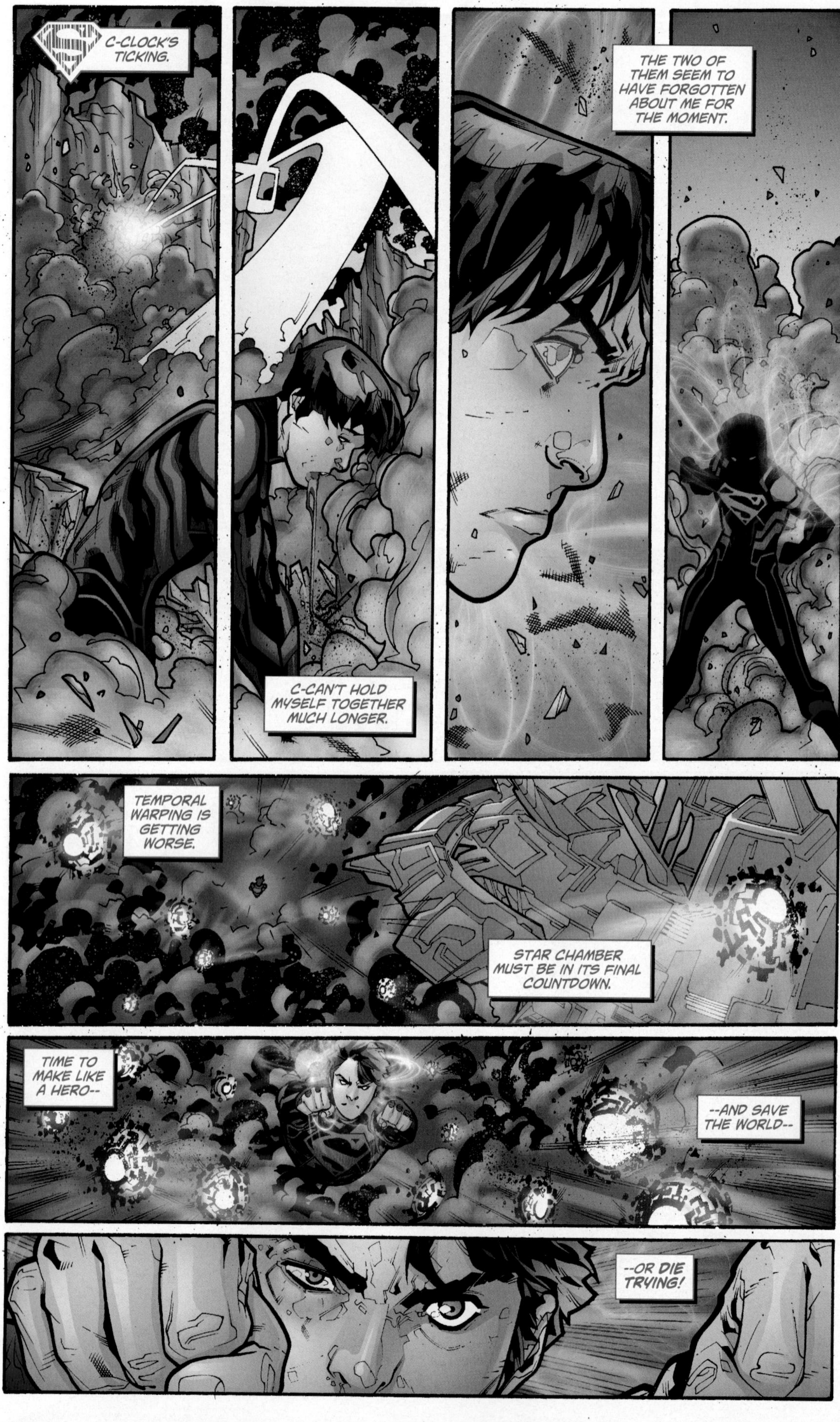
C-CLOCK'S TICKING.
C-CAN'T HOLD MYSELF TOGETHER MUCH LONGER.
THE TWO OF THEM SEEM TO HAVE FORGOTTEN ABOUT ME FOR THE MOMENT.
TEMPORAL WARPING IS GETTING WORSE.
STAR CHAMBER MUST BE IN ITS FINAL COUNTDOWN.
TIME TO MAKE LIKE A HERO--
--AND SAVE THE WORLD--
--OR DIE TRYING!

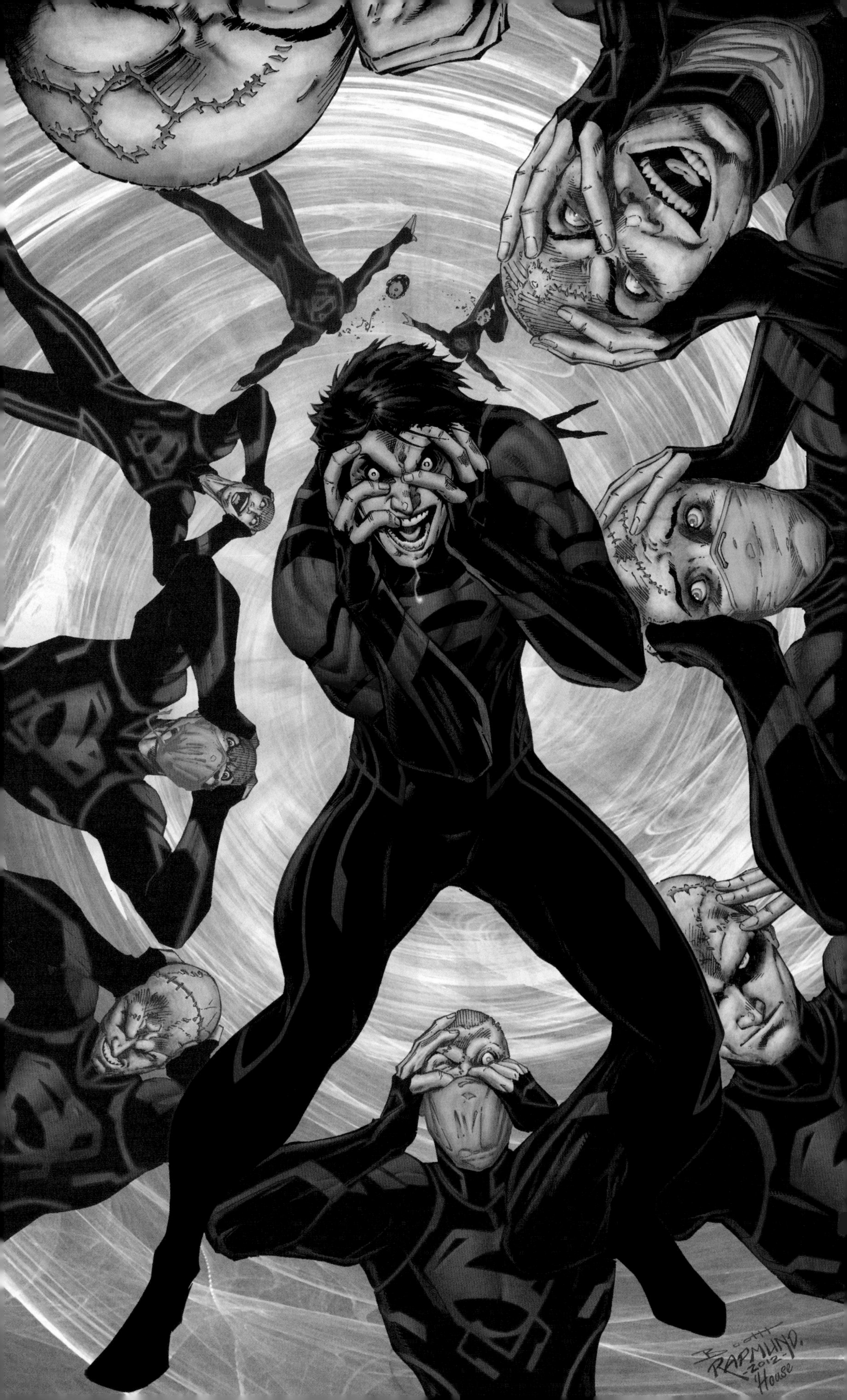
RAPMUND.
-2012-
House

MIND YOUR MANNERS

TOM DeFALCO, SCOTT LOBDELL & TONY LEE writers **R.B. SILVA & IBAN COELLO** pencillers **ROB LEAN & DENIS FRIETAS** inkers

cover art by **BRETT BOOTH, NORM RAPMUND & ANDREW DALHOUSE**

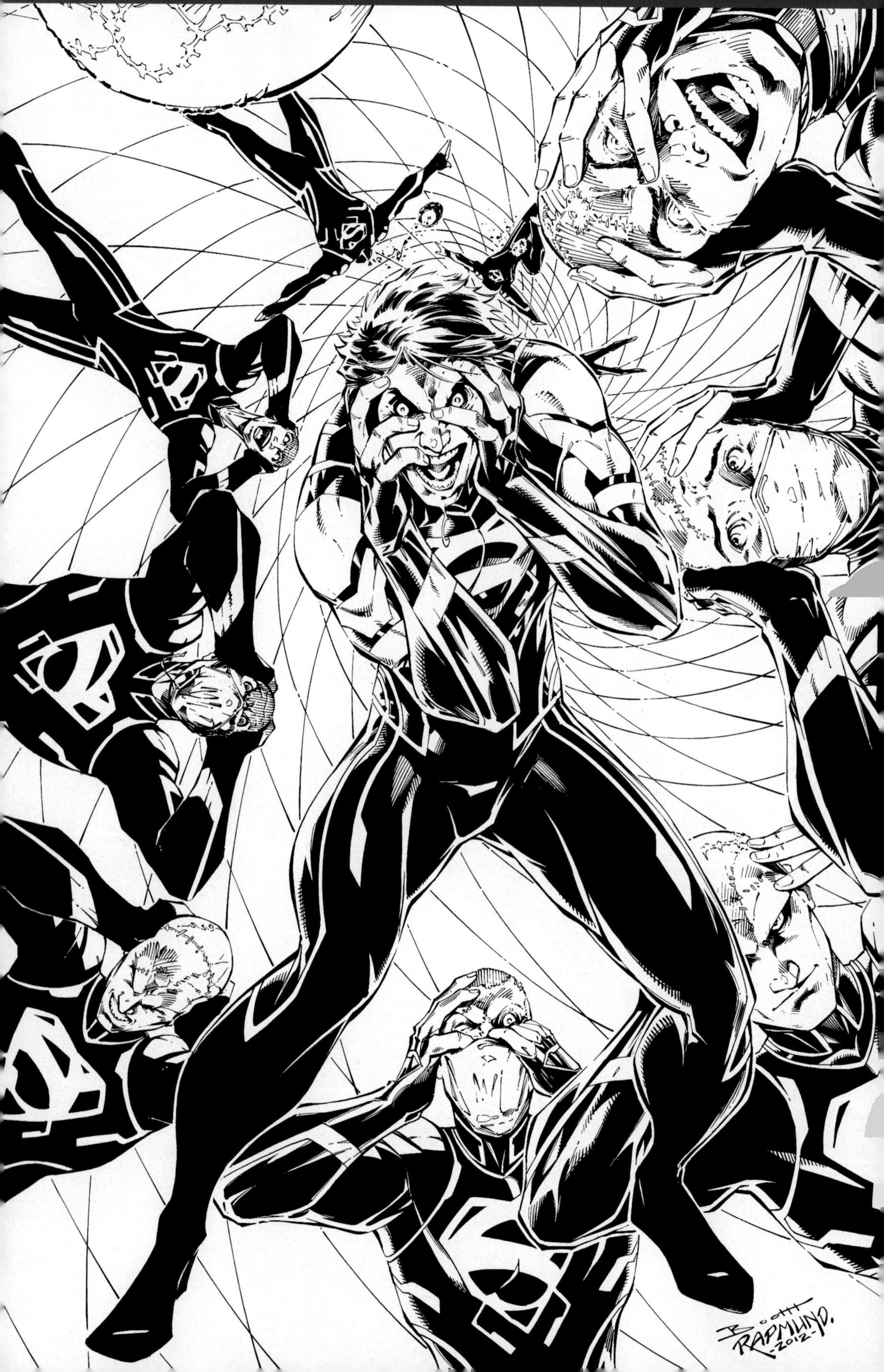

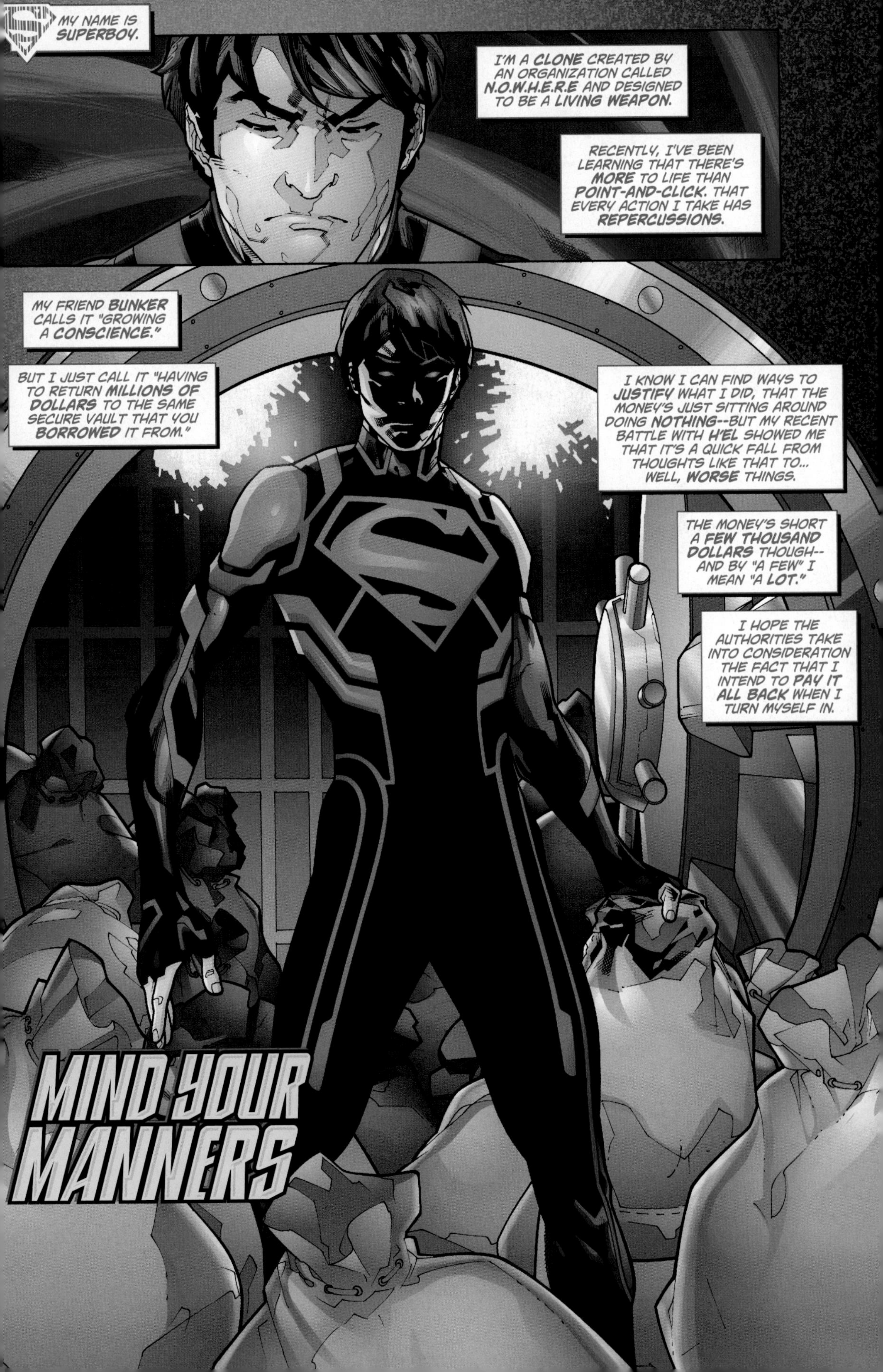
MY NAME IS SUPERBOY.
I'M A CLONE CREATED BY AN ORGANIZATION CALLED N.O.W.H.E.R.E AND DESIGNED TO BE A LIVING WEAPON.
RECENTLY, I'VE BEEN LEARNING THAT THERE'S MORE TO LIFE THAN POINT-AND-CLICK. THAT EVERY ACTION I TAKE HAS REPERCUSSIONS.
MY FRIEND BUNKER CALLS IT "GROWING A CONSCIENCE."
BUT I JUST CALL IT "HAVING TO RETURN MILLIONS OF DOLLARS TO THE SAME SECURE VAULT THAT YOU BORROWED IT FROM."
I KNOW I CAN FIND WAYS TO JUSTIFY WHAT I DID, THAT THE MONEY'S JUST SITTING AROUND DOING NOTHING--BUT MY RECENT BATTLE WITH H'EL SHOWED ME THAT IT'S A QUICK FALL FROM THOUGHTS LIKE THAT TO... WELL, WORSE THINGS.
THE MONEY'S SHORT A FEW THOUSAND DOLLARS THOUGH--AND BY "A FEW" I MEAN "A LOT."
I HOPE THE AUTHORITIES TAKE INTO CONSIDERATION THE FACT THAT I INTEND TO PAY IT ALL BACK WHEN I TURN MYSELF IN.
MIND YOUR MANNERS

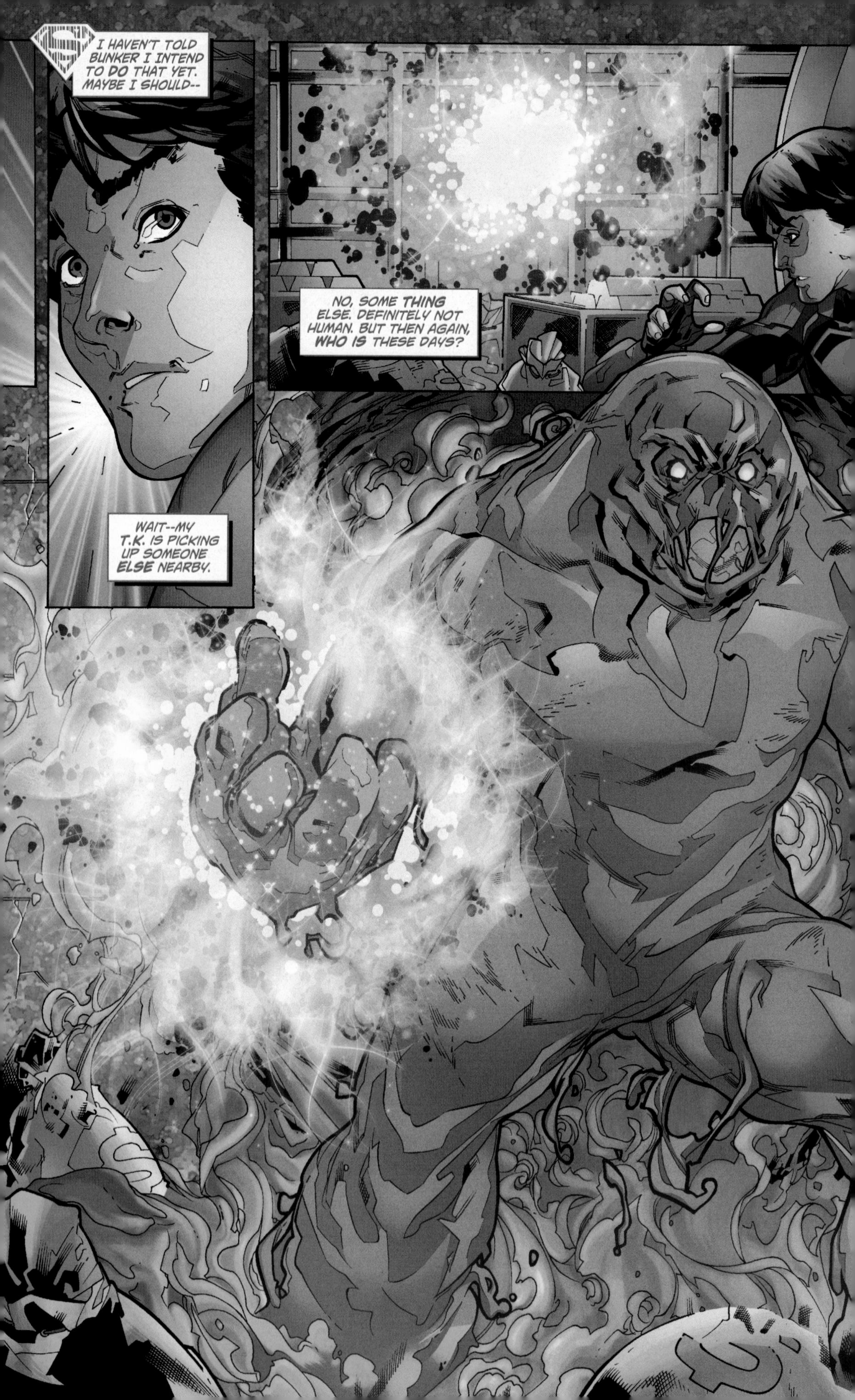
I HAVEN'T TOLD BUNKER I INTEND TO DO THAT YET. MAYBE I SHOULD--
NO, SOME THING ELSE. DEFINITELY NOT HUMAN. BUT THEN AGAIN, WHO IS THESE DAYS?
WAIT--MY T.K. IS PICKING UP SOMEONE ELSE NEARBY.

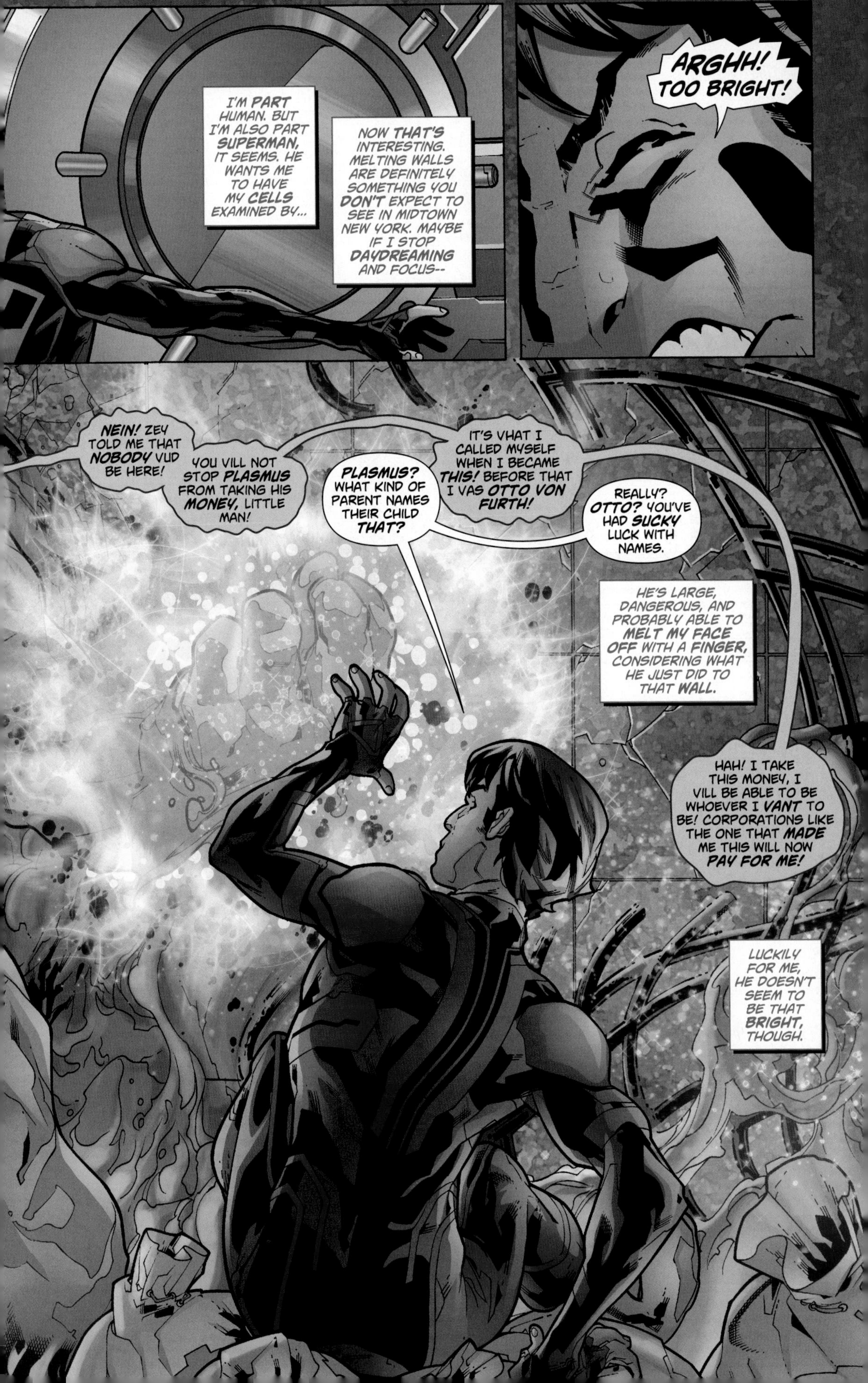
I'M PART HUMAN. BUT I'M ALSO PART SUPERMAN, IT SEEMS. HE WANTS ME TO HAVE MY CELLS EXAMINED BY...
NOW THAT'S INTERESTING. MELTING WALLS ARE DEFINITELY SOMETHING YOU DON'T EXPECT TO SEE IN MIDTOWN NEW YORK. MAYBE IF I STOP DAYDREAMING AND FOCUS--
ARGHH! TOO BRIGHT!
NEIN! ZEY TOLD ME THAT NOBODY VUD BE HERE!
YOU VILL NOT STOP PLASMUS FROM TAKING HIS MONEY, LITTLE MAN!
PLASMUS? WHAT KIND OF PARENT NAMES THEIR CHILD THAT?
IT'S VHAT I CALLED MYSELF WHEN I BECAME THIS! BEFORE THAT I VAS OTTO VON FURTH!
REALLY? OTTO? YOU'VE HAD SUCKY LUCK WITH NAMES.
HE'S LARGE, DANGEROUS, AND PROBABLY ABLE TO MELT MY FACE OFF WITH A FINGER, CONSIDERING WHAT HE JUST DID TO THAT WALL.
HAH! I TAKE THIS MONEY, I VILL BE ABLE TO BE WHOEVER I VANT TO BE! CORPORATIONS LIKE THE ONE THAT MADE ME THIS WILL NOW PAY FOR ME!
LUCKILY FOR ME, HE DOESN'T SEEM TO BE THAT BRIGHT, THOUGH.

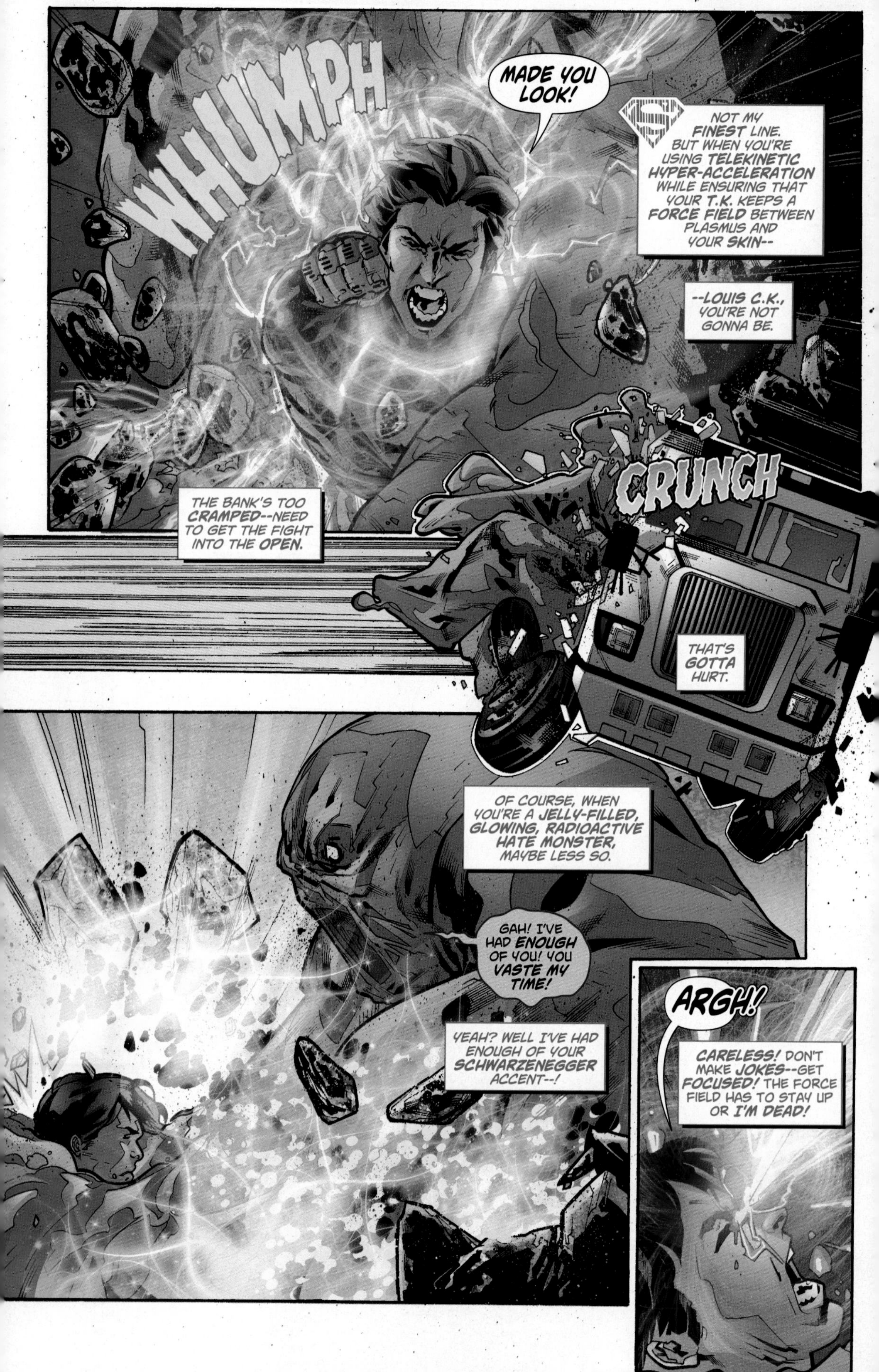
WHUMPH
MADE YOU LOOK!
NOT MY FINEST LINE. BUT WHEN YOU'RE USING TELEKINETIC HYPER-ACCELERATION WHILE ENSURING THAT YOUR T.K. KEEPS A FORCE FIELD BETWEEN PLASMUS AND YOUR SKIN--
--LOUIS C.K., YOU'RE NOT GONNA BE.
THE BANK'S TOO CRAMPED--NEED TO GET THE FIGHT INTO THE OPEN.
CRUNCH
THAT'S GOTTA HURT.
OF COURSE, WHEN YOU'RE A JELLY-FILLED, GLOWING, RADIOACTIVE HATE MONSTER, MAYBE LESS SO.
GAH! I'VE HAD ENOUGH OF YOU! YOU VASTE MY TIME!
YEAH? WELL I'VE HAD ENOUGH OF YOUR SCHWARZENEGGER ACCENT--!
ARGH!
CARELESS! DON'T MAKE JOKES--GET FOCUSED! THE FORCE FIELD HAS TO STAY UP OR I'M DEAD!

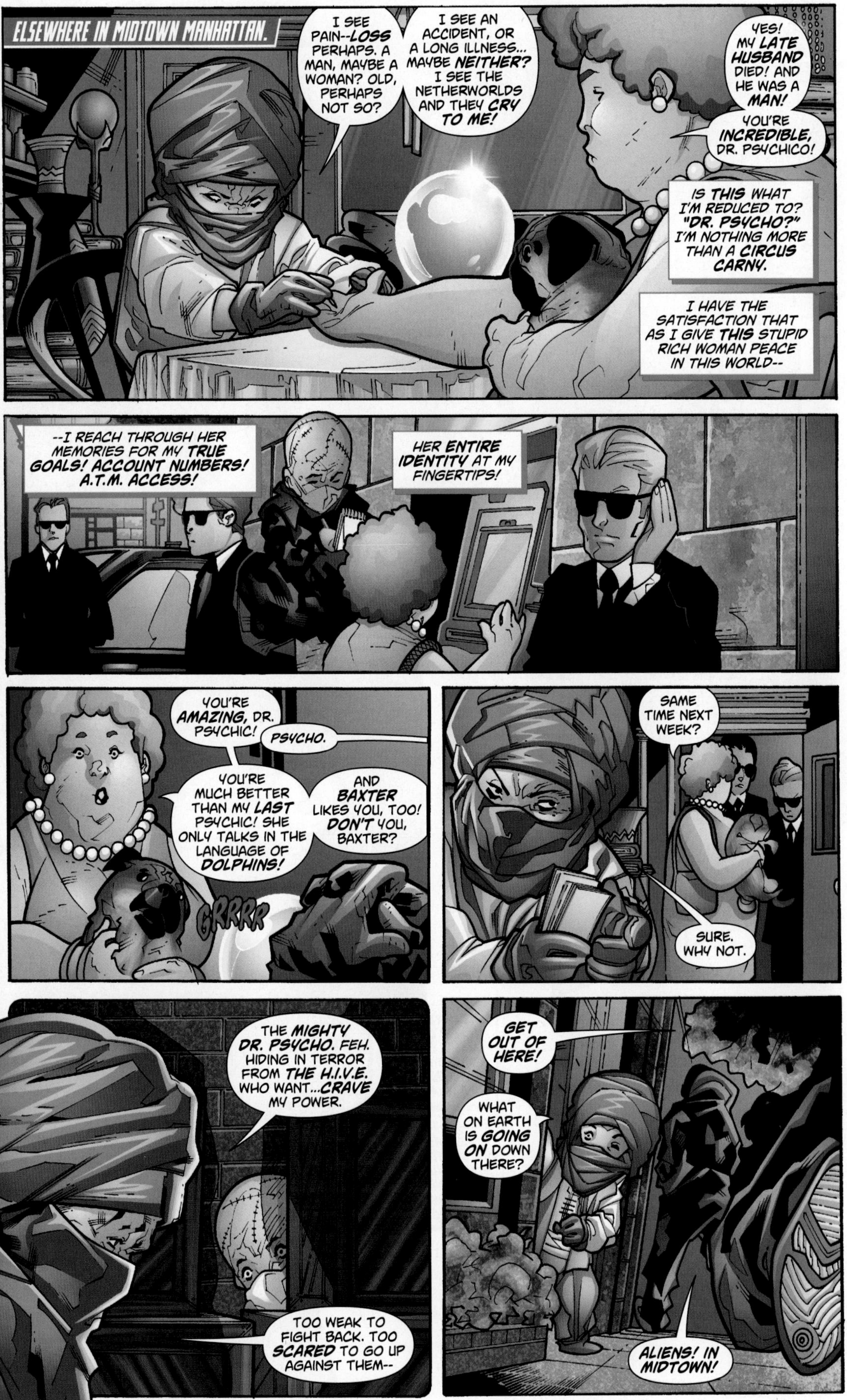
ELSEWHERE IN MIDTOWN MANHATTAN.
I SEE PAIN--LOSS PERHAPS. A MAN, MAYBE A WOMAN? OLD, PERHAPS NOT SO?
I SEE AN ACCIDENT, OR A LONG ILLNESS... MAYBE NEITHER? I SEE THE NETHERWORLDS AND THEY CRY TO ME!
YES! MY LATE HUSBAND DIED! AND HE WAS A MAN!
YOU'RE INCREDIBLE, DR. PSYCHICO!
IS THIS WHAT I'M REDUCED TO? "DR. PSYCHO?" I'M NOTHING MORE THAN A CIRCUS CARNY.
I HAVE THE SATISFACTION THAT AS I GIVE THIS STUPID RICH WOMAN PEACE IN THIS WORLD--
--I REACH THROUGH HER MEMORIES FOR MY TRUE GOALS! ACCOUNT NUMBERS! A.T.M. ACCESS!
HER ENTIRE IDENTITY AT MY FINGERTIPS!
YOU'RE AMAZING, DR. PSYCHIC!
PSYCHO.
YOU'RE MUCH BETTER THAN MY LAST PSYCHIC! SHE ONLY TALKS IN THE LANGUAGE OF DOLPHINS!
AND BAXTER LIKES YOU, TOO! DON'T YOU, BAXTER?
GRRRR
SAME TIME NEXT WEEK?
SURE. WHY NOT.
THE MIGHTY DR. PSYCHO. FEH. HIDING IN TERROR FROM THE H.I.V.E. WHO WANT...CRAVE MY POWER.
TOO WEAK TO FIGHT BACK. TOO SCARED TO GO UP AGAINST THEM--
GET OUT OF HERE!
WHAT ON EARTH IS GOING ON DOWN THERE?
ALIENS! IN MIDTOWN!

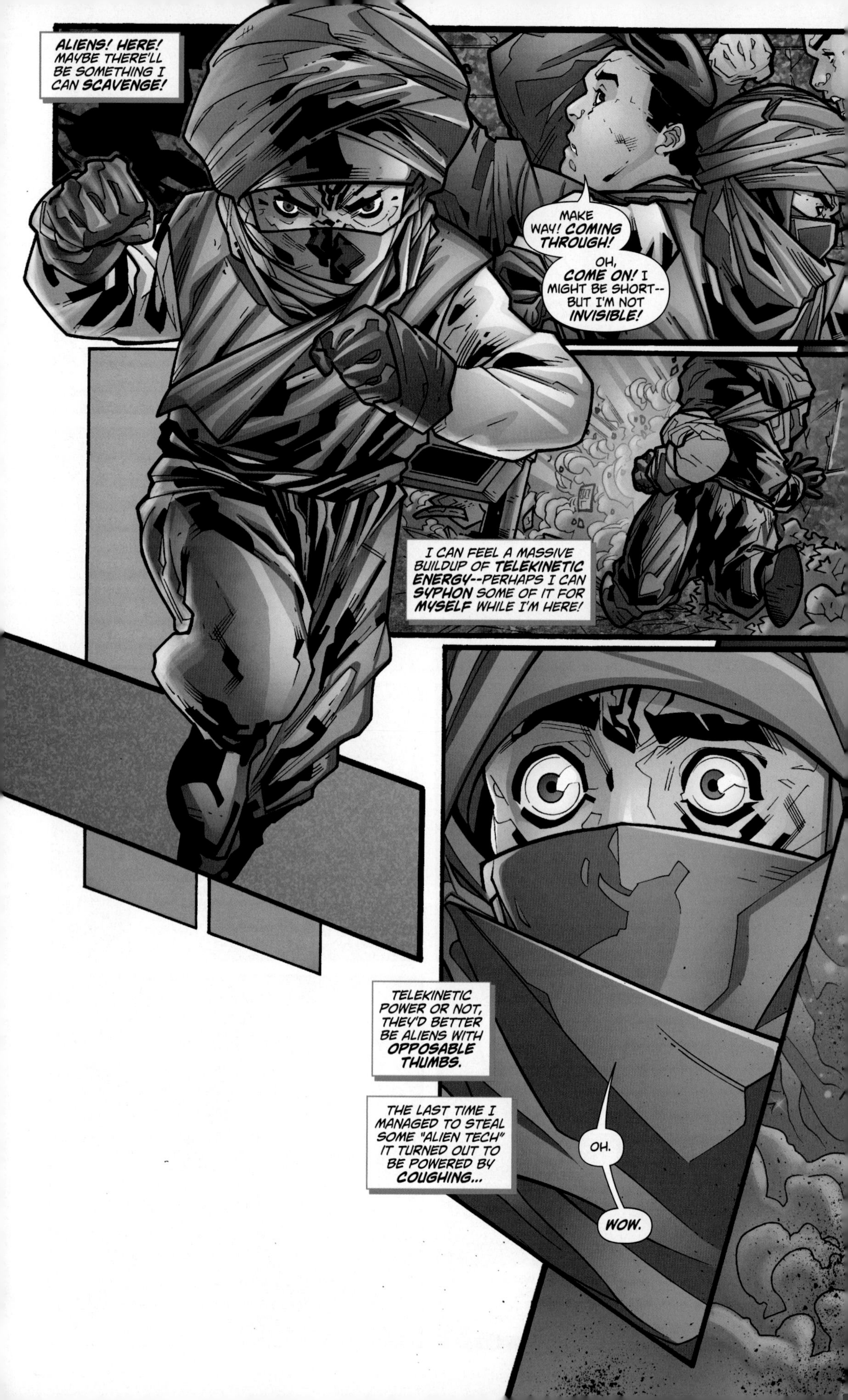
ALIENS! HERE! MAYBE THERE'LL BE SOMETHING I CAN SCAVENGE!
MAKE WAY! COMING THROUGH!
OH, COME ON! I MIGHT BE SHORT-- BUT I'M NOT INVISIBLE!
I CAN FEEL A MASSIVE BUILDUP OF TELEKINETIC ENERGY--PERHAPS I CAN SYPHON SOME OF IT FOR MYSELF WHILE I'M HERE!
TELEKINETIC POWER OR NOT, THEY'D BETTER BE ALIENS WITH OPPOSABLE THUMBS.
THE LAST TIME I MANAGED TO STEAL SOME "ALIEN TECH" IT TURNED OUT TO BE POWERED BY COUGHING...
OH.
WOW.

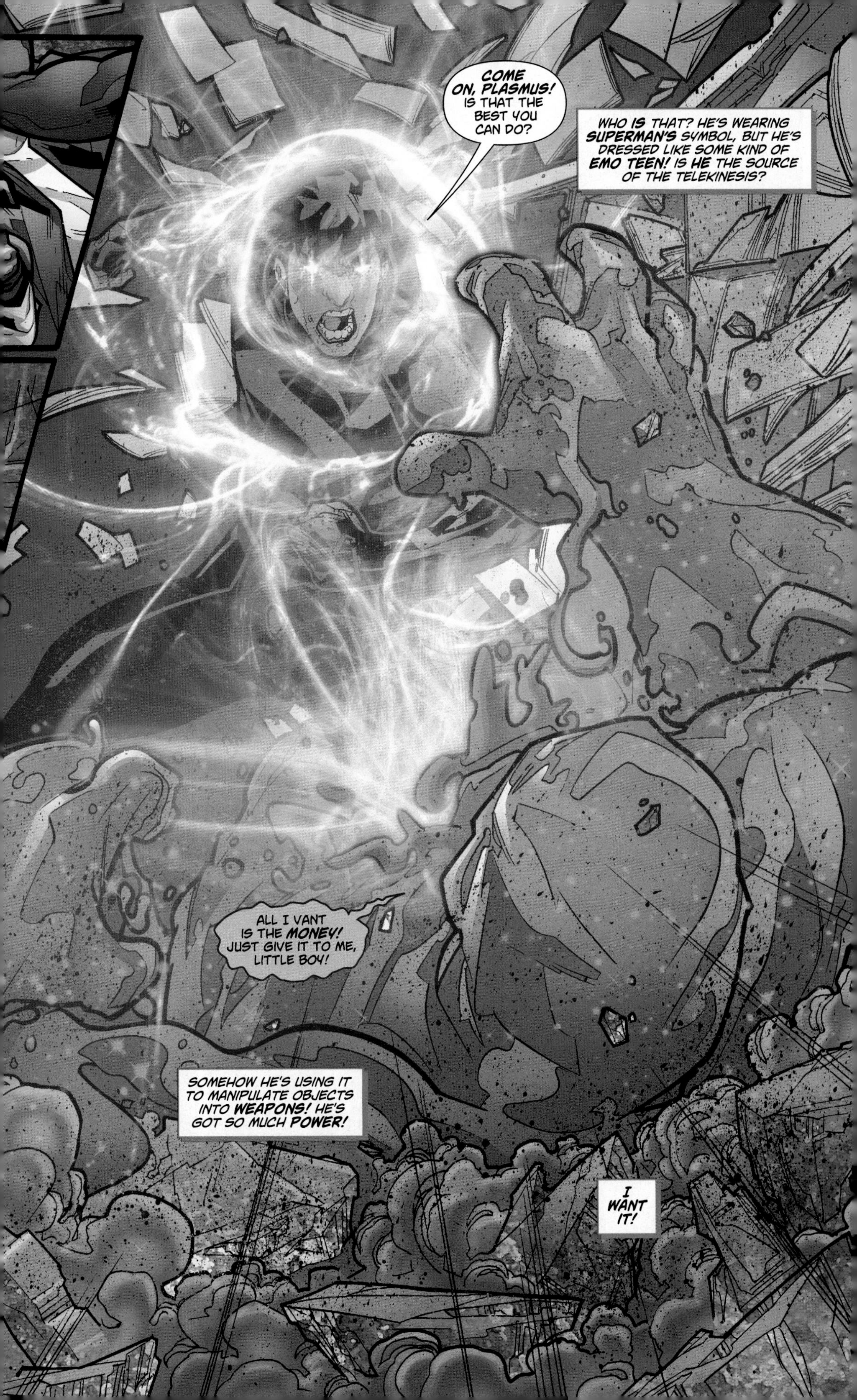
COME ON, PLASMUS! IS THAT THE BEST YOU CAN DO?
WHO IS THAT? HE'S WEARING SUPERMAN'S SYMBOL, BUT HE'S DRESSED LIKE SOME KIND OF EMO TEEN! IS HE THE SOURCE OF THE TELEKINESIS?
ALL I VANT IS THE MONEY! JUST GIVE IT TO ME, LITTLE BOY!
SOMEHOW HE'S USING IT TO MANIPULATE OBJECTS INTO WEAPONS! HE'S GOT SO MUCH POWER!
I WANT IT!

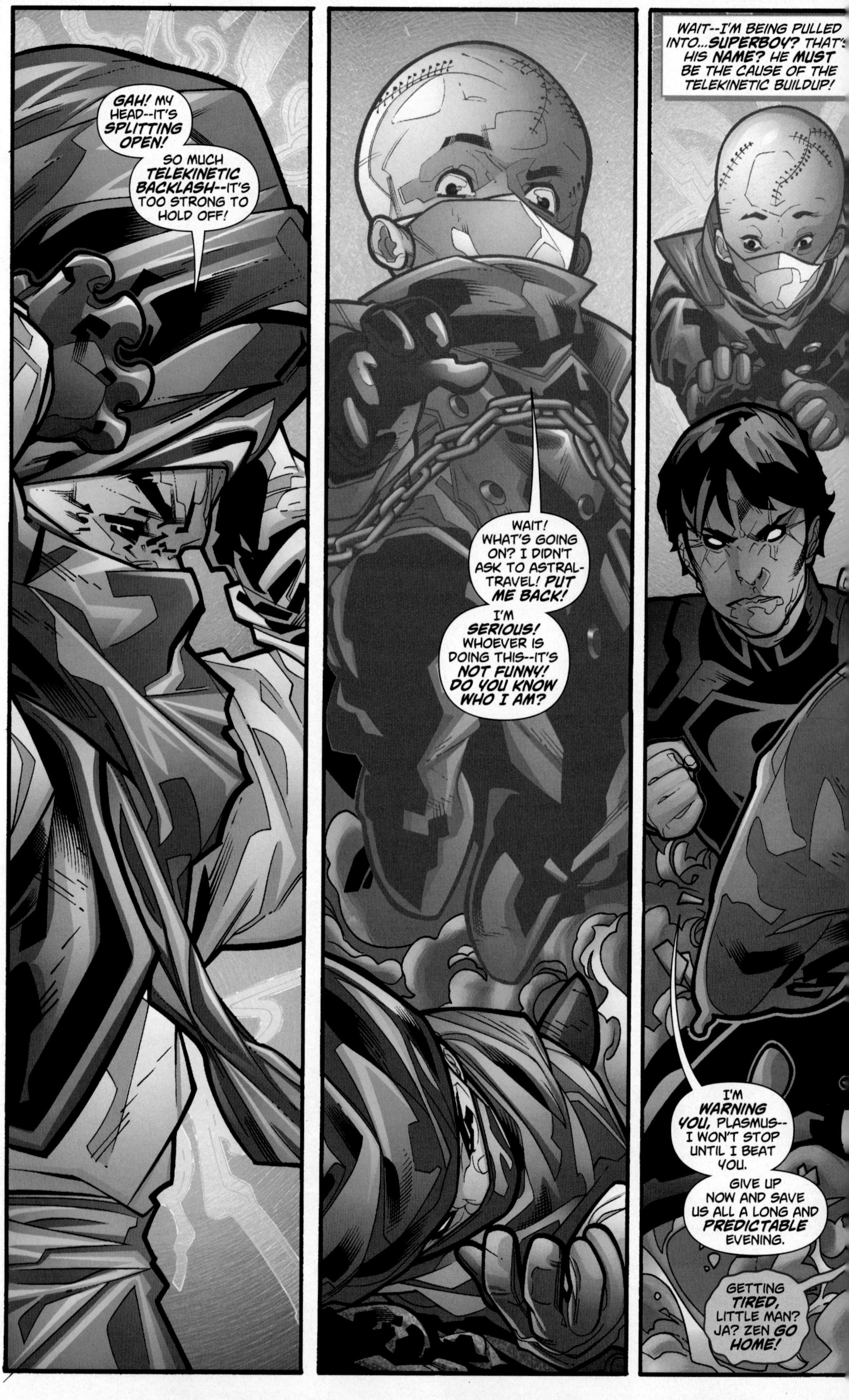
GAH! MY HEAD--IT'S SPLITTING OPEN!
SO MUCH TELEKINETIC BACKLASH--IT'S TOO STRONG TO HOLD OFF!
WAIT! WHAT'S GOING ON? I DIDN'T ASK TO ASTRAL-TRAVEL! PUT ME BACK!
I'M SERIOUS! WHOEVER IS DOING THIS--IT'S NOT FUNNY! DO YOU KNOW WHO I AM?
WAIT--I'M BEING PULLED INTO...SUPERBOY? THAT'S HIS NAME? HE MUST BE THE CAUSE OF THE TELEKINETIC BUILDUP!
I'M WARNING YOU, PLASMUS--I WON'T STOP UNTIL I BEAT YOU.
GIVE UP NOW AND SAVE US ALL A LONG AND PREDICTABLE EVENING.
GETTING TIRED, LITTLE MAN? JA? ZEN GO HOME!

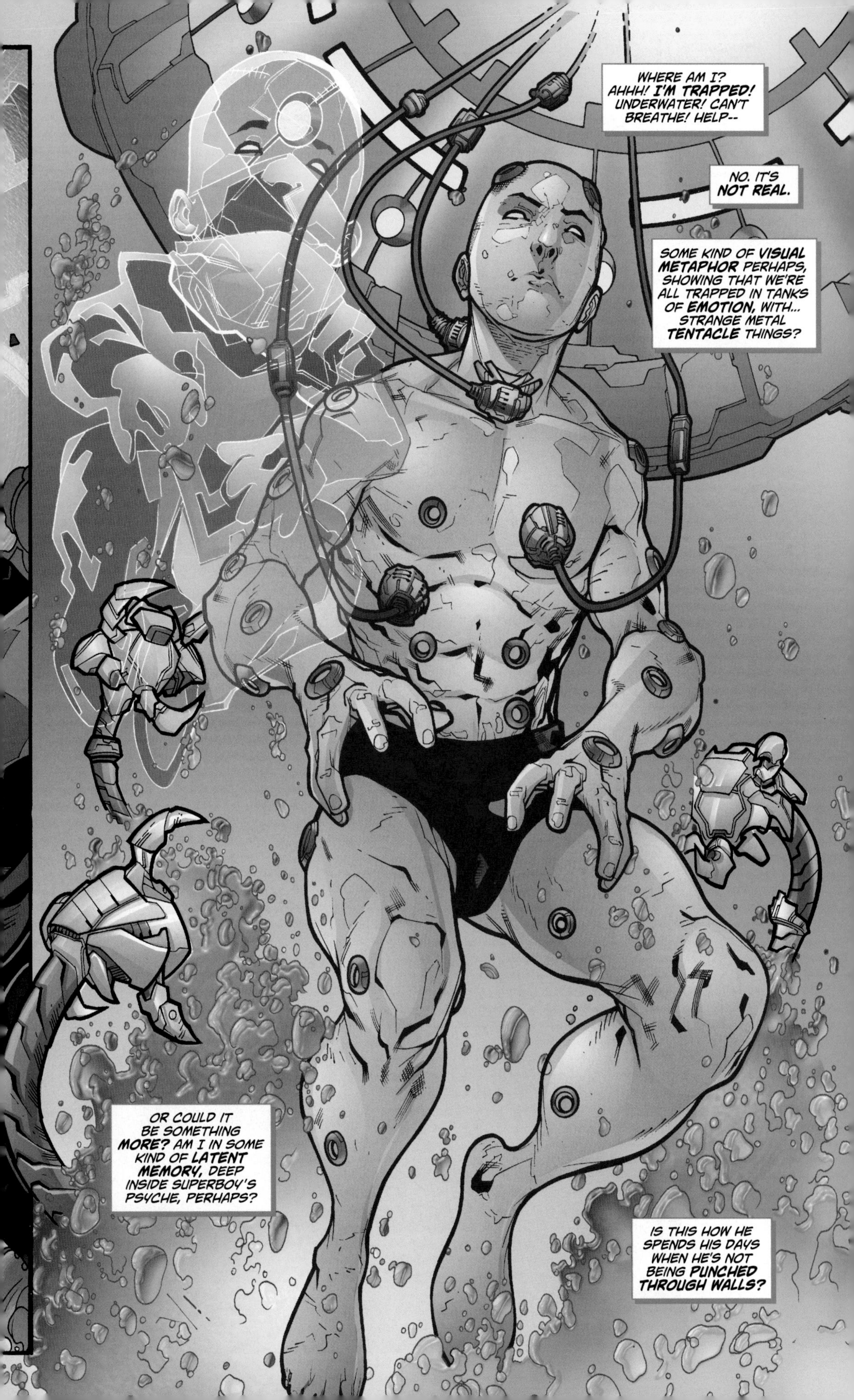
WHERE AM I? AHHH! **I'M TRAPPED!** UNDERWATER! CAN'T BREATHE! HELP--
NO. IT'S **NOT REAL.**
SOME KIND OF **VISUAL METAPHOR** PERHAPS, SHOWING THAT WE'RE ALL TRAPPED IN TANKS OF **EMOTION,** WITH... STRANGE METAL **TENTACLE** THINGS?
OR COULD IT BE SOMETHING **MORE?** AM I IN SOME KIND OF **LATENT MEMORY,** DEEP INSIDE SUPERBOY'S PSYCHE, PERHAPS?
IS THIS HOW HE SPENDS HIS DAYS WHEN HE'S NOT BEING **PUNCHED THROUGH WALLS?**

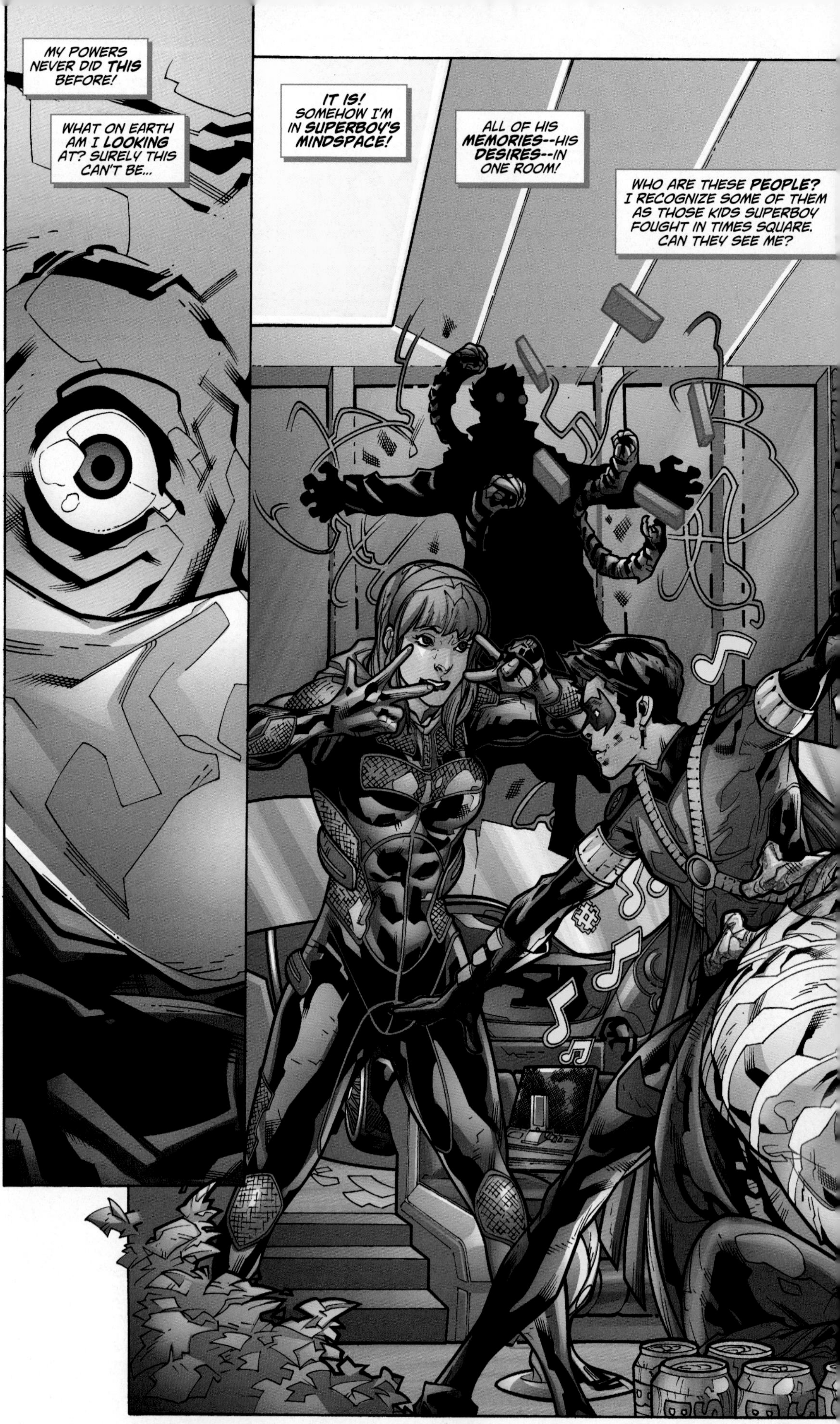
MY POWERS NEVER DID THIS BEFORE!
WHAT ON EARTH AM I LOOKING AT? SURELY THIS CAN'T BE...
IT IS! SOMEHOW I'M IN SUPERBOY'S MINDSPACE!
ALL OF HIS MEMORIES--HIS DESIRES--IN ONE ROOM!
WHO ARE THESE PEOPLE? I RECOGNIZE SOME OF THEM AS THOSE KIDS SUPERBOY FOUGHT IN TIMES SQUARE. CAN THEY SEE ME?

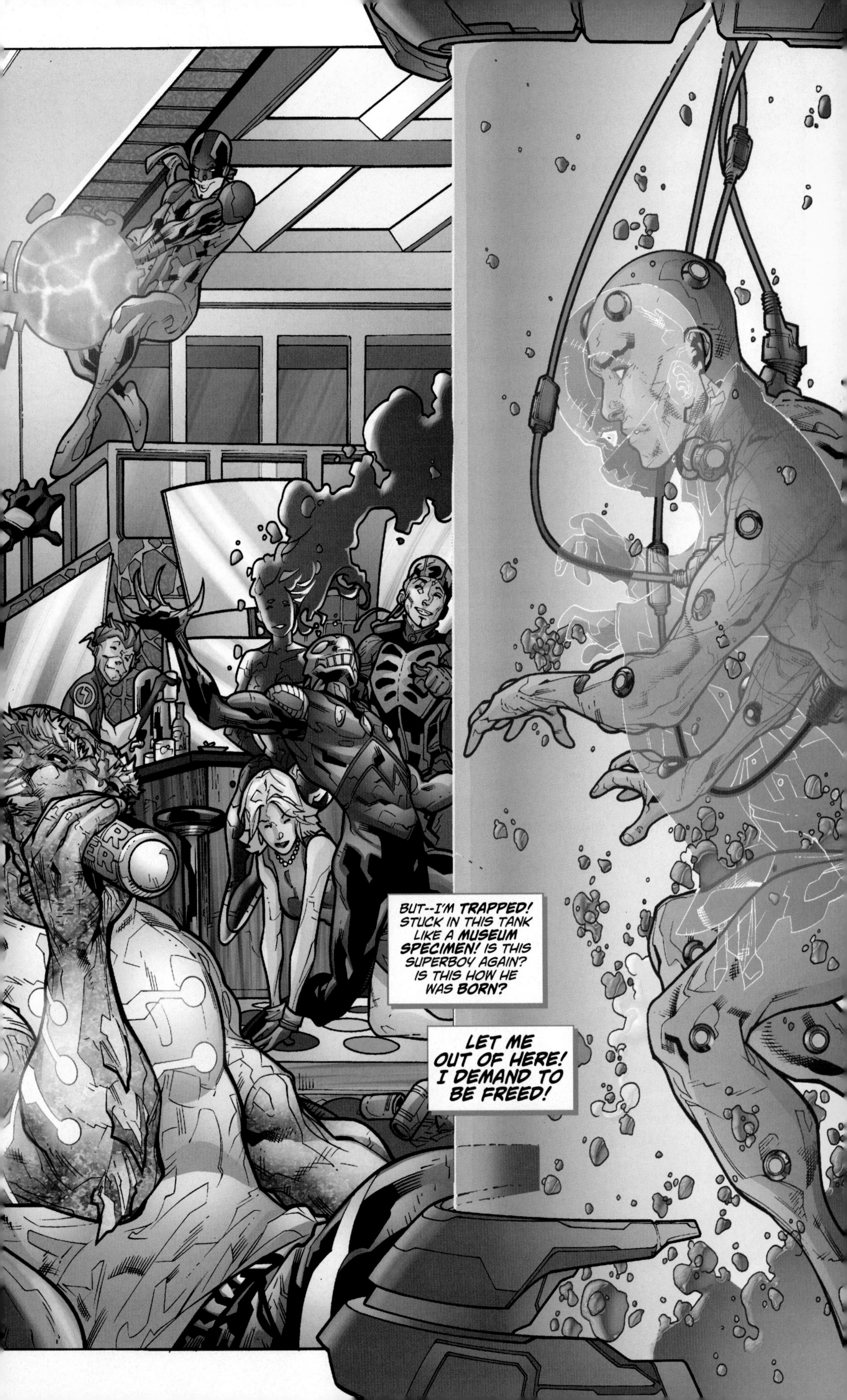

BUT--I'M **TRAPPED!** STUCK IN THIS TANK LIKE A **MUSEUM SPECIMEN!** IS THIS SUPERBOY AGAIN? IS THIS HOW HE WAS **BORN?**
LET ME OUT OF HERE! I DEMAND TO BE FREED!

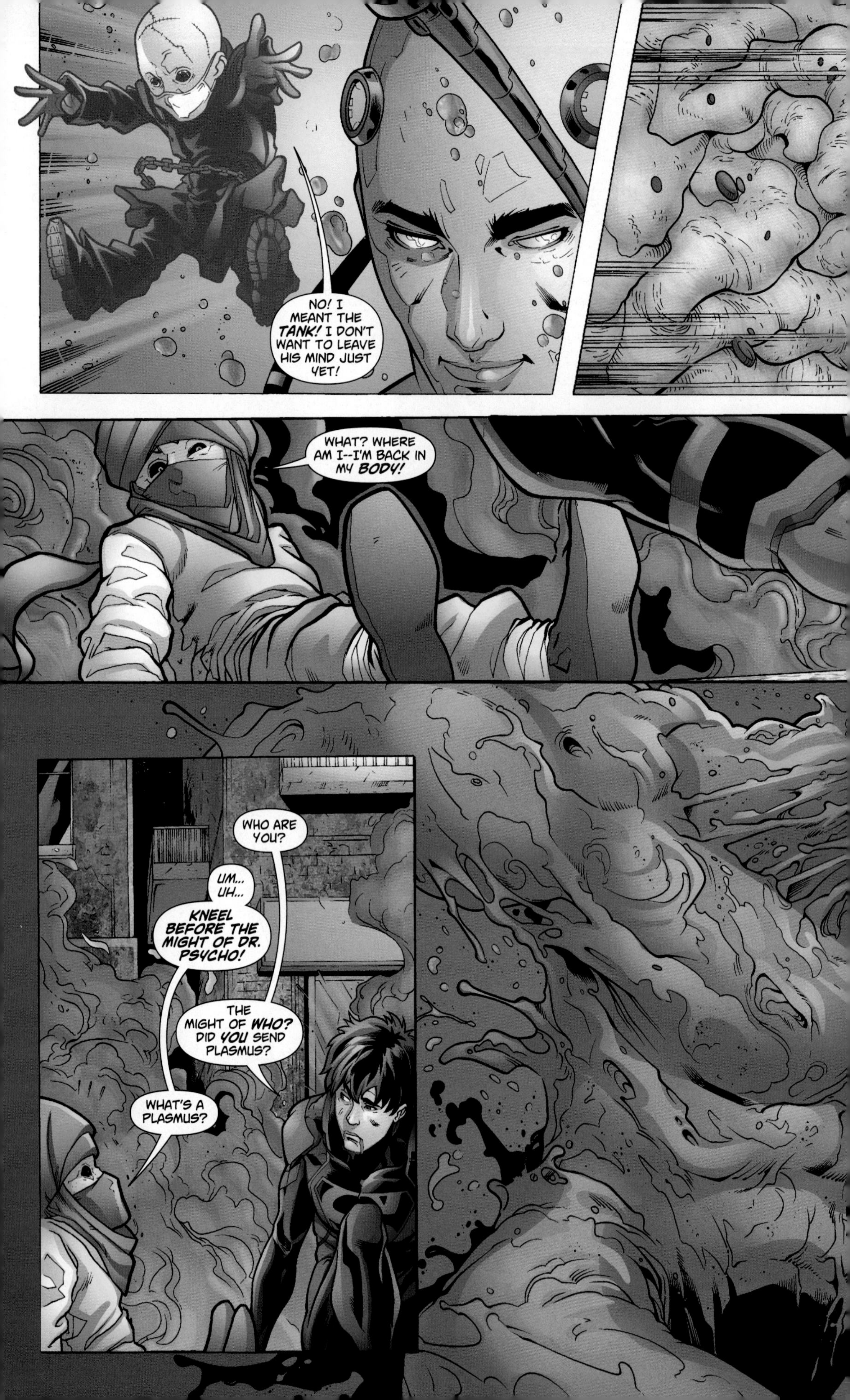
NO! I MEANT THE TANK! I DON'T WANT TO LEAVE HIS MIND JUST YET!
WHAT? WHERE AM I--I'M BACK IN MY BODY!
WHO ARE YOU?
UM... UH...
KNEEL BEFORE THE MIGHT OF DR. PSYCHO!
THE MIGHT OF WHO? DID YOU SEND PLASMUS?
WHAT'S A PLASMUS?

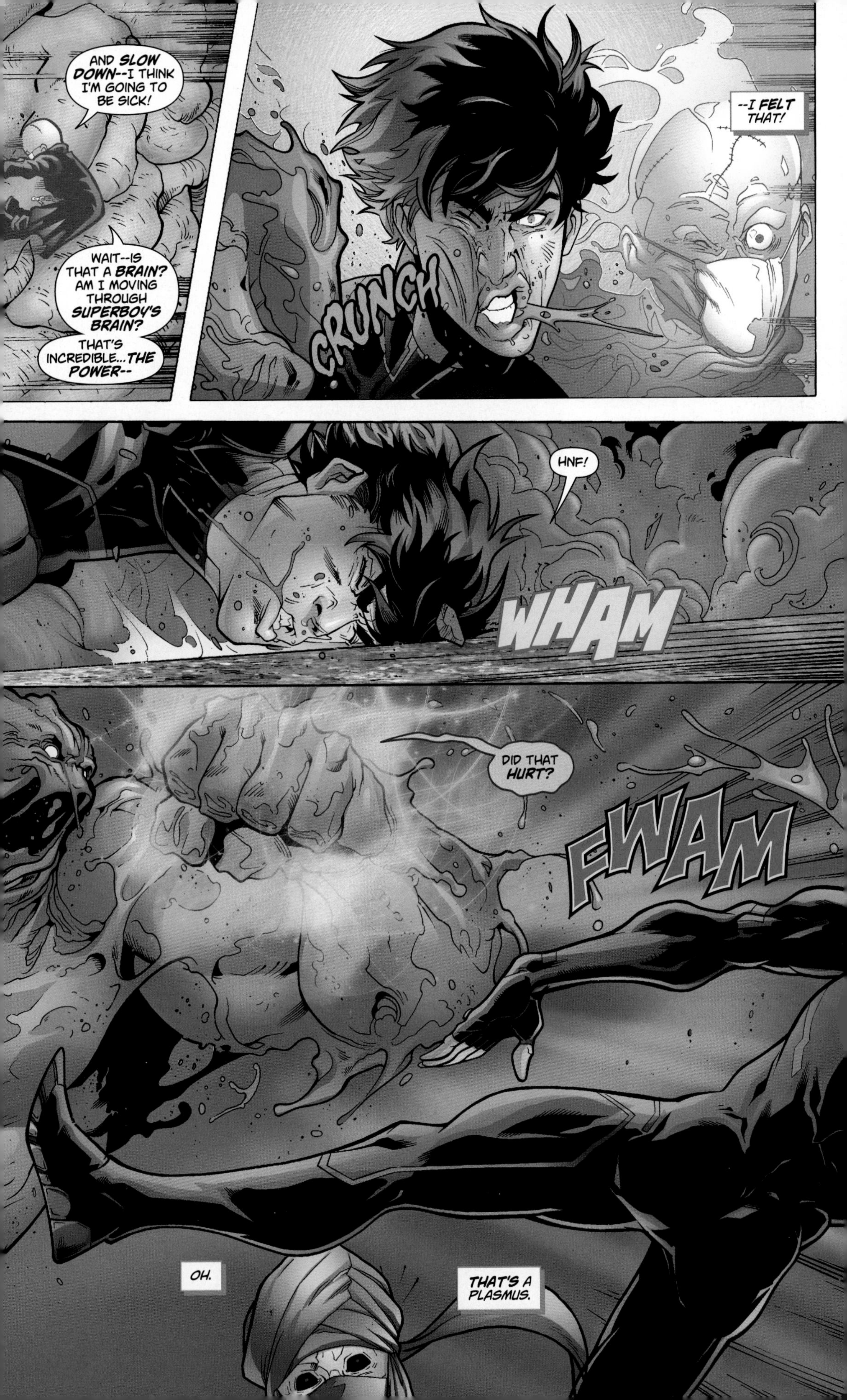
AND SLOW DOWN--I THINK I'M GOING TO BE SICK!
WAIT--IS THAT A BRAIN? AM I MOVING THROUGH SUPERBOY'S BRAIN?
THAT'S INCREDIBLE...THE POWER--
--I FELT THAT!
CRUNCH
HNF!
WHAM
DID THAT HURT?
FWAM
OH.
THAT'S A PLASMUS.

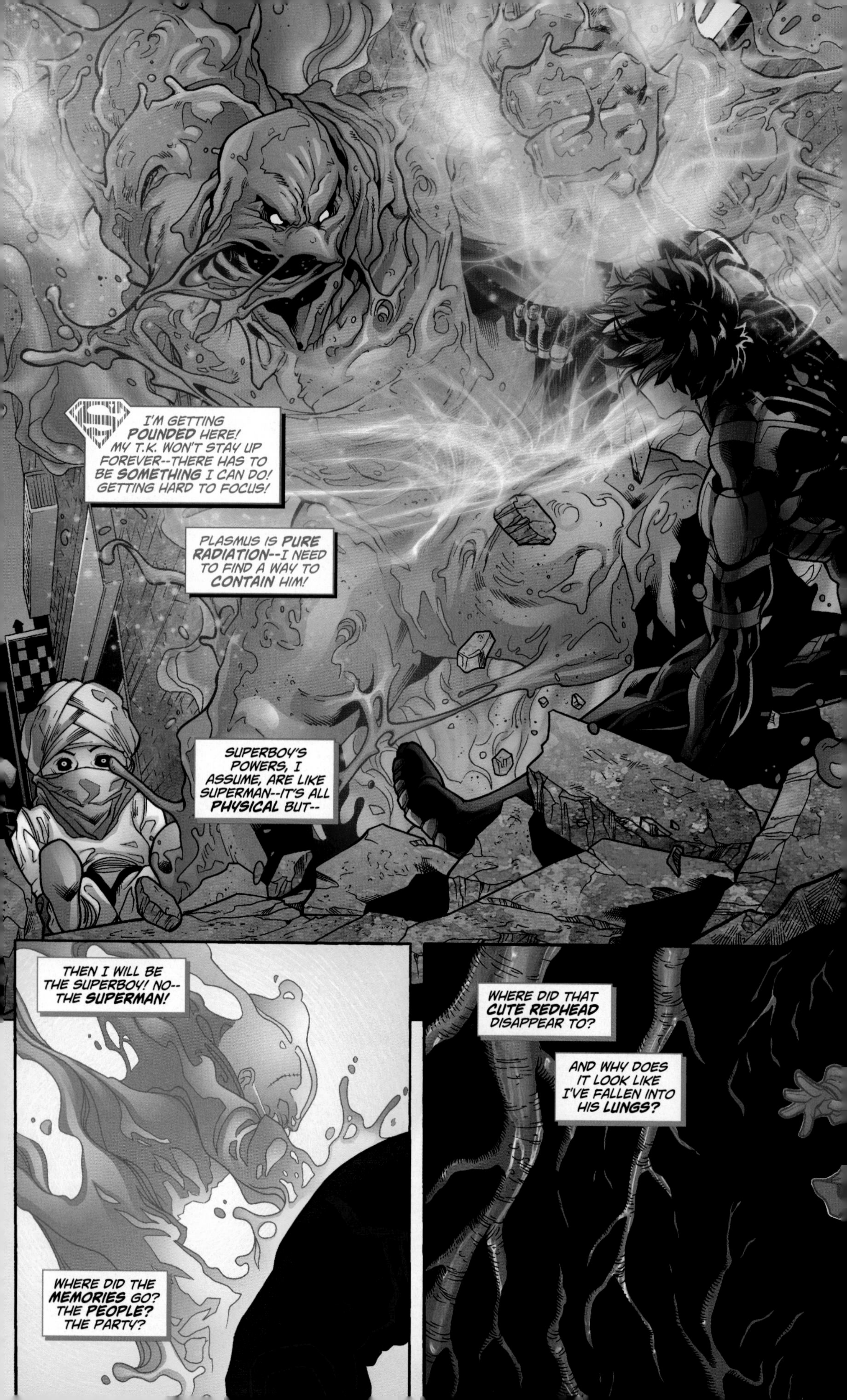
I'M GETTING POUNDED HERE! MY T.K. WON'T STAY UP FOREVER--THERE HAS TO BE SOMETHING I CAN DO! GETTING HARD TO FOCUS!
PLASMUS IS PURE RADIATION--I NEED TO FIND A WAY TO CONTAIN HIM!
SUPERBOY'S POWERS, I ASSUME, ARE LIKE SUPERMAN--IT'S ALL PHYSICAL BUT--
THEN I WILL BE THE SUPERBOY! NO--THE SUPERMAN!
WHERE DID THE MEMORIES GO? THE PEOPLE? THE PARTY?
WHERE DID THAT CUTE REDHEAD DISAPPEAR TO?
AND WHY DOES IT LOOK LIKE I'VE FALLEN INTO HIS LUNGS?

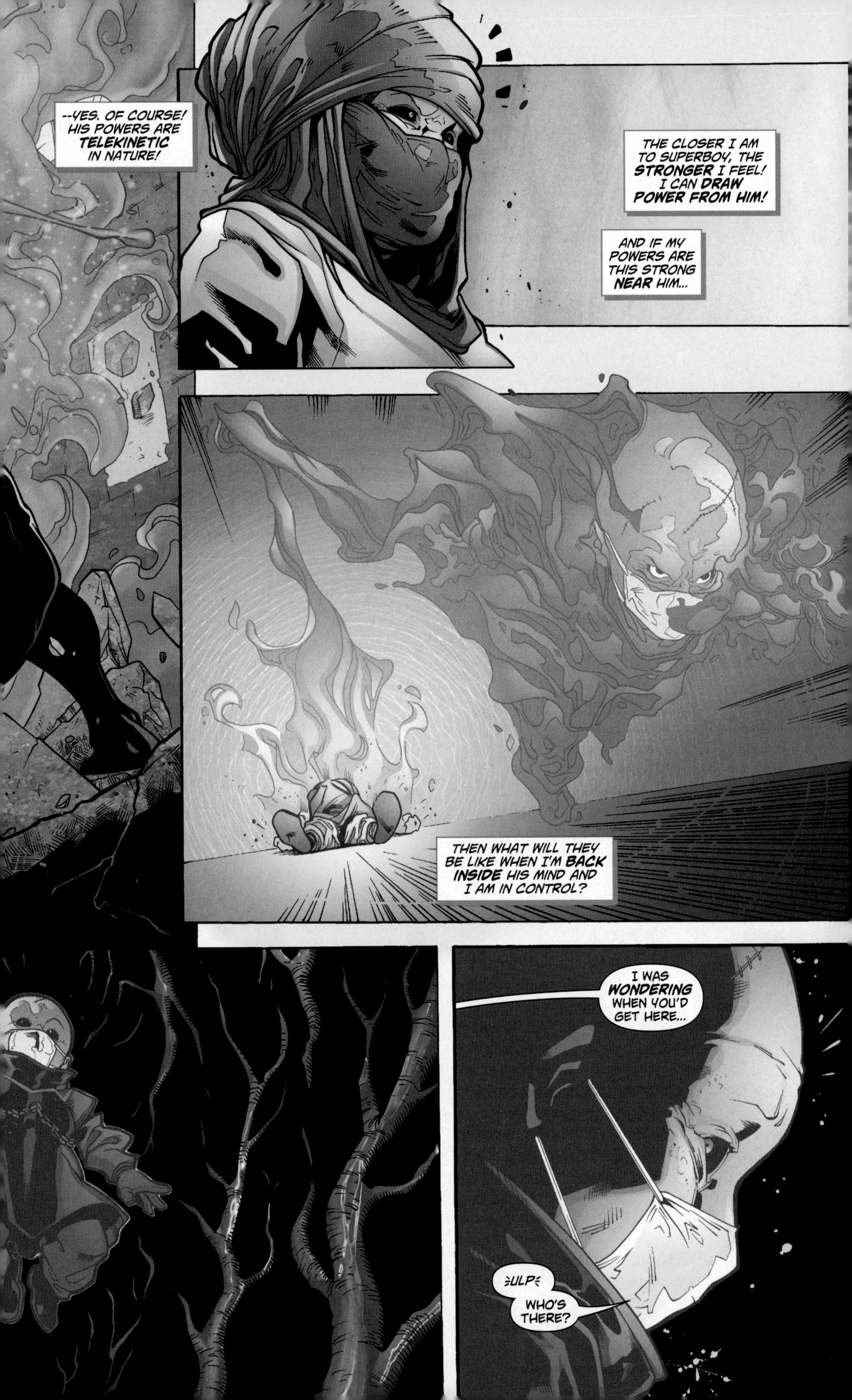
--YES. OF COURSE! HIS POWERS ARE TELEKINETIC IN NATURE!
THE CLOSER I AM TO SUPERBOY, THE STRONGER I FEEL! I CAN DRAW POWER FROM HIM!
AND IF MY POWERS ARE THIS STRONG NEAR HIM...
THEN WHAT WILL THEY BE LIKE WHEN I'M BACK INSIDE HIS MIND AND I AM IN CONTROL?
I WAS WONDERING WHEN YOU'D GET HERE...
ULP
WHO'S THERE?

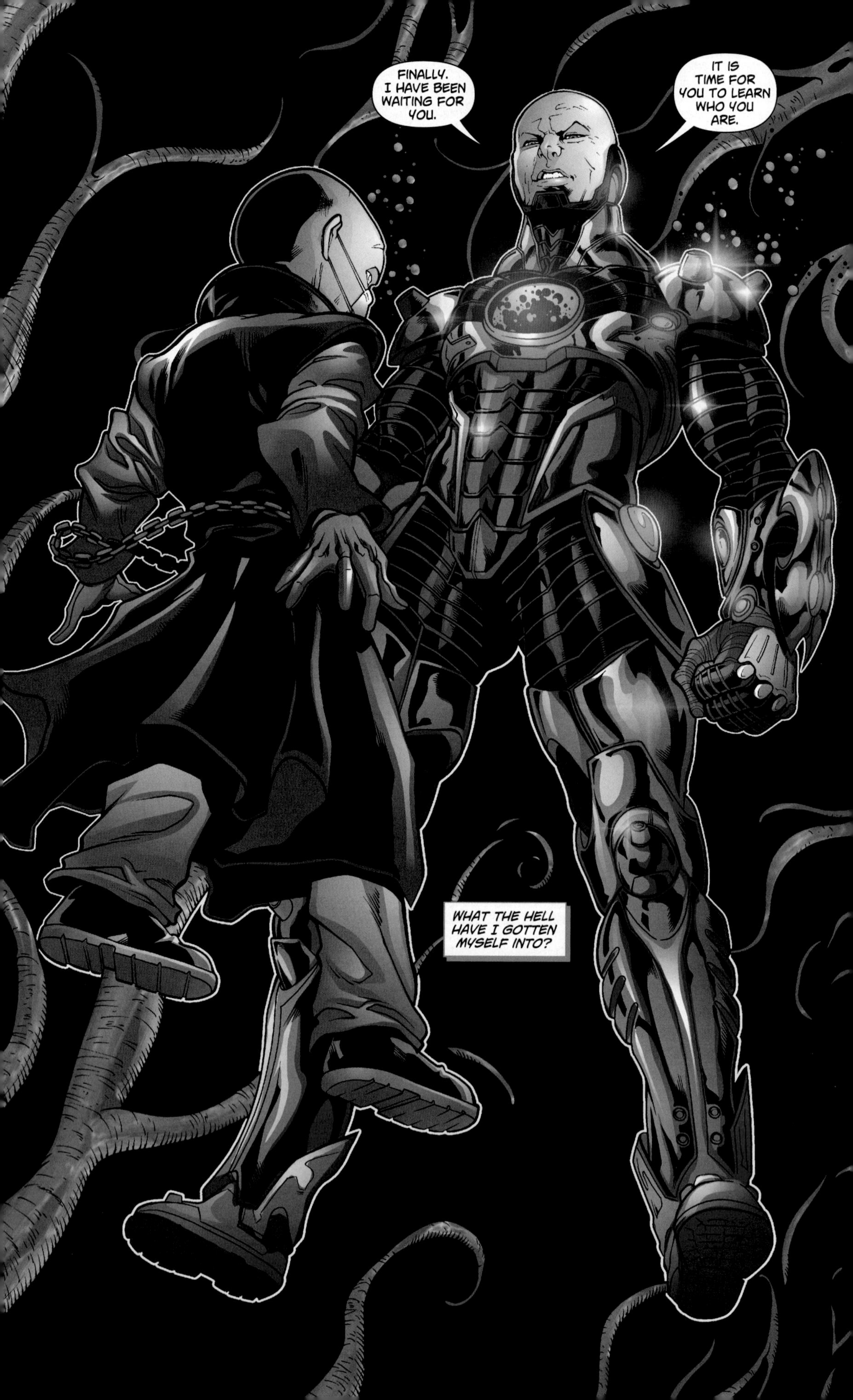
FINALLY. I HAVE BEEN WAITING FOR YOU.
IT IS TIME FOR YOU TO LEARN WHO YOU ARE.
WHAT THE HELL HAVE I GOTTEN MYSELF INTO?

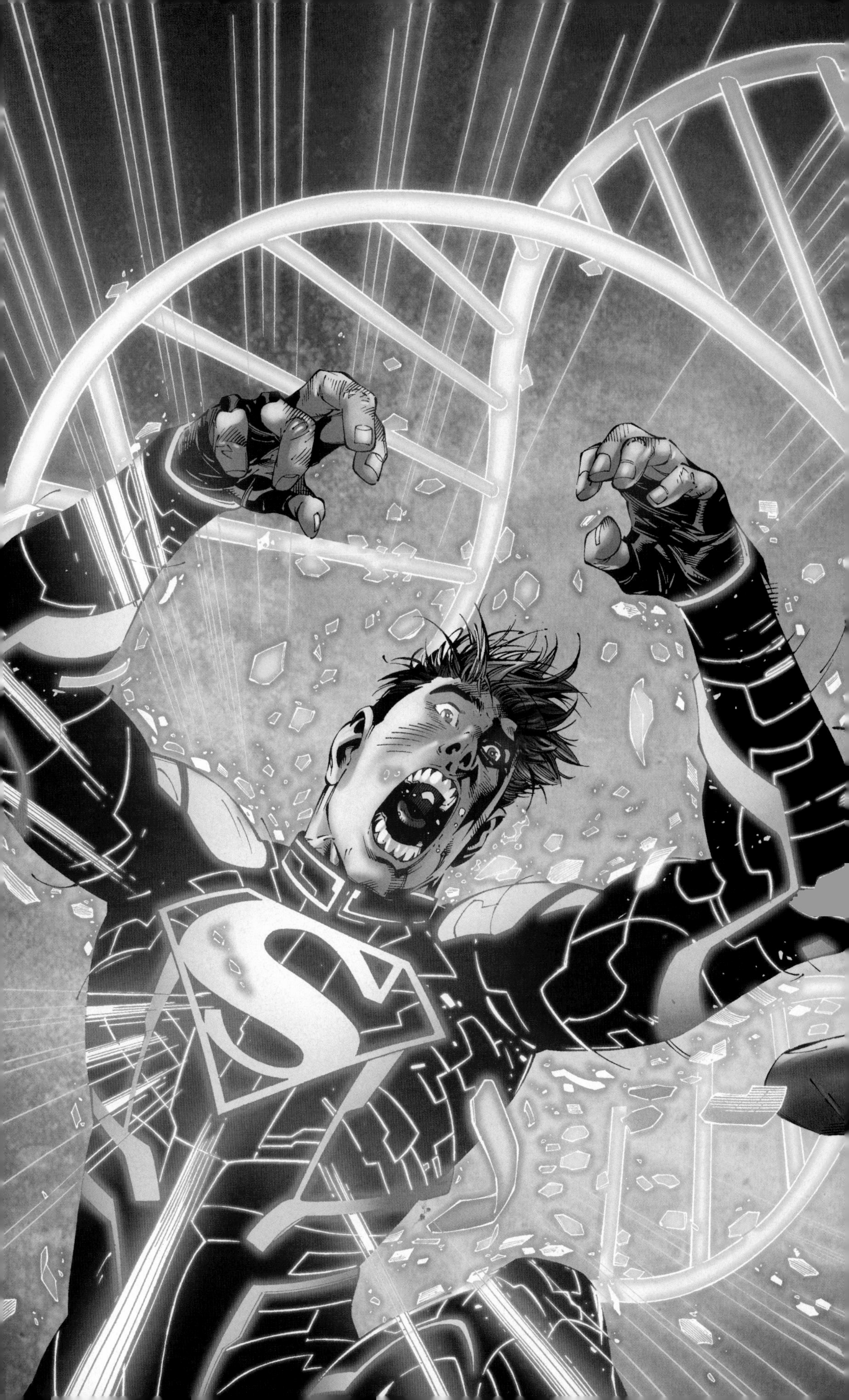

GONE BUT NOT FORGOTTEN

SCOTT LOBDELL writer **DIOGENES NEVES & R.B. SILVA** pencillers **VICENTE CIFUENTES & ROB LEAN** inkers

cover art by **ARDIAN SYAF, JAIME MENDOZA & BLOND**

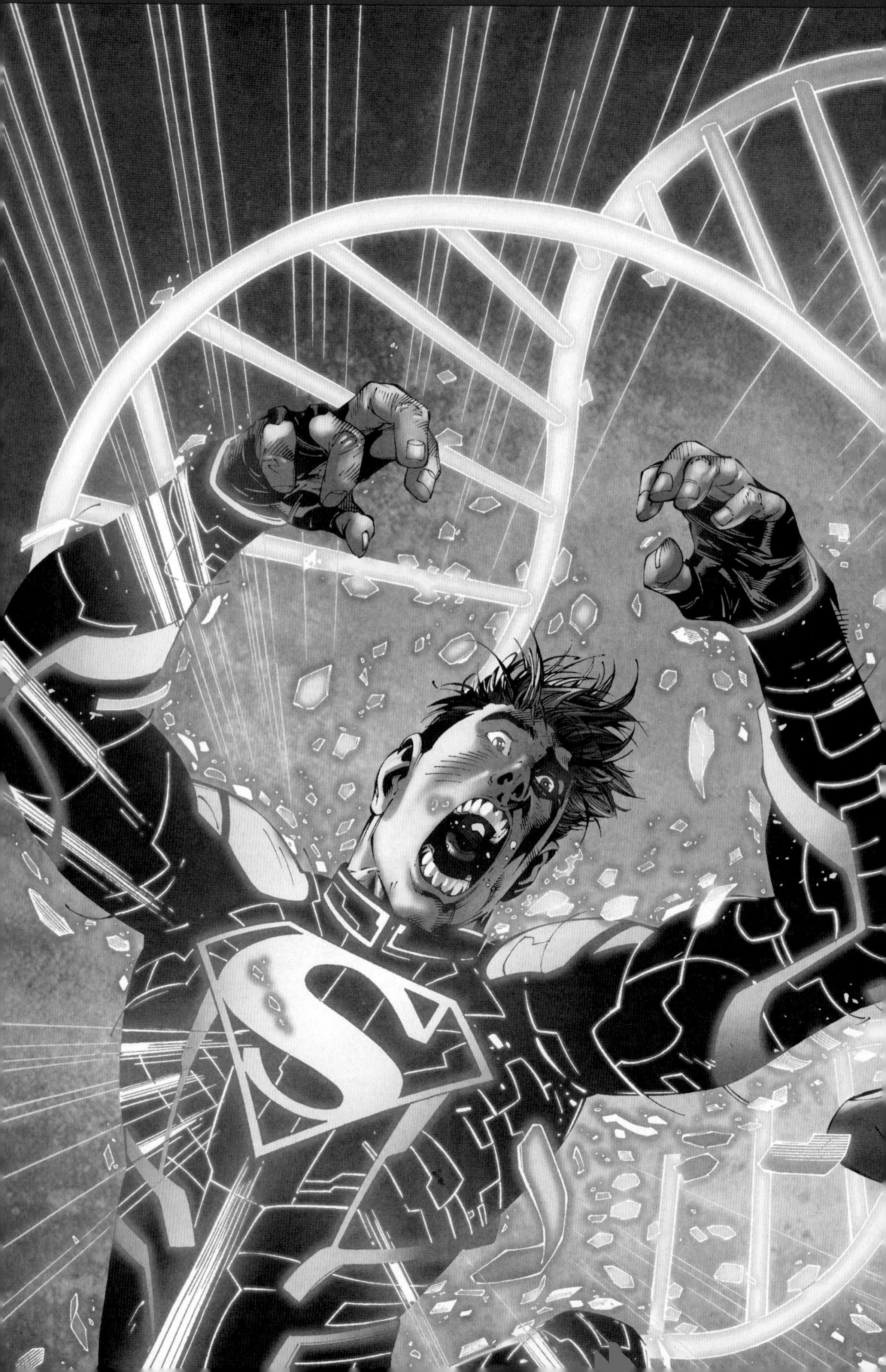

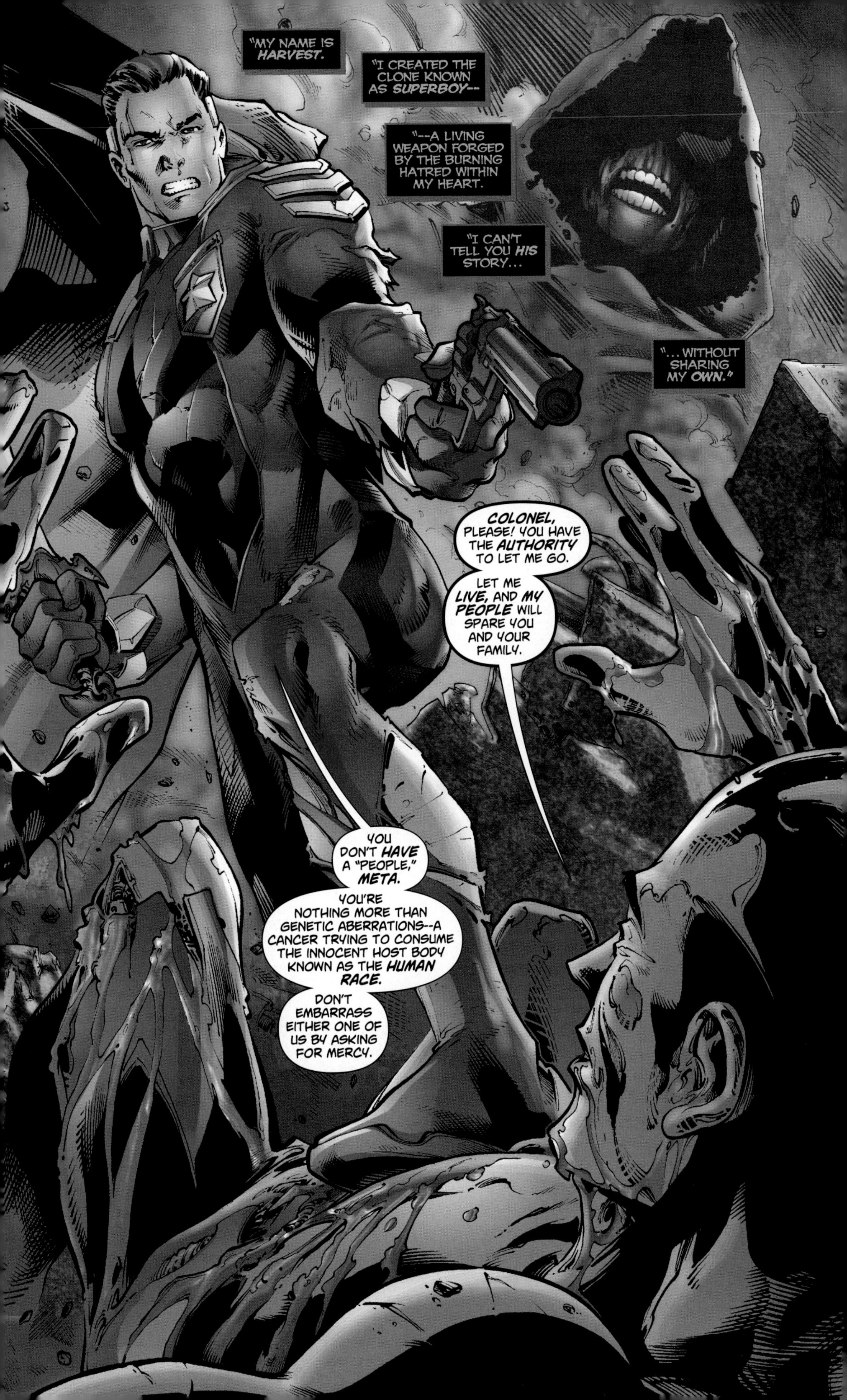
"MY NAME IS HARVEST.
"I CREATED THE CLONE KNOWN AS SUPERBOY--
"--A LIVING WEAPON FORGED BY THE BURNING HATRED WITHIN MY HEART.
"I CAN'T TELL YOU HIS STORY...
"...WITHOUT SHARING MY OWN."
COLONEL, PLEASE! YOU HAVE THE AUTHORITY TO LET ME GO.
LET ME LIVE, AND MY PEOPLE WILL SPARE YOU AND YOUR FAMILY.
YOU DON'T HAVE A "PEOPLE," META.
YOU'RE NOTHING MORE THAN GENETIC ABERRATIONS--A CANCER TRYING TO CONSUME THE INNOCENT HOST BODY KNOWN AS THE HUMAN RACE.
DON'T EMBARRASS EITHER ONE OF US BY ASKING FOR MERCY.

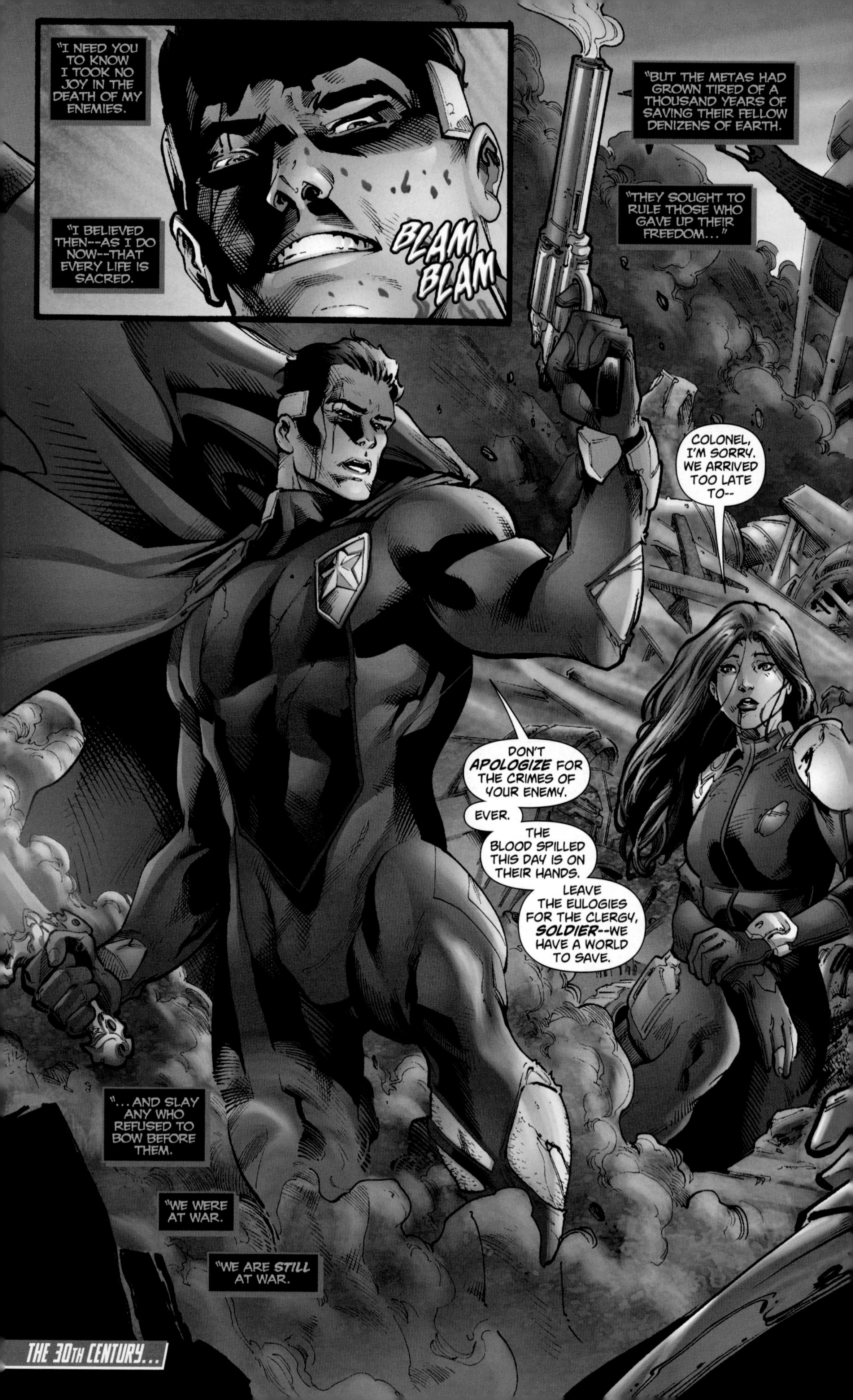
"I NEED YOU TO KNOW I TOOK NO JOY IN THE DEATH OF MY ENEMIES.
"I BELIEVED THEN--AS I DO NOW--THAT EVERY LIFE IS SACRED.
BLAM BLAM
"BUT THE METAS HAD GROWN TIRED OF A THOUSAND YEARS OF SAVING THEIR FELLOW DENIZENS OF EARTH.
"THEY SOUGHT TO RULE THOSE WHO GAVE UP THEIR FREEDOM..."
COLONEL, I'M SORRY. WE ARRIVED TOO LATE TO--
DON'T APOLOGIZE FOR THE CRIMES OF YOUR ENEMY.
EVER.
THE BLOOD SPILLED THIS DAY IS ON THEIR HANDS.
LEAVE THE EULOGIES FOR THE CLERGY, SOLDIER--WE HAVE A WORLD TO SAVE.
"...AND SLAY ANY WHO REFUSED TO BOW BEFORE THEM.
"WE WERE AT WAR.
"WE ARE STILL AT WAR.
THE 30TH CENTURY...

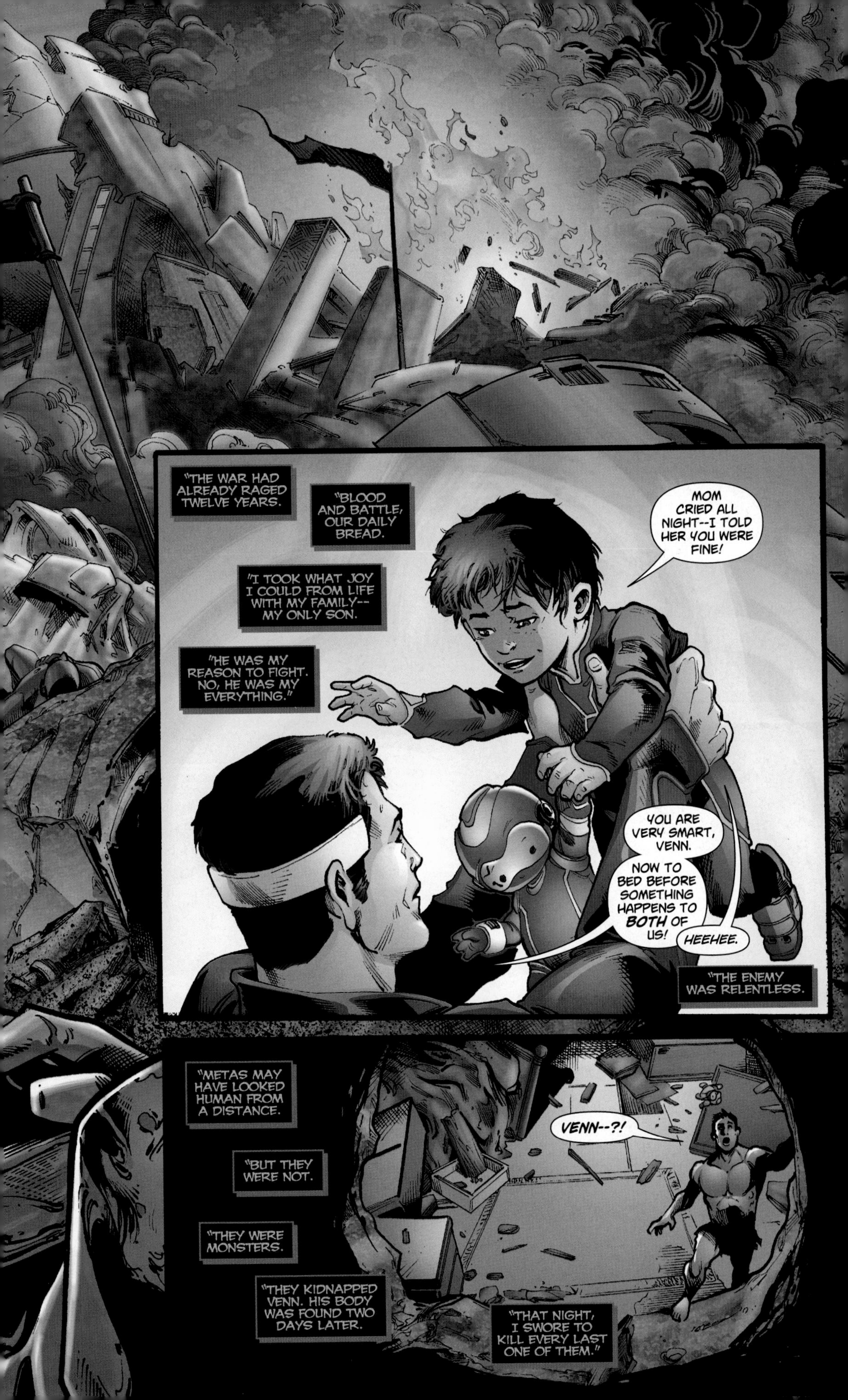
"THE WAR HAD ALREADY RAGED TWELVE YEARS.
"BLOOD AND BATTLE, OUR DAILY BREAD.
"I TOOK WHAT JOY I COULD FROM LIFE WITH MY FAMILY-- MY ONLY SON.
"HE WAS MY REASON TO FIGHT. NO, HE WAS MY EVERYTHING."
MOM CRIED ALL NIGHT--I TOLD HER YOU WERE FINE!
YOU ARE VERY SMART, VENN.
NOW TO BED BEFORE SOMETHING HAPPENS TO BOTH OF US!
HEEHEE.
"THE ENEMY WAS RELENTLESS.
"METAS MAY HAVE LOOKED HUMAN FROM A DISTANCE.
"BUT THEY WERE NOT.
"THEY WERE MONSTERS.
"THEY KIDNAPPED VENN. HIS BODY WAS FOUND TWO DAYS LATER.
VENN--?!
"THAT NIGHT, I SWORE TO KILL EVERY LAST ONE OF THEM."

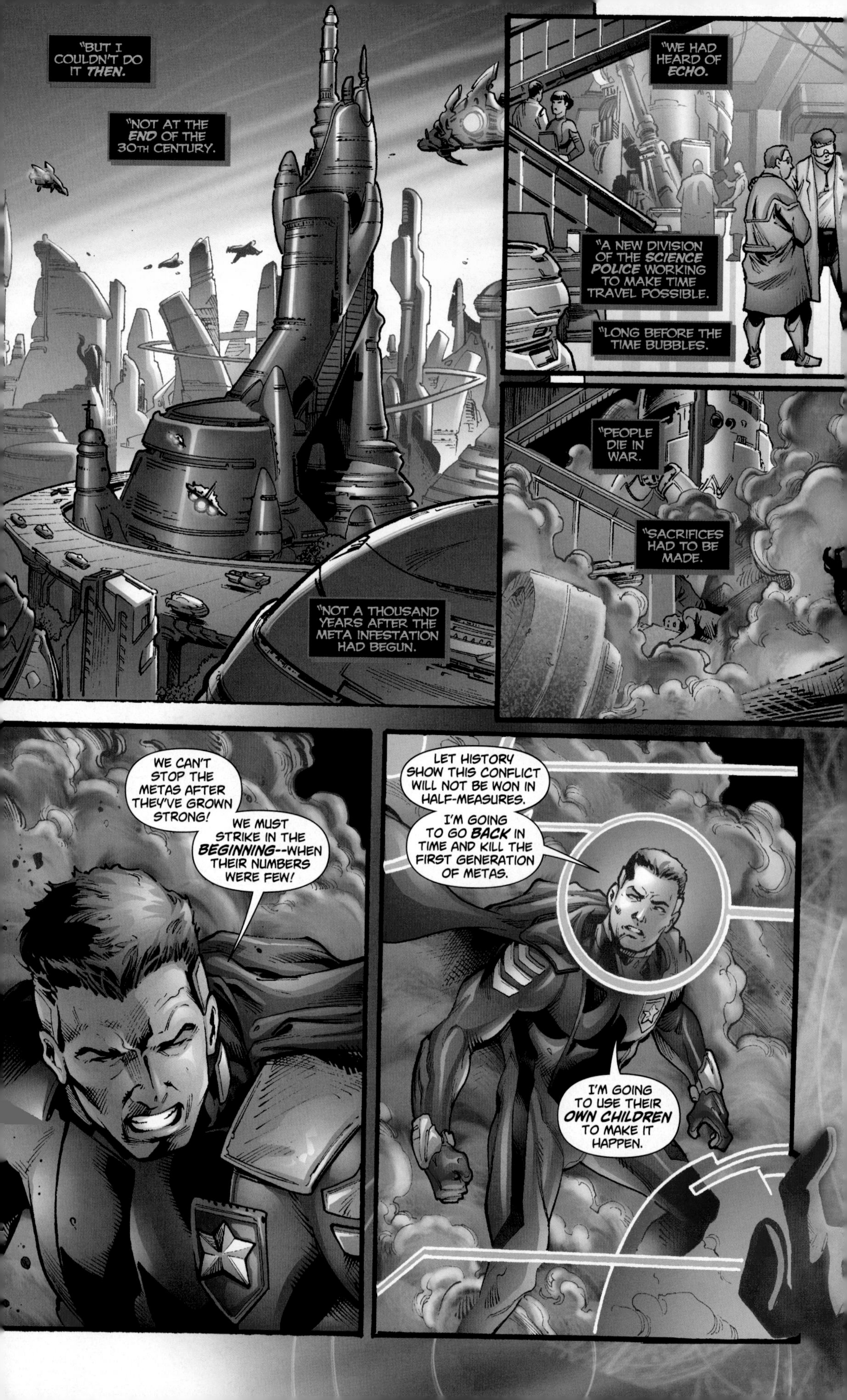

"BUT I COULDN'T DO IT THEN.
"NOT AT THE END OF THE 30TH CENTURY.
"NOT A THOUSAND YEARS AFTER THE META INFESTATION HAD BEGUN.
"WE HAD HEARD OF ECHO.
"A NEW DIVISION OF THE SCIENCE POLICE WORKING TO MAKE TIME TRAVEL POSSIBLE.
"LONG BEFORE THE TIME BUBBLES.
"PEOPLE DIE IN WAR.
"SACRIFICES HAD TO BE MADE.
WE CAN'T STOP THE METAS AFTER THEY'VE GROWN STRONG!
WE MUST STRIKE IN THE BEGINNING--WHEN THEIR NUMBERS WERE FEW!
LET HISTORY SHOW THIS CONFLICT WILL NOT BE WON IN HALF-MEASURES.
I'M GOING TO GO BACK IN TIME AND KILL THE FIRST GENERATION OF METAS.
I'M GOING TO USE THEIR OWN CHILDREN TO MAKE IT HAPPEN.

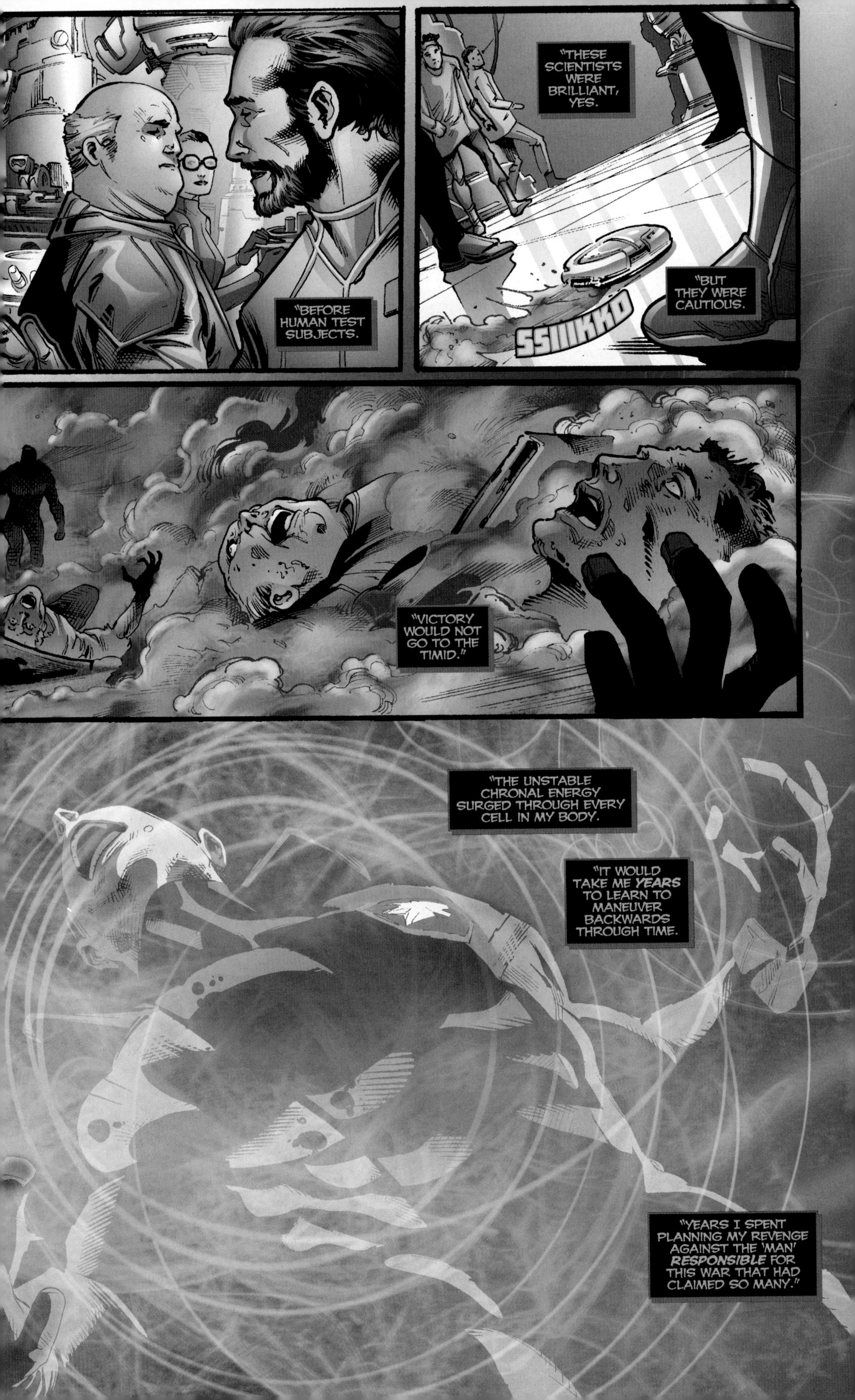
"BEFORE HUMAN TEST SUBJECTS.
"THESE SCIENTISTS WERE BRILLIANT, YES.
"BUT THEY WERE CAUTIOUS.
SSIIIKKD
"VICTORY WOULD NOT GO TO THE TIMID."
"THE UNSTABLE CHRONAL ENERGY SURGED THROUGH EVERY CELL IN MY BODY.
"IT WOULD TAKE ME *YEARS* TO LEARN TO MANEUVER BACKWARDS THROUGH TIME.
"YEARS I SPENT PLANNING MY REVENGE AGAINST THE 'MAN' *RESPONSIBLE* FOR THIS WAR THAT HAD CLAIMED SO MANY."

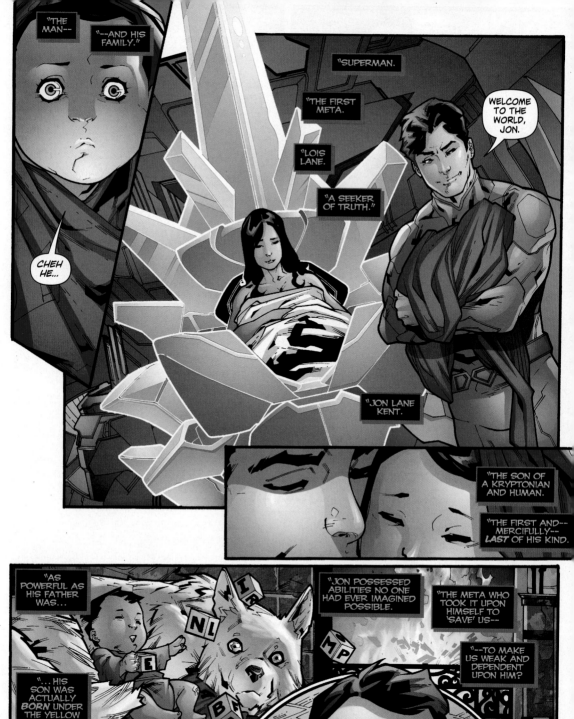

"THE MAN--

"--AND HIS FAMILY."

CHEH HE...

"SUPERMAN.

"THE FIRST META.

"LOIS LANE.

"A SEEKER OF TRUTH."

WELCOME TO THE WORLD, JON.

"JON LANE KENT.

"THE SON OF A KRYPTONIAN AND HUMAN.

"THE FIRST AND-- MERCIFULLY-- LAST OF HIS KIND.

"AS POWERFUL AS HIS FATHER WAS...

"JON POSSESSED ABILITIES NO ONE HAD EVER IMAGINED POSSIBLE.

"THE META WHO TOOK IT UPON HIMSELF TO 'SAVE' US--

"--TO MAKE US WEAK AND DEPENDENT UPON HIM?

"...HIS SON WAS ACTUALLY BORN UNDER THE YELLOW SUN.

"FOR A MOMENT HE WAS DISTRACTED FROM HIS MACHINATIONS.

"FOR A TIME, HE WAS HAPPY."

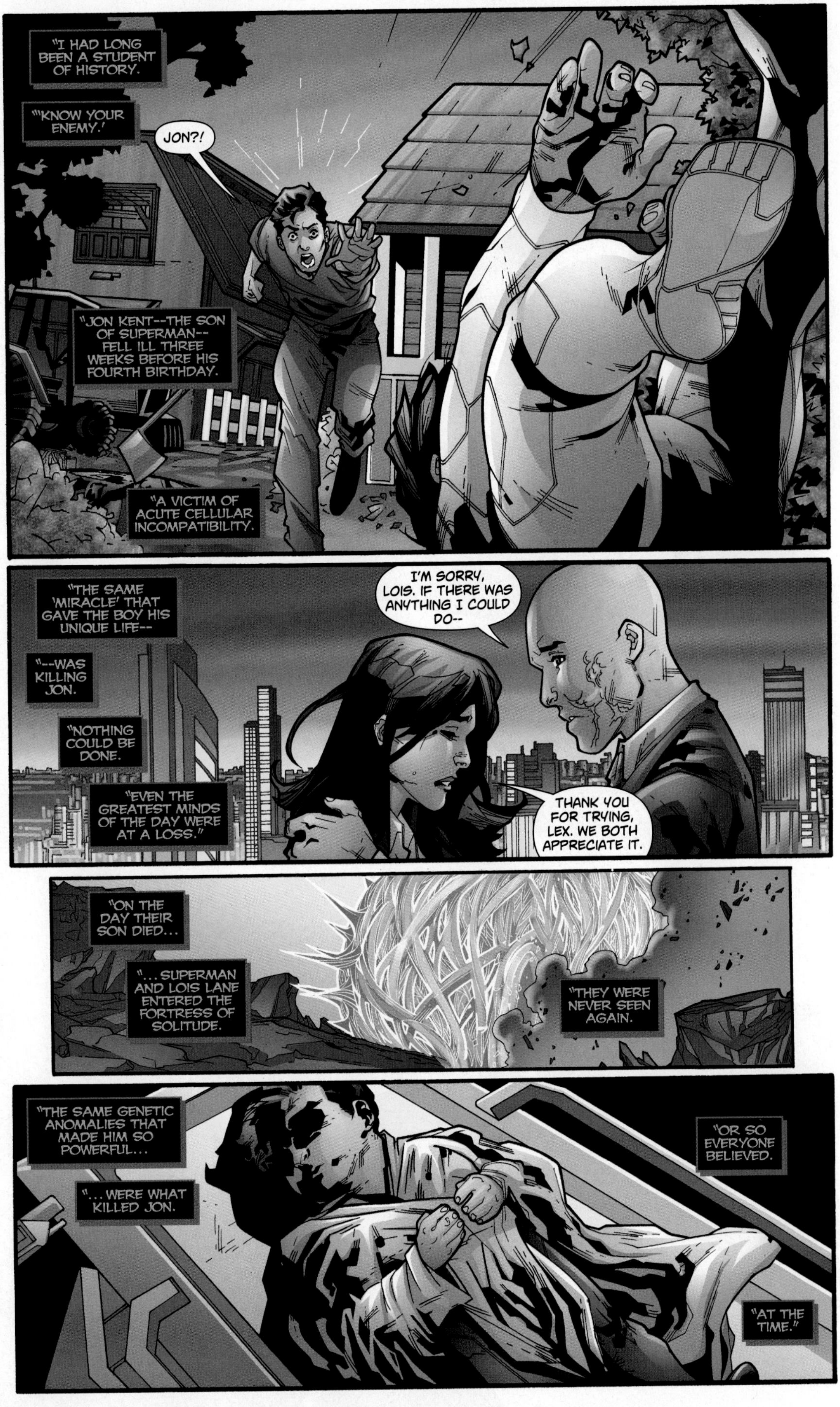
"I HAD LONG BEEN A STUDENT OF HISTORY.
"'KNOW YOUR ENEMY.'
JON?!
"JON KENT--THE SON OF SUPERMAN--FELL ILL THREE WEEKS BEFORE HIS FOURTH BIRTHDAY.
"A VICTIM OF ACUTE CELLULAR INCOMPATIBILITY.
"THE SAME 'MIRACLE' THAT GAVE THE BOY HIS UNIQUE LIFE--
"--WAS KILLING JON.
"NOTHING COULD BE DONE.
"EVEN THE GREATEST MINDS OF THE DAY WERE AT A LOSS."
I'M SORRY, LOIS. IF THERE WAS ANYTHING I COULD DO--
THANK YOU FOR TRYING, LEX. WE BOTH APPRECIATE IT.
"ON THE DAY THEIR SON DIED...
"...SUPERMAN AND LOIS LANE ENTERED THE FORTRESS OF SOLITUDE.
"THEY WERE NEVER SEEN AGAIN.
"THE SAME GENETIC ANOMALIES THAT MADE HIM SO POWERFUL...
"...WERE WHAT KILLED JON.
"OR SO EVERYONE BELIEVED.
"AT THE TIME."

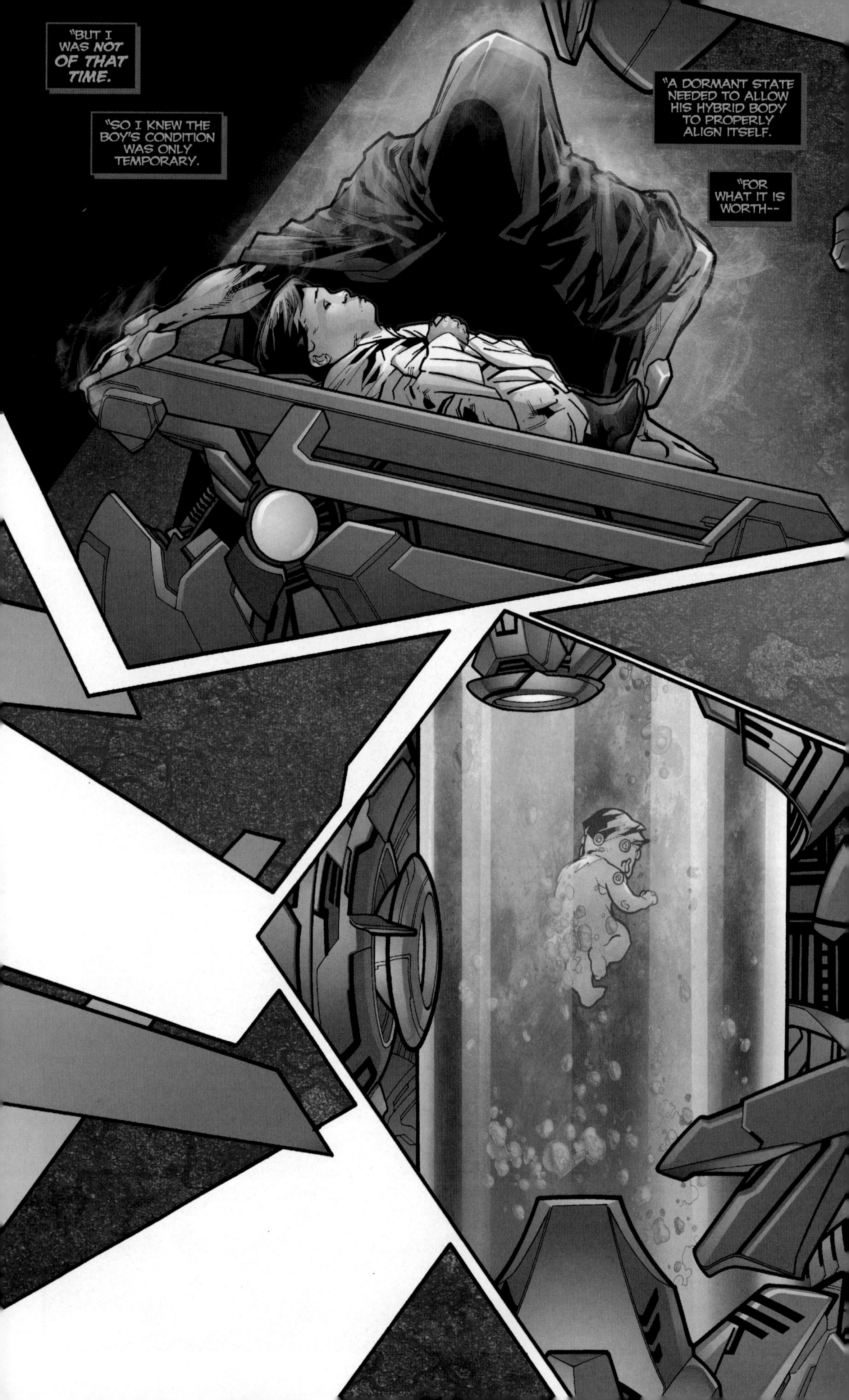
"BUT I WAS *NOT OF THAT TIME.*
"SO I KNEW THE BOY'S CONDITION WAS ONLY TEMPORARY.
"A DORMANT STATE NEEDED TO ALLOW HIS HYBRID BODY TO PROPERLY ALIGN ITSELF.
"FOR WHAT IT IS WORTH--

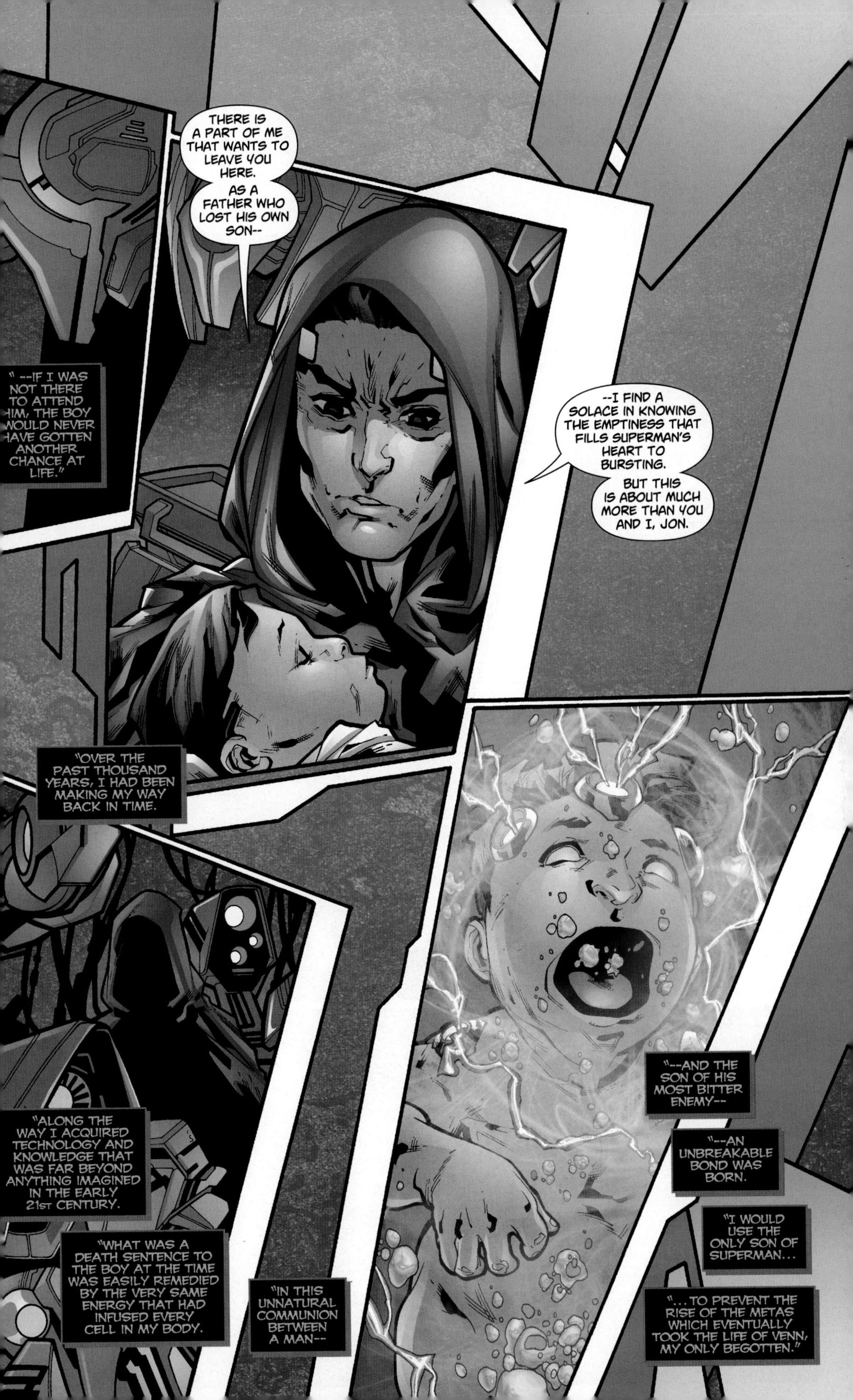
THERE IS A PART OF ME THAT WANTS TO LEAVE YOU HERE.
AS A FATHER WHO LOST HIS OWN SON--
--I FIND A SOLACE IN KNOWING THE EMPTINESS THAT FILLS SUPERMAN'S HEART TO BURSTING.
BUT THIS IS ABOUT MUCH MORE THAN YOU AND I, JON.
"--IF I WAS NOT THERE TO ATTEND HIM, THE BOY WOULD NEVER HAVE GOTTEN ANOTHER CHANCE AT LIFE."
"OVER THE PAST THOUSAND YEARS, I HAD BEEN MAKING MY WAY BACK IN TIME.
"ALONG THE WAY I ACQUIRED TECHNOLOGY AND KNOWLEDGE THAT WAS FAR BEYOND ANYTHING IMAGINED IN THE EARLY 21ST CENTURY.
"WHAT WAS A DEATH SENTENCE TO THE BOY AT THE TIME WAS EASILY REMEDIED BY THE VERY SAME ENERGY THAT HAD INFUSED EVERY CELL IN MY BODY.
"IN THIS UNNATURAL COMMUNION BETWEEN A MAN--
"--AND THE SON OF HIS MOST BITTER ENEMY--
"--AN UNBREAKABLE BOND WAS BORN.
"I WOULD USE THE ONLY SON OF SUPERMAN...
"...TO PREVENT THE RISE OF THE METAS WHICH EVENTUALLY TOOK THE LIFE OF VENN, MY ONLY BEGOTTEN."

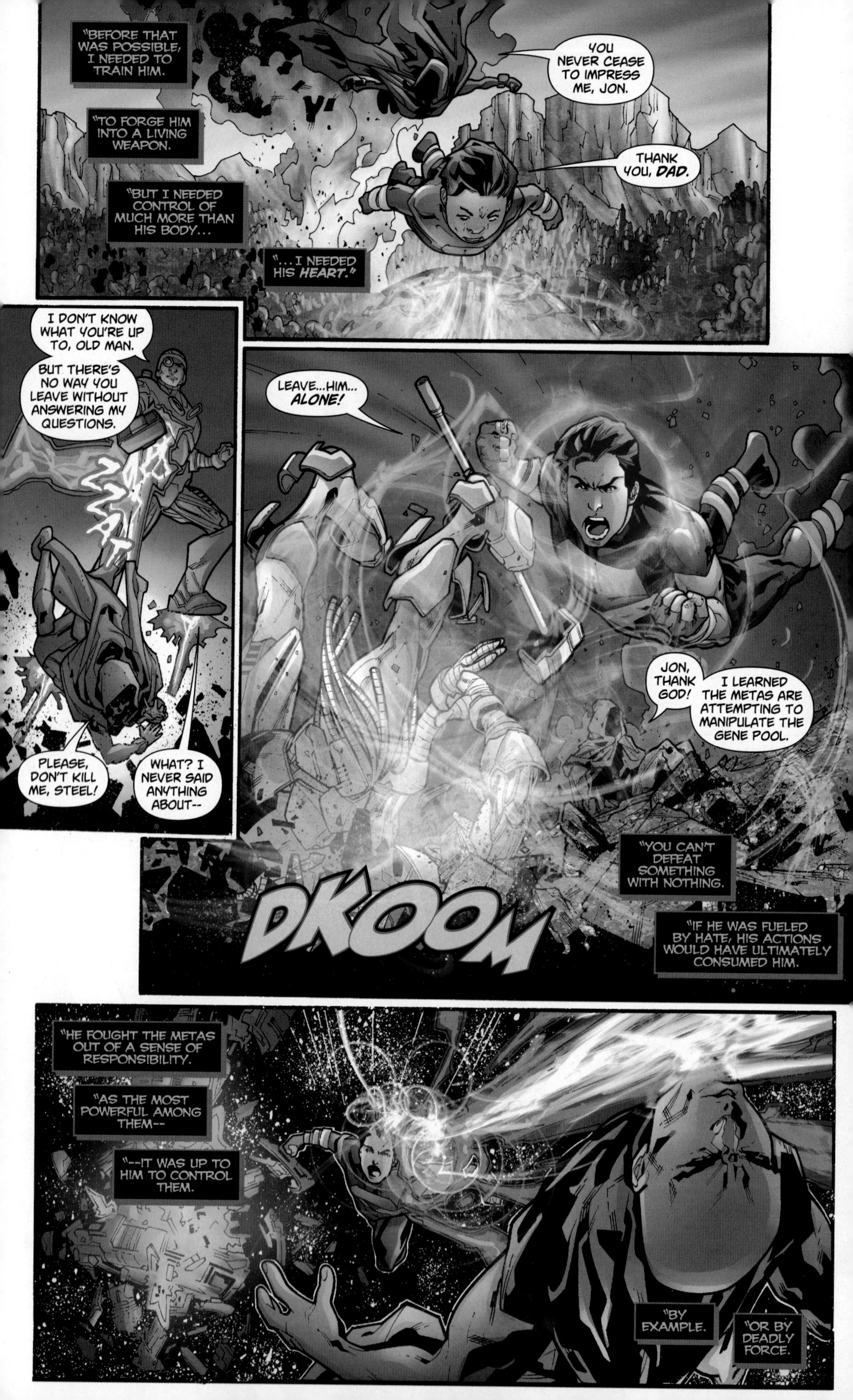
"BEFORE THAT WAS POSSIBLE, I NEEDED TO TRAIN HIM.
YOU NEVER CEASE TO IMPRESS ME, JON.
"TO FORGE HIM INTO A LIVING WEAPON.
THANK YOU, DAD.
"BUT I NEEDED CONTROL OF MUCH MORE THAN HIS BODY...
"...I NEEDED HIS HEART."
I DON'T KNOW WHAT YOU'RE UP TO, OLD MAN.
BUT THERE'S NO WAY YOU LEAVE WITHOUT ANSWERING MY QUESTIONS.
PLEASE, DON'T KILL ME, STEEL!
WHAT? I NEVER SAID ANYTHING ABOUT--
LEAVE...HIM... ALONE!
JON, THANK GOD!
I LEARNED THE METAS ARE ATTEMPTING TO MANIPULATE THE GENE POOL.
DKOOM
"YOU CAN'T DEFEAT SOMETHING WITH NOTHING.
"IF HE WAS FUELED BY HATE, HIS ACTIONS WOULD HAVE ULTIMATELY CONSUMED HIM.
"HE FOUGHT THE METAS OUT OF A SENSE OF RESPONSIBILITY.
"AS THE MOST POWERFUL AMONG THEM--
"--IT WAS UP TO HIM TO CONTROL THEM.
"BY EXAMPLE.
"OR BY DEADLY FORCE.

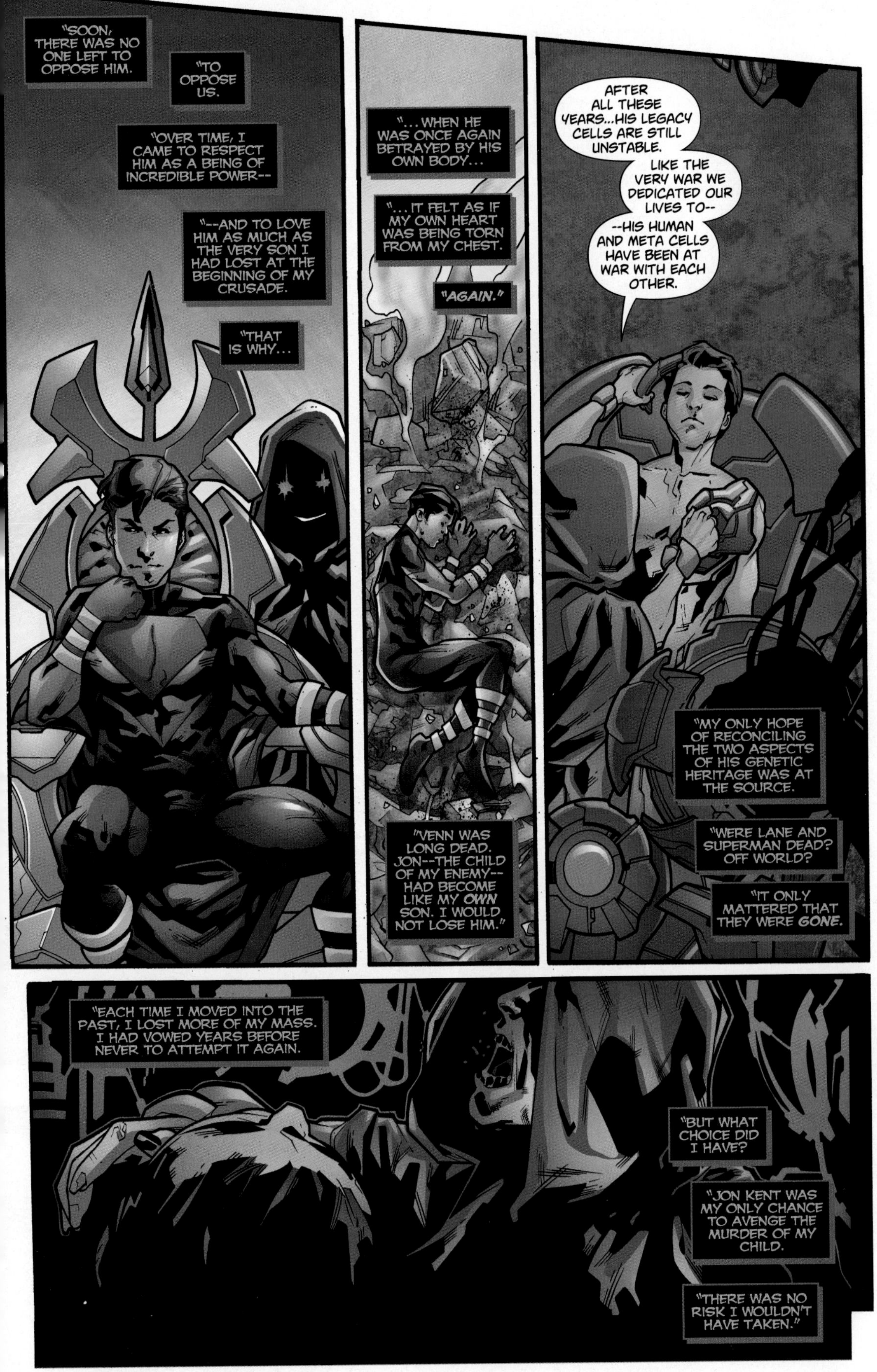
"SOON, THERE WAS NO ONE LEFT TO OPPOSE HIM.
"TO OPPOSE US.
"OVER TIME, I CAME TO RESPECT HIM AS A BEING OF INCREDIBLE POWER--
"--AND TO LOVE HIM AS MUCH AS THE VERY SON I HAD LOST AT THE BEGINNING OF MY CRUSADE.
"THAT IS WHY...
"...WHEN HE WAS ONCE AGAIN BETRAYED BY HIS OWN BODY...
"...IT FELT AS IF MY OWN HEART WAS BEING TORN FROM MY CHEST.
"AGAIN."
"VENN WAS LONG DEAD. JON--THE CHILD OF MY ENEMY--HAD BECOME LIKE MY OWN SON. I WOULD NOT LOSE HIM."
AFTER ALL THESE YEARS...HIS LEGACY CELLS ARE STILL UNSTABLE.
LIKE THE VERY WAR WE DEDICATED OUR LIVES TO--
--HIS HUMAN AND META CELLS HAVE BEEN AT WAR WITH EACH OTHER.
"MY ONLY HOPE OF RECONCILING THE TWO ASPECTS OF HIS GENETIC HERITAGE WAS AT THE SOURCE.
"WERE LANE AND SUPERMAN DEAD? OFF WORLD?
"IT ONLY MATTERED THAT THEY WERE GONE.
"EACH TIME I MOVED INTO THE PAST, I LOST MORE OF MY MASS. I HAD VOWED YEARS BEFORE NEVER TO ATTEMPT IT AGAIN.
"BUT WHAT CHOICE DID I HAVE?
"JON KENT WAS MY ONLY CHANCE TO AVENGE THE MURDER OF MY CHILD.
"THERE WAS NO RISK I WOULDN'T HAVE TAKEN."

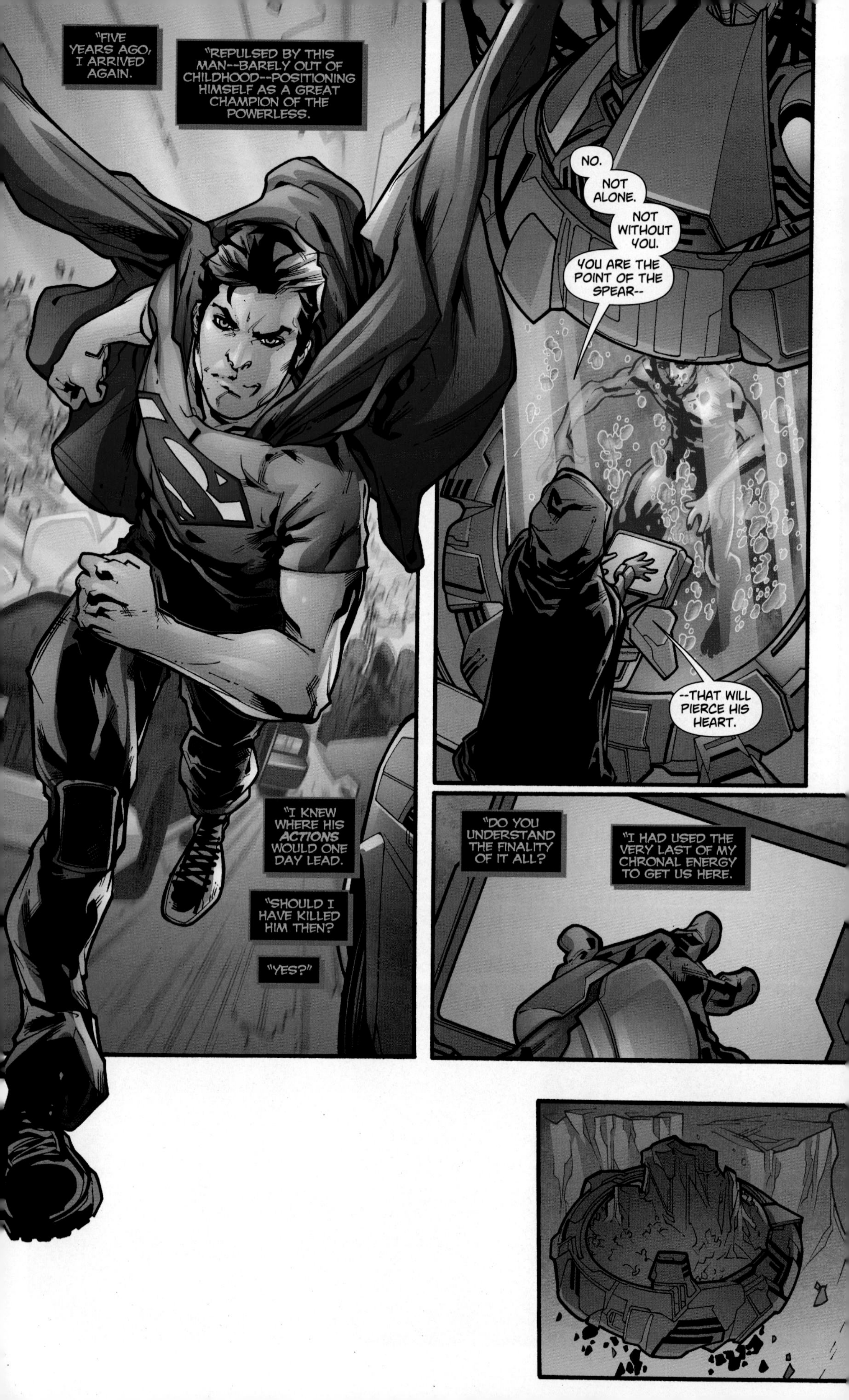
"FIVE YEARS AGO, I ARRIVED AGAIN.
"REPULSED BY THIS MAN--BARELY OUT OF CHILDHOOD--POSITIONING HIMSELF AS A GREAT CHAMPION OF THE POWERLESS.
"I KNEW WHERE HIS ACTIONS WOULD ONE DAY LEAD.
"SHOULD I HAVE KILLED HIM THEN?
"YES?"
NO.
NOT ALONE.
NOT WITHOUT YOU.
YOU ARE THE POINT OF THE SPEAR--
--THAT WILL PIERCE HIS HEART.
"DO YOU UNDERSTAND THE FINALITY OF IT ALL?
"I HAD USED THE VERY LAST OF MY CHRONAL ENERGY TO GET US HERE.

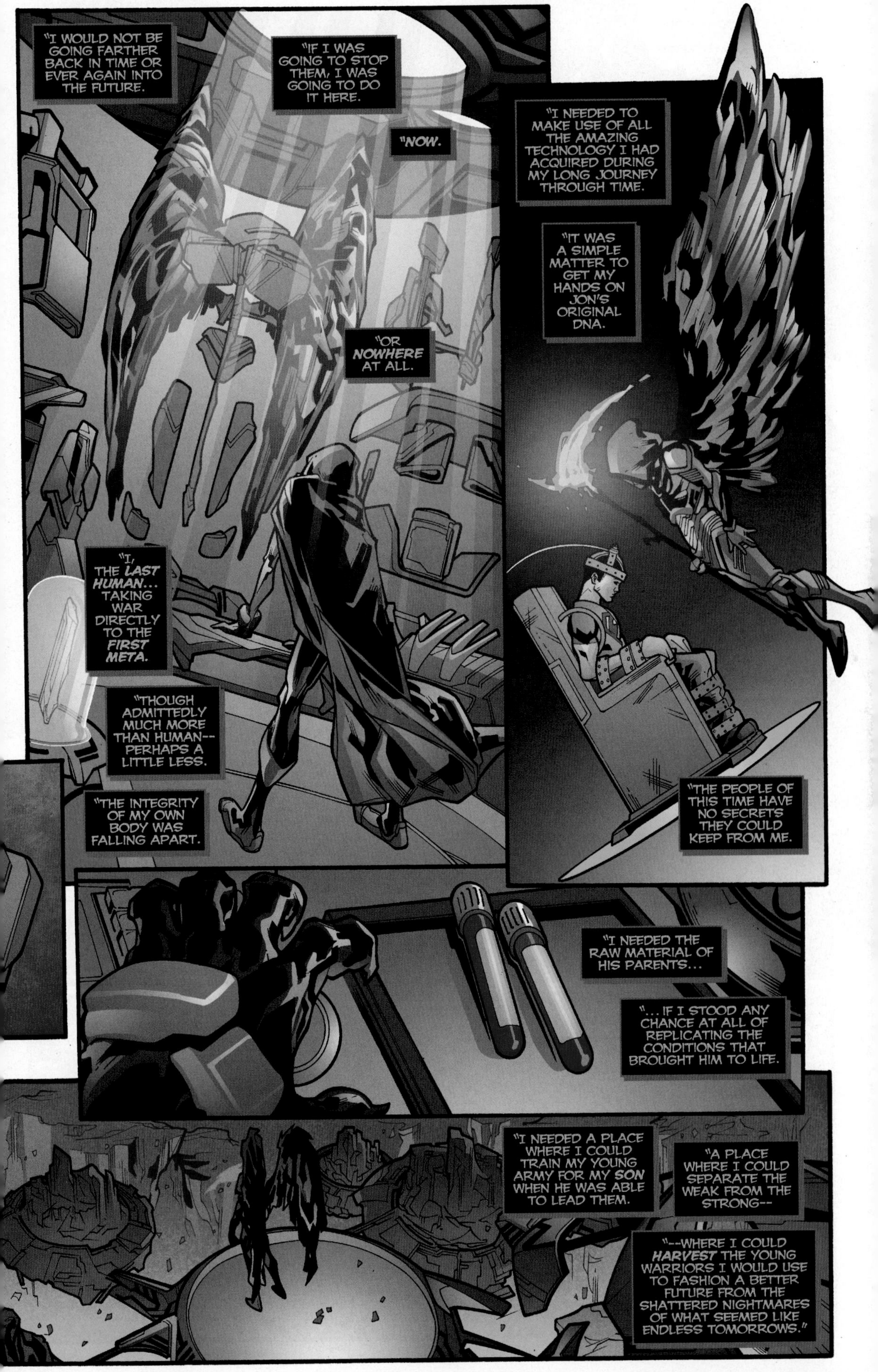
"I WOULD NOT BE GOING FARTHER BACK IN TIME OR EVER AGAIN INTO THE FUTURE.
"IF I WAS GOING TO STOP THEM, I WAS GOING TO DO IT HERE.
"*NOW*.
"OR *NOWHERE* AT ALL.
"I, THE *LAST HUMAN*... TAKING WAR DIRECTLY TO THE *FIRST META*.
"THOUGH ADMITTEDLY MUCH MORE THAN HUMAN--PERHAPS A LITTLE LESS.
"THE INTEGRITY OF MY OWN BODY WAS FALLING APART.
"I NEEDED TO MAKE USE OF ALL THE AMAZING TECHNOLOGY I HAD ACQUIRED DURING MY LONG JOURNEY THROUGH TIME.
"IT WAS A SIMPLE MATTER TO GET MY HANDS ON JON'S ORIGINAL DNA.
"THE PEOPLE OF THIS TIME HAVE NO SECRETS THEY COULD KEEP FROM ME.
"I NEEDED THE RAW MATERIAL OF HIS PARENTS...
"...IF I STOOD ANY CHANCE AT ALL OF REPLICATING THE CONDITIONS THAT BROUGHT HIM TO LIFE.
"I NEEDED A PLACE WHERE I COULD TRAIN MY YOUNG ARMY FOR MY *SON* WHEN HE WAS ABLE TO LEAD THEM.
"A PLACE WHERE I COULD SEPARATE THE WEAK FROM THE STRONG--
"--WHERE I COULD *HARVEST* THE YOUNG WARRIORS I WOULD USE TO FASHION A BETTER FUTURE FROM THE SHATTERED NIGHTMARES OF WHAT SEEMED LIKE ENDLESS TOMORROWS."

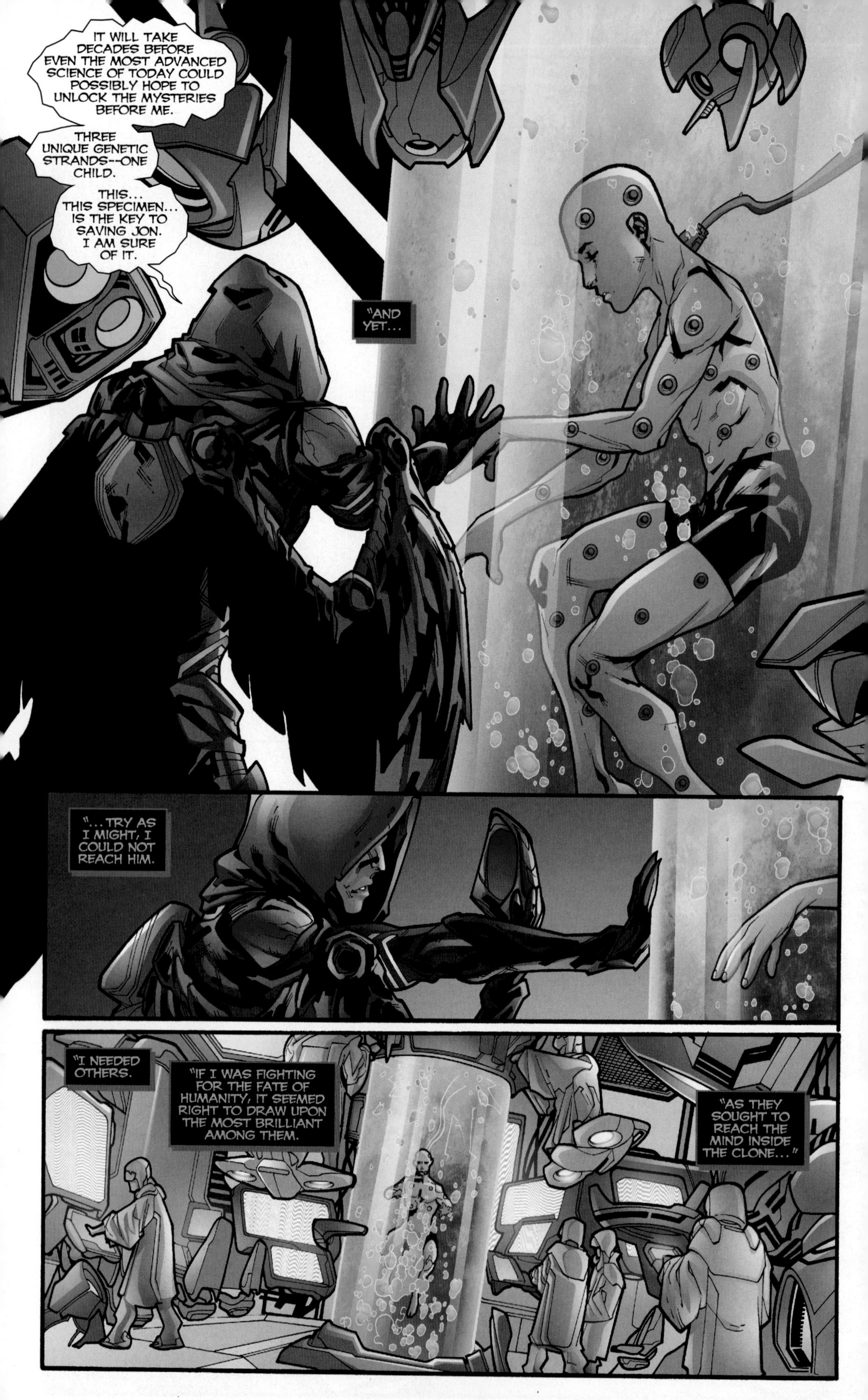

IT WILL TAKE DECADES BEFORE EVEN THE MOST ADVANCED SCIENCE OF TODAY COULD POSSIBLY HOPE TO UNLOCK THE MYSTERIES BEFORE ME.
THREE UNIQUE GENETIC STRANDS--ONE CHILD.
THIS... THIS SPECIMEN... IS THE KEY TO SAVING JON. I AM SURE OF IT.
"AND YET...
"...TRY AS I MIGHT, I COULD NOT REACH HIM.
"I NEEDED OTHERS.
"IF I WAS FIGHTING FOR THE FATE OF HUMANITY, IT SEEMED RIGHT TO DRAW UPON THE MOST BRILLIANT AMONG THEM.
"AS THEY SOUGHT TO REACH THE MIND INSIDE THE CLONE..."

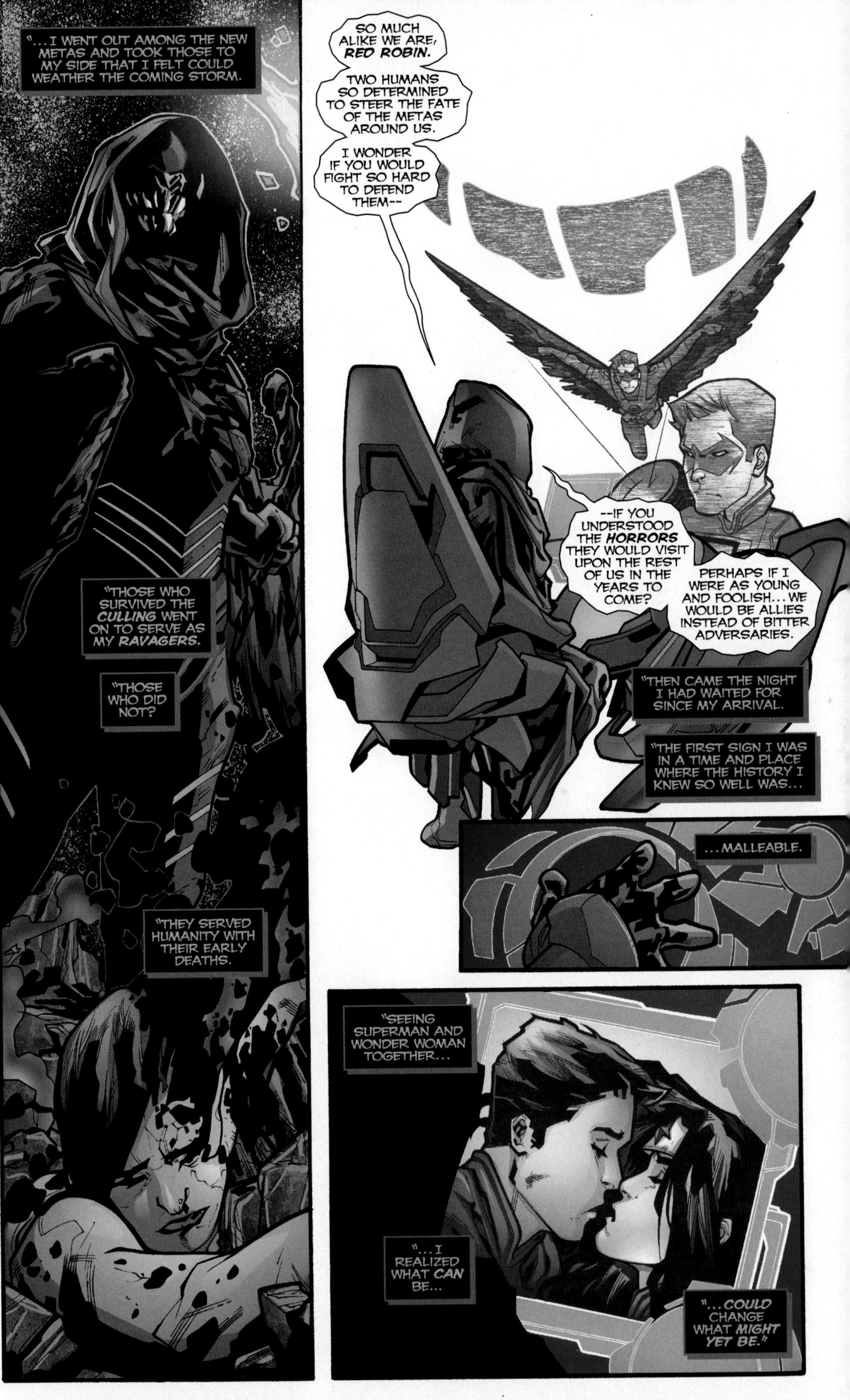
"...I WENT OUT AMONG THE NEW METAS AND TOOK THOSE TO MY SIDE THAT I FELT COULD WEATHER THE COMING STORM.
"THOSE WHO SURVIVED THE CULLING WENT ON TO SERVE AS MY RAVAGERS.
"THOSE WHO DID NOT?
"THEY SERVED HUMANITY WITH THEIR EARLY DEATHS.
SO MUCH ALIKE WE ARE, RED ROBIN.
TWO HUMANS SO DETERMINED TO STEER THE FATE OF THE METAS AROUND US.
I WONDER IF YOU WOULD FIGHT SO HARD TO DEFEND THEM--
--IF YOU UNDERSTOOD THE HORRORS THEY WOULD VISIT UPON THE REST OF US IN THE YEARS TO COME?
PERHAPS IF I WERE AS YOUNG AND FOOLISH... WE WOULD BE ALLIES INSTEAD OF BITTER ADVERSARIES.
"THEN CAME THE NIGHT I HAD WAITED FOR SINCE MY ARRIVAL.
"THE FIRST SIGN I WAS IN A TIME AND PLACE WHERE THE HISTORY I KNEW SO WELL WAS...
...MALLEABLE.
"SEEING SUPERMAN AND WONDER WOMAN TOGETHER...
"...I REALIZED WHAT CAN BE...
"...COULD CHANGE WHAT MIGHT YET BE."

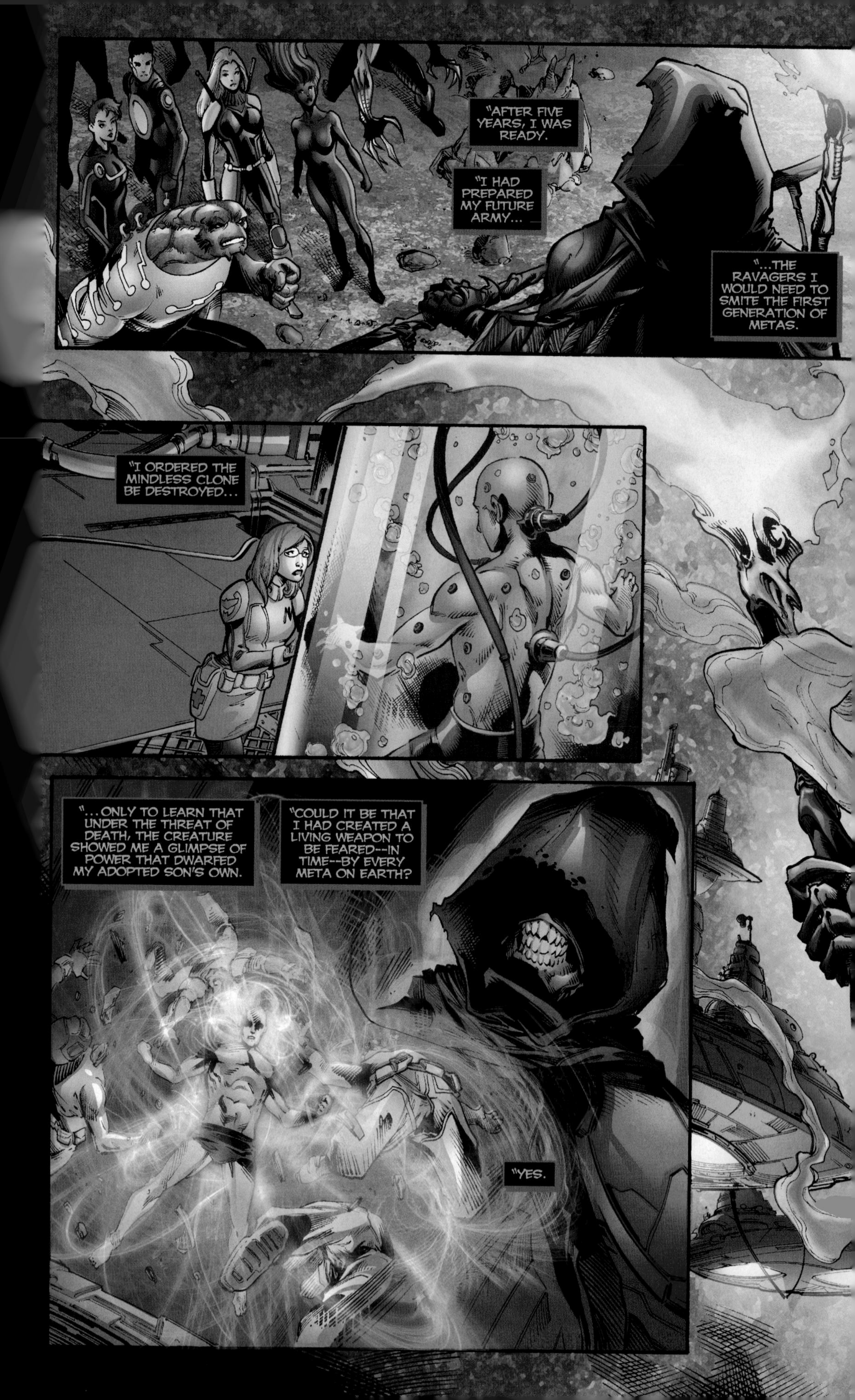
"AFTER FIVE YEARS, I WAS READY.
"I HAD PREPARED MY FUTURE ARMY...
"...THE RAVAGERS I WOULD NEED TO SMITE THE FIRST GENERATION OF METAS.
"I ORDERED THE MINDLESS CLONE BE DESTROYED...
"...ONLY TO LEARN THAT UNDER THE THREAT OF DEATH, THE CREATURE SHOWED ME A GLIMPSE OF POWER THAT DWARFED MY ADOPTED SON'S OWN.
"COULD IT BE THAT I HAD CREATED A LIVING WEAPON TO BE FEARED--IN TIME--BY EVERY META ON EARTH?
"YES.

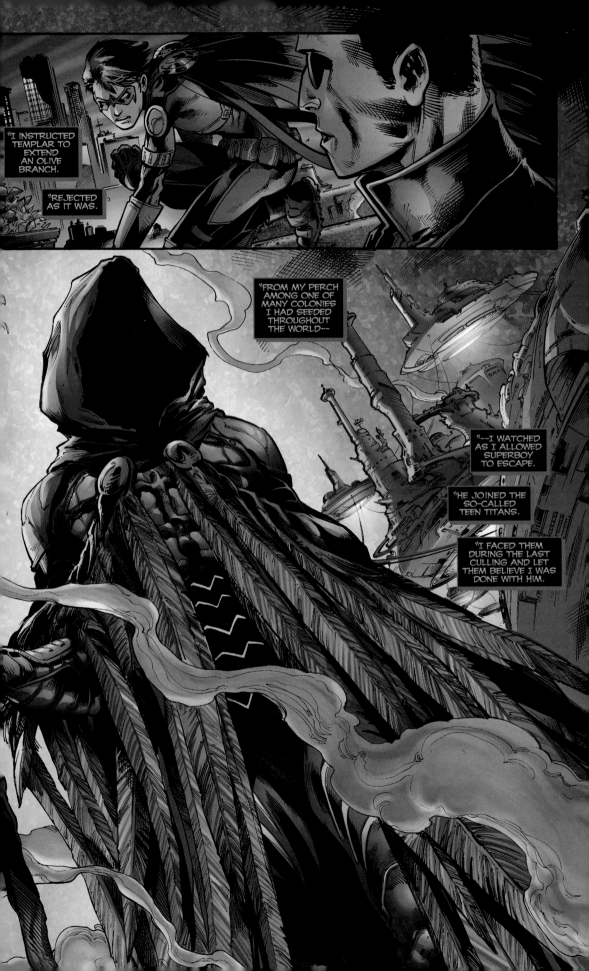

"I INSTRUCTED TEMPLAR TO EXTEND AN OLIVE BRANCH.

"REJECTED AS IT WAS.

"FROM MY PERCH AMONG ONE OF MANY COLONIES I HAD SEEDED THROUGHOUT THE WORLD--

"--I WATCHED AS I ALLOWED SUPERBOY TO ESCAPE.

"HE JOINED THE SO-CALLED TEEN TITANS.

"I FACED THEM DURING THE LAST CULLING AND LET THEM BELIEVE I WAS DONE WITH HIM.

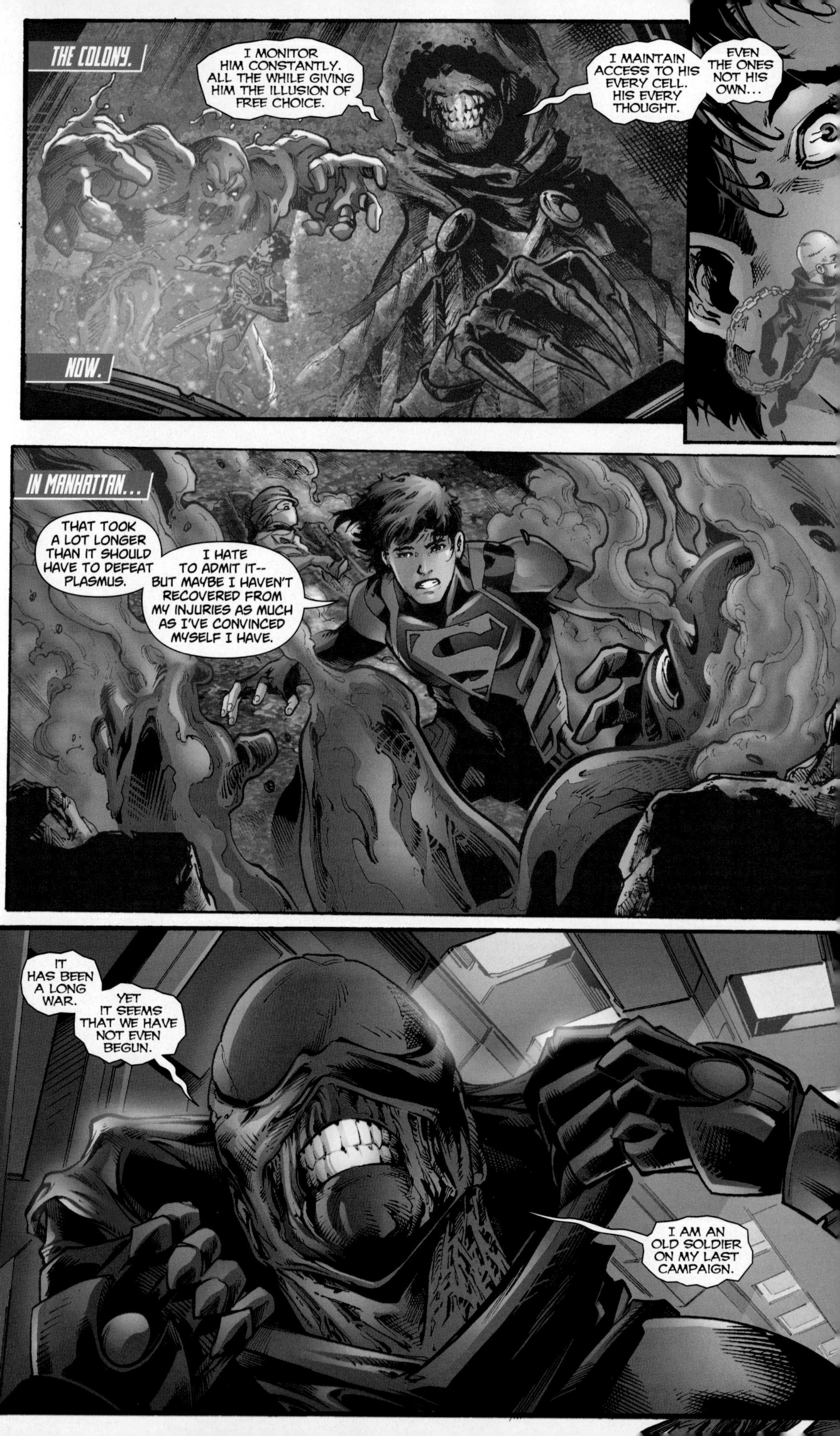
THE COLONY.
I MONITOR HIM CONSTANTLY. ALL THE WHILE GIVING HIM THE ILLUSION OF FREE CHOICE.
I MAINTAIN ACCESS TO HIS EVERY CELL. HIS EVERY THOUGHT.
EVEN THE ONES NOT HIS OWN...
NOW.
IN MANHATTAN...
THAT TOOK A LOT LONGER THAN IT SHOULD HAVE TO DEFEAT PLASMUS.
I HATE TO ADMIT IT-- BUT MAYBE I HAVEN'T RECOVERED FROM MY INJURIES AS MUCH AS I'VE CONVINCED MYSELF I HAVE.
IT HAS BEEN A LONG WAR.
YET IT SEEMS THAT WE HAVE NOT EVEN BEGUN.
I AM AN OLD SOLDIER ON MY LAST CAMPAIGN.

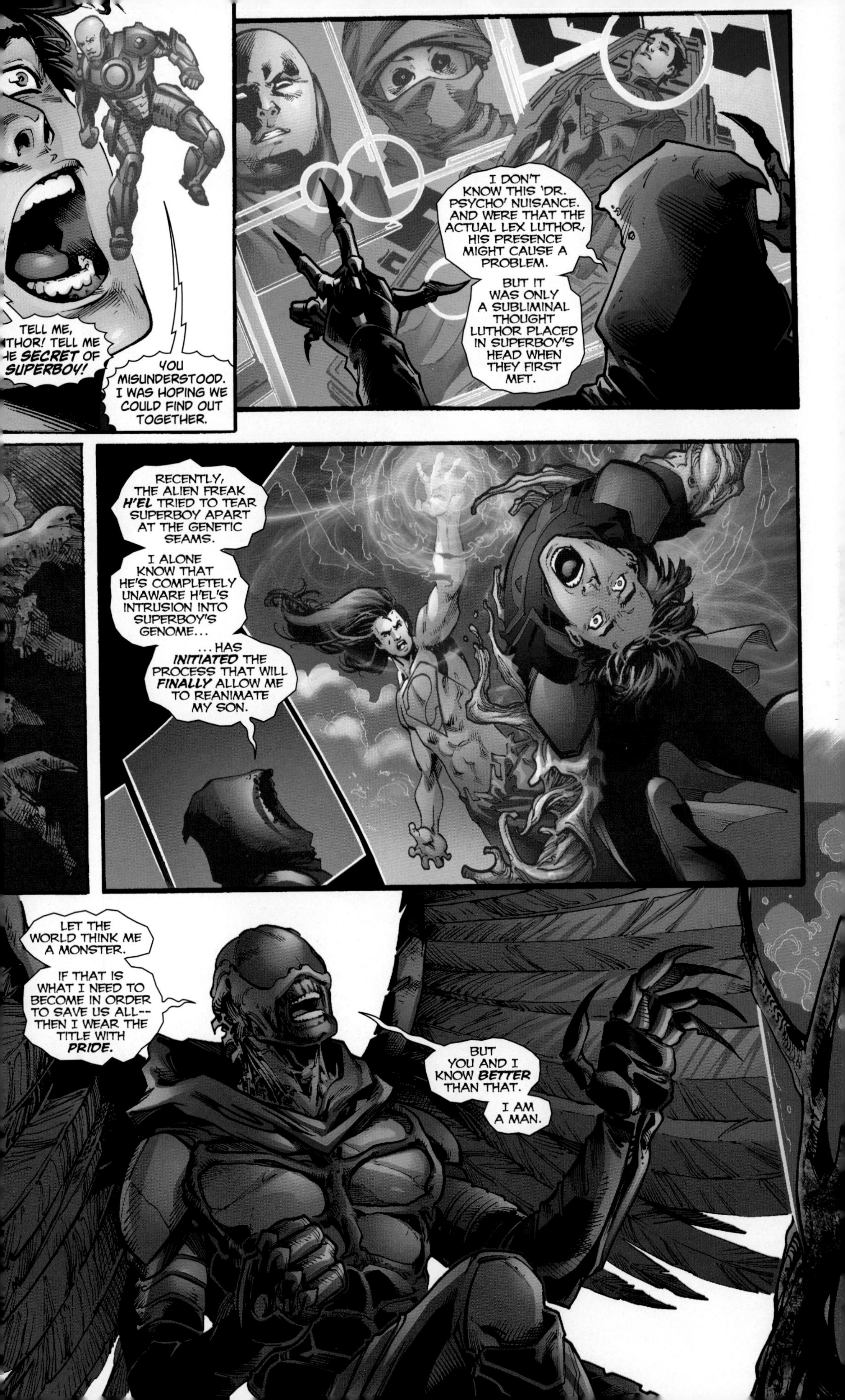

TELL ME, ...THOR! TELL ME ...HE SECRET OF SUPERBOY!
YOU MISUNDERSTOOD. I WAS HOPING WE COULD FIND OUT TOGETHER.
I DON'T KNOW THIS 'DR. PSYCHO' NUISANCE. AND WERE THAT THE ACTUAL LEX LUTHOR, HIS PRESENCE MIGHT CAUSE A PROBLEM.
BUT IT WAS ONLY A SUBLIMINAL THOUGHT LUTHOR PLACED IN SUPERBOY'S HEAD WHEN THEY FIRST MET.
RECENTLY, THE ALIEN FREAK H'EL TRIED TO TEAR SUPERBOY APART AT THE GENETIC SEAMS.
I ALONE KNOW THAT HE'S COMPLETELY UNAWARE H'EL'S INTRUSION INTO SUPERBOY'S GENOME...
...HAS INITIATED THE PROCESS THAT WILL FINALLY ALLOW ME TO REANIMATE MY SON.
LET THE WORLD THINK ME A MONSTER.
IF THAT IS WHAT I NEED TO BECOME IN ORDER TO SAVE US ALL--THEN I WEAR THE TITLE WITH PRIDE.
BUT YOU AND I KNOW BETTER THAN THAT.
I AM A MAN.

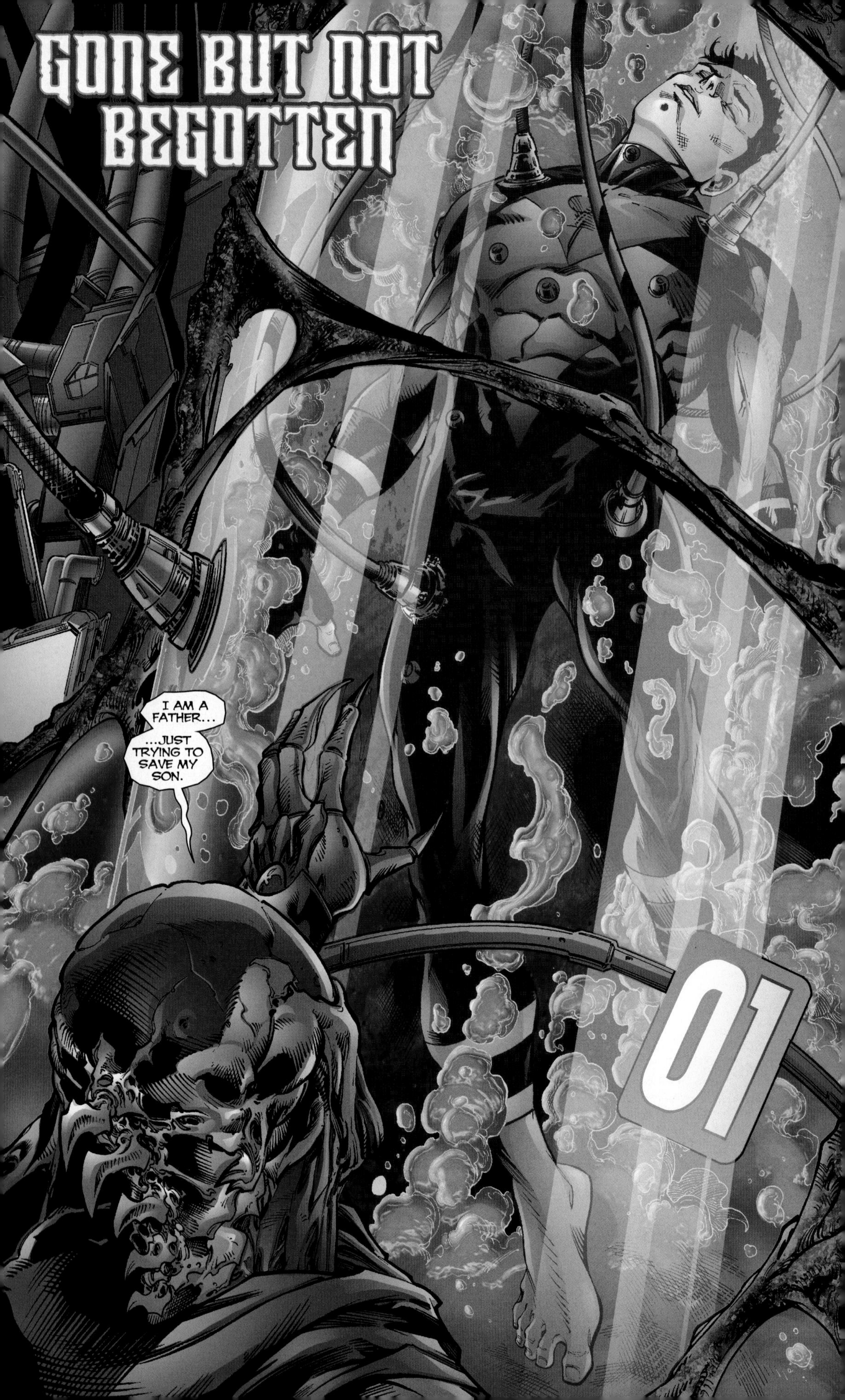
GONE BUT NOT BEGOTTEN
I AM A FATHER...
...JUST TRYING TO SAVE MY SON.
01

GOOD BOY

SCOTT LOBDELL writer KEN LASHLEY artist

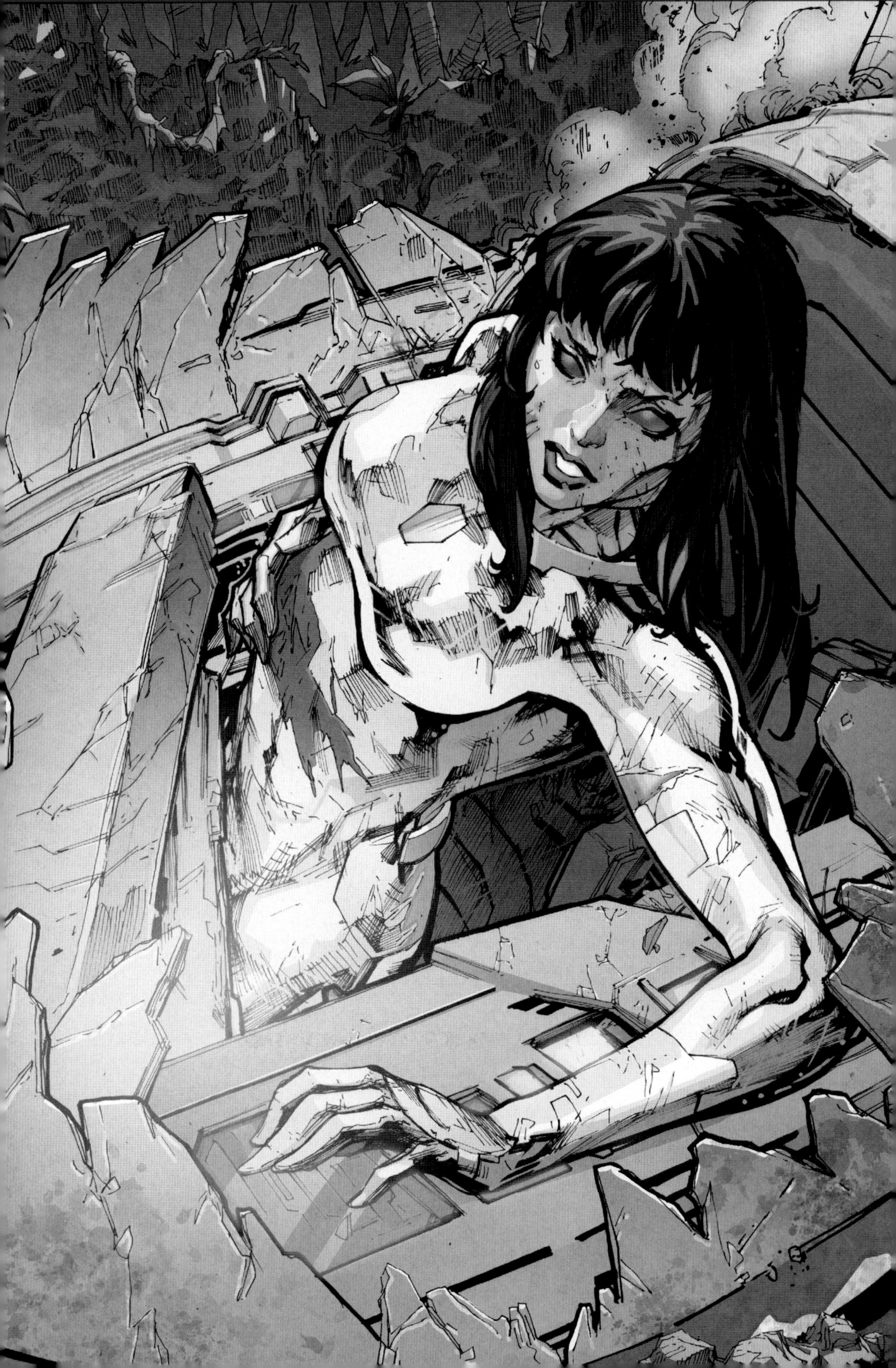

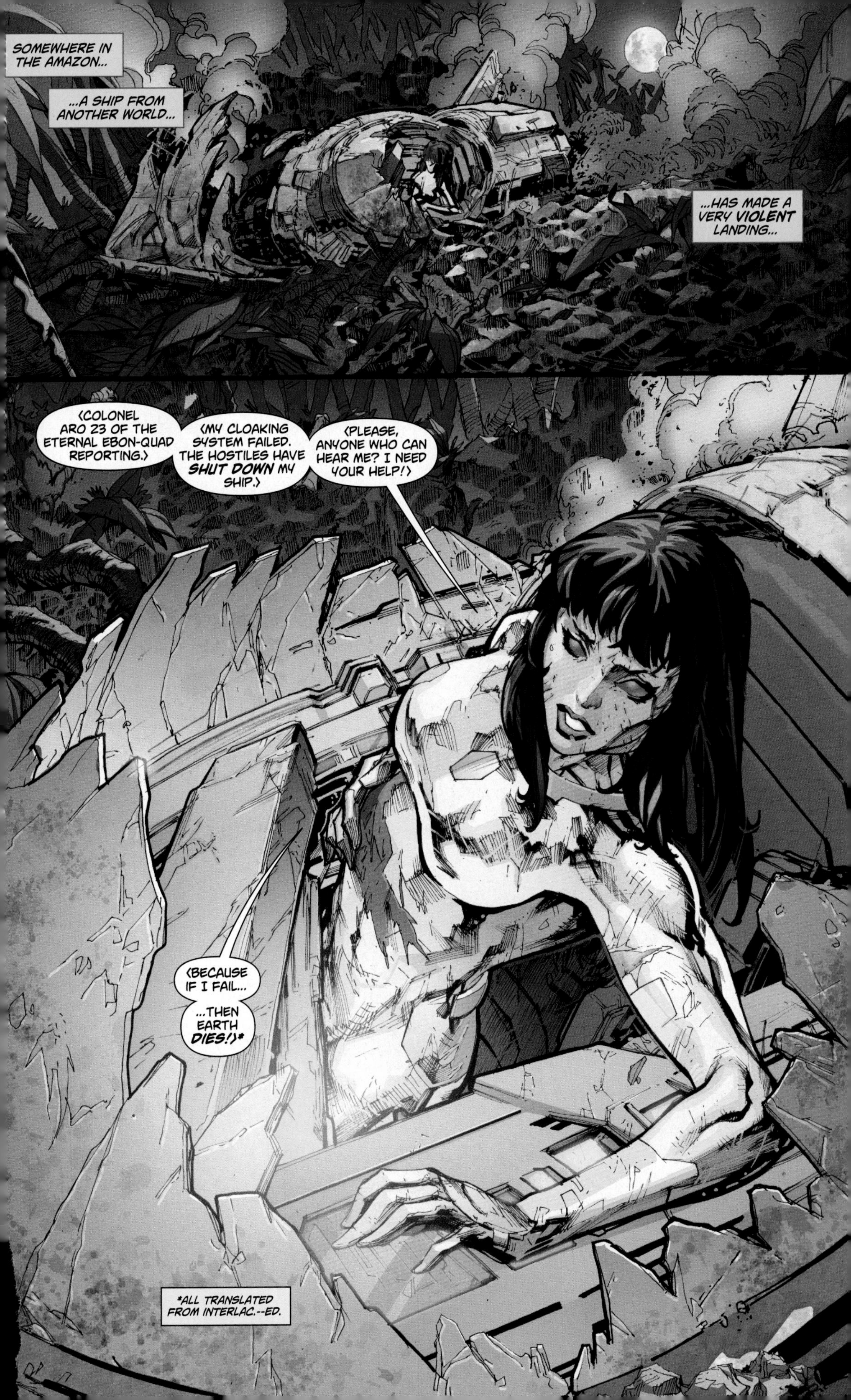
SOMEWHERE IN THE AMAZON...
...A SHIP FROM ANOTHER WORLD...
...HAS MADE A VERY VIOLENT LANDING...
‹COLONEL ARO 23 OF THE ETERNAL EBON-QUAD REPORTING.›
‹MY CLOAKING SYSTEM FAILED. THE HOSTILES HAVE SHUT DOWN MY SHIP.›
‹PLEASE, ANYONE WHO CAN HEAR ME? I NEED YOUR HELP!›
‹BECAUSE IF I FAIL...
...THEN EARTH DIES!›*
*ALL TRANSLATED FROM INTERLAC.--ED.

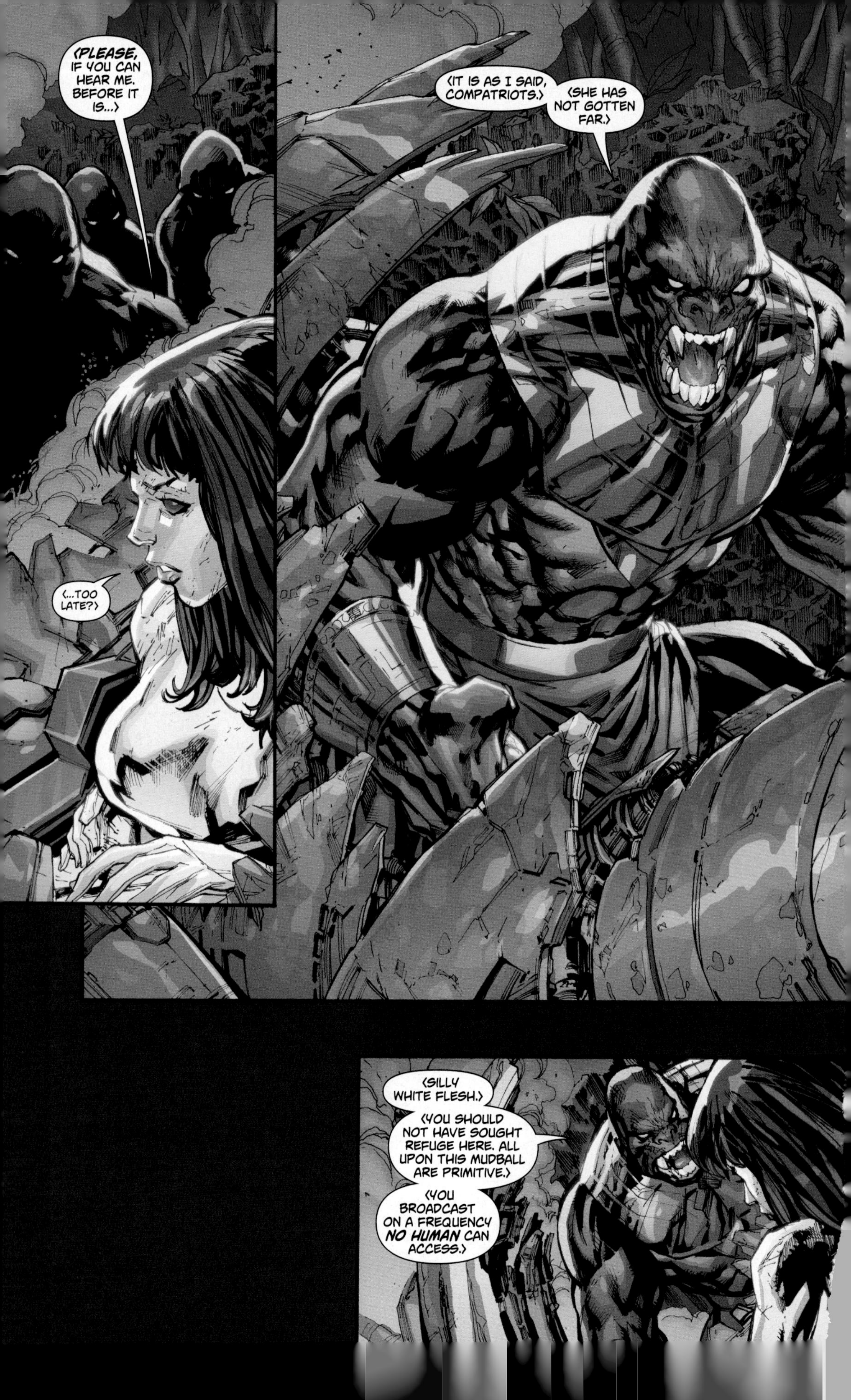
⟨PLEASE, IF YOU CAN HEAR ME. BEFORE IT IS...⟩
⟨...TOO LATE?⟩
⟨IT IS AS I SAID, COMPATRIOTS.⟩
⟨SHE HAS NOT GOTTEN FAR.⟩
⟨SILLY WHITE FLESH.⟩
⟨YOU SHOULD NOT HAVE SOUGHT REFUGE HERE. ALL UPON THIS MUDBALL ARE PRIMITIVE.⟩
⟨YOU BROADCAST ON A FREQUENCY NO HUMAN CAN ACCESS.⟩

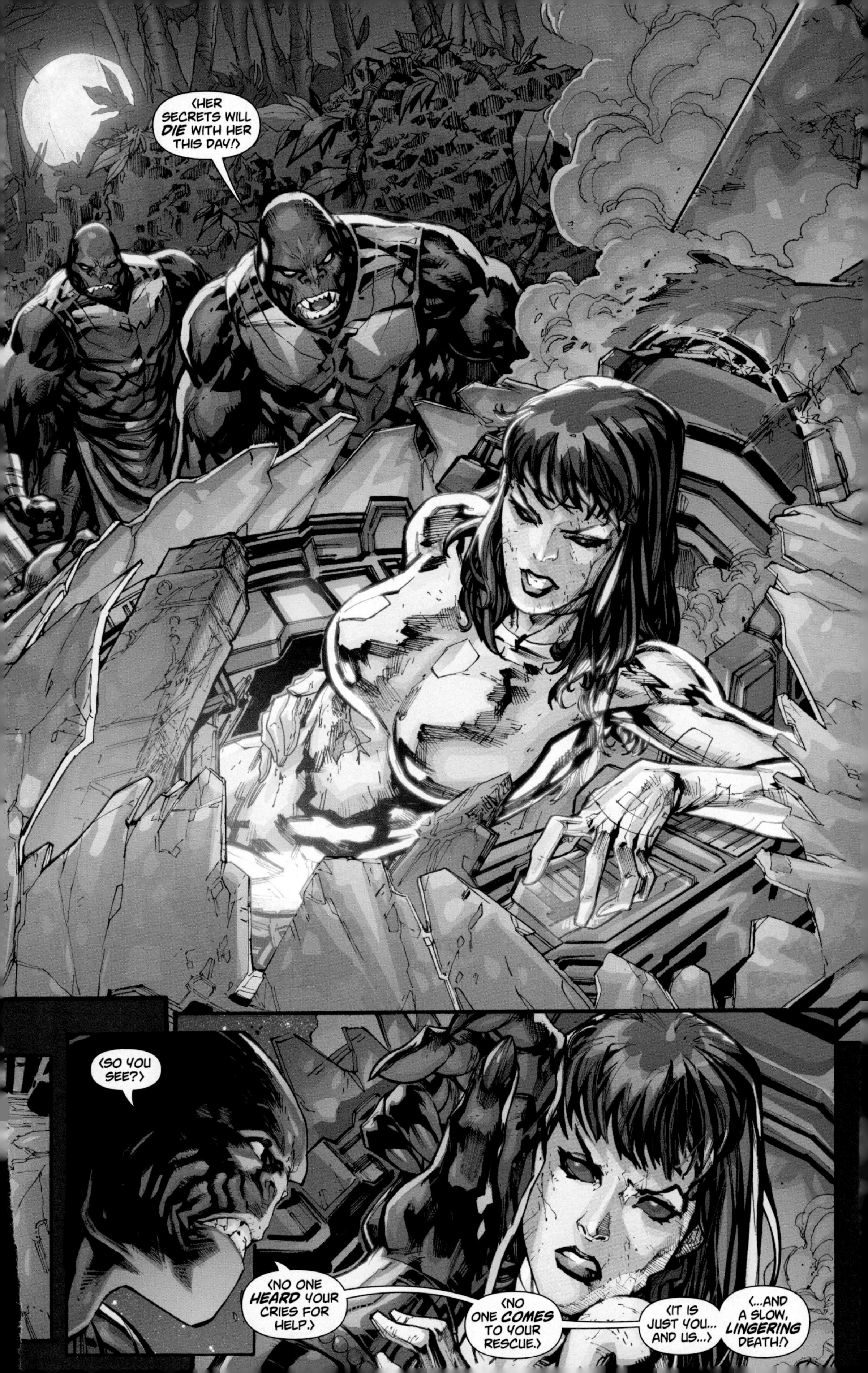

‹HER SECRETS WILL DIE WITH HER THIS DAY!›
‹SO YOU SEE?›
‹NO ONE HEARD YOUR CRIES FOR HELP.›
‹NO ONE COMES TO YOUR RESCUE.›
‹IT IS JUST YOU... AND US...›
‹...AND A SLOW, LINGERING DEATH!›

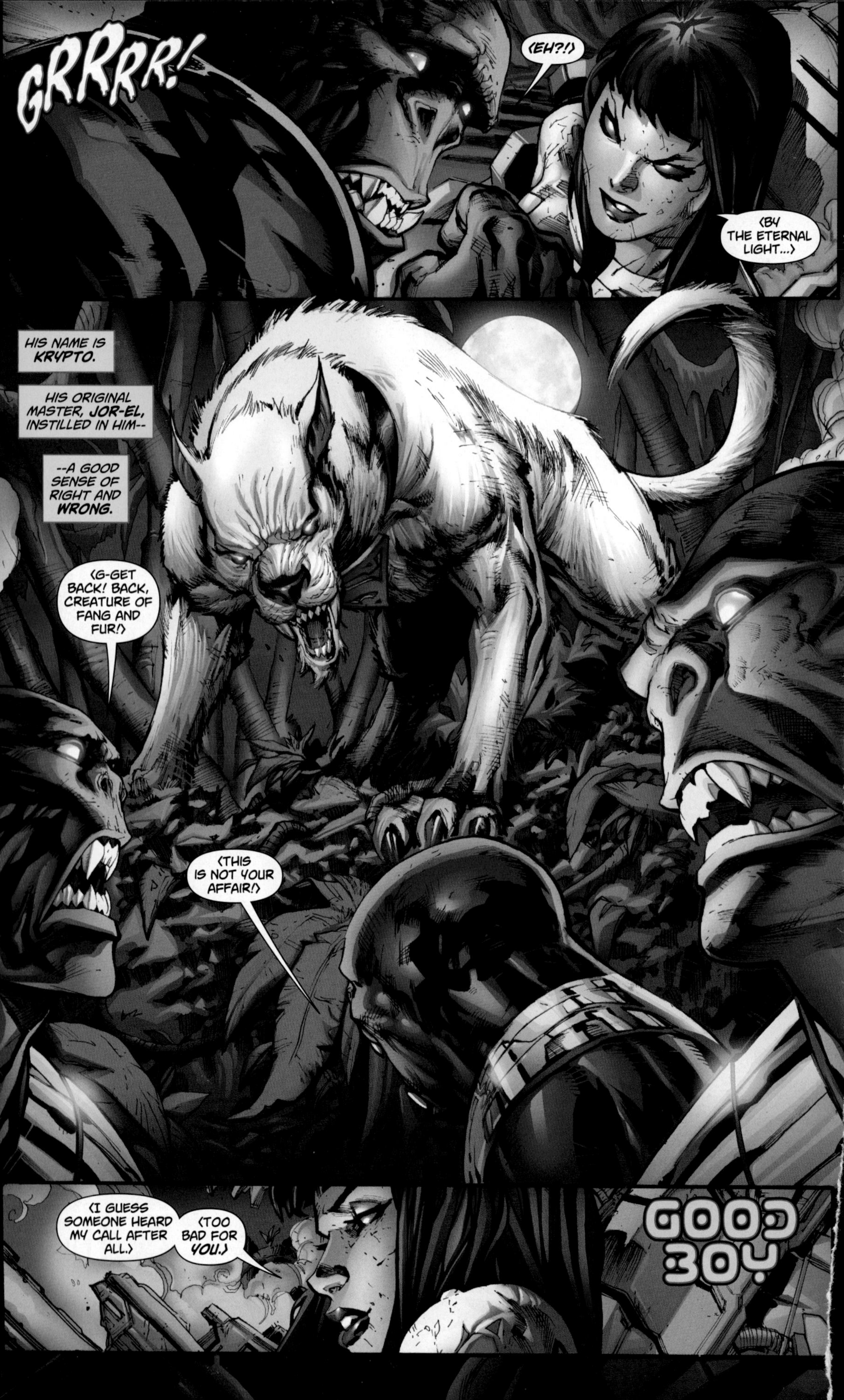
GRRRR!
‹EH?!›
‹BY THE ETERNAL LIGHT...›
HIS NAME IS KRYPTO.
HIS ORIGINAL MASTER, JOR-EL, INSTILLED IN HIM--
--A GOOD SENSE OF RIGHT AND WRONG.
‹G-GET BACK! BACK, CREATURE OF FANG AND FUR!›
‹THIS IS NOT YOUR AFFAIR!›
‹I GUESS SOMEONE HEARD MY CALL AFTER ALL.›
‹TOO BAD FOR YOU.›
GOOD BOY